This book charts the course of working- and middle-class radical politics in England from the continental revolutions of 1848 to the fall of Gladstone's Liberal government in 1874. Exploring the ways in which radicals used indigenous and continental nationalist sentiments to uphold class arguments, the author emphasizes the persistence of radical agitation after the fall of the Chartist mass platform and before the rise of organized socialism in the 1880s.

After Chartism traces the genealogy of English radicalism from its roots in Protestant Dissent and the seventeenth-century revolutions, a lineage acknowledged by middle- and working-class radicals alike in the nineteenth century. But it also underlines the extent to which this shared radical tradition was problematized by middle-class radicals' acceptance of classical liberal economics. The author traces the lineaments of this divide by contrasting middle- and working-class responses to the French, German, Italian, and Hungarian revolutions of 1848–9, to the Polish and Italian nationalism of the 1860s, and to the rise and fall of the Paris Commune in 1871. She argues that these years witnessed not the relentless liberalization of working-class radical protest in England, but rather a significant diminution of middle-class radicals' commitment to liberal economics. This accommodation contributed to the emergence of the 'new liberalism' of the 1880s, and helped to shape middle- and working-class responses to the early socialist movement.

Past and Present Publications

After Chartism

Past and Present Publications

General Editor: PAUL SLACK, *Exeter College, Oxford*

Past and Present Publications comprise books similar in character to the articles in the journal *Past and Present*. Whether the volumes in the series are collections of essays – some previously published, others new studies – or monographs, they encompass a wide variety of scholarly and original works primarily concerned with social, economic and cultural changes, and their causes and consequences. They will appeal to both specialists and non-specialists and will endeavour to communicate the results of historical and allied research in readable and lively form.

For a list of titles in Past and Present Publications, see end of book.

After Chartism

*Class and nation in English radical
politics, 1848–1874*

MARGOT C. FINN
Assistant Professor of History, Emory University

CAMBRIDGE
UNIVERSITY PRESS

Published by the Press Syndicate of the University of Cambridge
The Pitt Building, Trumpington Street, Cambridge CB2 1RP
40 West 20th Street, New York, NY 10011-4211, USA
10 Stamford Road, Oakleigh, Victoria 3166, Australia

First published 1993

Printed in Great Britain at the University Press, Cambridge

A catalogue record for this book is available from the British Library

Library of Congress cataloguing in publication data

Finn, Margot C.
  After Chartism: class and nation in English radical politics,
1848–1874 / Margot C. Finn.
       p.   cm. – (Past and present publications)
  Includes bibliographical references and index.
  ISBN 0 521 40496 7
  1. Radicalism – England – History – 19th century.   2. Working class –
England – Political activity – History – 19th century.   3. Middle
classes – England – Political activity – History – 19th century.
I. Title.   II. Series.
HN400.R3F56   1993
322′.2′094209034 – dc20   92–30241 CIP

ISBN 0 521 40496 7 hardback

UP

Contents

Illustrations

Acknowledgements

Various institutions have supported the research upon which this book is based. Fellowships from Columbia University, the Newberry Library, and the Woodrow Wilson Center in Washington DC allowed me to begin work on the project; a summer Faculty Development award from Emory College allowed me to complete it.

The owners and staffs of a host of archives and libraries have guided me through their collections with courtesy and patience. In London, I wish to acknowledge the Bishopsgate Institute, the British Library, the British Library of Political and Economic Science, the London Region National Graphical Society, the Public Record Office at Kew, the South Place Ethical Society, University College London, and the Athenaeum Collection at the University of London Library. I am grateful to the following provincial archives for their assistance during difficult economic times: the Archives Division of the Birmingham Reference Library, the Bodleian Library's Departments of Western Manuscripts and Printed Books, the Bradford Central Library, the Syndics of the Cambridge University Library, the Master and Fellows of Churchill College, the Mistress and Fellows of Girton College, Cambridge, the County Archivist of the Lancashire Record Office, the Liverpool City Libraries, the City of Manchester Leisure Services Committee, the Manchester Co-operative Union, the Modern Records Centre, the National Museum of Labour History and Labour Party Archives, the Sheffield City Archives, the Tyne and Wear Archives Department, the University of Liverpool Library, the University of Newcastle upon Tyne Special Collections, and the University Librarian and Library Archivist of the University of Sheffield. Richard Cobden's Papers are cited by courtesy of the Governors of Dunford House and F.A. Maxse's Papers by courtesy of A.J. Maxse, esq. Both are used with acknowledgements to the West Sussex Record Office and the County

Archivist. In Scotland, Mr Alex McAdam allowed me to use the John McAdam Papers in his possession at Bedlay Castle, and enlivened my visit with his own historical reflections. I am also grateful to the staffs at the Bibliothèque Historique de la Ville de Paris, the Fondazione Feltrinelli, the Istituto per la Storica del Risorgimento, and the International Institute for Social History in Amsterdam.

Several persons smoothed the early course of my research or my graduate career: in this respect, I am grateful to Robert O. Paxton, Anne Ramsay, and Michael Stanislawski. Gareth Stedman Jones steered me toward the consideration of liberalism; Miles Taylor kindly referred me to the George Dawson Collection; David Feldman offered helpful comments on class, national identity, and the vagaries of the historical profession. Steve Pincus offered a stream of insights on the character of seventeenth-century patriotism. Leonard Smith analysed my arguments and academic predicaments with intelligence and scathing humour as a graduate student, and continues to do so still.

A post-doctoral fellowship at the University of Chicago introduced me to rigorous intellectualism with a human face. Debates and discussions with my fellow Harper Instructors changed or sharpened a number of the arguments presented here. Fran Dolan deserves particular mention for combining an array of historical, literary, and feminist commitments with judicious infusions of hilarity. John Boyer, Jim Chandler, Jan Goldstein, Jim Grossman and Mark Kishlansky read my work, provided encouragement, and helped me to find permanent employment. I remember my time at Chicago with great warmth.

In Atlanta, I have enjoyed support from many generous colleagues. The members of the Emory University History Department have been consistently supportive of this project. Patrick Allitt read the bulk of the manuscript and provided a number of thoughtful suggestions; Michael Bellisles, James Melton, and Cynthia Patterson entertained my arguments on a variety of topics with great patience. Bill Beik, Mary Odem, Jonathan Prude, and Stephen White read and re-read chapters, offered sound advice, and talked politics, strategy, and ideas on countless occasions. Kate Gilbert improved the substance and the style of the manuscript significantly; Ellen Barnard checked references with speed and skill. Tina Brownley and Carole Hahn have given me wise counsel both at Emory and in Oxford. The members of the Atlanta Seminar in the Comparative History of Labor, Industrialization, Technology, and Society – and particularly Jon Schneer – created an ideal context for the completion of this project.

David Cannadine read an early draft of my first chapter and has read a number of subsequent versions, to my great benefit. William Davies and Paul Slack have been most helpful in assisting the progress of the manuscript toward publication.

Special mention must be made of a number of individuals who, at critical junctures, rescued either the manuscript or its author from crisis. My parents have been unfailingly generous in their support of all aspects of my education. With my brother and sister-in-law, they have tolerated my long absences, sudden changes of direction, and sustained obsession with books. No academic could wish for a warmer family circle from which to begin. William and Silvia Rodgers opened their home in London to me as a beginning research student, and have continued to do so ever since. In more than one way, they have helped to make this a book about social democracy. Peter Marsh rescued me in the eleventh hour from a career in biochemistry, an act of kindness (if not wisdom) for which I remain most grateful. Sheila Biddle – friend, critic, and boon companion – dispensed good cheer, good sense, and keen analysis of my arguments and prose. Her help saw me through this project at its nadir. Roy Foster unofficially assumed many of the duties of a dissertation advisor at an early stage in my research, reading repeated drafts of the manuscript and steering it toward publication with great forbearance for an often errant student, author, and neighbour.

This book grew from two essays that I wrote in graduate seminars in British history, essays in which I explored the internationalist sympathies of Keir Hardie ('The Man in the Cloth Kimono') and the contours of mid-Victorian politics ('The Grand Old Man and the Prince of Denmark: Gladstonian Liberalism and the Antic Disposition'). I have gained a full appreciation of the tolerance, encouragement, and insight with which these early forays into scholarship were met only as it has become my own lot to guide students through the labyrinths of modern British history. I was the recipient of boundless energy, perpetual wit, real acuity, and an indomitable will to understand the Victorians. These qualities, these interests and this avocation, do endure. This book is dedicated to the memory of Stephen Koss.

Abbreviations

BI	Bishopsgate Institute, London
BL, Add. MS	British Library, Additional Manuscript
BLPES	British Library of Political and Economic Science, London School of Economics
BODL	Bodleian Library, Oxford
HO	Home Office Papers, Public Record Office, Kew
IISG	International Instituut voor Sociale Geschiedenis, Amsterdam
LCL	Liverpool City Library, Archives Division
MCRL	Manchester Central Reference Library, Archives Division
MCU	Manchester Co-operative Union Library
MEPO	Metropolitan Police Papers, Public Record Office, Kew
T&WAD	Tyne and Wear Archives Department, Newcastle
WSRO	West Sussex Record Office, Chichester

Introduction

It is a truism, indeed it is a platitude, of Victorian labour history that the years which bridged the late Chartist movement and early socialism witnessed a fundamental discontinuity in the political development of the English working class. Upheld by Marx in the early nineteenth century as the harbinger of world revolution, English labour radicalism was denounced by Lenin in the early twentieth century as the captive of atavistic reformism. The intervening years saw not proletarian revolution but rather accommodation with a middle class itself bereft of true class consciousness. Thus 'a supine bourgeoisie', in a much-quoted phrase, 'produced a subordinate proletariat'. In doing so, some writers argue, it established a pattern of meliorist inter-class relations that has governed British political life to the present day.[1]

Painstakingly anatomized and trenchantly denounced by the editorial vanguard of the *New Left Review* from 1964, the 'profound caesura' of class politics in mid-Victorian England has, in the past three decades, become a basic premise of historical writing within the British left. Standing in sharp contrast to 'the great political ferment of 1815–48' and 'the continuous development of the modern labour movement and Labour Party ... with the rediscovery of socialism and the so-called "new" unionism of the 1880s', Eric Hobsbawm argues, 'the intervening decades were unlike either what went before or what came after'.[2] The defining characteristics of

---

[1] Perry Anderson, 'Origins of the Present Crisis', *New Left Review*, no. 23 (January-February 1964), pp. 26–51, citation from p. 36.

[2] Eric Hobsbawm, 'The Formation of British Working-Class Culture', in his *Worlds of Labour: Further Studies in the History of Labour* (London, 1984), p. 182. 'Profound caesura' is Anderson's phrase in 'Origins of the Present Crisis', p. 33. For a broader introduction to the polemics that surround this issue, see Perry Anderson's *Arguments within English Marxism* (London, 1980), and E.P. Thomp-

these years – the triumph of liberal economics, the growth of political reformism, and the diminution of social protest – are, however, more often invoked as established verities than explored as historical problems. Far more profound than the putative caesura engendered by the downtrodden (or insipid) force of English labour is the historiographical caesura of the mid-Victorian period, the dearth of scholarship which attempts to sketch the contours – much less to probe the mechanisms – of social conflict and conciliation in mid-Victorian England. E.P. Thompson has chronicled the growth of working-class militancy to 1832 at great length; Hobsbawm and others detail its renewed development from the 1870s.[3] Studies of Chartism abound; the secondary literature of late Victorian socialism is vast. A different logic governs the historiography of the intervening decades. For despite its pivotal role in the dominant theories of the discipline, the history of mid-Victorian working-class politics remains largely unwritten.[4]

Historians who employ the so-called labour aristocracy thesis to examine the social consensus of these years have offered a signal exception to this general rule of historiographical absence. Since the publication of Royden Harrison's *Before the Socialists* in 1965, the bulk of substantive inquiry into the post-Chartist era has followed this path.[5] Intent to underscore the divisions within labour that

son, 'The Peculiarities of the English', in Ralph Miliband and John Saville (eds.), *The Socialist Register: 1965* (London, 1965), pp. 311–62.

[3] E.P. Thompson, *The Making of the English Working Class* (Harmondsworth, 1963); Eric Hobsbawm, 'The Making of the Working Class 1870–1914', in his *Worlds of Labour*, pp. 194–213; Gareth Stedman Jones, 'Working-Class Culture and Working-Class Politics in London, 1870–1900: Notes on the Remaking of a Working Class', in his *Languages of Class: Studies in English Working Class History 1832–1982* (Cambridge, 1983), pp. 179–238.

[4] See the persuasive argument along these lines in Christopher Kent, 'Presence and Absence: History, Theory, and the Working Class', *Victorian Studies*, vol. 29 (Spring 1986), pp. 437–62. Three fine exceptions to this general rule of neglect which do not figure in the historiography of the labour aristocracy debate discussed below are Brian Harrison and Patricia Hollis, 'Chartism, Liberalism and the Life of Robert Lowery', *English Historical Review*, vol. 82 (July 1967), pp. 503–35; Martin Hewitt, 'Radicalism and the Victorian Working Class: The Case of Samuel Bamford', *Historical Journal*, vol. 34 (December 1991), pp. 873–92; and Stan Shipley, *Club Life and Socialism in Mid-Victorian London* (Oxford, 1971). See also the suggestive arguments of Harold Perkin, *The Origins of Modern English Society* (London, 1969).

[5] Royden Harrison, *Before the Socialists: Studies in Labour and Politics, 1861–1881* (London, 1965). Among the studies of the period that employ this basic framework, the most significant are Geoffrey Crossick, *An Artisan Elite in Victorian Society: Kentish London 1840–1880* (London, 1978); Robert Q. Gray, *The Labour Aristoc-*

militated against the development or expression of mature class consciousness, adherents of this broad school of analysis emphasize the strategic importance of a vocal, relatively secure labour élite situated from the 1850s at the interface between the working and the middle class. Skilled artisans located in trades largely untouched by mechanization and industrial pacemakers who occupied the higher echelons of the factory work force provide the pillars of labour aristocracy theory, forming a privileged stratum within the working class noted (if only in historical literature) for adherence to notions of independence and respectability that tied its value systems to those of the bourgeoisie, and thus deprived less affluent workers of a militant, class-conscious leadership capable of waging war against capital.[6] In its most orthodox interpretation, the labour aristocracy thesis directly links the social and economic fragmentation of the English factory proletariat to the political reformism of the wider English working class. Thus in John Foster's analysis, the sectional groupings and attendant false consciousness engendered by the industrial production process itself – most significantly by subcontracting and pacemaking – acted 'to obscure the reality of exploitation' and provide 'a ready channel for the penetration of ruling class attitudes and controls', thereby serving 'as a major prop to capitalist stability'.[7]

Social historians have subjected the claims of labour aristocracy theory to vigorous criticism, effectively demolishing the causal link that it posits between political reformism and the sectional divisions that separated labour aristocrats from labourers.[8] Recent trends in economic history, which underline the halting and piecemeal evolution of the British economy rather than its rapid industrial transformation, undercut those versions of the labour aristocracy thesis that

racy in Victorian Edinburgh (Oxford, 1976); and F.M. Leventhal, *Respectable Radical: George Howell and Victorian Working Class Politics* (Cambridge, Mass., 1971).

[6] Eric Hobsbawm, 'The Labour Aristocracy in Nineteenth-Century Britain', in his *Labouring Men: Studies in the History of Labour* (London, 1964), provides the most articulate and influential exposition of the argument; *idem*, 'The Aristocracy of Labour Reconsidered', in his *Worlds of Labour*, pp. 227–51, offers more recent reflections on this theme.

[7] John Foster, *Class Struggle and the Industrial Revolution: Early Industrial Capitalism in Three English Towns* (2nd edn, London, 1977), p. 4–5.

[8] See esp. Stedman Jones, 'Class Struggle and the Industrial Revolution', in his *Languages of Class*, pp. 25–75, and H.F. Moorhouse, 'The Marxist Theory of the Labour Aristocracy', *Social History*, vol. 3 (January 1978), pp. 61–82.

emphasize the instrumentality of factory production in the stabilization of class relations. Even within factory production, patterns of gender segregation, the retention of paternalist practices, and the escalation of ethnic tensions with the Irish now appear to have played a more significant role in the segmentation of the English work force than did the formation of a stable aristocracy of labour.[9] Variants of the labour aristocracy thesis that focus on skilled artisans rather than factory workers have similarly proven problematic, not least because skilled workers – far from consistently promoting political and industrial quiescence – typically stood at the forefront of Victorian radical movements. Reflecting social aspirations and cultural preferences that departed from the characteristic preoccupations of the employing class, the notions of thrift, respectability, and independence that informed the behaviour of many of these artisans are now seen to have represented values distinct to their station, rather than emblems of their embourgeoisement.[10]

Although historians have largely discarded the labour aristocracy thesis as a satisfactory blueprint for the analysis of mid-Victorian politics and social relations, their efforts to dismantle the theory's explanatory structures have done little to challenge its central contention that the years between Chartism and early socialism witnessed the liberalization of labour, the displacement of early class consciousness by a worldview that accepted the overarching framework of liberal economic mechanisms in the market and Liberal party politics in Parliament. Indeed, as scholars of the working class have turned away from essentially economic approaches to class

---

[9] N.F.R. Crafts, *British Economic Growth during the Industrial Revolution* (Oxford, 1985), and Raphael Samuel, 'The Workshop of the World: Steam Power and Hand Technology in Mid-Victorian Britain', *History Workshop Journal*, no. 3 (Spring 1977), pp. 6–72, detail the limits of Britain's industrial transformation. Patrick Joyce, *Work, Society and Politics: The Culture of the Factory in Later Victorian England* (Brighton, 1980), and Neville Kirk, *The Growth of Working Class Reformism in Mid-Victorian England* (London, 1985), emphasize the significance of ethnic barriers, family formations, and gender.

[10] For the contribution of skilled workers to radical politics and industrial struggles, see John Breuilly, 'Artisan Economy, Artisan Politics, Artisan Ideology: The Artisan Contribution to the 19th Century European Labour Movement', in Clive Emsley and James Walvin (eds.), *Artisans, Peasants and Proletarians 1760–1860* (London, 1985), pp. 187–225. The multi-valence of notions such as independence is ably demonstrated in Peter Bailey, ' "Will the Real Bill Banks Please Stand Up?": Towards a Role Analysis of Mid-Victorian Working-Class Respectability', *Journal of Social History*, vol. 12 (Spring 1979), pp. 336–53.

relations and adopted social, cultural, and political analyses in their stead, the purchase of the liberalization thesis has gained new strength. Whereas proponents of labour aristocracy theory located the origins of liberalization in a production process over which workers had little control, historians now find the seeds of liberal conviction rooted in working-class thought and speech itself. Thus Gareth Stedman Jones, in a particularly influential study of Chartist rhetoric, argues that liberal and libertarian tendencies both animated the language of Chartism and undermined the movement's ability to forge and maintain class struggle. In this view, the Chartists' preoccupation with corrupt, tyrannical, and repressive state institutions acted to distinguish their movement from bourgeois radicalism in the 1830s but promoted their incorporation within middle- and upper-class political structures in the 1840s and 1850s, when government ministers adopted liberal economic and political measures that tempered the class character of the state.[11]

This emphasis on the intersection of working-class radical culture with middle-class liberal politics – and hence on the considerable constraints placed on the development of working-class consciousness – is salutary, and fundamental to an understanding of the perception of social relations in Victorian England. For although the middle class had gained the franchise with the passage of the First Reform Act in 1832, its members remained (like the labouring population) largely excluded from the corridors of power throughout the century. Restricted to one seventh of the adult male population, concentrated disproportionately in the agricultural south, and pervaded by jobbery, intimidation, and corruption, the nineteenth-century electoral system consistently returned a House dominated by the landed and aristocratic interest. A shared abhorrence for this edifice of 'Old Corruption' linked reform-minded men of the middle and working class in the Victorian era as it had in the age of the French revolution.[12] Traditions of religious Dissent similarly acted to unite middle- and working-class reformers. Although opposition to the doctrines and perquisites of the Angli-

---

[11] Stedman Jones, 'Rethinking Chartism', in his *Languages of Class*, pp. 90–178. For other historians' variations on this theme of liberalization, see below, pp. 66, 238.

[12] Norman Gash, *Politics in the Age of Peel: A Study in the Technique of Parliamentary Representation 1830–1850* (London, 1953), details the persistence of landed and aristocratic rule; W.D. Rubinstein, 'The End of "Old Corruption" in Britain 1780–1860', *Past and Present*, no. 101 (November 1983), pp. 55–86, surveys its protracted demise.

can Church did not lead inevitably to oppositional political convictions, the legal disabilities suffered by Nonconformists of the middle class encouraged Dissenters to associate their cause both with the claims of the unenfranchised millions and with the fortunes of a Whig and Liberal political establishment that pledged to uphold the principles of civil and religious freedom.[13] Norms of orthography reflected these points of intersection between middle- and working-class culture. Working-class leaders, provincial manufacturers, and Nonconformists often joined in efforts to 'organize' public opinion and the 'laboring' population against the evils of a 'centralized' state; the Anglican élite, in contrast, 'organised' the resources of 'centralised' institutions such as the New Poor Law to meet the new demands of 'labour' in a commercial polity.[14]

More broadly, the burden of recent scholarship on class has underscored the extent to which shared beliefs in the legitimacy of parliamentary structures informed working-, middle-, and upper-class culture alike, containing labour's political vision securely within the compass of the nation-state. Embraced by historians who disagree deeply on the nature and meaning of class relations in England, the argument that national identities obscured or replaced class allegiances in the mid-Victorian period is now a commonplace of the literature. John Foster identified nationalist sentiment as an instrument of liberalization in his study of the labour aristocracy in Oldham, Northampton, and South Shields; Stedman Jones, while critiquing Foster's analysis of sectionalism, applauds his recognition of 'the vital role played by nationalism as an ideology capable of uniting the stratified work force on capitalist terms'.[15] Ross McKibbin's detailed exposition of the failure of Marxism to capture the allegiance of British labour similarly suggests the instrumental role of

[13] James E. Bradley, 'Whigs and Nonconformists: "Slumbering Radicalism" in English Politics, 1739–89', *Eighteenth Century Studies*, vol. 9 (1975), pp. 1–27, and Russell E. Richey, 'The Origins of British Radicalism: The Changing Rationale for Dissent', *Eighteenth Century Studies*, vol. 7 (1973–4), pp. 179–92, explore the relations between radicalism and Nonconformity. Edward Royle, *Victorian Infidels: The Origins of the British Secularist Movement 1791–1866* (Manchester, 1974), and *idem, Radicals, Secularists and Republicans: Popular Freethought in Britain, 1866–1915* (Manchester, 1980), documents the links forged between liberals, Dissenters, and artisanal radicals by shared conviction in the right to religious freedoms.
[14] For examples, see below, p. 69.
[15] Foster, *Class Struggle and the Industrial Revolution*, pp. 239–43; Stedman Jones, 'Class Struggle and the Industrial Revolution', in his *Languages of Class*, pp. 72, 74.

nationalist sentiment in combating working-class consciousness.[16] And Patrick Joyce, in a significant reevaluation of Victorian and Edwardian perceptions of labour, contrasts twentieth-century historians' preoccupation with the concept of class to contemporaries' emphasis on 'extra-proletarian identifications such as those of "people" and "nation"'.[17]

This book explores the liberalization process by tracing the national and international identities embraced by middle- and working-class English radicals in the decades that spanned the continental revolutions of 1848 and the electoral defeat of William Gladstone's Liberal government in 1874. In seeking to illuminate the contemporary meanings and impact of class in mid-Victorian England, it probes the relations between radical movements and the broader liberal culture of which these agitations ultimately formed a part, detailing the protracted evolution of English national consciousness and its interpenetration with radical traditions that stretched from the Puritan revolution to the early socialist movement. The chief concern of this endeavour is to explore the cultural and political construction of perceptions of class consciousness by radical activists, and the role played by radical, national, international, and class identities in mediating liberal popular politics after Chartism. Accepting the diminution of social and political protest in the mid-Victorian era as a given, this study does not purport to explain the origins of the phenomenon of reformism. Rather, it questions the nature and extent of liberalization in Victorian England by revealing the ways in which perceived class differences, by informing received national identities, changed the meaning of liberalism itself.

The approach adopted in this work has obvious limitations. Most problematic is the emphasis placed here on the cultural and political determination of class identity, rather than the significance of class as an economic formation. This interpretation of class privileges subjective sentiments over ostensibly objective realities, highlighting perceptions of class consciousness rather than the economic substance of class relations. It thus does little to illuminate our

[16] Ross McKibbin, 'Why Was There No Marxism in Great Britain?', in his *Ideologies of Class: Social Relations in Britain 1880–1950* (Oxford, 1990), pp. 1–41, esp. pp. 23–4.

[17] Patrick Joyce, *Visions of the People: Industrial England and the Question of Class, 1840–1914* (Cambridge, 1991), p. 11.

understanding of the workplace and the relations that obtained within the labour market between masters and their men.[18] Focusing on articulate spokesmen for the working class rather than upon the men and women whose interests they claimed to represent, this study perpetuates those conventions of historical writing that underline the role of articulate leaders and obscure the contributions of the anonymous workers who sustained their movements of social and political protest. Often themselves men of middle-class origins or education, the spokesmen for labour whose radical activities form the substance of this book must be understood to have manufactured working-class identities rather than simply to have reflected them.[19] A further limitation derives from the scope of national identity under consideration. Because uneven levels of economic development, linguistic barriers, religious differences, and distinctive legal structures lent different inflections to the radical traditions of Ireland, Scotland, and Wales, this study is narrowly concerned with the history of English national identity.[20] And because the mid-Victorian period saw a withdrawal of working-class women from the public arena of popular politics, this work is largely concerned with the aspirations and activities of English men.[21]

[18] For an intelligent analysis of the arguments against the approach to class adopted here, see *ibid.*, pp. 1–23 and *idem*, 'Work', in F.M.L. Thompson (ed.), *The Cambridge Social History of Britain 1750–1950*, 3 vols. (Cambridge, 1990), vol. II, pp. 158–68. The opposing side is best represented by James A. Epstein, 'Understanding the Cap of Liberty: Symbolic Practice and Social Conflict in Early Nineteenth-Century England', *Past and Present*, no. 122 (February 1989), pp. 75–118. The broader contours of this debate on the definition of class are surveyed in Neville Kirk, 'In Defence of Class: A Critique of Recent Revisionist Writing upon the Nineteenth-Century English Working Class', *International Review of Social History*, vol. 32 (1987), pp. 2–47.

[19] The designation of men such as Ernest Jones (a barrister) as 'working-class radical leaders' fits ill with the usage of orthodox Marxism, but has the virtue of capturing contemporary Victorian usage. It represents 'the self-description of the actors that one wishes to describe and analyze', a definition of class explored by Craig Calhoun, *The Question of Class Struggle: Social Foundations of Popular Radicalism during the Industrial Revolution* (Chicago, 1982), p. 18.

[20] This is not to deny that substantial overlap obtained among the various British national and radical identities. But the profound influence of Dissent, the radical cult of Cromwell, and the persistence of notions of 'the Englishman's birthright', discussed below, pp. 36–7, 41–6 all argue against the conflation of these national identities.

[21] For the influence of women on the course of English radicalism, see Dorothy Thompson, 'Women and Nineteenth Century Radical Politics', in Juliet Mitchell and Ann Oakley (eds.), *The Rights and Wrongs of Women* (London, 1976), pp. 112–38, and Jutta Schwarzkopf, *Women in the Chartist Movement* (New York,

The rationale informing the most significant of these analytical restrictions is developed more fully in the chapters that follow, but must be indicated briefly at the outset. Most importantly, the emphasis placed here on the cultural and political construction of class is not intended to deny or denigrate the contribution of economic determinants to class formation. The purpose of this approach is instead to demonstrate the ways in which class identities escaped the confines of the workplace and animated the wider social and political life of the Victorian nation. Nor is the emphasis placed on radical leaders intended to diminish the contributions of the men and women who underpinned their radical efforts. Rather, the role of leadership is given prominence because the records that leaders left allow a reconstruction of both the activities of working-class radical movements and the relations between these movements and middle-class radical agitations. When supplemented with documents that illuminate aspects of working- and middle-class oppositional culture, the rich collections of correspondence, the diaries, pamphlets, and autobiographies that record the efforts of radical leaders can reveal the broad patterns that governed class perceptions in the Victorian era, and the limits that constrained their expression.

This study emphasizes national and international identities both as a heuristic device and as a reflection of the dominant preoccupations of mid-Victorian radical culture. Between the revolutions of 1848 and the Paris Commune of 1871, continental Europe witnessed a succession of sporadic local uprisings and sweeping national revolutions that diverged sharply from the contemporary English experience. Informed or influenced by theories elaborated in the writings and speeches of such disparate figures as Louis Blanc, Louis Kossuth, Karl Marx, and Giuseppe Mazzini, insurgents in France, Germany, Italy, Hungary, and Poland articulated a constellation of political arguments that embraced the liberty of the individual, the sanctity of national independence, the social imperatives of the state, and the collective rights of international labour. These varied concepts and the movements they inspired enjoyed wide-ranging support in England, where they created a web of shared political interests that stretched from the working population through

1991). Trends in the wage form that helped to push women from the public and political spheres are discussed by Wally Seccombe, 'Patriarchy Stabilized: The Construction of the Male Breadwinner Wage Norm in Nineteenth-Century Britain', *Social History*, vol. 11 (January 1986), pp. 53–76.

middle-class politicians to Whig and Liberal grandees.[22] But they found a particular resonance in English radical circles. Within radical culture, this enthusiasm for continental causes, reinforced by the presence in England of thousands of exiled revolutionaries from the continent,[23] became intertwined with an indigenous debate on political economy, on the relationships among political institutions, social structures, and economic activities. Enveloped within a network of English radical traditions forged with the nation-state in the seventeenth century, these continental theories helped to inspire, regulate, and maintain the reform efforts of both middle- and working-class activists. In the nationalist and internationalist efforts of the 1860s – the Garibaldi agitations, the Anglo-Polish sympathy movement, the First International, and the suffrage movement of 1864–7 – they mobilized tens of thousands in movements of protest that spoke at once to class and patriotic identities. Although often overlapping with the concerns of Liberal party politicians, these efforts also underlined divisions among middle-class liberal reformers, and between liberal partisans and the more strident radicals of the working class. By the 1870s, contests among these varied groups over the meaning of patriotic politics had helped to transform fundamentally the character of English liberal culture.

Unlike the concept of the nation, the concepts of international brotherhood expounded in these years by English radicals lacked a secure ideological framework within which to operate. Their elaboration in the nineteenth century required the establishment of such parameters, the imaginative creation of internationalist goals, strategies, martyrs, and celebrations that could compete effectively with nationalist traditions for popular support. To a large extent, nationalism itself provided the scaffolding with which English radicals constructed these internationalist paradigms: in the varied radical agitations that exercised the nation from 1848, leaders of reform repeatedly co-opted nationalist rhetoric and institutions to

---

[22] For aristocratic and upper-class enthusiasm for continental causes within the Liberal party, see Ann Pottinger Saab, *Reluctant Icon: Gladstone, Bulgaria, and the Working Classes, 1856–1878* (Cambridge, Mass., 1991), and E.D. Steele, *Palmerston and Liberalism, 1855–1865* (Cambridge, 1991), esp. pp. 245–316.

[23] Bernard Porter analyses the emigration in *The Refugee Question in Mid-Victorian Politics* (Cambridge, 1979). At its peak in the early 1850s, the émigré community in England included roughly 4,500 French émigrés, a few hundred Italians, 2,500 Poles and Hungarians, and 1,300 Germans. *Ibid.*, pp. 14–15.

promote international campaigns.[24] As a well-entrenched historical tradition with bases of support in all classes, nationalism enjoyed a superior position in this ideological partnership, in which it ultimately prevailed. But the radical nationalist tradition neither dominated the dialogue entirely nor emerged from its victory unscathed.

Like internationalist concepts, the concept of class initially stood outside the English radical tradition. And like international identities, the identities of class were imagined constructions – imagined not in the sense that they lacked any material basis, but in that it required an heroic act of imagination for workers to regard their own existence primarily from their standpoint. Confronted daily by wide gradations of skill, trade unionization, wealth, status, residence, dialect, and education within their own ranks, few workers in the nineteenth century enjoyed Marx's lofty vantage point for the analysis of class relations. For just as national sentiments – despite the persistent claims of nationalist leaders – do not flow magically from shared territorial or linguistic experience, class consciousness does not spring immediately from the shared experience of economic exploitation. Like the nation, class must be inculcated. Its inculcation demands not only the creation of common platforms, visions, and voices, but the imposition or acceptance of a 'shared amnesia, a collective forgetfulness', as Ernest Gellner has written of national identity, that allows its adherents to celebrate their unanimity in the face of their conspicuous differences.[25] Endured in particularistic conditions and contexts, economic relations are not typically experienced as national or international phenomena: they require a major ideological reconfiguration to be recognized as such. In mid-Victorian England, the ritualized mechanisms by which this reconfiguration of working-class experience as working-class consciousness was accomplished drew from both indigenous and continental

[24] The use of 'nationalism' to describe these agitations offends against received historical conventions of definition, conventions most ably defended by Eric Hobsbawm, *Nations and Nationalism since 1789: Programme, Myth, Reality* (Cambridge, 1990), esp. pp. 43–5, 101–30. The usage adopted here, in which patriotism – the term used most commonly by contemporaries – is essentially conflated with nationalism – a term that began to enter the Victorian vocabulary in *ca.* 1848 – is defended below, pp. 17–18. For Victorian uses of 'nationalism' and 'nationalist' to describe the concerns of radical patriotism, see below, pp. 154, 168.

[25] Ernest Gellner, 'Nationalism and the Two Forms of Cohesion in Complex Societies', in his *Culture, Identity, and Politics* (Cambridge, 1987), pp. 6–28, citation from p. 6. Gellner here builds upon the arguments of Ernest Renan's *Qu'est-ce qu'une nation?* (Paris, 1882).

political traditions, from both patriotic and fraternal ideologies. The common but false antithesis in historical writing between nationalism and internationalism acts to obscure the two concepts' fundamental interrelation in this process. In doing so, it masks their mutual contribution to both class formation and liberal popular politics in the industrial era.

1 · *Nation and class in the English radical tradition*

Nations and classes have long (if warily) coexisted in Britain, but national history and class analysis have proven difficult to combine in even the subset of British historiography devoted exclusively to England. In the halcyon decades of political narrative that stretched from David Hume and Thomas Babington Macaulay to J.H. Plumb, the *History of England* figured as a normative topic of inquiry, a unifying, national subject transcending socio-economic distinctions and self-evidently worthy of multi-volume endeavour.[1] Displaced, however, in the 1960s from the centre of historical scholarship, the received verities of the English nation gave way to forms of social history that privileged sectional analysis. In this new historiographical climate, as one disgruntled observer warned, scholars of gender, locality, and above all class threatened to render national history obsolete.[2] More recently, renewed historical interest in the phenomenon of nationalism and mounting disillusion with the predictive powers of Marxism have restored much of the status quo. A succession of Labour party defeats and popular enthusiasm for foreign wars waged by Tory governments have underlined the enduring ideological appeal of the nation in Britain. Once unwilling to acknowledge the significance of national identity for the labouring population, social historians beating a reluctant retreat from class now routinely turn in mid-flight to embrace the English nation.[3]

---

[1] Hume's six volume *History of England* appeared in 1759–62, Macaulay's five volume *History* in 1848–62. Plumb's volume on the eighteenth century in the Pelican *History of England* was first published in 1950.

[2] Gertrude Himmelfarb, 'Is National History Obsolete?', in her *The New History and the Old* (Cambridge, Mass., 1987), pp. 121–42.

[3] See, for example, Raphael Samuel's preface to the three volumes of essays collected under his editorship, *Patriotism: The Making and Unmaking of British National Identity* (London, 1989), vol. I, pp. x–xvii. The 'British National Identity' of the subtitle proves, in the essays themselves, to be essentially English: only four

If the trends and demands of contemporary politics have encouraged scholars to temper sectional analysis with integrative national
histories, the characteristic preoccupations and activities of English
persons in past centuries cast the limitations inherent in the common
dichotomy between class and nation into sharp relief. For although
Marxists have been reluctant to construct national narratives and
proponents of national history correspondingly loath to acknowledge the force of class interests in national history, generations of
English radical activists have willingly deployed patriotic devices
together with class ideologies in movements of social, economic, and
political protest. Tracing their distinctive English identity to Puritan
Dissent, the Country Party tradition, and the institution of Parliament, eighteenth- and nineteenth-century agitators were fully alive
to the radical potential of the English nation. Expanded in the
French revolutionary era to accommodate new concepts of international brotherhood, the national idiom cherished by these radical
leaders informed the evolution of class politics in the serried popular
movements that reached from the London Corresponding Society to
Chartism. The resulting amalgam of class, national, and internationalist sentiment shaped the contours of public debate on the
role of the working class in English political culture for decades,
creating a dialogue between the working and upper classes that
mediated the growth of parliamentary democracy in Britain.

STATE FORMATION AND THE ENGLISH NATION

Nineteenth-century partisans of English radical movements drew
upon a broad and often disparate array of intellectual genealogies,
historical narratives, martyrologies, and fictions in constructing
their political programmes, but the English radical traditions to
which they ultimately pledged allegiance derived their lineage, in the
first instance, from the institutions of the nation-state. The broad
character and chronology of medieval and early modern government growth are thus central to an understanding of mid-Victorian
radical activity. These political developments in turn provide a

of the fifty-seven articles deal extensively with Ireland, Scotland, or Wales. For
an important corrective to this view, see Miles Taylor, 'John Bull and the
Iconography of Public Opinion in England *c*. 1712–1929', *Past and Present*, no.
134 (February 1992), pp. 93–128.

framework within which the peculiar evolution of English nationalist ideology may best be understood. Fostered, like radicalism itself,
by the process of state formation, nationalist idioms first gained
currency in the spiritual and institutional upheaval of the Protestant
Reformation. Rendered increasingly strident by the course of the
seventeenth-century revolutions and bolstered by the substantial
resources of the British military establishment, the patriotic edifice
created in these years served to promote a vision of the nation
at once bellicose, imperial, and xenophobic. The appeal exerted by
this distinctive sense of patriotism reached to persons at all social
levels within the state, generating an entrenched consciousness of
national identity that long predated class consciousness in English
society.

Viewed from a European perspective, English state formation is
conspicuous for its early genesis, its parliamentary focus, and its
relative success. Conventional historical wisdom holds that nation
and state evolved in tandem from at least the fifteenth century in
both France and England, but the prominence and sweeping claims
of parliamentary government have encouraged successive generations of historians to concede priority to the formation of the
English nation-state. For whereas state formation in both France
and Spain entailed absolutist efforts to control highly scattered and
particularistic bases of authority, English monarchs faced an
increasingly centralized opposition from a Parliament that was
essentially of their own making.[4] G.R. Elton's classic delineation of
this process underlines the importance of the sixteenth-century
expansion of central bureaucracy; other scholars find powerful
motives for English state formation among seventeenth-century
county and village élites.[5] The shrinking frontiers of England abroad
further reinforced these local and national efforts to define the state
and its functions more clearly. Possessed of French territories from
1066, England suffered humiliating defeats throughout the fifteenth

---

[4] Hugh Seton-Watson, *Nations and States: An Enquiry into the Origins of Nations
and the Politics of Nationalism* (London, 1977), pp. 17–49; John Breuilly, *Nationalism and the State* (Manchester, 1982), pp. 53–7; Philip Corrigan and Derek Sayer,
The Great Arch: English State Formation as Cultural Revolution (Oxford, 1985),
pp. 15–28.

[5] G.R. Elton, *The Tudor Revolution in Government: Administrative Changes in the
Reign of Henry VIII* (Cambridge, 1953); Michael Braddick, 'State Formation and
Social Change in Early Modern England: A Problem Stated and Approaches
Suggested', *Social History*, vol. 16 (January 1991), pp. 1–17.

century only to be severed from the continent entirely with the loss of Calais in 1558.

Recent scholarship on the wider British context of state formation has tempered traditional assumptions about the easy triumph of English government institutions by emphasizing the extent to which Ireland, Scotland, and Wales resisted full absorption by a predatory English state.[6] But even in this view the sixteenth and seventeenth centuries emerge as a period of rapidly expanding English dominion. The concentration of wealth, population, and administrative structures enjoyed by England in this period, Hugh Kearney persuasively argues, inaugurated a new era in British history marked by the formation of a dominant 'English empire'.[7] The Tudor incorporation of Wales in 1536, Cromwell's subjection of Ireland in 1650, and the Scottish Act of Union of 1707 formalized the rule of the English state over the Celtic periphery. Failing to obliterate substantial cultural and economic distinctions among the four nations, these developments nonetheless succeeded in constructing an administrative union of remarkable resilience and force. As John Brewer's analysis of the eighteenth-century state clearly demonstrates, England's transformation from 'a minor, infrequent, almost inconsequential participant' in European warfare into 'the military *Wunderkind* of the age' rested securely upon the foundations of Tudor–Stuart government growth.[8]

If political structures reified the process of state formation, an expansion of national consciousness further accelerated the emergence of a distinctive English identity in the early modern period, lending ideological coherence and legitimacy to the government's varied efforts to unite disparate human forces within a single realm. Here again the relative precocity of English developments within a wider European context is significant. Already in the fifteenth century English delegates to the Council of Constance (1414–17) were determined to uphold their nation's sense of cultural autonomy

[6]   See esp. Robin Frame, *The Political Development of the British Isles 1100–1400* (Oxford, 1990); Brian P. Levack, *The Formation of the British State: England, Scotland, and the Union 1603–1707* (Oxford, 1987); Keith Robbins, *Nineteenth-Century Britain: England, Scotland, and Wales, the Making of a Nation* (Oxford, 1989).

[7]   Hugh Kearney, *The British Isles: A History of Four Nations* (Cambridge, 1989), pp. 106–27.

[8]   John Brewer, *The Sinews of Power: War, Money and the English State, 1688–1783* (New York, 1989), pp. xiii, 3–24.

against the competing claims of France. 'Whether a nation be understood as a people marked off from others by blood relationship and habit of unity, or by peculiarities of language (the most sure and positive sign and essence of a nation in divine and human law)', they proclaimed, 'or whether a nation be understood, as it should be, as a territory equal to that of the French nation, England is a real nation.'[9] By breaking from the cosmopolitan embrace of the Catholic Church, Henry VIII further underlined English national consciousness, employing statutory law to secure religious allegiance within the compass of a strictly national state. In this context, 'the patriotic aspects of the Reformation', as Christopher Hill suggests, 'must have struck contemporaries far more forcibly than any doctrinal change'.[10] The successful marriage of the doctrine of the ancient constitution, which depicted the English past as a timeless continuum of custom and usage derived from the common law, to the apocalyptic vision of England as an elect nation of godly Protestants brought the identity of England to the centre of public attention in the seventeenth century.[11] Not least among the myriad ideological demons unleashed by this potent union was early English nationalism.

Scholars conventionally date the emergence of Western nationalism from the later eighteenth century, and tend to discount English involvement in this ostensibly continental phenomenon. 'By some definitions of nationalism, the English (dodging for the moment an awkward question, by counting the Scots and Welsh as honorary Englishmen) never properly experienced it at all', Geoffrey Best asserts. 'What the British inherited from so much history that they did not have to bother about the theory of it, the French, Germans, Italians, and continental others . . . had to invent in passionate haste when revolution hit them.'[12] Hugh Seton-Watson's analysis, while

[9] Cited by Ralph A. Griffiths, 'The Later Middle Ages', in Kenneth O. Morgan (ed.), *The Oxford Illustrated History of Britain* (Oxford, 1984), p. 222.
[10] Christopher Hill, *Reformation to Industrial Revolution: A Social and Economic History of Britain 1530–1780* (London, 1967), p. 21.
[11] J.G.A. Pocock, 'England', in Orest Ranum (ed.), *National Consciousness, History, and Political Culture in Early Modern Europe* (Baltimore, 1975), pp. 98–117. G.R. Elton discusses the political forces that contributed to this development in his 'English National Selfconsciousness and the Parliament in the Sixteenth Century', in Otto Dann (ed.), *Nationalismus in vorindustrieller Zeit* (Munich, 1986), pp. 73–82.
[12] Geoffrey Best, *Honour among Men and Nations: Transformations of an Idea* (Toronto, 1982), p. 12.

acknowledging the extended political genealogy of English national consciousness, similarly asserts that 'English nationalism never existed, since there was no need for either a doctrine or an independence struggle' in England.[13] Associating nationalism inextricably with the excesses of French revolutionary politics or with the seeds of fascism, this line of argument fits neatly with the secular preoccupations of twentieth-century historians but fails to illuminate the significance of nationalism for earlier English generations. For religion, as Sir Lewis Namier was fond of saying, 'is a sixteenth-century word for nationalism'.[14] Nineteenth-century English usage of the term captured precisely this relationship. The *Oxford English Dictionary* in 1836 defined nationalism not as a political doctrine but rather as the conviction that some nations are the objects of divine election.[15]

Viewed from this perspective, England may be seen to boast a rich nationalist heritage rooted in the Calvinist distinction between favoured and condemned nations. In this English variant of nationalist development, dubbed 'holy nationalism' by Conor Cruise O'Brien, ancient Israel figured as the original template of the elect nation, England as its modern embodiment. 'So tender a care hath HE alwaies had of that England', John Lyly observed of God in 1580, 'as of a new Israel, His chosen and peculiar people.'[16] The appearance and increasing accessibility of vernacular translations of the Bible encouraged the elaboration of this line of argument and fostered a belief among educated English Protestants that their nation enjoyed a peculiar covenant with the deity. John Aylmer, a royal tutor and later Bishop of London, expressed this growing conviction succinctly in 1559. 'God is English', he wrote in the margins of his *Harborowe for Faithfull and Trewe Subiectes*.[17] New cultural practices lent this ideology substance, enabling nationalist

[13] Seton-Watson, *Nations and States*, p. 34. Breuilly advances the same thesis in his *Nationalism and the State*, pp. 53–7.
[14] Cited by Hill, *Reformation to Industrial Revolution*, p. 23.
[15] Anthony D. Smith, *Theories of Nationalism* (London, 1971), p. 167.
[16] Conor Cruise O'Brien, *God Land: Reflections on Religion and Nationalism* (Cambridge, Mass., 1988), pp. 1–22; *The Complete Works of John Lyly*, ed. R. Warwick Bond, 3 vols. (Oxford, 1902), vol. II, p. 205, cited by Hans Kohn, 'The Genesis and Character of English Nationalism', *Journal of the History of Ideas*, vol. 1 (January 1940), p. 73.
[17] Patrick Collinson, *The Birthpangs of Protestant England: Religious and Cultural Change in the Sixteenth and Seventeenth Centuries* (New York, 1988), pp. 1–27, citation from p. 4.

sentiment to permeate the quotidian life of the common people. Designed to create a new, Protestant sense of current and historical time, the cycle of religious services, processions, bonfires, and bell ringing that marked the Elizabethan and early Stuart calendar both celebrated and forged English national identity. Elaborate commemorations of the defeat of the Spanish Armada, the discovery of the Gunpowder Plot, and Prince Charles Stuart's return from Spain in 1623 both removed the Protestant calendar from the annual Christological cycle of the continent and underlined England's status as an elect nation guarded by particular Providence.[18]

As the ceremonial dates recognized by the new national calendar suggest, fear of continental Catholic aggression was central to the emergence of early English nationalism. Itself suspect as a foreign innovation in the age of Henry VIII, Protestantism gained its enduring linkage to English nationality with Mary Tudor's unpopular Spanish marriage. In this highly charged political context, Patrick Collinson notes, 'the initial, legislative repudiation of the papal nexus steadily widened its implications until anti-Catholicism, founded on the formal proposition that the Pope is none other than the Antichrist, became the sheet-anchor of England's nationhood'.[19] Threatened alike by continental missionaries and domestic recusants, England appeared as a beleaguered isle in the vast Anti-Popery literature that flourished from the Elizabethan era. Depicting the English people's timeless struggle against an Antichrist whose most recent and diabolic forms were Spain and the Papacy, the successive editions of John Foxe's *Acts and Monuments* (1563, 1570, 1583, 1587) laid the groundwork of an immensely popular national hagiography in which Catholicism consistently figured as a foreign importation. Gaining new currency under the Stuarts, this coherent tradition of national self-representation fed the flames of political division throughout the Civil War, and beyond.[20]

---

[18] David Cressy, *Bonfires and Bells: National Memory and the Protestant Calendar in Elizabethan and Early Stuart England* (London, 1989).

[19] Collinson, *Birthpangs of Protestant England*, pp. 10–11. These pervasive, persistent fears of Catholic aggression, like the later depiction of the Stuart Court as a centre of foreign values, argue against Seton-Watson's claim that England lacked a struggle for independence and hence a nationalist identity.

[20] Carol Z. Wiener, 'The Beleaguered Isle: A Study of Elizabethan and Early Jacobean Anti-Catholicism', *Past and Present*, no. 51 (May 1971), pp. 27–62; Robin Clifton, 'The Popular Fear of Catholics during the English Revolution', *Past and Present*, no. 52 (August 1971), pp. 23–55; Peter Lake, 'Anti-Popery: The Structure of a Prejudice', in Richard Cust and Ann Hughes (eds.), *Conflict in Early*

Foxe's *Acts and Monuments* depicted the English as only one among several elect nations that composed a wider Protestant Church, but the Interregnum and its aftermath served to endow the English nation with the status of pre-eminent election.[21] Under Cromwell and the Rump Parliament, Dutch Protestants – depicted in sermons as Stuart sympathizers seduced by the twin evils of monarchy and Mammon – eclipsed the Catholic Spanish in the fearful popular imagination, a circumstance that encouraged English divines to hail their nation as first among even the Protestant elect. The Navigation Acts and Anglo-Dutch Wars testified to the force of this particularistic vision, which expanded further under the later Stuarts and lent English national identity a martial inflection that was to mark the radical tradition deeply. Intent to portray the Dutch as regicides, republicans, and religious fanatics, the Anglican Royalists who surrounded Charles II renewed warfare against the Dutch to protect a Protestant nation whose interests and identity were narrowly English in definition.[22]

Economic developments, most notably the expansion of the British empire, enlarged the scope and preoccupations of English national identity in the course of the eighteenth century. Economic historians have long recognized the nationalist character of Parliament's control over early modern trade,[23] but social historians have only recently begun to explore more popular expressions of English economic patriotism in this period. Opposition to Catholic Spain, central to the religious nationalism of earlier centuries, helped to catalyse the emergence of this secular variant of national conscious-

---

Stuart England: Studies in Religion and Politics 1603–1642 (London, 1989), pp. 72–106.

[21] William Haller, *Foxe's Book of Martyrs and the Elect Nation* (London, 1963), which mistakes Foxe's meaning by depicting England's elect status as both exclusive and permanent, nonetheless captures the work's partisan potential – realized only in the later seventeenth century – as an instrument of nationalism. Richard Bauckham details Foxe's actual intentions in his *Tudor Apocalypse* (Appleford, 1978), pp. 70–90, 156–7.

[22] S.C.A. Pincus analyses the evolution of English national identity in this context in 'Protestantism and Patriotism: Ideology and the Making of English Foreign Policy 1650–1665' (PhD thesis, Harvard University, 1990), esp. pp. 97–129, 454–64. For the significance of Protestant militarism, see Timothy George, 'War and Peace in the Puritan Tradition', *Church History*, vol. 53 (December 1984), pp. 492–503.

[23] For examples, see Edgar Furniss, *The Position of the Laborer in a System of Nationalism: A Study in Labor Theories of the Later English Mercantilists* (Boston, 1920) and, more recently, Rondo Cameron, *A Concise Economic History of the World: From Paleolithic Times to the Present* (New York, 1989), pp. 154–9.

ness as well. Welcomed with public rejoicing at its outbreak in October 1739, war with Spain captured the patriotic imagination when Vice-Admiral Edward Vernon and his men defeated the Spanish forces at Porto Bello in November. A popular hero commemorated in poems, ballads, prints, and anniversary celebrations, Vernon figured as a commercial patriot, instrumental at one and the same time in defending domestic liberties and expanding foreign markets.[24] In the ensuing decades, France and its burgeoning empire largely displaced Spain as the focus of English national enmity and patriotic pride, as the victories of the Seven Years' War (1756–63) demonstrated anew that God was English. 'No nation', a Sussex shopkeeper expounded in 1759, 'had ever greater occasion to adore the Almighty Disposer of all events than Albion, whose forces meet with success in all quarters of the world.'[25] The aftermath of war saw the elaboration of myriad cultural stereotypes that served to entrench English Gallophobia in the popular mind of the English nation, a development that was especially pronounced among the lower and middle ranks of society.[26]

The negative force of chauvinist antagonism to the continent provided the nucleus of patriotic ideology in England, but eighteenth-century English nationalism drew strength from more positive sources of identification as well. British triumphs in the European theatre of war encouraged English patriots both to denigrate French culture and to glorify their own nation in the apotheosis of the king.[27] More broadly, the changing structure of economic life, the growth of transport mechanisms, and the extension of communication networks encouraged the perception of national unities among otherwise disparate populations of Britons. If, as Karl Deutsch argued in his classic anatomy of the sociology of nationalism, 'membership in a people essentially consists . . . in the ability to communicate more effectively, and over a wider range of subjects,

---

[24] Kathleen Wilson, 'Empire, Trade and Popular Politics in Mid-Hanoverian Britain: The Case of Admiral Vernon', *Past and Present*, no. 121 (November 1988), pp. 74–109. As Wilson is careful to note, in this instance British – not English – identity dominated the discourse on the nation.

[25] Cited by Roy Porter, *English Society in the Eighteenth Century* (Harmondsworth, 1982), p. 21.

[26] Gerald Newman, *The Rise of English Nationalism: A Cultural History 1740–1830* (New York, 1987), pp. 63–84.

[27] Linda Colley, 'The Apotheosis of George III: Loyalty, Royalty and the British Nation 1760–1820', *Past and Present*, no. 102 (February 1984), pp. 94–129.

with members of one large group than with outsiders', the proliferation of newspapers, directories, maps, canals, and turnpikes that marked England in the later eighteenth century underpinned a further expansion of national identity. Although government officials proved reluctant to construct an all-inclusive state nationalism upon these foundations, their subjects seized patriotic opportunities with alacrity. In the years from 1750 to 1830, as Linda Colley has clearly demonstrated, 'almost all sectional interest groups in Britain resorted to nationalist language and activism to advance their claims to wider civic recognition'.[28]

Provincial identities and localism clearly endured alongside the patriotic national consciousness that evolved in England from the sixteenth century. Distinguishing England from greater Britain and estranging even England's constituent units from each other, parochial definitions of the nation were especially tenacious among the working classes, and persisted into the Victorian age. The Scottish hatter James Burn, recounting at mid-century his youthful exploits as a beggar boy, recalled his acquaintance with three highwaymen who 'formed a *trio* of nationalities, one was Yorkshire, another Scotch, and the third Irish'.[29] The Forest of Dean colliers evinced a correspondingly narrow vision of the nation, referring to the forest as 'the country' and to persons born beyond the pale of Gloucestershire as 'foreigners'. 'Confusion to all foreigners' was a popular toast of local rioters determined to rid the mines of workers from outside the forest in 1829–31.[30] But although local patriotisms continued to flourish beyond the eighteenth century, their grip on even plebeian culture was increasingly tempered by the wider claims of the nation. Rooted in the political structures of the state, disseminated by partisans of the elect nation, and consolidated through diplomacy and warfare, national identity emerged in England well before it flourished on the continent. In the decades of revolutionary ferment that followed the events of 1789, English national identity expanded in myriad directions, but retained intact its peculiar early modern foundations.

---

[28] Karl W. Deutsch, *Nationalism and Social Communication: An Inquiry into the Foundations of Nationality* (London, 1953), pp. 70, 75; Linda Colley, 'Whose Nation?: Class and National Consciousness in Britain 1750–1830', *Past and Present*, no. 113 (November 1986), pp. 97–117, citation from p. 116.

[29] James Dawson Burn, *Autobiography of a Beggar Boy* (London, 1855), p. 99.

[30] Chris Fisher, *Custom, Work and Market Capitalism: The Forest of Dean Colliers, 1788–1888* (London, 1981), pp. 47–8, 104.

NATIONALISM AND INTERNATIONALISM

Historians of the English Reformation and revolution underline the nationalist tenor of these early modern experiences, but theorists of nationalism typically locate the origins of this phenomenon in the confluence of three later eighteenth-century revolutions. Together the Enlightenment revolution of intellect, the industrial revolution of the economy, and the French revolution of 1789 constitute a received trinity of forces widely recognized as crucial to the emergence of European nationalism. Each of these three forces, moreover, contributed to the articulation of internationalist ideologies that emerged alongside the new nationalist doctrines. Often ignored in historical analysis, this interpenetration of nationalism and internationalism was of central importance to the evolution of England's distinctive radical tradition.

Although otherwise distinctive in their intentions, preoccupations, and emphases, each of the three dominant interpretations of eighteenth-century nationalism underscores the significance of notions of popular sovereignty, and thus helps to illuminate the patriotic genealogy of the English radical tradition. To Hugh Seton-Watson, concerned with the intellectual ancestry of the phenomenon, the 'essence' of nationalism 'is very simple: it is the application to national communities of the Enlightenment doctrine of popular sovereignty'.[31] Ernest Gellner, although intent to demonstrate that nationalism is a necessary response to industrial transformation, similarly emphasizes sovereignty. Nationalism in his definition 'is primarily a political principle, which holds that the political and the national unit should be congruent'.[32] Scholars of the French revolutionary era display the same basic preoccupation. Otto Dann's survey of European nationalism in the aftermath of 1789 traces its explosive growth to the union of two distinct concepts of the nation: ' "nation" as a group of people of identical origin, and "nation" as a collective holder of sovereignty'.[33]

Novel in its democratic inflection and intensity, the new emphasis on political sovereignty that enveloped European national identity in this period nonetheless drew sustenance from earlier traditions of

[31] Seton-Watson, *Nations and States*, p. 445.
[32] Ernest Gellner, *Nations and Nationalism* (Ithaca, N.Y., 1983), p. 1.
[33] See his introduction to Otto Dann and John Dinwiddy (eds.), *Nationalism in the Age of the French Revolution* (London, 1988), p. 3.

nationalist thought. Rousseau and Herder, pioneering exponents of Enlightenment nationalism, emerged from the Protestant cultures of Calvinist Geneva and German Pietism. Saturated with references to the ancient nation of Israel, Rousseau's political treatises sought to transfer emotive religious loyalties from the elect nation of the Protestant apocalyptic tradition to a sovereign nation of civic patriots who embodied the General Will.[34] Herder's exaltation of nations as the natural and inviolable divisions of the human race and the idealization by Kant – again a Pietist – of self-determination and self-legislation further politicized national identity, and substantially widened the audience to which nationalist ideology could appeal.[35]

If Enlightenment philosophy provided a theoretical underpinning for the democratization of national consciousness, the French revolution furnished the most telling illustration of this new concept of the sovereign nation. Its abolition of orders, destruction of guilds, and repeated attempts to frame a constitution suited to popular government marked an end to Ancien Regime institutional forms and signalled the origin of the society of the citizen. The concept of the nation was integral to the politics of this new revolutionary state, ever-present in an environment in which the human representatives of government were ever-changing. The Declaration of the Rights of Man and the Citizen was emphatic: 'The principle of sovereignty resides essentially in the Nation', it asserted, 'no body of men, no individual, can exercise authority that does not emanate expressly from it.'[36] Just as changes in the character of annual ceremonial observance fostered national consciousness in early modern England, the integration of politics with popular culture in a cycle of revolutionary festivals that celebrated patriotic heroes and events consolidated French national culture in the revolutionary era. Here the influence of Enlightenment philosophy is again evident, for the

---

[34] For the Protestant origins of Enlightenment nationalism, see O'Brien, *God Land*, pp. 43–63, esp. pp. 49–51, and Gellner, *Nations and Nationalism*, pp. 40–1. Ann Cohler explores Rousseau's theories in *Rousseau and Nationalism* (New York, 1970).

[35] Elie Kedourie, *Nationalism* (London, 1960), esp. pp. 24–32, 54–62.

[36] Cited in *ibid.*, p. 12. Lynn Hunt, *Politics, Culture, and Class in the French Revolution* (Berkeley, 1984), pp. 1–119, and Clive Emsley, 'Nationalist Rhetoric and Nationalist Sentiment in Revolutionary France', in Dann and Dinwiddy (eds.), *Nationalism*, pp. 39–52, explore French revolutionary nationalism in greater depth.

replacement of authoritarian politics by the rule of shared political culture was of central importance in the nationalist writings of both Herder and Rousseau.[37]

If commercial expansion fostered the growth of English national consciousness, changing economic structures arguably contributed to the virulence of nationalist identification in revolutionary France. Ernest Gellner identifies the transition from agrarian to urban and industrial society as a crucial stage in the formation of nationalism, arguing that modern economies – which must breach the boundaries of local communities and violate time-honoured traditions – require nationalist ideologies to reconcile their populations to short-term deprivations experienced in the midst of rising social, economic, and political expectations. Nationalism, in this view, functions as a mechanism by which human society insulates itself against the adverse effects of its own structural development.[38] Miroslav Hroch's detailed analysis of the social composition of nationalist movements lends credence to this pairing of patriotic activism and economic change, finding small urban and rural craft producers and traders to have been especially receptive to the early claims of nationalism.[39] In revolutionary France, these small producers formed the backbone of the sans-culottes of 1792–4. Threatened by economic crisis and military invasion, the sans-culottes used the direct exercise of popular sovereignty in the streets to uphold a political vision in which price controls would secure the fundamental economic unity of the nation.[40]

Intellectual, political, and economic developments combined to foster national consciousness in revolutionary France, but they also served to propel nationalism beyond French borders in this period. The sans-culottes' interpretation of the revolutionary triad of liberty, equality, and fraternity had emphasized the domestic application of popular sovereignty, but competing strains of patriotic

---

[37] Mona Ozouf analyses the function of these festivals in *La Fête révolutionnaire 1789–1799* (Paris, 1976). For Herder, Rousseau and national culture in this context see F.M. Barnard, 'National Culture and Political Legitimacy: Herder and Rousseau', *Journal of the History of Ideas*, vol. 44 (April–June 1983), pp. 231–53.

[38] Gellner, *Nations and Nationalism*, pp. 8–52.

[39] Miroslav Hroch, *Social Preconditions of National Revival in Europe: A Comparative Analysis of the Social Composition of Patriotic Groups among the Smaller European Nations*, trans. by Ben Fowkes (Cambridge, 1985), pp. 136–7.

[40] For the sans-culottes' response as an effort to resist the individuation of property, see esp. William H. Sewell, *Work and Revolution in France: The Language of Labor from the Old Regime to 1848* (Cambridge, 1980), pp. 100–13.

argument evolved within the Jacobin context and challenged this local orientation. Already in December 1791 Anacharsis Cloots had proposed that French armies offer neighbouring peoples revolutionary constitutions and *assignats*, a policy which he told the Jacobin Club would establish Paris at the centre of a universal republic that welded the human family into a single, French nation. Expelled from the Jacobin Club in 1792 for their avowed support of conquest, the Girondins embarked upon a policy of expansionist warfare which, when perpetuated by the Thermidorian Convention in 1794, established new meanings and imperatives for the revolutionary nation. Conceived as 'la Grande Nation', France now embodied, if only in the French imagination, both the triumph of one people over its oppressive monarchy and, more broadly, the archetype of all subsequent national liberations. The soldiers of the French revolutionary armies thus figured not only as citizens of France, but as fraternal saviours charged with the forced liberation of subject peoples throughout Europe.[41] Brought to fruition under Napoleon, the sweeping vision of a universal French nation aroused resistance from both monarchs and their domestic detractors, often forcing reform-minded patriots to choose between domestic and foreign tyranny. Already deeply marked by Gallophobia, national consciousness in Britain gained new life from the threat of French revolutionary nationalism of this variety, which acted to unite much of society against reform and behind the established nation-state.[42]

Powerful and pervasive, this chauvinist interpretation of the French revolution was not, however, the only international manifestation of national consciousness to emerge from the revolutionary years. Adumbrated in December 1790, Maximilien Robespierre's definition of fraternity rooted popular sovereignty firmly in the universal rights of male citizens, creating the groundwork for a political theory in which both national identity and international brotherhood could coexist. Drawing his inspiration from the cosmopolitan ideals of Enlightenment luminaries such as Diderot, who

[41] Florence Gauthier, 'Universal Rights and National Interest in the French Revolution', in Dann and Dinwiddy (eds.), *Nationalism*, pp. 27–38; Jacques Godechot, 'Nation, patrie, nationalisme et patriotisme en France au xviiie siècle', *Annales historiques de la Révolution française*, vol. 43 (October–December, 1971), pp. 481–501, esp. pp. 498–501.

[42] Colley, 'Whose Nation?'; Clive Emsley, *British Society and the French Wars, 1793–1815* (London, 1979); H. T. Dickinson (ed.), *Britain and the French Revolution 1789–1815* (Basingstoke, 1989).

disparaged 'those narrow and malicious minds ... who can only think of their petty societies – their nations',[43] Robespierre founded his national policy on a conception of human nature that recognized the fundamental unity of mankind. The thirty-fifth article of his draft Declaration of Rights, presented to the Convention on 24 April 1793, proclaimed that 'The men of all countries are brothers and the different peoples should help one another, according to their means, as if they were citizens of the same state.' But Robespierre, crucially, departed from chauvinist revolutionaries in disavowing the construction of a universal political system. Declaring that 'whoever oppresses one nation declares himself the enemy of all others', article thirty-six of his draft Declaration endorsed a nationalist ideology that denounced military annexation and envisioned in its stead a spontaneous international fraternity of self-governing nations.[44] Visionary and impracticable in the context of its time, Robespierre's union of national and international consciousness endured long after the patriot's execution in 1794, becoming a rallying cry for generations of radical reformers.[45]

In England as in France, the insistent realities of militant nationalism obscured the appeal of fraternal nationality in the revolutionary era, but these years nonetheless saw English thinkers contribute to a liberal expansion of the scope of internationalist thought. Investing international relations with a profound moral imperative, English exponents of classical political economy elaborated a theory of commercial brotherhood that proved increasingly persuasive as trade and industry increased. The provenance of the term internationalism attests to this intellectual ancestry, and to its ethical inflection in the liberal tradition. Jeremy Bentham, a staunch advocate of the independent nation as the basis of legitimate government, coined internationalism in 1789 to advance the arguments of his *Introduction to the Principles of Morals and Legislation*. Predicated upon the twin principles of utility and free trade, Benthamite internationalism envisioned a world-wide reign of peace ensured by a liberal 'Euro-

---

[43] Cited by Thomas J. Schlereth, *The Cosmopolitan Ideal in Enlightenment Thought: Its Form and Function in the Ideas of Franklin, Hume, and Voltaire, 1694–1790* (Notre Dame, 1977), p. 44.
[44] For Robespierre's Declaration of Rights and its broader significance for nationalism, see Gauthier, 'Universal Rights', esp. pp. 28, 33.
[45] Lloyd S. Kramer, 'The Rights of Man: Lafayette and the Polish National Revolution, 1830–1834', *French Historical Studies*, vol. 14 (Fall 1986), pp. 521–46, and below, pp. 122–4.

pean fraternity' of nations.[46] Although political developments precluded the realization of these goals, the efforts of the international peace movement secured liberal internationalism a wide audience and talented leadership in the ensuing decades.[47]

Pacifist ideals inspired thousands of English liberals, but the tenets of liberal internationalism also drew strength from social and economic relations. For although commercial rivalry, like revolutionary politics, militated against free trade between France and England, the wider structural interdependence of the two nations' economies encouraged even bellicose militants of the propertied classes to recognize international interests alongside national identities. Integrated capital markets joined financial interests in England, France, and the Netherlands by the later eighteenth century; intermarriage among commercial dynasties consolidated these monetary unions and gave them social expression. The very mechanisms, indeed, which promoted national consciousness by tempering parochialism acted as well to expand citizens' identities beyond national frontiers.[48] Railways and the telegraph, transport and communication networks, combined to generate overlapping reticulations of consciousness in which nationalism and internationalism were intertwined. To speak, as is common, of 'nationalism and its opposite and corrective, internationalism'[49] is therefore imprecise. Nationalism and internationalism were not opposed historically so much as they were contingent.

Widely current in diverse schools of historical writing, the misplaced antithesis between nationalist and internationalist identity

---

[46] Carlton J.H. Hayes, *The Historical Evolution of Modern Nationalism* (New York, 1931), pp. 129–30; Jeremy Bentham, 'Principles of International Law', in John Bowring (ed.), *The Works of Jeremy Bentham* (Edinburgh, 1843), vol. II, pp. 535–60.

[47] J.A. Hobson, *Richard Cobden: The International Man* (London, 1919), offers an excellent case-study of liberal internationalism, and W.H. van der Linden, *The International Peace Movement, 1815–1874* (Amsterdam, 1987) surveys its wider context.

[48] Larry Neal, *The Rise of Financial Capitalism: International Capital Markets in the Age of Reason* (Cambridge, 1991); Charles A. Jones, *International Business in the Nineteenth Century: The Rise and Fall of a Cosmopolitan Bourgeoisie* (New York, 1987). F.S.L. Lyons surveys these themes more broadly in *Internationalism in Europe 1815–1914* (Leyden, 1963).

[49] Best, *Honour among Men and Nations*, p. xii. Friedrich Meinecke, *Cosmopolitanism and the Nation State*, trans. by Robert B. Kimber (Princeton, 1970), offers a pioneering analysis of 'the complex process of confrontation and union' (p. 21) that governed the relation between cosmopolitan and nationalist tendencies in the nineteenth century.

draws particular strength from the enduring legacy of classical Marxism. Guided by a dogged determination to stand Hegel on his head, the young Marx and Engels rejected the state's claim to function as an embodiment of the nation's sovereignty, emphasizing instead the primacy of the abstract, universalized category of civil society. Anchoring nationalism in the material needs of modern industry, they recognized it as a progressive or historical force when nationalist development promoted centralization and economic growth on a large scale, and more particularly the development of factory production and class conflict. In this dialectical interpretation, nationalism laid the foundation for class consciousness only to be superseded by it.[50]

Central to Marx's economic formulation of nationality was his ascription of national consciousness to the bourgeoisie, and corresponding equation of internationalism with working-class consciousness. Unable to construct a meaningful interpretation of middle-class nationalism without resorting to concepts of political sovereignty, Marx offered a theoretically impoverished (if at times historically perceptive) analysis in which national identity functioned as a Janus-faced instrument of intra-class rivalry and inter-class oppression. 'However much the individual bourgeois fights against the others, as a *class* the bourgeoisie have a common interest, and this community of interest, which is directed against the proletariat inside the country, is directed against the bourgeois of other nations outside the country', he argued in 1845. 'This the bourgeois calls his *nationality*.'[51] Propelled forcefully by the logic of its shared economic interests, Marx's idealized proletariat was largely impervious to the claims of nationality. At most, nationalist identity represented a temporary obstacle to international class consciousness: 'large-scale industrial labour, large-scale subjection to capital ... has stripped him of every trace of national character', the *Communist Manifesto* famously proclaimed, 'but the proletariat

[50] For the Hegelian influence, see Z.A. Pelczynski, 'Nation, Civil Society, State: Hegelian Sources of the Marxian Non-Theory of Nationality', in Pelczynski (ed.), *The State and Civil Society: Studies in Hegel's Political Philosophy* (Cambridge, 1984), pp. 262–78. The best introduction to the wider problem of the relation between Marxism and nationalism is still Horace B. Davis, *Nationalism and Socialism: Marxist and Labor Theories of Nationalism to 1917* (New York, 1967).

[51] Karl Marx, 'Draft of an Article on Friedrich List's Book *Das nationale System der politischen Okonomie*', cited and discussed in Roman Szporluk, *Communism and Nationalism: Karl Marx versus Friedrich List* (New York, 1988), p. 35.

of each country must, of course, first of all settle matters with its own bourgeoisie'.[52] In this view workers' long-term interests lay emphatically with internationalism. 'The nationality of the worker is neither French, nor English, nor German, it is *labour*', Marx concluded. 'His government is neither French, nor English, nor German, it is *capital*.'[53]

It is fashionable to deride these simplistic assumptions, which the events of the twentieth century reveal to have been exceptionally myopic. But it is also mistaken to attribute early Marxism's failure to engage seriously with nationalism solely to materialist theory's philosophical deficiencies. For the antagonism that Marx and Engels evinced toward nationalism derived in large measure from their nineteenth-century context, from the cut and thrust of radical polemic in which they enmeshed their lives. Their subsequent deification as theorists mysteriously elevated above the petty demands of history obscures the extent to which the two Germans recognized nationalist movements' significance for class politics. As Roman Szporluk clearly demonstrates, their refusal to immerse themselves in the maelstrom of contemporary nationalist aspiration reflected both an avowed distaste for bourgeois ideologies (other than their own) and a recognition of the need to distinguish their theory from alternative, nationalist critiques of political economy with which it contended for popular support. By dismissing the ability of nationalism to function as what Szporluk calls 'a third party on the battlefield where Marxism met capitalism', Marx and Engels sought to create a bipolar opposition between socialism and capitalism.[54] This ideological sleight of hand lent their theory the appearance of great clarity and coherence. But in a world of radical politics ruled by triangular relations among labour, capital, and the nation-state it can only have reduced the popular appeal of Marxist argument.

Although both Marx and Engels tempered their opposition to nationalism as they grew older, the legacy of their early hostility lived on in the divisive campaigns waged by their successors. The much-publicized polemics of V.I. Lenin and Rosa Luxemburg represent only the most visible portion of an extended debate which

[52] 'Manifesto of the Communist Party', in *Karl Marx, Frederick Engels: Collected Works* (New York, 1975–), vol. VI, pp. 494–5.
[53] Marx, 'Draft of an Article', cited by Szporluk, *Communism and Nationalism*, p. 35.
[54] *Ibid.*, p. 14.

has had the net effect of retrospectively erecting a rigid barrier between nationalist and internationalist movements of the nineteenth century. If men and women, as Eric Hobsbawm astutely suggests, 'did not choose collective identifications as they chose shoes, knowing that one could only put on one pair at a time', Marxist historians have traditionally been doctrinaire in their refusal to acknowledge the mutuality of class, confessional, and national identities.[55] Yet it is also the Marxist tradition which offers, in the work of Ber Borochov, by far the most systematic effort to explicate the troubled historical relations of nation, class, and internationalism in the modern period.

A Jewish socialist and nationalist who died in the Russian revolution, Borochov offered a materialist analysis of national identity in his much-neglected classic, 'The National Question and the Class Struggle'. Two aspects of production, relations of production and conditions of production, provide the basis for his discussion of nationalism. Relations of production are familiar from classical Marxist writing: these are the relations described in pre-industrial societies by terms such as caste, rank, and order and in industrial societies by class. Relations of production vary with the level of economic sophistication achieved by a given society but are essentially constant among different societies at the same stage of development. Conditions of production, on the other hand, vary substantially from society to society, regardless of the stage of economic growth attained. Geographical, anthropological, and historical in origin, conditions of production fashion peoples in pre-modern societies; under industrialism they forge nations. Class struggle arises from discrepancies in the relations of production, national struggles from those in the conditions of production.[56]

Central to this interpretation is the recognition that nationalism is a political force with direct relevance for class formation. Conditions of production, Borochov argues, spring from the territory but soon evolve to include political institutions, culture, and nationalism itself. These conditions can and do occlude relations of production; nationalism can and does obscure the significance of class. Yet class

[55] Hobsbawm, *Nations and Nationalism*, p. 123. The Lenin–Luxemburg debates are well illustrated in Horace B. Davis (ed.), *The National Question: Selected Writings by Rosa Luxemburg* (New York, 1976).
[56] Ber Borochov, 'The National Question and the Class Struggle', in *Nationalism and the Class Struggle: A Marxian Approach to the Jewish Problem*, ed. Abraham G. Duker (Westport, Conn., 1972), pp. 136–40.

formation can occur only in a national context, for it is only a perception of his inferior position within an ordered social and economic environment that enables the worker to perceive the logic of sustained class struggle:

> It is false to accept the widespread fallacy which claims that the proletariat has no relation with the national wealth and therefore has no national feelings and interests. No class in society is outside the conditions of production of that society . . . the territory has its value for the proletariat . . . as a place in which to work.

Industrial class struggle, Borochov argues, 'can take place only where the worker toils . . . where he has already occupied a certain workplace', for 'as long as the worker does not occupy a definite position, he can wage no struggle'.[57]

Borochov's interpretation provides a basic framework for the integrated analysis of the phenomena of class, nationalism, and internationalism. Like labour aristocracy theory, Borochov's model argues against the depiction of workers as a monolithic social and economic unit, for it suggests that even workers who share the same relations of production may experience different conditions of production. His reasoning, moreover, predicts an increase, not a diminution, of national sentiment with industrialization: conditions of production gain rather than lose importance as workers unite in efforts to readjust the relations of production. Yet Borochov's theory also recognizes the full significance of the development of internationalism for nationalism and class. Internationalism, in this view, entails not only a belief in the right of other peoples to delimit and control their own particular territory or conditions of production, but also a perception of shared relations of production among widely various industrial societies. Rather than constituting two entirely antagonistic forms of ideology, one reflecting false consciousness and the other class consciousness, nationalism and internationalism are two different aspects of a single process of production, engaged in a perpetual dialectic. Thus 'on the one hand, the capitalistic system appears as international, and destroys all boundaries between tribes and peoples and uproots all traditions, while on the other hand, it is itself instrumental in the intensification of international struggle and heightens national self-consciousness'.[58]

[57] *Ibid.*, pp. 157, 159.   [58] *Ibid.*, p. 160.

The precise historical configuration of class thus reflects the confluence of economic experiences, national identities, and internationalist sentiments. Like class and nation, to which it is closely tied, internationalism finds a real and important basis in the production process; like these forces too, internationalism is a learned pattern of thought and behaviour rather than an instinctive response to the social and economic conditions imposed by industrialism. In continental Europe, commercial expansion and Enlightenment thought laid the groundwork for the emergence of this belief system in the later eighteenth century even as they established the economic and philosophical foundations of continental nationalism.

Yet although internationalism fed upon a nationalist base, it is the coeval development of internationalism and class that emerges most clearly from an analysis of national identity that embraces both the early modern period and the English nation. For in England national consciousness predated internationalism not by decades but by centuries, becoming embedded in English political culture not with industrialism or Enlightenment philosophy but with the Protestant confessional state. In sharp contrast to nationalism, internationalism failed to flourish in the early modern period.[59] Its appearance as a significant and persistent ideological force in England dates from the later eighteenth century. The twofold significance of this period lies in the coincidence of the French and industrial revolutions, in the tentative and often inchoate articulation of class concepts within a political framework governed by debates on both the nature of sovereignty and the nature of man. Repeated and amplified in the English response to the continental revolutions of 1848, this interchange of class, national, and international idioms was curious, but not aberrant. Its origins lay in the development from the early modern period of a tradition of radical politics in England that was both national and popular in appeal. The persistence and growth of this English radical tradition in the face of class and internationalism helped to shape the peculiar configuration of Europe's first proletariat.

[59] This is not to deny the internationalist tendencies of early Protestantism, which are discussed by Patrick Collinson, 'England and International Calvinism 1558–1640', in Menna Prestwich (ed.), *International Calvinism 1541–1715* (Oxford, 1985), pp. 197–223. But English Calvinism became increasingly insular in its second generation, a process noted by Christopher Hill, 'The Protestant Nation', in *The Collected Essays of Christopher Hill, vol. II: Religion and Politics in 17th Century England* (Brighton, 1986), pp. 30–1.

THE NATION IN THE ENGLISH RADICAL TRADITION

Radicalism is an amorphous term in English history, comprising a diverse and contradictory array of persons, concepts, and strategies. Employed from the seventeenth century to denote 'going to the root', the adjective 'radical' was coupled with 'reform' by 1786, became a noun signifying 'an advocate of radical reform' by 1802, and produced 'radicalism' itself by 1820.[60] Nineteenth-century usage embraced both middle- and working-class reformers, both liberal and socialist philosophies. Within the propertied classes, the 'Philosophic Radicals' surrounding James and John Stuart Mill advocated classical political economy and the democratization of government in the twenties and thirties; more influential in the later nineteenth century was what one middle-class socialist termed 'the old school of Radicals of the Cobden–Bright period, the advanced men of the sixties and seventies ... a well marked type, intellectually and otherwise'.[61] Among the lower classes, the spectrum of allegiance described by radicalism was more varied and fluid. To Joseph Gutteridge, Coventry silk weaver and sometime carpenter, the terms ' "Revolutionist" or "Radical" ' applied equally to parliamentary reformers, infidel sectarians, and the Owenite socialists, of whom he was one.[62] Thomas Wood, a mechanic born in 1822, embraced 'the extreme of Radicalism, or Chartism as it was then called', as an apprentice; G.J. Holyoake, who subscribed to both Chartism and Owenism in his youth, joined with the 'Radical' trade unionists of the Reform League to promote suffrage extension in 1867.[63]

Faced with this diverse pattern of contemporary usage, twentieth-century historians have constructed two basic schools of radical

---

[60] Arthur E. Bestor, 'The Evolution of the Socialist Vocabulary', *Journal of the History of Ideas*, vol. 9 (June 1948), pp. 261–2.

[61] Joseph Hamburger, *Intellectuals in Politics: John Stuart Mill and the Philosophic Radicals* (New Haven, 1965); Ernest Belfort Bax, *Reminiscences and Reflections of a Mid and Late Victorian* (London, 1918), p. 227.

[62] Valerie E. Chancellor (ed.), *Master and Artisan in Victorian England: The Diary of William Andrews and the Autobiography of Joseph Gutteridge* (New York, 1969), p. 126.

[63] The Autobiography of Thomas Wood', in John Burnett (ed.), *Annals of Labour: Autobiographies of British Working-Class People 1820–1920* (Bloomington, 1974), p. 308; George Jacob Holyoake, *Sixty Years of an Agitator's Life*, 2 vols. (London, 1893), vol. I, p. 268.

interpretation. The more traditional view traces the origins of English radicalism to the succession of agitations for parliamentary reform which began in the later eighteenth century. Emphasizing radical opposition to parliamentary corruption and aristocratic patronage, and underlining the prominence within radical movements of gentlemanly (if not genteel) leaders such as John Wilkes and John Cartwright, this body of analysis imbues radicalism with a reformist tenor rendered all the more conspicuous by its contrast to the successful revolutions of the Americans and the French.[64] More recent approaches to radicalism have generated a second broad school of interpretation, which endows the radical tradition with a more extended, capacious, and subversive genealogy. Proponents of this view typically find the ideological provenance of English radicalism in the seventeenth-century revolutions, and trace its lineage to Tory dissidents as well as to the Whigs. Acknowledging the importance of parliamentary agitations for radical movements, their analysis also recognizes the radical implications of religion, non-parliamentary popular politics, and economic conflict.[65]

Historians who critique this second school rightly note that its anachronistic nomenclature can distort the contemporary meaning of early English dissidence. By treating early modern oppositional ideologies as foreshadowings of later, more modern radical programmes, the premature radicalization of seventeenth- and early eighteenth-century discourse can promote a whiggish view of history which both prizes arguments from the context in which they were formulated and privileges radical politics over more common conservative allegiances.[66] Yet no history of Victorian radicalism can

---

[64] The classic text is Simon Maccoby, *English Radicalism 1762–1785: The Origins* (London, 1955). More recent interpretations which retain this chronology include John Brewer, *Party Ideology and Popular Politics at the Accession of George III* (Cambridge, 1976), and Joseph O. Baylen and Norbert J. Gossman (eds.), *Biographical Dictionary of Modern British Radicals*, 2 vols. (Sussex, 1979–84), vol. I, pp. 1–7.

[65] Linda Colley, 'Eighteenth-Century English Radicalism before Wilkes', *Transactions of the Royal Historical Society*, 5th ser., vol. 31 (1981), pp. 1–19; Gary Stuart De Kray, *A Fractured Society: The Politics of London in the First Age of Party, 1688–1715* (Oxford, 1985); Margaret and James Jacob (eds.), *The Origins of Anglo-American Radicalism* (London, 1984); Gregory Claeys, *Citizens and Saints: Politics and Anti-Politics in Early British Socialism* (Cambridge, 1989), esp. pp. 23–35.

[66] Lotte Mulligan and Judith Richards, 'A "Radical" Problem: The Poor and the English Reformers in the Mid-Seventeenth Century', *Journal of British Studies*, vol. 29 (April 1990), pp. 118–46, oppose the radical designation for the seventeenth

ignore the extended ideological lineage of the English radical tradition. For if twentieth-century historians debate the chronological origins of English radicalism, nineteenth-century radical activists consistently located their ideological roots in the Puritan revolution. The ballad of 'The White Hat' is characteristic, invoking the memory of Hampden, Pym, and Cromwell to celebrate the followers of Henry Hunt and advance a radical reform of Parliament in 1819 (Ill. 1)[67]. Later exponents of the radical tradition persistently adduced the same antecedents. The London secularist leader Charles Bradlaugh was typical in prefacing his exposition of English republican principles in the 1870s with a lecture on Oliver Cromwell.[68] Rural radicalism boasted the same heritage. Joseph Arch, leader of the Agricultural Labourers' Union in 1872, attributed his followers' resolve to the circumstance that their seventeenth-century 'forefathers had stood up for the threatened liberties of England, and with scythes and pitchforks and clubbed muskets had beaten back the King's Life Guards till the cannon mowed them down'.[69]

Arch's autobiography points not only to radicalism's seventeenth-century origins but also to its close association with English national sentiment. For his depiction of the agricultural labourers' plight spoke equally to their economic exploitation and to the tradition of the elect nation. 'These white slaves of England stood there with the darkness all about them', Arch recalled of his late-night speeches to the workers, 'like the Children of Israel waiting for some one to lead them out of the land of Egypt.'[70] Drawing its assumptions from the ideological armoury of the nation, English radicalism was, like English nationalism, a product of state formation. Marked by their inveterate patriotism, parliamentarianism, and Protestantism, the oppositional traditions forged in the early modern period guided and at times constrained the radical endeavour of subsequent generations of reformers. But as the example of Joseph Arch and the

---

century; J.C.D. Clark, *English Society 1688–1832: Ideology, Social Structure and Political Practice during the Ancien Regime* (Cambridge, 1985), p. 348, critiques but ultimately upholds the deliberately anachronistic use of 'radicalism' to describe early modern popular movements.

[67] 'The White Hat' (London, [1819]), BODL, Harding Ballads, B.11 (4162).

[68] Printed Announcement of Lectures, February 1875, BI, Charles Bradlaugh Collection, item 415.

[69] Joseph Arch, *From Ploughtail to Parliament: An Autobiography* (London, 1898; repr. London, 1986), p. 92.

[70] *Ibid.*, p. 71.

THE WHITE HAT.

Printed by J. Evans and Sons, Long-lane, London.

IN sixteen hundred and forty-one,
  The Radicals had some famous fun ;
Till with King Charles they so merrily sped,
They first took his crown, and then his head.
  Then hey for Radical Reform,
    To raise in England a glorious storm ;
  Till every man his dinner has got,
  For twopence the loaf, and a penny the pot.

Hampden and Pim, with their Radical shears,
Cropt the bishops, and sliced the peers ;
While Oliver kick'd the mace with an air,
And set his own rump in the Speaker's chair.
  Then hey for Radical Reform, &c.

Oliver wore a broad-brimm'd hat :
It was not *white* but no matter for that;
For so very broad its brim was grown,
That it cover'd the altar, & capp'd the throne.
  Then hey for Radical Reform, &c.

Oliver then grew proud and high;
He look'd on his comrades rather shy ;
He spit in their faces, and cut them all,
Till they humbly cried, God save King Noll!
  Then hey for Radical Reform, &c.

In eighteen hundred and nineteen,
Again shall be what before has been ;
Until we reform both Church and State,
As in sixteen hundred and forty-eight.
  Then hey for Radical Reform, &c.

Hampden and Pim were not half so good
As Doctor Watson and Thistlewood ;
And Lawyer Pearson as learnedly spoke
As ever did Mr. Solicitor Coke.
  Then hey for Radical Reform, &c.

And there's Henry Hunt, the cock of us all,
Will do the job much better than Noll ;
Whose Beaver was never so broad or flat,
As our King Harry the Ninth's White Hat.
  Then hey for Radical Reform, &c.

And Oliver had not Harry's way,
In making harangues from a one horse *chay* ;
Or, when he had reach'd his private ends,
In cutting his inconvenient friends.
  Then hey for Radical Reform, &c.

We'll have no pension, place, nor court,
No King nor Regent to support ;
No priests to feed, no taxes to pay :
And we'll go to the devil our own way.
  Then hey for Radical Reform, &c.

A Parliament shall be held once a year,
Without the presence of bishop or peer ;
And every man be his own law-maker,
In right of his single vote and acre.
  Then hey for Radical Reform, &c.

Reform like this we Radicals choose, [lose ;
Who have something to gain & nothing to
Unlike Sir Frank, and the Whiggish train,
Who have something to lose and nothing to
  Then hey for Radical Reform, &c. [gain.

Now march, my boys, in your Radical rage ;
Handle your sticks, and flourish your flags ;
Till we lay the Throne and the Altar flat,
With a whisk of Harry the Ninth's White Hat.
  And hey for Radical Reform,
    To raise in England a glorious storm ;
  And level each proud aristocrat,   [Hat.
  With a whisk of Harry the Ninth's White

1 'The White Hat'

agricultural labourers suggests, national sentiment also served to
sustain and widen radical activism in these years. Protestant monarchs sought to restrict their subjects' loyalties to a single, unified
state through reformed belief, but Protestant religion ultimately
succeeded in widening the scope of social and political argument
within the consolidated state system.

Partisan elaboration of the homiletic resources of the Hebrew Bible lay at the heart of English Protestantism's radical impulse, just as it was central to the evolution of English nationalism. Elevating the religion of English men and women over continental Catholicism to erect what one historian has aptly described as 'a towering scaffold of moral nationalism', the image of Israel and the concept of election inspired introspection and reform rather than complacence within the English polity.[71] Addressing 'all the inhabitants of this land' in *England's Summons* (1613), Thomas Sutton told the English people that 'God hath opened the windows of heaven wider and offered more grace unto you ... than to all the nations under the canopy and roof of heaven', but noted that despite this peculiar favour, 'you still persist in your gray and ancient sins'. James Jones's sermon, *London's Looking-Back to Jerusalem* (1630), struck a correspondingly sober note, warning that God 'hath honoured this nation of ours above all nations of the world; for shame, let us not out-sin all the nations of the world, for if we out-act them in sin, we must out-suffer them in punishment'.[72] The radical implications of this religious conception of English nationhood became increasingly obvious under the Stuarts, but were evident even in the Elizabethan era. Already in 1589, Martin Marprelate disparaged those persons who 'were obedient subjects to the Queen and disobedient traitors to God and the realm'.[73] Under the Stuarts, the competing claims of monarchical loyalty, religious conviction, and allegiance to the state were increasingly problematic.

The emergence in the 1620s of a perceived opposition between Court and Country buttressed the radical ideology of the elect nation with an explicitly political programme. Initially signifying merely the monarch, his entourage, and his officials, the Court came in these years to symbolize tyranny, decadence, corruption, effeminacy, Catholicism, and foreign influences in general – all but the xenophobia remaining persistent objects of radical odium into the twentieth century. In sharp contrast to the Court, representatives of the Country interest claimed to stand for ancient English liberties

---

[71] Michael McGiffert, 'God's Controversy with Jacobean England', *American Historical Review*, vol. 88 (December 1983), pp. 1151–74. McGiffert qualifies his argument in *ibid.*, vol. 89 (October 1984), pp. 1217–18, but does not alter his argument about Jacobean Protestant nationalism.

[72] Cited in *ibid.*, p. 1218. See also Collinson, *Birthpangs of Protestant England*, pp. 17–27.

[73] Cited by Hill, 'The Protestant Nation', in *Collected Essays*, p. 28.

and rights, including notably the rights of property, confirmed by law. As one proponent of their cause explained in 1629:

> being chosen for the Country, they are to be all for the Country, for the Liberty of the Subject, for the Fredome of Speech, & to gain as much and as many Priviledges for the Subject from the King, as is possible. And if they stand stiffley out in the deniall of Subsidies, to save their owne & their Countries purses, then they are excellent Patriots, good Commonswealthsmen, they have well & faithfully discharg'd the trust reposed in them by their City or Country.

Typically denoted 'the Country interest' by contemporaries, these men were also described by their peers as 'patriots' and 'parliamentarians'.[74]

Exacerbated by English and Protestant defeats abroad and by monarchical opposition at home, Country Party opposition – its adherents later insisted – was instrumental in precipitating the English Civil War.[75] The defining characteristics of this ideology are noteworthy, for the Country Party, if only in spite of itself, helped to give birth to the English radical tradition. Manly, patriotic, and Protestant, the Country was drawn not from the *nouveaux riches* but from the ruling class itself. Frequently noble and almost inevitably landed, its adherents were the pillars of Stuart society, men acutely conscious of the political mechanisms that must be mastered to lend the elect nation firm institutional foundations. Not surprisingly, their arguments more often took the form of conservative pleas for the restoration of ancient rights embodied in common law than in calls for innovative reform. Even in the republicanism of the Interregnum this tradition was profoundly backward-looking, based on Machiavelli, Livy, and Polybius rather than common justice, decency, or reason.[76]

---

[74] Perez Zagorin, *The Court and the Country: The Beginning of the English Revolution* (London, 1969), pp. 33–9, 72. 'Country' was not necessarily synonymous with nation: as Zagorin points out on p. 33, it also denoted the county for which Members of Parliament held their seats.

[75] Twentieth-century historians, in contrast, debate the role of the Country Party in crystallizing disaffection. Zagorin's *Court and Country* is the classic statement of the Country's revolutionary impact; the opposing side is well represented by Conrad Russell, *Parliament and English Politics, 1621–1629* (Oxford, 1979).

[76] Zagorin, *Court and Country*, pp. 83–90; J.G.A. Pocock, *The Ancient Constitution and the Feudal Law: A Study of English Historical Thought in the Seventeenth Century* (Cambridge, 1957). On Interregnum republicanism, see Blair Worden, 'Classical Republicanism and the Puritan Revolution', in Hugh Lloyd-Jones,

It is, however, short-sighted to dismiss English radicalism as the product of a blind and inexplicable adherence to antique aristocratic conceptions of society informed by empty national myths and the arcane wisdom of classical historians. Aristocratic ideals of culture, society, and government proved remarkably resilient in England, but they failed in even the early modern period to monopolize discussion on the conduct of the English state. Nor did their representatives necessarily seek to do so. In the course of the 1640s, protracted disputes with the Crown forced members of both Houses to appeal to the common people for arms, men, and monies. Determined to concentrate political power in their own hands for their own purposes, the Lords and Commons nonetheless repeatedly claimed to act as representatives of a sovereign nation. As Edmund Morgan has argued, these men 'invented the sovereignty of the people in order to claim it for themselves – in order to justify their own resistance, not the resistance of their constituents singly or collectively, to a formerly sovereign king'. Conservative in intention, this ploy was radical in consequence, for 'popular sovereignty, like divine right, had a life and a logic of its own that made demands on those who used it'.[77] If English oppositional strategies were from an early date confined to a single set of institutions, English oppositional leaders were relatively quick to broaden the range of their support within the wider population. Long before this was the case on the continent, radical politics in England purported to be national.

Here again the radical consequences of the conservative Country Party and Civil War traditions are crucial, and an emphasis on the neoclassical proclivities of the governing élite perhaps misleading. Convinced of their own superior claims to rule, Country and Commonwealth politicians were not loath to court the common people when it suited their ends to do so. As David Underdown has suggested, seventeenth-century popular politics was not tolerated by aristocratic Englishmen so much as it was inspired by them.[78] In this discourse with the larger nation, the great men of England made few allusions to the great minds of the classical polis: consistently,

Valerie Pearl, and Blair Worden (eds.), *History and Imagination: Essays in Honour of H.R. Trevor-Roper* (London, 1980), pp. 182–200.

[77] Edmund S. Morgan, *Inventing the People: The Rise of Popular Sovereignty in England and America* (New York, 1988), pp. 50, 90.

[78] David Underdown, *Revel, Riot, and Rebellion: Popular Politics and Culture in England 1603–1660* (Oxford, 1985), esp. pp. 106–45.

their model of virtuous government was provided by ancient England, not by ancient Greece. Couched in the rhetoric of the freeborn Englishman who suffered now under a Norman Yoke, their language was the language of patriotism. During the Forced Loan controversy of 1626–8, the Earl of Lincoln appealed *To All True-Hearted Englishmen*; John Lilburne's attack on arbitrary rule was *Englands Birth-Right Justified* (1645). More circumspect but no less eloquent was a gentlemanly response to the disputed election of Great Marlow in 1640. Sir Simonds D'Ewes – no radical he – confided in his diary 'that the poorest man ought to have a voice, that it was the birthright of the subjects of England'.[79]

Divinely sanctioned, Parliament figured in these debates as the chief repository and defence of the political birthrights of the elect nation. Diverse Leveller patriots, petitioning the House of Commons in 1647, underlined the singular providence of England's system of sovereignty, asserting that 'God hath blessed them with their first desires, making this Parliament most free and absolute of any Parliament that ever was ... with power sufficient to deliver the whole Nation from all kind of oppression and grievance ... and to make it the most absolute and free nation in the world.'[80] In Parliament, the Country interest had found a natural forum in which to voice its patriotic opposition to the king's intended tyranny; in Parliament, the representatives of a sovereign people found Charles I guilty of high treason against the English nation and authorized his execution. With the exile of the Stuarts, diffuse theories of English popular rights merged with the concept of the elect nation to forge a godly enthusiasm for radical change which appealed to individuals of all social levels. The Leveller, Digger, Ranter, and Quaker movements of these years hardly typified the experience of revolution, but their efflorescence nonetheless illustrated Parliament's unwitting contribution to the development of radical forces beyond its ken and control. And if concepts of social and economic equality and notions of democratic politics failed to prevail in the Commonwealth and Protectorate, neither did their

---

[79] Cited in *ibid.*, p. 132. For the important theory of the Norman Yoke in the radical tradition, see Christopher Hill, 'The Norman Yoke', in John Saville (ed.), *Democracy and the Labour Movement: Essays in Honour of Dona Torr* (London, 1954), pp. 11–66.

[80] *To the Right Honourable and Supreme Authority of This Nation, the Commons in Parliament Assembled* [1647] reprinted in William Haller (ed.), *Tracts on Liberty in the Puritan Revolution 1638–1647*, 3 vols. (New York, 1934), vol. III, pp. 399–400.

opponents succeed in expunging their marks from the evolving
radical tradition.[81]

The extremism of the radical sects is a commonplace of seventeenth-century historiography, but the extent to which more moderate Englishmen expounded radical ideals of freedom and the nation
is perhaps not emphasized enough. Oliver Cromwell, 'God's Englishman', although unwilling to subscribe to Leveller extremes,
promoted both the radical trajectory and the nationalist tenor of his
times. Centred in 1642 on objections to the king's attempts to stifle
parliamentary authority, the burden of the 'Good Old Cause' had
shifted by 1653 to the mission of constructing a godly nation.
Drawing, predictably, upon the imagery of ancient Israel and its
liberation from Egyptian bondage, Cromwell's concern for the
preservation of the ancient constitution gave way increasingly to a
preoccupation with religious freedom and natural law contractua-
lism: by 1656, he had proclaimed that 'Liberty of conscience is a
natural right.'[82] Expanding the foundations of English liberty from
historic birthrights to natural laws, this line of argument nonetheless
retained the fundamental equation of religious and national liberties
established in the sixteenth century. Cromwell spoke compellingly in
this vein in 1657, defining religion and 'the Civil Liberty and Interest
of the Nation' as the twin human concerns of divine authority. 'If
anyone whatsoever think the interest of Christians and the interest
of the Nation inconsistent or two different things', he concluded, 'I
wish my soul may never enter into their secrets.'[83]

In recent years, scholars have sought to de-radicalize the political
legacy of the Civil War and Interregnum period. On the political
right, their arguments focus on the profoundly conservative beliefs
of the leading figures of that great euphemism, 'the Great Rebellion';
on the left, critics dismiss the revolution as 'the least bourgeois

---

[81] Christopher Hill, *The World Turned Upside Down: Radical Ideas during the English Revolution* (Harmondsworth, 1972).

[82] J.S.A. Adamson, 'Oliver Cromwell and the Long Parliament', in John Morrill (ed.), *Oliver Cromwell and the English Revolution* (New York, 1990), pp. 88–98; Anthony Fletcher, 'Oliver Cromwell and the Godly Nation', in *ibid.*, pp. 209–33; Johann Sommerville, 'Oliver Cromwell and English Political Thought', in *ibid.*, pp. 234–58, esp. pp. 241, 255. For a broader development of these themes, see R.C. Richardson and G.M. Ridden (eds.), *Freedom and the English Revolution: Essays in History and Literature* (Manchester, 1986).

[83] *The Letters and Speeches of Oliver Cromwell, with Elucidations by Thomas Carlyle*, ed. Sophia C. Lomas, 3 vols. (London, 1904), vol. III, pp. 30–1.

revolution of any major European country', 'like some infantile trauma driven deep into the national subconscious'.[84] A mere recitation of the events of these years helps to put the former school of argument into perspective: employing a backward-looking, conservative, and at times reactionary ideology, the leaders of the English revolution executed a reigning monarch, abolished the institution of monarchy and the House of Lords, and used the national legislature to violate the property rights of their opponents – far more stringent measures than the socialist Labour party of the twentieth-century has ever ventured. Assisted by an army of their own creation, they maintained control over much of the nation for over a decade, effectively subjugated Ireland, waged wars, and entered into diplomatic relations with foreign governments. Unsuccessful in the final analysis, this was nonetheless a revolution.

It was not, however, a class revolution, and its designation as even 'the least pure bourgeois revolution of any major European country' is misguided. Orchestrated by wealthy landed grandees, the English revolution was supported – and opposed – by individuals from all levels of society. Its ultimate effect may have been the creation of conditions under which capitalist production could (and quite visibly did) flourish, but it neither emanated from a commercial class nor was primarily concerned with capitalist growth.[85] If any single adjective encapsulates the social composition and ideological preoccupations of the revolution, it is 'national' and not 'bourgeois'. Here the approach of the *New Left Review* is less than illuminating. Arguing that the incomplete character of bourgeois class formation necessarily precluded an effective revolution in the seventeenth century, its proponents claim that this failure in turn dictated the birth of an immature, acquiescent working class under industrialism. In this view, the reformism of Victorian workers derives from the pale legacy of the Puritan revolution, from the 'lack of any

---

[84] For the former school of argument, see for example Robert Ashton, 'Tradition and Innovation in the Great Rebellion', in J.G.A. Pocock (ed.), *Three British Revolutions: 1641, 1688, 1776* (Princeton, 1980), pp. 208–23. For the latter school, see Anderson, 'Origins of the Present Crisis', p. 28, and Tom Nairn, 'The English Working Class', *New Left Review*, no. 24, (March–April 1964), pp. 43–57, citation from p. 47.

[85] This is an argument essentially conceded by Anderson and Nairn. Gareth Stedman Jones offers an intelligent reappraisal of the concept of bourgeois revolution in 'Society and Politics at the Beginning of the World Economy', *Cambridge Journal of Economics*, vol. 1 (March 1977), pp. 77–92.

revolutionary tradition within English culture'.[86] Tom Nairn thus identifies the failure of the English middle class to elaborate Jacobin principles in the seventeenth century as the source of workers' subsequent inability to develop class consciousness, for 'while the [French] bourgeoisie made a living museum of the revolutionary tradition, it remained a living inspiration, a promise surviving every defeat, to the masses'.[87]

This line of analysis has the virtue of freeing English workers from the full burden of their mammoth historical failure as a conscious class, but it is rather less successful as historical explanation than as apologia. As the ease with which the Restoration was accomplished suggests, the Civil War and the Interregnum did not effect a permanent or complete transformation of national political ideals in England: the vast majority of the population welcomed the return of the Stuarts in 1660. But the revolution did witness a politicization of society – even at its lower levels – which bore lasting effects. Monarchy, aristocracy, patriarchy, and property were not over-turned completely with the revolution, but they endured a process of scrutiny and interrogation that cast their status of naturalized privilege into doubt. If the bulk of the English people remained wedded to the institutions of the state from the Restoration, they did so with a new awareness of the uses to which these national instruments could be put.[88] The subversive function of Parliament and the law in the revolution established an enduring conviction in the creative potential of English institutions and the ability of even a tradition-bound ideology to challenge and alter the hierarchical society which upheld it. J.G.A. Pocock has argued that the concept of the elect nation was dethroned with the Restoration, leaving the ancient constitution in a position of unrivalled ideological supremacy.[89] From the vantage point of popular politics, however, the elect nation and the ancient constitution must be described as enjoying a symbiotic alliance from this period. Their union created an abiding sense of historically determined English national rights opposed to the Catholic tyrannies of continental Europe, vested in

[86] Perry Anderson, 'Components of the National Culture', *New Left Review*, no. 50 (July–August 1968), pp. 3–57.
[87] Nairn, 'English Working Class', p. 46.
[88] Underdown, *Revel, Riot, and Rebellion*, pp. 286–8; Tim Harris, *London Crowds in the Reign of Charles II: Propaganda and Politics from the Restoration until the Exclusion Crisis* (Cambridge, 1987).
[89] Pocock, 'England', p. 115.

the common law and Parliament, and accessible to popular appeal by all members of society. These convictions, enshrined in the living museum of the revolutionary tradition, remained the guiding precepts of English radicalism to the later eighteenth century.

The Exclusion Crisis and revolution of 1688–9 reinforced this body of belief, if only inadvertently. Scholars now discount the influence of John Locke's contractual theory of government as a motive force in the Glorious Revolution, underlining the reluctance of even Whig politicians to glorify the 'revolution principles' on which their own political ascendancy was founded.[90] But the prelude to this political settlement served both to affirm and to enrich the radical aspirations established by republicans and Levellers in the Puritan revolution. Algernon Sidney's *Court Maxims*, written in 1665, spoke eloquently to the persistence of dissent – celebrating civil strife, disparaging hereditary inequality, and upholding the laws of nature and human reason.[91] In the circle of dissidents surrounding Lord Shaftesbury, formerly a member of Cromwell's Council of State, the Whigs' left wing recalled the Leveller legacy with pride, and sought to extend its political purchase to resist new Stuart tyrannies. Virulently hostile to the associated evils of Popery and absolute monarchy, of which France served as the paradigmatic example, the oppositional ideology elaborated by these men drew with equal alacrity upon the claims of historical birthrights and the logic of natural laws. Given substance in the petitioning campaign that sought to force Charles II to assemble Parliament in 1679–80, this line of analysis extended popular sovereignty to elector and non-elector alike, wedding religious Nonconformists and artisans securely to the radical project. When Charles II blocked the electoral process by dismissing the Oxford Parliament in 1681, the logical conclusion of this radical philosophy was renewed revolution, for 'the moral choice between freedom and slavery could, from a political standpoint, lead in only one direction'.[92]

In the aftermath of 1688, disaffected elements among both the

---

[90] J.P. Kenyon, *Revolution Principles: The Politics of Party 1689–1720* (Cambridge, 1977).

[91] Jonathan Scott, *Algernon Sidney and the English Republic, 1623–1677* (Cambridge, 1988), esp. pp. 186–206.

[92] Richard Ashcraft, *Revolution Politics and Locke's Two Treatises of Government* (Princeton, 1986), esp. pp. 143–4, 160–4, 175, 185–210, 309–10, citation from p. 207.

political élite and the artisanate continued to agitate for the civil and religious liberties denied by the revolution settlement. Central to the maintenance of a national revolutionary tradition in these years was the association of persons of both parties, Whig and Tory, with Country Party principles of government. Far from being reduced to the creed of a discredited fringe of fanatics, Country Party traditions continued to be articulated by much of the political nation.[93] Although Whig politicians viewed their party's revolutionary heritage with considerable embarrassment as they attained parliamentary ascendancy under Walpole, Whig apologists could exploit a popular vein of revolutionary patriotism when they chose to do so. Daniel Defoe's *True-Born Englishman* (1701) and *Jure Divino* (1706) were characteristic, defending the English subject's right to resist both domestic tyranny and foreign political influences.[94] Tory politicians, proscribed from the centre of politics with the Hanoverian succession, assumed the mantle of the Country Party from the early eighteenth century. Increasingly identified with the English national interest in opposition to a whiggish cosmopolitanism that embraced both foreign wars and foreign exiles from the Palatine, they became associated in the popular mind with the rule of law and the Englishman's birthright. Popular demonstrations in London to protest the Whig and Hanoverian successions played upon these ties with considerable success.[95]

In the ensuing decades, as Linda Colley has demonstrated, Tory patriotism served both to maintain a xenophobic revolutionary tradition at the forefront of popular politics and to reinforce the concept of parliamentary accountability to the public, 'exploiting English nationalism's potential as a bridge between the gentleman politician and the mobility'.[96] Given the patriotic resonance and

---

[93] For the continued radicalism of the political élite, see Mark Goldie, 'The Roots of True Whiggism 1688–94', *History of Political Thought*, vol. 1 (1980), pp. 195–234; for artisanal radicalism, see Gary Stuart De Kray, 'Political Radicalism in London after the Glorious Revolution', *Journal of Modern History*, vol. 55 (December 1983), pp. 585–617. Kathleen Wilson details the extra-parliamentary radical ramifications of the Glorious Revolution in 'Inventing Revolution: 1688 and Eighteenth-Century Popular Politics', *Journal of British Studies*, vol. 28 (October 1989), pp. 349–86.

[94] Kenyon, *Revolution Principles*, pp. 58, 114.

[95] Linda Colley, *In Defiance of Oligarchy: The Tory Party 1716–60* (Cambridge, 1982), pp. 90–3; Nicholas Rogers, 'Popular Protest in Early Hanoverian London', *Past and Present*, no. 79 (May 1978), pp. 70–100, esp. pp. 91–5.

[96] Colley, *In Defiance of Oligarchy*, pp. 174, 153.

wide currency of the revolutionary tradition in England, it was possible for a Tory London alderman in 1747 to uphold the achievements of Oliver Cromwell and proudly proclaim 'I am a Jacobite upon republican principles.' Predictably, Tory rhetoric cultivated nostalgia for the vanishing customs of the old English countryside, but the appeal of popular Tory nationalism was equally evident in urban centres, which retained considerable political autonomy even in the age of Walpole. London, Norwich, Coventry, Newcastle, Bristol, Birmingham, Manchester, and Leeds were foci of Tory patriotism; the election cry of Bristol's popular crowd in 1754 was 'No Naturalization! No Jews! No French Bottle-Makers! No Lowering Wages to 4d. a Day and Garlick!'[97]

The speeches, tracts, and agitations endorsed by politicians of the governing class from Bolingbroke, author of the *Idea of the Patriot King* (1749), to the elder Pitt and Lord George Gordon later in the century ensured the perpetuation of a national ideal which embraced, at one and the same time, revolution, patriotism, Protestantism, and popular rights.[98] David Hume's historical writings lent considerable cachet to this constellation of patriotic ideals, normalizing the nation as the motive force in England's revolutionary history. In his interpretation, Stuart monarchs erred in refusing to 'regard national privileges as ... sacred and inviolable', Puritans rightly 'made the privileges of the nation ... a part of their religion', and 'generous patriots' such as Pym and Sir John Eliot defended ancestral prerogatives 'animated with a warm regard to liberty'.[99] More popular historians and polemicists laboured, with great success, throughout the eighteenth century to convert the Civil War intransigents–Hampden, Sidney, Milton, Ludlow, and Vane – into patriotic symbols of Country Party respectability whose positive contribution to the nation's preservation was axiomatic.[100]

[97] Cited in *ibid.*, pp. 102, 100, 155. Nicholas Rogers analyses the persistence of urban political autonomy in *Whigs and Cities: Popular Politics in the Age of Walpole and Pitt* (Oxford, 1989).

[98] Isaac Kramnick, *Bolingbroke and His Circle: The Politics of Nostalgia in the Age of Walpole* (Cambridge, Mass., 1968); Marie Peters, *Pitt and Popularity: The Patriot Minister and London Opinion during the Seven Years' War* (Oxford, 1980).

[99] David Hume, *The History of England*, 6 vols. (London, 1778), vol. V, pp. 236, 177, 159.

[100] Peter Karsten, *Patriot-Heroes in England and America: Political Symbolism and Changing Values over Three Centuries* (Madison, 1978), pp. 13–56; Blair Worden, 'The Commonwealth Kidney of Sir Algernon Sidney', *Journal of British Studies*, vol. 24 (January 1985), pp. 27–40.

Couched in the political language of a bygone era, this rhetorical tradition was given substance in common life through the constant function of the rule of law. Here again the legacy of the seventeenth century is crucial, for it was in response to the repeated constitutional crises provoked by the Stuarts that the precepts of the rule of law were articulated and enacted in the legislative code. Originally intended to secure gentry wealth from the king's supposed tyranny, English justice as it emerged from the Civil War years required an obsessive adherence to legal forms, fixed rather than indeterminate offences, and strictly observed rules of evidence. Administered with great pomp and circumstance by landed government officials at the assizes, it was fiercely defensive of property, the owners of which were alone eligible to serve as justices, judges, and members of its most vaunted institution, the jury.[101]

Yet as both the poor and the affluent were anxious to proclaim, the rule of law was the common property of the English nation. However illusory it might prove in practice, equality before the law was guaranteed by English legislative theory. Knowledge of even the minutiae of the common law was surprisingly current in the population at large, and the courts were not infrequently used, with the full complicity of their officials, to protect the lesser from the great. Not unlike the nation, the law in consequence 'became something more than a creature of a ruling class – it became a power with its own claims, higher than those of prosecutor, lawyers, and even the great scarlet-robed assize judge himself'.[102] Informed by the revolutionary tradition, the rule of law effectively upheld the social and economic dominance of landed property and large-scale commercial wealth, but it did so only in the name of a wider political nation to which it was, by its own frequent admission, ultimately accountable.

The implications for English radicalism of this broad-ranging ideological concession are twofold. On the one hand, the close articulation of law and Parliament in England, like the shared assumptions of Whig and Tory high politics, allowed and encouraged the elaboration of a vibrant political culture with bases of support at

---

[101] Douglas Hay, 'Property, Authority and the Criminal Law', in Douglas Hay, Peter Linebaugh, John Rule, E.P. Thompson, and Cal Winslow (eds.), *Albion's Fatal Tree: Crime and Society in Eighteenth-Century England* (London, 1975), pp. 17–63, esp. pp. 33–9. For the association between liberty and property that underpinned this system, see H.T. Dickinson, *Liberty and Property: Political Ideology in Eighteenth-Century Britain* (London, 1977).

[102] Hay, 'Property, Authority and the Criminal Law', p. 33.

all levels of society. Long before this was the case on the continent, law and parliamentary politics in England represented twin attributes of a united nation-state, enjoying already in the eighteenth century what John Brewer terms a 'conjugal bond' in English popular perception. In the Wilkite movement of the 1760s and 1770s, popular leaders advanced from traditional pleas for the law's general accountability to the public to radical arguments for specific reforms of the institution of Parliament itself.[103]

Wilkes was an unscrupulous rake of limited democratic vision, but he stood at the front of a long line of gentlemanly politicians, increasingly popular and increasingly radical, who courted the common people with the ancient constitution, revolution principles, and the rule of law. Major John Cartwright, born to a landed family and tracing his intellectual lineage to the 'true Whigs' of the eighteenth-century Commonwealth tradition, called for annual Parliaments, equal electoral districts, the secret ballot, and universal manhood suffrage in *Take Your Choice* (1776). In its second edition (1777), his pamphlet advocated the remaining two points of what would later be known as the Charter, the abolition of property qualifications and the institution of salaries for Members of Parliament.[104] 'Orator' Henry Hunt and Sir Francis Burdett employed, nay flaunted, the same tradition in the early nineteenth century. Hunt's insistence on the constitutionality of the mass platform and of his own independence as a landed proprietor was axiomatic; Burdett, eluding arrest for several days in 1801, submitted to the authorities only while engaged in the sacred activity of reading Magna Carta aloud to his young son.[105]

In establishing the groundwork for later radical movements these men and their popular following contributed to an oppositional tradition which sought to reassess the distribution of power, wealth, and labour in English society. In this sense, the revolutionary

[103] John Brewer, 'The Wilkites and the Law, 1763–74: A Study of Radical Notions of Governance', in John Brewer and John Styles (eds.), *An Ungovernable People: The English and Their Law in the Seventeenth and Eighteenth Centuries* (London, 1980), p. 128.

[104] Naomi Miller, 'John Cartwright and Radical Parliamentary Reform 1808–1819', *English Historical Review*, vol. 83 (October 1968), pp. 705–28; Caroline Robbins, *The Eighteenth-Century Commonwealthsman: Studies in the Transmission, Development, and Circumstance of English Liberal Thought from the Restoration of Charles II to the War with the Thirteen Colonies* (Cambridge, Mass., 1959).

[105] John Belchem, 'Henry Hunt and the Evolution of the Mass Platform', *English Historical Review*, vol. 93 (October 1978), pp. 739–73.

tradition of the rule of law and Parliament exercised a radical influence on the politics of the English nation. Equally, however, it was the revolutionary tradition that restricted the compass of popular politics, even as it moved to the left. Jeremy Bentham, himself preoccupied with the legal regulation of society, was quick to recognize this limitation. 'There is but one thing which those in this country look upon as repugnant to happiness, which is arbitrary power, despotism', he remarked, 'and they think that to abolish despotism, it is sufficient to establish laws.'[106] Indeed, the precedent and the hagiography of the Civil War years had established a conviction that the common law and the House of Commons could together alter the structure of society: as John Brewer and John Styles suggest, popular interpretations of the rule of law 'go far towards explaining why popular criticism remained within the parameters of legal debate'. These political assumptions lay at the heart of Chartism, and were at once the source of its liabilities as a class movement and its enduring significance as a national agitation.[107]

CLASS AND EARLY INTERNATIONAL SENTIMENT IN ENGLAND

The history of political radicalism in England from the Civil War to the French revolution suggests that the dominant interpretations of nationalism require considerable revision. Sociologists conflate the rise of nationalism with the rise of industry and assert that nationalist sentiment functions by infusing an essentially agrarian labour force with modern values of social consensus. The English experience from the 1620s demonstrates the ability of nationalist ideals to emerge and flourish in an agrarian society, inspiring oppositional politics among both the social élite and the immiserated. Ultimately, as sociologists suggest, nationalism may serve to bind society as a whole to common values, but it did so in England only by encouraging a high level of political argument and conflict at all social levels from a relatively early date. Contrary to classical liberal and Marxist

---

[106] Cited by John Brewer and John Styles, 'Introduction', in Brewer and Styles (eds.), *An Ungovernable People*, p. 11.

[107] *Ibid.*, p. 16. Stedman Jones, 'Rethinking Chartism', in his *Languages of Class* anatomizes the constraints placed on Chartism by this radical heritage, a point also discussed below, pp. 133, 140–1.

expectations, moreover, English nationalist sentiment did not initially issue from Enlightenment principles or the commercial machinations of the rising bourgeoisie. Rather, its origins lay in the highly conservative ideology of the Country Party tradition, a tradition that delimited the nation within parameters set by property rights, Protestant religion, and political sovereignty. In a perceptive analysis of the emergence of modern nationalism, Benedict Anderson dates from the later eighteenth century the appearance of the nation as 'an imagined community . . . imagined as both inherently limited and sovereign'.[108] In England, the radical tradition and the sinews of the state had combined to create an imagined national identity already in the seventeenth century.

The common assumptions of internationalism similarly require revision in light of the English historical experience. In both liberal theory and French revolutionary thought, nationalism gives birth effortlessly to internationalism: secure in the enjoyment of his political and economic independence, the hypothetical citizen recognizes a natural, universal brotherhood of nations. Classical Marxist analysis is correspondingly simplistic: stripped of his national identity by the remorseless advance of industry, the worker identifies himself as a proletarian, and the proletariat has no country. History in England followed a different path. With its rule of law and its political birthrights, the nation significantly preceded liberalism and long outlasted the peasant proprietor, the handloom weaver, and the political shoemaker, establishing the conditions of production within which relations of production came to be interpreted. The institutions of the state ensured that nationalism in England was not only an imagined community but a daily experience of common life, a living museum of the revolutionary tradition. *Job Nott's Advice*, the counsel of an anti-Jacobin artisan to his 'brother artificers', spoke eloquently to this perception in the 1790s:

> We have long enjoyed that Liberty and Equality which the French have been struggling for: in England, ALL MEN ARE equal; all who commit the same offences are liable to the same punishment. If the *very poorest and meanest man* commits a murder, he is hanged with a hempen halter, and his body dissected. If the *Richest*

[108] Benedict Anderson, *Imagined Communities: Reflections on the Origins and Spread of Nationalism* (London, 1983), p. 15.

Nobleman commits a murder, *he* is hanged with a hempen halter, and his body is dissected – *all are equal here*.[109]

The patriotic tenor of *Job Nott's Advice* is predictable, but its timing was ironic. For the social, economic, and political changes of the later eighteenth century produced a breach of epic proportions in the English national tradition, introducing the concepts of class and internationalism into English radical argument. Neither concept required the wholesale abandonment of existing national idioms: from the start, class and internationalist agitations marshalled national institutions and rhetoric to their own ends. Factory owners and journeymen clothiers in the West Riding thus invoked the nation in 1806 to urge, respectively, the free market economy of the classical economists and the corporatist ideal of the Commonwealth tradition. Middle-class witnesses brought before a parliamentary committee investigating the condition of the woollen industry insisted that 'the right of every man to employ the Capital he inherits, or has acquired, according to his own discretion, without molestation or obstruction ... is one of those privileges which the free and happy constitution of this Country has long accustomed every Briton to consider as his birthright'. Clothiers and journeymen articulated a different vision of the nation, calling for protective legislation against the free play of capital in the factory system 'if it be found injurious to the state'.[110]

Similarly, early internationalist sentiment both drew sustenance from and posed a threat to national ideals of social harmony. As E.P. Thompson's *Making of the English Working Class* successfully demonstrates, the articulation of artisanal and early industrial radicalism in England was shaped by a broadly European context; triggered by the forces of the industrial revolution, it was informed by the nationalist and internationalist ideals of the French revolution. Under this continental aegis, the years from 1789 saw the refraction of transnational ideals of government and society by England's insular, xenophobic radical tradition.[111] As the authorities were quick to perceive at the time, these developments

---

[109] Cited by Hay, 'Property, Authority and the Criminal Law', p. 39.
[110] Cited by John Smail, 'New Languages for Labour and Capital: The Transformation of Discourse in the Early Years of the Industrial Revolution', *Social History*, vol. 12 (January 1987), pp. 53, 58.
[111] Thompson, *Making of the English Working Class*, pp. 102–85.

threatened a received and much-vaunted belief in England's historic identity as a national unit, putting the concept of the elect nation to question and suggesting in its stead two alternative visions of society, one governed by a universal brotherhood of nations and the other ruled by international war between the classes. In this manner, the combined forces of economic and political revolution challenged both the old régime and the radical tradition that stood opposed to it.

Within middle- and upper-class Whig and Dissenting circles, enthusiasm for the national and international implications of France's revolutionary moment, although cut short by the Terror, gave rise to a wave of new radical impulses that vexed and invigorated liberal culture throughout the nineteenth century. The Whig élite mounted a particularly diverse array of responses to the revolution, generating both Edmund Burke's conservative nationalist reaction and Charles James Fox's cosmopolitan defence of the French events.[112] In Richard Price, the Whigs' Dissenting wing found a Nonconformist conscience in which patriotism, international brotherhood, and the revolutionary tradition could peacefully coexist. Defining the nation as a 'community ... protected by the same laws, and bound together by the same civil policy', his *Discourse on the Love of Our Country* cautioned English patriots 'to distinguish between the love of our country and that spirit of rivalship and ambition which has been common among nations'. Tracing national sentiment to the elemental forces of human nature, underlining the citizen's imperative 'to liberalize and enlighten' the public, denouncing debt, vice, and corruption, and dismissing offensive warfare as inherently unjust, Price's *Discourse* bore the characteristic impress of liberal individualism. But Price, like succeeding generations of Dissenting radicals, embraced the Enlightenment's fraternal conception of the nation without discarding its Puritan antecedents. His call for the recovery of England's lost liberties – notably freedom of conscience and political representation – adduced Montesquieu, Fenelon, and Turgot against the

---

[112] Frank O'Gorman, *The Whig Party and the French Revolution* (London, 1967), and John Derry, 'The Opposition Whigs and the French Revolution', in Dickinson (ed.), *Britain and the French Revolution*, pp. 39–59, illuminate Whig responses; the intellectual impact on the élite is discussed in Seamus Deane, *The French Revolution and Enlightenment in England: 1789–1832* (Cambridge, Mass., 1988).

forces of 'priestcraft and tyranny' only after invoking the spirits of Milton, Sidney, and Locke.[113]

Among artisans, workers, and their political allies, the radical impact of the French revolution proved both deeper and more enduring than within the middle and upper classes. In Thomas Paine the radical tradition found an exponent who expanded the horizons of labour's revolutionary vision beyond England to the continent, beyond Dissent to secularism, and beyond politics to economics. Effecting 'a bridge between the older traditions of the whig "commonwealthsman" and the radicalism of Sheffield cutlers, Norwich weavers, and London artisans', Paine's *Rights of Man* (1791–2) became, in the words of E.P. Thompson, 'a foundation-text of the English working-class movement'.[114] Himself a man of small property and libertarian proclivities alternately drawn and repelled by the claims of classical political economy, Paine laid the groundwork upon which members of the London Corresponding Society and its offshoots constructed English ideologies of class that spoke at once to national freedoms, international rights, and economic justice. The example of John Thelwall, the democratic agitator arrested for sedition in 1794 with Horne Tooke, Thomas Hardy, and Francis Place, illustrates the expansive radical vision of Paine's more extreme disciples. Imprisoned in Newgate, Thelwall wrote poems celebrating the patriotism of Hampden and Sidney; upon his release, he championed Kosciusko's efforts to liberate the Polish nation. More troubled than Paine by the consequences of commercial and industrial growth, Thelwall by 1796 had advanced a radical critique of political economy that privileged the political rights of labour, questioned the sanctity of property, and problematized the notion of free contracts between master and man.[115]

[113] Richard Price, *A Discourse on the Love of Our Country, Delivered on Nov. 4 1789. At the Meeting House in the Old Jewry, to the Society for Commemorating the Revolution in Great Britain* (London, 1790), pp. 6–8, 12, 15–16, 20, 27, 30–4, 38. J.G.A. Pocock contextualizes Price's *Discourse* within the Country tradition in 'The Varieties of Whiggism from Exclusion to Reform: A History of Ideology and Discourse', in his *Virtue, Commerce, and History* (Cambridge, 1985), pp. 286–7, and Isaac Kramnick locates Price within the debate on liberal individualism in *Republicanism and Bourgeois Radicalism: Political Ideology in Late Eighteenth-Century England and America* (Ithaca, N.Y., 1990), pp. 204–6.

[114] Thompson, *Making of the English Working Class*, pp. 94, 90.

[115] *Ibid.*, pp. 136, 159, and Iain Hampsher-Monk, 'John Thelwall and the Eighteenth-Century Radical Response to Political Economy', *Historical Journal*, vol. 34 (March 1991), pp. 1–20.

Scholars now approach the issue of class consciousness with considerable caution, rightly questioning the extent to which the bulk of the labouring population imbibed new revolutionary values and underscoring both the persistence of craft production and the reluctance of artisans to extend their radical political claims to those below them.[116] Historical analysis has benefited greatly from these refinements, but in the process something crucial has been lost. Economic conditions in the later eighteenth and early nineteenth centuries were not conducive to the formation of a monolithic working class in England, yet class was a commonplace of political argument by the early Chartist period.[117] A reconceptualization, however tentative and limited, of national privileges as human rights and of particularistic historical freedoms as abstract international liberties informed this development: Paine's most influential work was entitled the *Rights of Man* and not, as might well have been the case a generation earlier, the *Briton's Birthright*. Liberty, equality, fraternity, and the rights of man did not create class and internationalism in England, but given the peculiar development of English political radicalism from the seventeenth century they were a necessary prelude to the articulation of these novel concepts.[118]

Under the younger Pitt and his successors, governmental reaction to this challenge was swift, brutal, and effective, mobilizing broad sectors of the population – Church and King mobs, spies and informers, Evangelical lady tract writers, parliamentary orators, and the military – in a counterrevolutionary movement of sweeping proportions. If strident demands lodged by radical leaders preoccupied the public mind in these revolutionary years, loyalty and conservatism characterized the public behaviour of the great mass of

---

[116] Calhoun, *Question of Class Struggle*, offers a sustained discussion of class in Thompson's work and an alternative interpretation of its role in popular radicalism. For the broader debate on class, see above, pp. 2–11.

[117] Asa Briggs, 'The Language of "Class" in Early Nineteenth-Century England', in Asa Briggs and John Saville (eds.), *Essays in Labour History* (London, 1960), pp. 154–72.

[118] Gregory Claeys provides an excellent discussion of Enlightenment and French revolutionary contributions to the evolution of English internationalism in 'Reciprocal Dependence, Virtue and Progress: Some Sources of Early Socialist Cosmopolitanism and Internationalism in Britain, 1750–1850', in Frits van Holthoon and Marcel van der Linden (eds.), *Internationalism in the Labour Movement, 1830–1940*, 2 vols. (Leiden, 1988), vol. I, pp. 235–58.

the population.[119] But the ideological exchange forged in this era between continental revolutions and domestic movements for political and economic reform nonetheless proved tenacious. Despite its conspicuous success in reducing the popular appeal of radical agitation, government repression failed to stem the continued expansion of popular radical ideals. Debating societies located in alehouses offered a convivial institutional base within which ultra-radicals elaborated a revolutionary culture that extended from Pitt's Reign of Terror to Chartism, and beyond. Using religious rhetoric and Dissenting ministers' licences to protect themselves from prosecution, English Jacobins evaded the edicts of the government to develop new democratic, infidel, and socialist perspectives that widened the ideological scope and claims of the radical tradition in the decades after 1794.[120]

The revival of large-scale popular agitation in the years of distress that followed the Napoleonic Wars saw renewed emphasis placed by radicals upon indigenous national traditions. Samuel Bamford, silk weaver and parliamentary reformer, thus captured a widely current radical conviction when he asserted that government repression would inevitably break the radical activist's spirit 'unless the nation become his pioneer'.[121] The political genealogy from which Bamford traced his radical sympathies attested to this constriction of the radical tradition, mixing national and international influences, but underscoring the English elements of his political lineage. Heir to a family of seventeenth-century Roundheads, a Jacobite grandfather, a 'Christian patriot' uncle, and a Jacobin father, Bamford claimed to have been 'born a Radical'. Although he noted that his father was a devotee of Paine's *Rights of Man*, he emphasized the formative influence exerted on his own development by Milton's poetry and the *Pilgrim's Progress*. Surpassed in the Chartist era by a new

[119] Robert R. Dozier, *For King, Constitution, and Country: The English Loyalists and the French Revolution* (London, 1983), offers a good description of the counter-revolutionary movement; Clark, *English Society*, esp. pp. 315–48, details the persistence of conservative values and expectations.
[120] Iain McCalman, 'Ultra-Radicalism and Convivial Debating Clubs in London, 1795–1838', *English Historical Review*, vol. 102 (April 1987), pp. 309–33; *idem, Radical Underworld: Prophets, Revolutionaries and Pornographers in London, 1795–1840* (Cambridge, 1988); Thompson, *Making of the English Working Class*, pp. 711–46.
[121] Samuel Bamford, *Passages in the Life of a Radical*, 2 vols. (London, 1844), vol. I, pp. 111–12.

generation of radicals, Bamford continued in old age to affirm his allegiance to 'THE NATION! . . . the only party I will ever serve.'[122]

At the height of their popularity in 1838–42, the men and women who pledged to support the six points of the Charter – universal manhood suffrage, the secret ballot, equal electoral districts, annual Parliaments, the abolition of property qualifications, and payment of MPs – lent new life to the national myths revered by earlier generations of English radicals. Newcastle's *Northern Liberator* was characteristic, seeking in 1839 to instruct its readers in the Protestant revolutionary tradition by offering a Chartist rendition of the *Pilgrim's Progress* in which 'Radical' replaced 'Christian' as protagonist.[123] More broadly, these years saw working-class strategists, backed by tens of thousands of adherents, exploit to the full the radical implications of popular constitutionalist idioms – the right to bear arms, the right to petition Parliament, and ultimately the right to resist tyranny. The Chartists' rhetorical strategy, as James Epstein has clearly demonstrated, limited the ability of radicals to endorse novel political agendas – most notably property redistribution and female emancipation – that lay outside the received constitutional tradition. Accompanied by a diminution of internationalist sentiment and a constriction of the breadth of English oppositional vision, this tactic nonetheless deepened the appeal of radicalism precisely by locating political debate within received national parameters, the legitimacy of which no class within the state could dismiss out of hand.[124]

If early Chartist argument adhered primarily to received nationalist norms, later Chartism broke substantial new ideological ground. For although it suffered losses of both vigour and membership in the mid-forties, the Chartist movement expanded its political preoccupations significantly in this period, combining a renewed commitment to international radicalism with a persistent rejection of middle- and upper-class economic doctrines. Chartist leaders now sought to buttress their faltering agitation by proclaiming again England's solidarity with the oppressed classes and nationalities of the continent. Significantly, this extension in the range of internation-

---

[122] *Ibid.*, pp. 8, 52, 234–5, and *idem, Early Days* (London, 1849), pp. 20–1, 40, 43, 100, 192–4.

[123] Maxine Berg, *The Machinery Question and the Making of Political Economy 1815–48* (Cambridge, 1980), p. 288.

[124] James A. Epstein, 'The Constitutional Idiom: Radical Reasoning, Rhetoric, and Action in Early Nineteenth-Century England', *Journal of Social History*, vol. 23 (Spring 1990), pp. 553–74.

alism was reinforced by the physical presence in England of émigré radicals from the continent. Julian Harney's Chartist Society of Fraternal Democrats, established in 1846, was only one example of this trend, uniting English working-class radicals with exiled social and political activists from Poland, Italy, Germany, and France.[125] What had begun in the Jacobin era as an abstract alliance between English and continental democracy was transformed by the Chartist leadership into an active collaboration between English and continental agitators.

Parallel to the development of these international ties was a sharpening of Chartists' antagonism to the economic orthodoxies of middle-class radicalism. Opposition to the tenets of liberal political economy – Malthusian population theory, freedom of both trade and the labour market, the wages fund theory and the laws of supply and demand – had underpinned labour radicalism from the struggle for parliamentary reform in 1830–2 to the Plug Riots of 1842,[126] but succeeding years saw an intensification of these hostilities. Robert Owen's reconceptualization of political economy was central to this process, introducing new theories of collective social and economic identity into a radical tradition hitherto preoccupied with efforts to free the individual from the depredations of a corrupt aristocratic state that had usurped the nation's sovereignty. Although Owen himself disparaged state institutions, his followers consistently politicized his socialism, using his theories as 'ideological raw material' needing to be 'worked up by them into different products'.[127]

Of equal significance was the dramatic triumph of the Anti-Corn Law League in 1846. Established by Manchester manufacturers and merchants in 1839, the League commanded huge resources – its coffers in 1843 contained £50,000 – and a national following of tens of thousands under the able leadership of John Bright, Richard Cobden, J.B. Smith, and George Wilson. Their success in forcing the repeal of laws that protected English cereals from foreign compe-

[125] Henry G. Weisser, *British Working-Class Movements and Europe: 1815–1848* (Manchester, 1975), pp. 134–54.

[126] I.J. Prothero, *Artisans and Politics in Early Nineteenth-Century England: John Gast and His Times* (Folkestone, 1979), pp. 267–327; Robert Sykes, 'Early Chartism and Trade Unionism in South-East Lancashire', in James A. Epstein and Dorothy Thompson (eds.), *The Chartist Experience: Studies in Working-Class Radicalism and Culture, 1830–60* (London, 1982), pp. 152–93.

[127] Thompson, *Making of the English Working Class*, p. 789; Gregory Claeys, *Machinery, Money and the Millennium: From Moral Economy to Socialism 1815–1860* (Princeton, 1987), pp. 132–65.

tition made the Anti-Corn Law campaigns a formative moment in the consolidation of middle-class consciousness, a triumph over aristocratic forces to which middle-class radicals returned again and again in their efforts to reform the institutions of the state. More even than a defeat of the landed interest, however, repeal of the Corn Laws represented a major step toward the Manchester School's achievement of international peace and prosperity through the abolition of political intervention in domestic markets and diplomatic intervention abroad.[128] From the outset, Chartist activists sought to thwart the achievement of these goals. Although no less hostile than members of the League to the aristocratic interests protected by the Corn Laws, Chartists rejected the League's wider ambition to extend free trade to labour relations. Hissing, heckling, and physical abuse, which became increasingly common Chartist tactics at League rallies in the forties,[129] drove a wedge between middle- and working-class reformers that widened significantly in the late Chartist movement of 1848–58.

In choosing to pursue these divisive tactics, Chartist activists also problematized their relation to the radical tradition from which they drew their inspiration. For their rejection of liberal conceptions of laissez-faire not only alienated working-class radicals from middle- and upper-class leaders, men whose social groups had since the age of Hampden and Pym provided popular movements with parliamentary leadership. It also forced them to reassess the radical conception of the nation-state, a conception that prioritized political freedoms and largely ignored issues of social and economic justice. In the heady atmosphere of revolution generated by the events of 1848, Chartists drew upon the resources of the international radical community to meet these new demands. Without abandoning the national identities that linked them to middle-class radicals, they embraced French revolutionary theories that propelled the radical tradition beyond its Puritan and Jacobin roots to the politics of class.

[128] Norman McCord, *The Anti-Corn Law League, 1838–1846* (London, 1958), is the standard work, but the movement's ideological stance is best approached from Richard Francis Spall, Jr, 'Free Trade, Foreign Relations, and the Anti-Corn Law League', *International History Review*, vol. 10 (August 1988), pp. 405–32.

[129] Lucy Brown, 'Chartists and the Anti-Corn Law League', in Asa Briggs (ed.), *Chartist Studies* (London, 1959), pp. 342–71; Wendy Hinde, *Richard Cobden: A Victorian Outsider* (New Haven, 1987), pp. 65, 69–71, 75, 87–8. The force of the antagonism generated in this struggle, which is often downplayed by historians, was typically emphasized in contemporaries' memoirs. See for example George Howell MS Autobiography, BI, Howell Collection, vol. A, part 7.

2 · English radical responses to the revolutions of 1848–1849

But were there no excuses for the mass? Was there no excuse in the spirit with which the English upper classes regarded the continental revolutions? No excuse in the undisguised dislike, fear, contempt, which they expressed for that very sacred name of Liberty, which has been for ages the pride of England and her laws . . .?

. . . If there had been one word of sympathy with the deep wrongs of France, Germany, Italy, Hungary – one attempt to discriminate the righteous and God-inspired desire of freedom, from man's furious and self-willed perversion of it, we would have listened to them. But, instead, what was the first, last, cardinal, crowning argument? . . . it was with the profits of the few that revolutions interfered; with the Divine right, not so much of kings, but of money-making.[1]

In *Alton Locke*, his fictional recreation of the life and times of a Chartist tailor, the Anglican clergyman and social reformer Charles Kingsley sought both to explain the underlying causes of popular disaffection and to wean the working class from radical politics. Kingsley's delineation of his protagonist's radical genealogy was astute, neatly capturing the patriotic tropes of late Chartist culture. A Dissenter heir to 'old Puritan blood', Alton Locke drew his inspiration from Milton's writings, Foxe's *Book of Martyrs*, and the 'patriots' of the Hebrew Bible. 'Moses leading his people out of Egypt . . . Jehu executing God's vengeance on the kings – they were my heroes, my models', Locke asserted, 'they mixed themselves up with the dim legends about the Reformation-martyrs, Cromwell and Hampden, Sidney and Monmouth, which I had heard at my

[1] Charles Kingsley, *Alton Locke, Tailor and Poet: An Autobiography* (London, 1850), chap. 32.

mother's knee'.[2] But if Kingsley's portrait of the English radical tradition was perceptive, *Alton Locke*'s critique of the upper-class reaction against the revolutions of 1848 was nonetheless misleading. A sustained diatribe against both commercial growth and the political apathy of the parliamentary establishment, Kingsley's novel ignored the enthusiasm with which significant sectors of the Victorian middle class welcomed the continental revolutions as a spur to their own reform efforts. Reducing the highly diverse array of responses mounted by English radicals in 1848 to a monolithic bourgeois backlash against the visceral demands and physical force of the Chartists, his analysis caricatured a complex historical moment in which working- and middle-class reformers were alternately swept together and driven apart by patriotic radical convictions.

Like the French revolution of 1789, the continental revolutions of 1848 marked English radical culture deeply, forcing reformers to reassess the relations among time-honoured national traditions and wider European political developments. In France, the February revolution brought the fall of monarchy and declaration of the Second Republic, the institution of universal manhood suffrage, abolition of the death penalty, and an end to slavery in the colonies. Hungarian patriots wrestled with the Austrian government for national independence from March, a struggle that Italian nationalists soon joined to the south. In the early months of 1848, English support for these continental reform initiatives united much of the Liberal left wing, Dissent, and the Chartist movement. But this tide of patriotic internationalist optimism proved shortlived. As in the eighteenth century, the expansion of French revolutionary politics beyond received English notions of popular sovereignty and republican virtue drove a wedge between popular radicals and more affluent reformers; as in the eighteenth century, draconian state reprisals against radical demonstrations embittered relations among radicals, reformers, and government officials. Class concepts, only inchoate in 1789, further complicated this response to revolution, but they did so without disrupting entirely patterns of inter-class collaboration established by earlier generations of English radicals. Mixing liberalism with democracy, socialism with nationalism, the revolutionary doctrines unleashed in 1848 did not shatter the

---

[2]   *Ibid.*, chaps. 1, 4.

English radical tradition, but they rendered its claim to speak equally for all classes within the state increasingly problematic.

EARLY CHARTIST RESPONSES TO 1848

> Forty-eight with all its stories –
> France's rise and Austria's fall –
> Italy's recovered glories –
> Fair Palermo's shattered wall;
> Thus do nations preach to you, Men,
> How to raise a fallen state –
> Prate no more of Eighty-two, Men –
> Think – oh think of Forty-Eight![3]

Recent scholarship has sought to divest the Chartist movement of much of the revolutionary aura with which it was imbued in the nineteenth century. Emphasizing internecine rivalries within the Chartist leadership, the ideological ties that linked Chartism to middle-class liberalism, or the inability of Chartists steeped in the radical political tradition to generate meaningful critiques of industrial capitalism, these approaches effectively distance late Chartism from the full-blooded revolutions of continental Europe.[4] Deflating the Chartists' more extravagant claims for the transformational power of their political vision, they rightly underline the considerable obstacles that parochial identities, national allegiances, and human frailty posed to the success of the Chartist movement. Unless tempered with an understanding of contemporary perceptions of Chartism, however, their emphasis on the inherent limitations of the Chartists' programme and organization can obscure the movement's enduring impact on nineteenth-century politics and social relations. For if historians gifted with hindsight see in late Chartism a

---

[3] 'Past and Present', *Irish Felon*, 1 July 1848.

[4] David Large, 'London in the Year of Revolutions, 1848', in John Stevenson (ed.), *London in the Age of Reform* (Oxford, 1977), pp. 177–211, and Henry G. Weisser, *April 10: Challenge and Response in England in 1848* (Lanham, 1983), emphasize the reformist tenor of Chartism in 1848. Joel Wiener offers an astute analysis of the tensions within the Chartist leadership in *William Lovett* (Manchester, 1989), pp. 51–6; Dorothy Thompson, *The Chartists: Popular Politics in the Industrial Revolution* (New York, 1984), pp. 332–5, emphasizes the essential overlap between Chartism and liberalism; and Stedman Jones, 'Rethinking Chartism', in his *Languages of Class*, underlines the ideological limitations of Chartism as a critique of modern industry.

beleaguered, riven, and insular agitation, contemporaries were united in the belief that the English and continental radical movements were of a revolutionary piece in 1848. Together the revival – however brief – of large-scale demonstrations, the threat and indeed incidence of physical violence, and the considerable ideological expansion of working-class political argument served to convince Victorian observers of the subversive character, unity, and scope of Chartist demands in 1848.

Stretching from the meliorist to the militant wings of the movement, Chartist support for the French revolutionaries was deep, widespread, and immediate. The news of Louis Philippe's abdication galvanized the February meeting of Julian Harney's Fraternal Democrats. 'Frenchmen, Germans, Poles, Magyars, sprang to their feet, embraced, shouted, and gesticulated in the widest enthusiasm', Thomas Frost recalled in his memoirs. 'Then the doors were opened, and the whole assemblage descended to the street, and, with linked arms and colours flying, marched to the meeting-place of the Westminster Chartists, in Dean Street, Soho.'[5] The *Northern Star*, guiding light of the national organization, was quick to endorse this international fraternization, calling on 26 February for English participation, through support for the Charter, in a broadly European struggle for freedom spearheaded by France.[6] Chartist clubs and localities embraced this charge with enthusiasm. In March Salford Chartists demonstrated to celebrate the February revolution; in London, working men swiftly deputed Chartist leaders to carry their congratulations to the Provisional Government in Paris.[7]

The sweeping dimensions of this response emerge clearly from John Saville's detailed analysis of government reactions to the Chartist revival of 1848. Placing the state's response to Chartism securely within a European framework, Saville locates the radical challenge of this year 'within the triangle of revolutionary Paris, insurgent Ireland, and a revitalized native Chartist movement in

---

[5] Thomas Frost, *Forty Years' Recollections: Literary and Political* (London, 1880), pp. 128–9.

[6] *Northern Star*, 26 February 1848.

[7] For Salford, see Charles Gibson to Sir George Grey, 13 March 1848, HO 45/ 2410B, item 42. The Chartists dispatched to Paris included Julian Harney, Ernest Jones, and W.J. Linton, who travelled with Mazzini. See *Reasoner*, 22 March 1848, pp. 231–2; *Northern Star*, 4 and 11 March 1848; William James Linton, *Threescore and Ten Years: 1820 to 1890 Recollections* (New York, 1894), pp. 103–4.

London and the industrial North'.[8] Shared enthusiasm for the February revolution, he argues, served to unite Chartists with Irish nationalists throughout the United Kingdom, an alliance that posed an unprecedented threat to the government. The concentration of Chartist riots and disturbances in areas of England with substantial Irish populations – London and the industrial towns of Lancashire and the West Riding – made the practical implications of this ideological union palpably evident to the authorities.[9] In London over 10,000 persons met on 6 March to protest the income tax and give 'thundering cheers for the brave Parisians and the People's Charter', a demonstration that led to three days of rioting. The following week saw Ernest Jones and Philip McGrath, Chartist delegates recently returned from attendance on the French Provisional Government, at the centre of a demonstration of 20,000 that ended with the looting of shops in Camberwell. Although London workers failed to rise during the Kennington Common protest of 10 April, disturbances by textile workers in Bradford, Manchester, and Liverpool in the next weeks ended only after the government had deployed tens of thousands of special constables, policemen, and military troops.[10]

Within the general population, critics of radicalism were haunted by the articulation between these waves of unrest and the continental revolutions. In Sheffield, the Reverend Thomas Kerns termed the sacrilege of Chartist Sunday meetings 'an exotic in England ... foreign to the best feelings of the English character' and concluded that the practice 'has been imported from the Continent'.[11] The flood of correspondence dispatched to the Home Office by troubled citizens made middle-class opinion on this issue abundantly clear. J.H. Mann, an anxious denizen of Kentish Town, urged Sir George Grey to limit political meetings to the parish and thereby disabuse 'the public mind as well as Foreign nations ... as to the extent of the

---

[8] John Saville, *1848: The British State and the Chartist Movement* (Cambridge, 1987), p.1.

[9] *Ibid.*, pp. 73–4, 120–1; W.J. Lowe, 'The Chartists and the Irish Confederates: Lancashire, 1848'. *Irish Historical Studies*, vol. 24 (November 1984), pp. 172–96; D.N. Petler, 'Ireland and France in 1848'. *Irish Historical Studies*, vol. 25 (November 1985), pp. 493–505.

[10] David Goodway, *London Chartism 1838–1848* (Cambridge, 1982), pp. 71–2; Saville, *1848*, pp. 88–9, 102–65.

[11] Thomas Kerns, *Chartist Sunday Meetings: Correspondence between the Rev. Thomas Kerns, M.D., Incumbent of Brightside, and the Chartists of Sheffield* (Sheffield, [1848]), not paginated.

numbers claimed by the Chartists'.[12] Respectable men and women were outraged by Chartist efforts to replace indigenous national allegiances with a broad range of foreign and subversive values in which international patriotism loomed especially large. W.W. Weston's denunciation of G.W.M. Reynolds, whose speech at Trafalgar Square had incited the riots of 6 March, was typical:

> the mob orator and sub Leader of the Chartists is an Avowed Atheist, and a scoffer of all things honest and proper men call good, he is a Naturalized Frenchman, and he has been in the Paris National Guard, and he has been heard to say that if the French invaded England he would be the first to hoist the Republican Flag, he is in the pay of the *Weekly Dispatch* as a writer of Revolutionary articles ... and he is also quite likely to be in the pay of some of the lowest Republican clubs in Paris.

'The respectable classes of the community', Weston concluded with feeling, 'may well shudder at a Mob led by such a *patriot* as this.'[13]

Although the historical associations of 1789 and the Provisional Government's declaration of universal manhood suffrage ensured that France enjoyed pride of place in the English response to 1848, Chartist leaders – like their more alarmist detractors – made little effort to distinguish among the varied currents of continental radicalism in the first months of 1848. Rather, working-class radicals subsumed the democratic, national, and socialist aspects of the revolutions of France, Germany, Italy, Austria, and Hungary under the banner of a single popular movement, of which English radicalism was a constituent part. Enlightenment conceptions of fraternity and natural rights were central to this internationalization of the continental revolutions. William Lovett, a moderate Chartist anxious to revive both parliamentary reform and inter-class collaboration, characteristically predicated his support for universal manhood suffrage on the logic that '*all* belonging to the great brotherhood of man – *all* have, consequently, equal claims to ... determine ... the nature of the laws they are called upon to obey'.[14] Meshing easily with radical distaste for aristocratic corruption, these arguments gave particular prominence to notions of sovereignty that had guided liberal and nationalist aspiration in the first French revolu-

---

[12] Mann to Grey, 12 April 1848, HO 45/2410A, item 355.
[13] Weston to Grey, [1848], HO 45/2410A, item 345.
[14] William Lovett, *Justice Safer than Expediency: An Appeal to the Middle Classes on the Question of the Suffrage* (London, 1848), p. 3.

tion. The Chartist editor C.G. Harding urged all reformers to endorse universal manhood suffrage 'to reconquer for the people that sovereignty which a selfish and wicked oligarchy have usurped'. Predictably, the *Republican* journal that Harding launched in 1848 bore the subtitle *A Magazine Advocating the Sovereignty of the People*.[15]

The persistent emphasis in Chartist rhetoric on popular sovereignty demonstrates the enduring significance of Enlightenment theories for English reform ideology, and the fundamental compatibility of liberal, nationalist, and internationalist ideals with aspects of the English radical tradition. Yet the impact of liberal Enlightenment thought on working-class radicalism in 1848 is easily overestimated. If natural rights theory aided the absorption of continental influences by English radicals, it neither dethroned the established radical canon nor precluded the elaboration of new lines of radical analysis. Trygve Tholfson has argued that 'Enlightenment liberalism' laid the groundwork for cross-class reformism in mid-Victorian England, providing 'the intellectual foundations of both working-class radicalism and the middle-class ideology to which it was directed', but the burden of late Chartist polemic argues against this thesis.[16] Superimposed upon English radical patriotism, liberal political concepts were viewed at second hand by English radicals. To reduce the radical response in 1848 to a common core of liberal or Enlightenment belief is as misguided as to ascribe Chartist reactions of that year exclusively to class.

Inspired by republican, anti-Catholic, and nationalist impulses, the Italian revolutions offered Chartist internationalists as much scope for nostalgic reflection as for liberal panegyric, encouraging working-class radicals to assimilate the exploits of Italian patriots with the historic moments of the Commonwealth rather than the recent achievements of commercial society. 'Shame, million-fold shame to the coward nation, that beholds unmoved the struggles of brave martyr peoples to win the liberty which is their birthright, the nationality, the unity, which alone can strengthen them', the Chartist wood engraver William James Linton expostulated in contemplating the Milanese revolution. Linton, who invoked the spirits of

---

[15] *The Republican: A Magazine Advocating the Sovereignty of the People* (1848), pp. 141–2.

[16] Trygve Tholfson, *Working Class Radicalism in Mid-Victorian England* (New York, 1977), p. 26.

Shakespeare, Milton, Wyclif, and Hampden, expressed no sympathy for liberal laissez-faire, a policy which he associated with the English government's refusal to intervene on behalf of revolutionary nations in 1848. His critique of this policy excoriated the 'diplomatic filth and commercial sordidness' that prevented 'the countrymen of Elizabeth and Cromwell' from participating in European battles for freedom.[17] France's February revolution emerged from Linton's interpretation as a nationalist event with Chartist and Commonwealth connotations. 'For a nation to be free, it is sufficient that she wills it', he urged in commending the declaration of the French Republic. 'Gather, O ye enslaved millions! to assert the Nation's will – the People's Charter, the foundation stone of the Commonwealth!'[18]

Underlining the seventeenth-century origins of English radicalism, patriotic interpretations of 1848 allowed Chartist internationalists to defend continental liberty without endorsing English liberalism. Far more than an exercise in political nostalgia, however, Chartist emphasis on nationality provided an ideological instrument for the extension of English radical traditions. English conceptions of nationality forged in the Commonwealth era had few intrinsic affiliations with theories of class conflict. But they swiftly acquired class meanings in the context of 1848, for Chartist internationalists wilfully ignored distinctions between national and economic liberation in their interpretations of the continental revolutions. In the bills posted by the South Lancashire and Cheshire Chartists in April, patriotic sentiments thus prefaced attacks on class oppression and support for the rights of labour. Noting that all European states were now consumed 'with a desire for freedom, and a patriotic energy necessary to its achievement', these Chartist delegates described the continental nations 'preparing to throw off the degrading bonds that have so long rendered them, as ourselves, the slaves of class distinction – of Class usurpation'. In this view, the task confronting Chartists and their 'patriotic brethren' on the continent entailed economic justice as well as popular sovereignty. 'CITIZENS, The day of your emancipation is drawing nigh', the posters announced. 'Labour's jubilee is being proclaimed over the world.'[19]

---

[17] *Republican* (1848), pp. 122–3.   [18] *Ibid.*, p. 103.
[19] Printed poster, 'The South Lancashire and Cheshire Chartist Delegates to the People', HO 45/2410B, item 47.

The economic implications of Chartists' expanding notions of patriotism were especially evident in their enthusiasm for French conceptions of democratic socialism. Proudhon, Cabet, and Saint-Simon all found advocates among the English working class, but it was Louis Blanc's organization of labour that commanded the allegiance of English Chartists in 1848. Less utopian than the works of his socialist compatriots, Blanc's *Organisation du travail* (1840) offered a sustained denunciation of the poverty and moral degradation that attended economic individualism and free competition, and provided concrete political proposals for the alleviation of this social and economic distress. Under his plan, democratically organized 'social workshops' financed by the state and protected by government legislation would supplant capitalist competition, moralize the production process, and ultimately lead to the extinction of poverty. Charged by the Provisional Government with drafting the decree that guaranteed the right to labour, and associated with the National Workshops that provided tens of thousands of workers with temporary employment throughout the spring, Blanc emerged from the revolution of 1848 as a champion of the rights of labour much loved by the Parisian working classes.[20]

His reputation was equally high among English workers. Translated into English, Blanc's *Organisation of Labour* became a key text for Chartist polemic in 1848, providing reformers schooled in a radical tradition that privileged state institutions with a potential parliamentary mechanism for economic change. Radical leaders were fully alive to the popular appeal of Blanc's doctrines, and worked to infuse democratic socialism into their own campaigns. Thomas Allsop, an advocate of both the Charter and socialist economics, urged Robert Owen to 'above all things . . . in some way associate yourself with the French organization of Labour so as to give your recommendations all the effect of example'. 'In the present time your association with Lords and Ladies will be injurious to you', he cautioned, 'Louis Blanc and Albert are far better introductions to the notice of the English workmen'.[21]

This enthusiasm for Blanc's democratic theories, widely current in Chartist circles, served to temper English radicals' libertarian ten-

---

[20] Sewell, *Work and Revolution*, pp. 232–6, 243–55.
[21] Allsop to Owen, 30 March 1848, MCU, Robert Owen Collection, item 1590. Albert Martin was a member of the Provisional Government of working-class origin.

dencies, encouraging Chartists to supplement their traditional diatribes against the corruption and expense of the aristocratic state
with calls for government intervention on behalf of the labouring
population. In April G.J. Holyoake, like Allsop a Chartist with
Owenite sympathies, warned his audience at London's John Street
Institution against accepting facile attacks lodged by the '*Economist*
and cent per cent people' against socialism, and proclaimed that
working-class radicals, if successful in winning the Charter, 'would
organize labour with it':

> We are told that to organize labour implies an authority, and
> authority would be tyranny . . . Away, then, with the jargon about
> tyranny. No people are so much humbugged by terms as the
> English. If I am to live under a tyranny, it is better that I live under
> a tyranny which secures me Freedom, Intelligence, and Com-
> petence, than under a liberty which dooms me to Oppression,
> Ignorance, and Starvation.[22]

These arguments were the stuff of Chartist aspiration in the provinces as well. An estimated 12,000 Sheffield Chartists under the
leadership of Isaac Ironside met in Paradise Square on 13 March to
endorse an address which congratulated the Provisional Government and affirmed the principle that 'Society owes to every individual permanent remunerative employment, according to choice,
capacity, and public necessities'. Ironside reported at the following
week's meeting that he had dispatched a letter to Lord John Russell
suggesting the establishment of an 'Organisation of Labour' in
England.[23]

Sovereignty, nationality, and economic justice were the characteristic preoccupations of Chartists determined to wrest universal
manhood suffrage from the English government in the first months
of 1848. Guided by these principles, working-class radicals greeted
the continental revolutions with enthusiasm, and used continental
paradigms to their own ends. In the rich body of argument generated in this initial response to the revolutions, Chartists' invocation
of continental ideology followed a twofold pattern of usage. On the
one hand, much of the attention that the continental revolutions
commanded in the Chartist movement reflected political preoccupations endemic to English radicalism from the seventeenth century
and was expressed in the language and symbolism of the existing

[22] *Reasoner*, 19 April 1848, pp. 284–5.
[23] *Sheffield and Rotherham Independent*, 18 and 25 March 1848.

nationalist radical tradition. The continental emphasis in the late
Chartist movement thus provides material for a case-study of
ideological appropriation, an historical instance in which working-
class radicals grafted continental rhetoric, imagery, and precedent to
received national memories. On the other hand, however, it represented a significant and new departure on the part of English radical
leaders, a process of assimilation and accommodation in which they
adopted and elaborated subversive social theories from the continent. Often intertwined in practice, these two patterns of usage held
distinctly different implications for Chartist collaboration with
radicals of the middle class.

MIDDLE-CLASS RESPONSE AND REACTION

> Though the nations yet bow down
>   To the sceptre and the crown –
> Though they bend the fawning knee
>   To a titled luxury;
> More contemptible than this
>   To behold a people kiss
> The mire-bedraggled tatters hanging bare
>   Of the rabble in the street,
>   And sit slavering at the feet
> Of the ignorant and hungry *proletaire* . . .
> Oh, beware of mob-idolatry
> — beware.[24]

Although middle-class support for the continental revolutions was
far less sweeping than that of the Chartists, radical enthusiasm for
the events of 1848–9 was evident at all levels of English bourgeois
society. Liberal intellectuals, inspired by longstanding family traditions of opposition to Catholic 'despotism', the historical teachings of Thomas Arnold, and sympathies born of travel on the
continent, were naturally – if only briefly – attracted to the revolutionary cause. Benjamin Jowett journeyed from Oxford to Paris in
the midst of France's initial upheaval and marched, with a revolutionary column, around the Place de la Concorde; Arthur Hugh
Clough responded to the fall of the Roman Republic with the
stirring lines of 'Say Not the Struggle Nought Availeth'. A.V. Dicey,

[24] 'A Warning Voice to the Parisians', *The Puppet Show*, 1 April 1848, pp. 17–18.

doyen of liberal legal thought, was only thirteen in 1848, but it was to France's February revolution that he later traced the first stirrings of his political conscience.[25]

Beyond the pale of liberal Oxbridge, the continental revolutions found their most substantial middle-class support among the ranks of Dissent and within the bohemian precincts of London's literati. Here international sympathies born in the era of the first French revolution were consolidated by social and political alliances with Polish and Italian exiles who had sought refuge in England in the thirties and forties. The People's International League, established in 1847 to 'embody and manifest an efficient Public Opinion in favour of the right of every People to self-government and the maintenance of their own Nationality', lent institutional support to these pervasive radical sentiments in the months before the February revolution.[26] Embracing the Italian patriot Giuseppe Mazzini, the Polish nationalist Charles Stolzman, and the moderate Chartists Thomas Cooper and W.J. Linton, the League's membership rolls reveal as well the characteristic social and cultural formations from which middle-class radical internationalism drew its strength for decades. Thornton Hunt, the son of Leigh Hunt and later a Chartist leader, and Douglas Jerrold, an associate of Charles Dickens and the father-in-law of Henry Mayhew, were men of letters whose membership testified to the radical and international sympathies of literary London's bohemian subculture.[27] More numerous and influential were the Nonconformists, who formed the backbone of both the People's International League and the wider middle-class radical movement of which it was a part. The social reformer William Howitt was a Quaker, but Unitarians clearly predominated. W.J. Fox, the spiritual leader of South Place Chapel, joined the League alongside William Shaen, James Stansfeld, S.M. Hawkes, Henry

---

[25] Christopher Harvie details these and other instances of academic internationalism, and the wider context of liberal engagement in continental politics, in *The Lights of Liberalism: University Liberals and the Challenge of Democracy 1860–86* (London, 1976), pp. 33–4, 97–104.

[26] 'Address to the Council of the People's International League', 1847, T&WAD, Joseph Cowen Jr Collection, 634/A8.

[27] Harry W. Rudman, *Italian Nationalism and English Letters: Figures of the Risorgimento and Victorian Men of Letters* (New York, 1940), traces the evolution of literary internationalist sympathy; Christopher Kent conveys the characteristic tone of this radical subculture in 'The Whittington Club: A Bohemian Experiment in Middle-Class Social Reform', *Victorian Studies*, vol. 18 (September 1974), pp. 31–55.

Solly, and the younger Peter Alfred Taylor. Shaen (a solicitor), Solly
(a Unitarian preacher), and Stansfeld (a brewer) were all young men
sympathetic to the moral force Chartism of William Lovett. Taylor,
scion of the Courtauld family nexus, represented a family of
Unitarian manufacturers that traced its radical ancestry from the
political influence of Richard Price in 1789 to the Corn Law
agitation of the 1840s.[28]

Mazzini's departure for Italy with the outbreak of the revolutions
disrupted the operations of the People's International League, which
concluded its activities in 1848 by sending an address of congratulations to the French Provisional Government.[29] But the League's
demise hardly signalled an end to middle-class radical zeal, for the
next months saw a continued escalation of bourgeois internationalism alongside efforts to unite middle- and working-class reform
movements. The People's League established by William Lovett in
April included Howitt, Shaen, and Stansfeld of the People's International League among its members, and sought to promote the six
points of the Charter with petitions to Parliament. Warning the
citizens of London that the constitutional privileges secured by
Magna Carta, the Petition of Right, the Habeas Corpus Act, the Bill
of Rights, and the Act of Settlement were now threatened by an
aristocratic class antipathetic to the continental revolutions, the
League grounded its arguments for universal manhood suffrage in
Enlightenment internationalism, adducing 'the great brotherhood of
humanity' as justification for its reform efforts.[30]

Within the confines of chapel culture, these political aspirations
found zealous spiritual advocates, as the early events of 1848
captivated the Nonconformist conscience as fully as they had
engaged the sympathies of the Chartist internationalists. Although
embarrassed in retrospect by the power and form of his youthful
emotions, Henry Solly – Dissenter, member of the People's Inter-

[28] For membership and participation in the League, see 'Minutes of the Provisional
Committee of the People's International League', Istituto Giangiacomo Feltrinelli
Milan, William James Linton Papers, VI, fols. 18–20. The younger Unitarians'
sympathy for Chartism and the League is discussed in J.L. and Barbara Hammond, *James Stansfeld: A Victorian Champion of Sex Equality* (London, 1932), pp.
7–15, and M.J. Shaen, *William Shaen: A Brief Sketch* (London, 1912), pp. 16–18.
For Taylor's radical heritage, see D.C. Coleman, *Courtaulds: An Economic and
Social History*, 3 vols. (Oxford, 1969–80), vol. I, pp. 203–39.
[29] Linton, *Threescore and Ten Years*, p. 103.
[30] 'The People's League: Circulars', Birmingham Reference Library, William Lovett
Collection, fols. 288–90.

national League, and self-proclaimed friend of the working classes –
recalled the impact of the February revolution with great clarity:

A vast number of English Liberals and Radicals hailed it with joy,
for they regarded it as an almost bloodless triumph of a struggle
for constitutional freedom against bureaucratic despotism ...
Among others who were carried away by the great wave of
enthusiastic sympathy, which rolled over England, were many of
the most active and intelligent members of my congregation and
myself ... we seemed to be entirely in the right at that stage ... in
giving expression to our sympathy *as citizens or individuals* – but
we were lamentably and flagrantly wrong ... in holding a meeting
in the chapel after the morning service the first Sunday succeeding
the Revolution, and then and there agreeing to an address as an
utterance of that sympathy ... how I could have been a cordially
consenting party to having a meeting after the service at all, I
cannot understand – except by remembering the extraordinary
and contagious force of such occasions, as well as my earlier
Chartist antagonism to oppression and political injustice of every
kind.

Locally, Solly's 'grievous indiscretion' cost him dearly, as a 'new and
influential' member departed for a more moderate congregation.[31]
But at the national level his sympathies were endorsed by the
leadership of militant Dissent. Edward Miall's *Nonconformist* compared the corruption of Louis Philippe's system of government to
the iniquitous privileges of England's Established Church, and
greeted the February revolution as an 'impressive moral spectacle –
a ... sublime illustration of the inherent impotence of wrong'.[32]

Beneath this broad layer of middle-class radical enthusiasm a
more discriminating attitude towards the continental revolutions
was, however, apparent. Although fully developed only in the
aftermath of the Paris June Days, the lineaments of this response
were evident in the distinctly different patterns of national preference exhibited by middle- and working-class radicals from the spring
of 1848. For Chartists, France – with its adoption of universal
manhood suffrage – was the overwhelming centre of attraction in
these months; for middle-class reformers, interest in the liberal and
national revolutions of Germany, Italy, and later Hungary far

[31] Henry Solly, *These Eighty Years: Or, The Story of an Unfinished Life*, 2 vols.
(London, 1893), vol. II, pp. 40–1, 44.
[32] *Nonconformist*, 1 March 1848, p. 135.

surpassed sympathy for the February revolution.[33] 'I quite agree with you that what ever becomes of France *Germany* & Italy will have great reason to rejoice in the times', Bessie Rayner Parkes, a granddaughter of the Unitarian radical Joseph Priestley, wrote to Barbara Leigh Smith in March. 'Indeed I think it is in those two countries alone that real progress will be made.'[34] The basis for this preference emerges clearly from both private correspondence and the newspaper press. For whereas France's Provisional Government, as Richard Cobden explained to John Bright, 'find themselves in a sad mess with their Communist notions', the revolutions 'have been political throughout Germany, *where alone there has been real revolution*'. 'The German revolution is essentially political', the *Illustrated London News* likewise instructed its readers, but 'the French revolution is essentially social, and occurred at its own time, without reference to the wants or sympathies of other nations'. In consequence, while the paper looked 'with some hope to the termination of the troubles of Germany', it could only 'feel something akin to despair when we reflect upon the troubles of France'.[35]

This analysis, although delivered in the autumn, was fully consonant with the broad spectrum of middle-class opinion from the first weeks of the revolution. Whether issued by conservatives, moderates, or radicals, these interpretations of the continental revolutions upheld a relentless demarcation between social and economic relations, on the one hand, and political life on the other. The London *Times*, anatomizing the decrees of the Provisional Government in March, was explicit. 'There are no fictions so wild as those which are

---

[33] Unlike Italy and Hungary, Germany failed to retain substantial support among middle-class radicals and found little support in working-class circles at any point. Arnold Ruge complained with some justice to G.J. Holyoake that the German cause had been neglected 'whilst the poor Magyars, who have neither principles nor good will for any other emancipation but that of the 4 millions of "noble Magyars", and the Italians, who do not pretend that they aim at anything but their *independence* and a *Republic* ... have the sympathy of the English'. Ruge to Holyoake, 1853, MCU, George Holyoake Collection, item 619.

[34] Bessie Rayner Parkes to Barbara Bodichon, 30 March 1848, Girton College Archives, Cambridge, Bessie Rayner Parkes Papers, V/21. In a subsequent letter to Bodichon, Parkes discounted the possibility that the French were capable of forming 'a *true* Republic' (29 April 1848, V/22). For her Unitarian ancestry, see Olive Banks, *The Biographical Dictionary of British Feminists: Volume One, 1800–1930* (Brighton, 1985), p. 27.

[35] Cobden to Bright, 21 March 1848, WSRO, Richard Cobden Papers, vol. 30, fol. 26; Cobden to Bright, 1 November 1848, BL, Richard Cobden Papers, Add. MS 43,649, fols. 88–9; *Illustrated London News*, 7 October 1848, pp. 209–10.

engendered by a paroxysm of popular enthusiasm', it proclaimed, 'and none so fatal as those which extend their influence from the political rights of men to their social condition, and having remodelled the constitution of the state seek to regenerate the whole fabric of society'.[36] Ostensibly rooted in public utility and hostile to political abstractions, this pervasive response to the French revolution derived – despite middle-class reformers' frequent protestations to the contrary – from dogged adherence to the claims of a system of political theory. For although the disciples of Adam Smith, as Maxine Berg has argued, sought to create 'a discipline apart', a set of principles 'tied neither to a wider social theory nor to a political vision', their economic reasoning had successfully penetrated the full range of bourgeois social and political thought by the Victorian period.[37] Successful in harmonizing otherwise disparate middle-class arguments, an acceptance of classical political economy and the doctrine of separate social and political spheres acted to sever liberal reformers decisively from working-class radicals in 1848.

The newspapers of Anglican and metropolitan reform, proffering analyses of 1848 that ranged between the extremes of educated contempt and Christian condemnation, were no less determined than the *Times* to denounce the Provisional Government's lapse from classical economics. The *Morning Chronicle* advocated moderate reform of England's electoral system, but condemned all efforts to effect social reform through politics:

> The evil consequences of interfering with the unalterable laws of labour are equally obvious to every person of reflecting mind. If the supply exceeds the demand, the utmost that the State can do with prudence is – what is done through the medium of the Poor-Law in England – save the suffering from the last extremity of want. Capital, the only regular source of employment, may be diverted, but can hardly be created, by a Government ... M. LOUIS BLANC's schemes for abolishing *concurrence*, and putting all who live by labour on an equality, is the heterogenous compound of Owenism, Socialism, St. Simonism, Fourierism, and all other *isms* which have taken the perfectibility of the human species as their

---

[36] *Times*, 1 March 1848, p. 5.
[37] Berg, *Machinery Question*, pp. 37–8. For the broader penetration of social and political discourse by political economy and the doctrine of separate spheres with regard to gender, see Catherine Hall and Leonore Davidoff, *Family Fortunes: Men and Women of the English Middle Class 1780–1850* (London, 1987).

starting point ... Fancy a man contending, not merely that competition is the root of all evil in the world, but that it can and ought to be suppressed.[38]

The Christian Socialists associated with Charles Kingsley were equally determined to separate the spheres of politics and economics. The prospectus of their *Politics for the People* initially defied conventional middle-class wisdom in proclaiming that politics, 'when they become POLITICS FOR THE PEOPLE ... are found to take in a very large field: whatever concerns man as a social being must be included in them'. But the articles that followed discarded this novel argument with alacrity. Kingsley chastised the Chartists for falling 'into just the same mistake as the rich of whom you complain – the very mistake which has been our curse and our nightmare – I mean, the mistake of fancying that *legislative* reform is *social* reform'.[39] And J.M.F. Ludlow, who had travelled eagerly to France at the outset of the revolution, soon recognized the fundamental error of French social politics. 'They fancy that society is to be regenerated by an improved social machinery; as if a machine, however perfect, can ever itself produce any moral good', he stormed, 'As sure as there is a God, he will avenge himself on them.'[40]

The organs of provincial radicalism, more often amenable than metropolitan papers to the claims of both Dissent and the Chartists, were initially less harsh in their judgement. An ally of the Chartist Isaac Ironside, Robert Leader of the *Sheffield and Rotherham Independent*, was sceptical but not damning of the French organization of labour in March. Warning that 'a republican government will prove itself no better as a manufacturer than our own; and a government cannot manufacture at the public expense without destroying more capital than it creates', Leader nonetheless accepted Louis Blanc's National Workshops as a temporary expedient in a time of revolution.[41] The judgement of the *Newcastle Chronicle*, nothing loath to see the fall of the French monarchy, was more sober. The paper dismissed Blanc's projects for the organization of labour as 'bold experiments, opposed to the established doctrines of political economy and the general principles of trade, and so fraught

---

[38]   *Morning Chronicle*, 2 March 1848, p. 4.
[39]   *Politics for the People*, 6 May 1848, p. 1; 13 May 1848, p. 28.
[40]   Ludlow to Sir Charles Forbes, March 1848, Cambridge University Library, John Malcolm Forbes Ludlow Correspondence and Papers, Add. MS 7348/10.
[41]   *Sheffield and Rotherham Independent*, 4 March 1848, p. 8. Leader's contact with Ironside is discussed below, p. 93.

with difficulties on every side, that they must, under the most favourable circumstances, prove a source of great embarrassment to the Provisional Government and their successors, whilst the consequences of failure are of a character which it is fearful to contemplate'.[42]

These prophecies of doom were soon rewarded, for in the eyes of the middle class the Paris June Days merely served to confirm a sacred assumption challenged by the February revolution, graphically illustrating the gross folly inherent in linking social and economic issues with politics. The four days of insurrection, precipitated by the National Assembly's decision of 21 June to dissolve the National Workshops, forced Louis Blanc into English exile, leaving 1,500 workers dead, 12,000 insurgents imprisoned, and the hopes of European labour in tatters.[43] In sharp contrast to a wide spectrum of Chartists, middle-class reformers were virtually unanimous in denouncing at one and the same time Blanc's *Organisation of Labour*, the National Workshops, and French social politics. 'The two men whose wild and pernicious theories tended most speedily to the dissolution of the social fabric were M. LOUIS BLANC and M. DUCLERC', the *Morning Chronicle* concluded in the wake of the insurrection. 'The one, the creator of those nests of sedition and gulphs of public credit, the *ateliers nationaux*: the other, the unblushing advocate of a system of finance at once the most delusive and the most iniquitous ever propounded in a civilized community.'[44]

So pervasive was this analysis that by July even those middle-class radicals who in March had dismissed the *Times* as reactionary had come to echo its pragmatic views. Distaste for continental social theories resounded through their reaction, laying the foundations for later middle-class arguments that demonstrable economic success, not abstract political rights, should govern access to the franchise in England. In Sheffield Robert Leader's *Independent* sounded a sorrowful note, cautioning readers that 'the condition of France will long be a warning to the rest of the world, and will tend to make nations which enjoy liberty and moderate prosperity, careful how they adopt the political or social theories of the

---

[42] *Newcastle Chronicle*, 31 March 1848, p. 4.
[43] Sewell, *Work and Revolution*, pp. 271–2.
[44] *Morning Chronicle*, 3 July 1848, p. 4; 5 July 1848, p. 4. Duclerc, the French Minister of Finance, proposed the nationalization of the railways on 17 May 1848.

French'.[45] The *Manchester Times*, associated through John Bright with the Manchester School, had earlier urged suffrage extension as both a right and a palliative for 'the wide-spread pauperism that lies like a corroding and crumbling cancer at the base of society', but by July it discerned the roots of 'the great misfortune for France' in 'the temporary supremacy of ardent theorists' committed to government expenditure.[46]

The spectre of communism now haunted hitherto radical middle-class publications, bearing an impress that was to mark English reform movements for decades to come. The Provisional Government had sealed its own fate when it 'pledged itself to find occupation for the unemployed, and encouraged communism, and with that view established national workshops', the *Newcastle Chronicle* explained late in June. 'It has now risen again in dreadful disarray, and under the ominous cry of establishing a new "Social and Democratic Republic", has produced one of the most disastrous insurrections ever recorded.'[47] Transfixed by the red flag, Miall's *Nonconformist* swiftly followed suit. An early proponent of the February revolution, it now located the ideological origins of the slaughter of June in 'Association – Communism – the red flag – the republic, social and democratic.'[48]

The depth and intensity of this pervasive reaction to the French revolution are fully comprehensible only when viewed alongside middle-class responses to the contemporary Chartist agitation. For like the Chartists themselves, middle-class reformers were quick to identify an essential affinity between the two movements. Even before the June Days, middle-class radicals equated the English cry for the six points of the Charter with the French proclamation of the rights of labour. In responding to the English face of this European threat, middle-class observers again upheld a strict dichotomy between political and social life, a division of spheres that underpinned their rejection of the concept of class. The reform-minded *Birmingham Journal* neatly encapsulated these concerns in its analysis of European radicalism. Having identified the Provisional Government's contravention of the laws of supply and demand as

[45] *Sheffield and Rotherham Independent*, 8 July 1848, p. 8.
[46] *Manchester Times*, 11 March 1848, p. 5; 8 April 1848, p. 4; 1 July 1848, p. 4.
[47] *Newcastle Chronicle*, 30 June 1848, p. 4.
[48] *Nonconformist*, 5 July 1848, p. 495. For the concept of the social and democratic republic, see below, pp. 87–8.

'the elements of a conflagration which cannot be quenched but in blood' in March, the *Journal*'s editors proceeded to conflate 'Communism and Chartism' in April:

> We do not think that sufficient attention has been paid to the double character of the revolutionary movement throughout Europe, it is both political and social, and these elements should be most carefully distinguished. In Germany, Italy, Hungary and Poland, the political element is predominant; in France, among the Repealers of Ireland and the Chartists of England, the social element is most conspicuous; revolt is directed not so much against any particular form of government as against those social laws which determine the relations between the employer and the employed. Communism is at open war with Economic Science. Such a contest involves not merely the interests but the safety of every man in the community; should the principles of FOURRIER [*sic*] and LOUIS BLANC prevail, it will be necessary to construct society afresh on a totally new basis, and to alter all the individual relations between man and man.

In the face of this 'momentous and appalling issue', the duty of all middle-class friends of the working masses was no less clear than urgent. As only the plain truths of political economy could disabuse English workers of the social theories of the French revolution, the newspaper proclaimed 'it to be a mere delusion to divert them from this enquiry by political discussions which have no bearing whatever on the momentous questions really at issue'.[49]

Failure to maintain this strict demarcation between social and political spheres could only lead to perpetual class conflict. 'We do not apprehend the repetition of an insurrection on so gigantic a scale as that which has recently been crushed', the *Birmingham Journal* reported in response to the June Days. 'But we do dread the complete dissolution of the bonds by which society is held together; we do dread a continuous war of the classes.'[50] Harriet Martineau and Charles Knight, well practised in the art of infusing working-class literature with the theories of Bentham and Adam Smith, recognized the same potential for class war in the Chartist movement and the February revolution, and launched the *Voice of the People*, a supplement for distribution with popular newspapers, to

[49] *The Birmingham Journal and Commercial Advertiser*, 11 March 1848, p. 4; 15 April 1848, p. 4.
[50] *Ibid.*, 15 July 1848, p. 4.

combat class theories of society with a nationalist analysis that underlined the role of the propertied classes in preserving popular sovereignty. 'The "Populus" of the Romans, the "Peuple" of the French, the "People" of the English, each, in the broad and comprehensive sense of the term, means the whole community – the nation', they argued in explaining their title to readers. Only 'by an abuse of the term' was the word people 'used to designate what we too exclusively call the working classes'. From this perspective, it was 'not a very difficult matter to trace the present domination of a section of the people in Paris to the opinions which have been current in French literature for ten or twelve years'. For the February revolution was 'based upon a systematic attempt to raise a portion of the industrious classes – the non-capitalist portion – into the belief that they are exclusively "The People" '.[51]

As a corrective to class sentiment, bourgeois reformers responding to the revolutions of 1848 urged a recognition of the community of interests binding the middle and the working class, a limited degree of reform, and the time-honoured heroes of English patriotism. Henry Vincent, in the course of delivering lectures sympathetic to Cobden's liberal reformism in Sheffield in April, 'proceeded to notice the leading men of the liberal party – Pym, Eliot, Hampden, Sir Henry Vane, Coke, and Cromwell'.[52] Knight and Martineau, turning the Chartist popularity of 'Mourir pour la patrie' to their own ends, preferred 'with the original, to give a *Paraphrase*, that we think better suited to *our* condition and *our* hopes'. Aptly entitled 'For Our Country To Live', the resulting nationalist anthem was redolent with the ethic of self-help and the tenets of pacific liberalism:

> By household Laws, and Public Order,
> Old England calls to works of Peace, –
> Work, to the Land's remotest border,
> Till Justice reign, till Crime shall cease.

[51] *The Voice of the People: A Supplement to All Newspapers*, 22 April 1848, p. 1. Knight and Martineau had previously written such instructive tracts for the working class as *The Tendency of Strikes and Sticks to Produce Low Wages, Letters to the Working People on the New Poor Law*, and *Political Economy Tales*. See S.E. Finer, 'The Transmission of Benthamite Ideas 1820–50', in Gillian Sutherland (ed.), *Studies in the Growth of Nineteenth-Century Government* (London, 1972), p. 24.
[52] *Sheffield and Rotherham Independent*, 8 April 1848, p. 2.

For our Country to live! for our Country to live!
  Is the task that our Rights and our Duties shall give.

Yes! we must work; the high, and the lowly, –
  Work for our land, with hearts outpoured.
England and Peace! the call is holy,
  To win the world without the sword.
For our Country to live! for our Country to live!
  Is the task that our Rights and our Duties shall give.

Not surprisingly, the original version, printed above this 'paraphrase', was rendered for readers only in French.[53]

Public lecturers on the middle-class reform circuit returned to the lessons of the nation repeatedly in their efforts to grapple with the threat posed to their own radical traditions by French theories and insurrections in 1848. George Dawson, a Congregationalist minister and popular orator, was alternately inspired and chagrined by the continental events, whose nationalist aspects he associated with England's own historic struggles in the age of Milton. Dawson was fully alive to the industrial tensions of his day and not unsympathetic to working-class radicalism, but 'almost entirely disagreed with the political economy of the Provisional Government of France', for 'he had no faith in the utility of a Government pottering and tinkering at workmen's wages, or talking about the hour at which a man should leave his work'. Crafted to 'make a clear distinction between the political and the social causes of the revolutions', his lecture at the Manchester Athenaeum reminded English reformers that their own national heritage precluded the necessity of a radical revolution for freedom. 'Our forefathers did that for us long ago', Dawson concluded, 'and in nothing does England [act] more wisely, than in showing to Europe that all the great changes which continental peoples are obliged to carry by force, can now, in this country, be carried by . . . manly straightforward speech'.[54]

---

[53] *Voice of the People*, 22 April 1848, p. 12. The contrast between the two versions is striking. The lines of the original are: 'Pour la voix du canon d'alarme / La France appelle ses enfants. / Allons, dit le soldat, aux armes! / C'est ma mere, je la défends. / Mourir pour la patrie! – Mourir pour la patrie . . . ' etc.

[54] Typescript of a lecture on 'The French Revolution', 29 March 1848, Birmingham Reference Library, George Dawson Collection, vol. 17, fols. 242–3; typescript of a lecture on 'The Present State of Europe', [1848–9], Dawson Collection, vol. 11, fols. 493–4.

CHARTISTS AND THE DEMOCRATIC AND SOCIAL REPUBLIC

> Dark days have fall'n, yet in the strife,
>   They bate no hope sublime,
> And bravely works the fiery life –
>   Their hearts pulse thro' the time,
> As grass is greenest trodden down,
>   So suffering makes men great;
> And this dark tide shall grandly crown
>   The men of Forty-eight.
>   Hurrah!
> For the men of Forty-eight.[55]

Viewed from the perspective of mass agitation, the experience of Chartism after July 1848 is the experience of defeat. Alarmed by the escalation of unrest at home, in Ireland, and on the continent, the British authorities conducted a summer campaign of repression that had by autumn eviscerated the Chartist movement. Among the several hundred activists arrested in these months, the leadership was especially hard hit. Ernest Jones and Peter McDouall, national orators and organizers par excellence, each received prison terms of two years; Bradford, Manchester, and other provincial towns saw a succession of local leaders picked off by the forces of the state. In London, Feargus O'Connor, himself under parliamentary investigation for financial mismanagement of the Chartist Land Company, sought to limit this damage by severing Chartism from both its physical force and its continental associations. His antipathy for foreign brands of radicalism, evident since the early years of the movement, now found expression in repeated, increasingly shrill, denunciations of socialist schemes and the organization of labour.[56]

While eroding the popular base of the Chartist movement, O'Connor's tergiversations, and his later syphilitic decline, acted to

---

[55] Gerald Massey, 'The Men of Forty-Eight', *Friend of the People*, 25 January 1851, p. 56.
[56] Saville, *1848*, pp. 161–3; John Belchem, '1848: Feargus O'Connor and the Collapse of the Mass Platform', in Epstein and Thompson (eds.), *The Chartist Experience*, pp. 275–6. Writing to a fellow Chartist in 1843, O'Connor confessed 'that much as I love liberty and hate oppression I would greatly prefer another consignment in York Castle to the enjoyment of that description of freedom which I would be likely to receive at the hands of foreign arbitrators'. O'Connor to Thomas Allsop, 1 July 1843, BLPES, Thomas Allsop Collection, Coll. Misc., 525/2, fol. 2.

expand the ideological horizons of working-class radicalism. For as O'Connor abandoned the European arena for a more insular, British theatre of reform, a host of lesser leaders advanced their competing claims to lead English radicals alongside their continental brethren. Six figures were especially prominent in this group: George Julian Harney, George Jacob Holyoake, William James Linton, James Bronterre O'Brien, G.W.M. Reynolds, and – upon his release from prison in 1850 – Ernest Jones provided the nucleus of an alternative working-class radical leadership in the late Chartist movement. Although none could rival O'Connor's earlier popularity with the masses, each worked in his own way to preserve working-class radical politics into the fifties, and beyond. And each, unlike O'Connor, continued to proclaim the fundamental identity of English and continental politics, remaining true to international sympathies born in earlier decades and consolidated by the events of 1848. Schooled in the traditions of the first French revolution, Bronterre O'Brien composed works on both Gracchus Babeuf (1836) and Robespierre (1859); Julian Harney, a sailor in his youth, signed his articles in the radical press 'L'Ami du Peuple', after Marat. The wood engraver Linton and Holyoake, who as a youth had worked in Birmingham as a whitesmith, co-edited the *Cause of the People* (1848), which drew its inspiration from George Sand's *Cause du Peuple* and its motto from Mazzini. Ernest Jones had, at the tender age of twelve, sought to join the forces of the Polish revolution of 1830, and Reynolds had entered English radical politics under the influence of French republicanism.[57]

Inspired equally by English and continental radical ideals, these rivals for the Chartist leadership – in stark contrast to both O'Connor and middle-class radicals – continued to defend French revolutionary politics in the aftermath of the June Days. Nor were they alone among the reduced ranks of the working-class movement in so doing. Thomas Cooper, the moderate reformer who served as

---

[57] Alfred Plummer, *Bronterre: A Political Biography of Bronterre O'Brien 1804–1864* (London, 1971), pp. 59–72; John Saville, *Ernest Jones: Chartist* (London, 1952), pp. 12, 20–1; Louis James and John Saville, 'George William MacArthur Reynolds (1818–1879)', in Joyce M. Bellamy and John Saville (eds.), *The Dictionary of Labour Biography* (London, 1976), vol. III, pp. 146–7; A.R. Schoyen, *The Chartist Challenge: A Portrait of George Julian Harney* (London, 1958), esp. p. 14; Joseph McCabe, *Life and Letters of George J. Holyoake*, 2 vols. (London, 1908), vol. I, p. 127; Francis B. Smith, *Radical Artisan: William James Linton 1812–98* (Manchester, 1973), pp. 53–9.

the model for Kingsley's Alton Locke, departed sharply from his middle-class allies in demanding that English radicals recognize the economic imperatives of the poor alongside their political rights. Although committed to an alliance with Cobden and Bright by April, Cooper was still steadfast to his Chartist origins in July, upholding Blanc's associative principles against 'the slaughterous opposition of the *bourgeoisie*, or shopocrats' of France and England. 'We shall see Louis Blanc uppermost again, yet, I trust; and (let us hope) Lamartine brought out again in his genuine shape', he wrote to a radical colleague. 'All that he has wanted was decision to stand by little Louis Blanc, instead of permitting him to be laughed down, just with the idea of keeping peace.'[58]

As in their initial response to the continental revolutions, Chartists who persisted in defending French revolutionaries after June intermingled social, economic, and political ideals in a body of argument that linked new continental slogans with the enduring catchwords of the English radical tradition. G.W.M. Reynolds's efforts to reinvigorate the English theory of the Norman Yoke with Proudhon's dictum 'property is theft' and Blanc's 'rights of labour' typify this confluence of ideologies. Arguing that 'when William the Conqueror seized upon some Saxon's estate and gave it to one of his Norman ruffians, this was theft – and the property thus acquired by the Norman noble was robbery', he urged all 'true patriots and earnest reformers' to pursue a social and political programme that called for the abolition of primogeniture and the recognition of the rights of labour.[59] In his *Political Instructor* (1849–50), Reynolds cultivated the perceived connection between Chartism and the continental cause assiduously, impressing his readers graphically with the fundamental interrelation of the European movements. Interspersed with his sketches of Thomas Cooper, William Lovett, Julian Harney, Ernest Jones, and Bronterre O'Brien were illustrated biographies of Giuseppe Mazzini, Louis Blanc, George Sand, and Louis Kossuth.[60]

If middle-class radicals were relentless in demarcating distinct social and political spheres and in distinguishing socialist from nationalist revolutions in the aftermath of the June Days, Chartist

[58] Thomas Cooper to Thomas Tatlow, 19 April and 4 July 1848, BI, Thomas Cooper Collection.
[59] *Reynolds's Political Instructor*, 26 January 1850, p. 90.
[60] *Ibid.*, 24 November 1849 to 30 March 1850.

ideologues were equally determined to champion social politics through appeals to nationalist sentiment. *The Democratic and Social Almanac for 1850*, presented to readers of the *Weekly Tribune* in December 1849, advanced this cause with a calendar in which the celebrated figures and events of 1789 and 1848 enriched the national litany of patriots of England's radical tradition. The birth and death dates of noted radicals supplied by the almanac provide a checklist for centuries of radical allegiance, extending from Wat Tyler, Hampden, Milton, and Cromwell to Wilkes, Cartwright, Paine, Robespierre, Cobbett, Queen Caroline, and Fourier. Events of radical portent noted in its pages ranged from the institution of trial by jury to the passage and suspensions of Habeas Corpus, the execution of Louis XVI, the Polish revolution of 1830, the trial of the Welsh Chartist John Frost, and the Paris June Days. In addition to contrasting the expense of government in royal Britain and republican America, an exercise that reflected conventional radical obsessions, the *Democratic and Social Almanac* reprinted the 'Socialist's Catechism' by Louis Blanc.[61]

Radical traditions of patriotism, liberty, and birthright continued to guide Chartist perceptions of politics in the wake of the Paris June Days, but they played only a secondary role in the evolving ideology of Chartist leaders other than O'Connor in these months. To account for the shared failure of English radicalism and European revolution in 1848, Chartist leaders were compelled to reassess the essentially political notions of national sovereignty embodied in the six points. Forced by state reprisals to abandon the mass platform, they espoused a programme of education and propaganda in the radical press both to explain the past disasters of the movement and to ensure its future success. Their new pedagogic imperative linked the collapse of Chartism inextricably to that of the continental revolutions. 'The fate of LOUIS BLANC, ALBERT, BARBES, and others', Bronterre O'Brien proclaimed in November 1848, 'ought to be a warning to all Chartists how impossible it is for enlightened friends of working men to serve them, if the working men are not themselves enlightened.'[62]

Meshing easily with the moral-force message espoused by moderates such as Lovett and Cooper – who traced the fall of the republics in France, Italy, and Hungary to an uneducated electorate, and

[61] *The Democratic and Social Almanac for 1850* (London, 1849), pp. 2–22.
[62] *Power of the Pence*, 18 November 1848, p. 27–8.

urged fellow reformers 'to labour earnestly for the increase of intelligence in our own fatherland'[63] – this line of analysis none-theless served to distinguish Chartist argument from middle-class political opinion. For Chartist leaders espoused an agenda of popular enlightenment that set their educational programme in direct opposition to received bourgeois interpretations of 1848. Far from abandoning their earlier linkage of social, economic, and political issues, they argued that its incomplete development had led to the downfall of the European revolutions. Here again Chartist activists, in refusing to demarcate social and political spheres, declined to distinguish between social and political revolutions. 'Nothing can be easier', O'Brien declared, 'than to prove that, had the people of France, of many parts of Italy, of Berlin, Dresden, and other places, understood their *social* as well as their *political* rights, no counter-revolution could possibly have been successful.'[64]

By 1850, indeed, a consensus had emerged in Chartist circles that a radical programme which failed, in England or on the continent, to take cognizance of social rights was doomed to fail the working class. The received emblems of national identity remained central to this radical vision, but equal emphasis now fell on a new, social conception of sovereignty. Citing Saint-Just's maxim that 'those who make half revolutions, dig a grave for themselves', Julian Harney argued that the European counter-revolutions 'must be attributed to popular folly, or rather to popular ignorance':

> In demanding representative institutions, universal suffrage, free-dom of the press, trial by jury, and the usual order of 'Reforms' advocated by mere political agitators, the people of Continental Europe were ignorant of the all-important fact that such 'reforms' are utterly valueless, unless associated with such social changes as will enable the great body of the community to command the actual sovereignty of society ... With the experience of other nations to guide them, it would be culpable in the highest degree for the Democrats of this country to neglect the duty of enlighten-ing the masses as to their social rights, while agitating for the enactment of the political franchise embodied in the People's Charter.[65]

---

[63] *Cooper's Journal: Or, Unfettered Thinker and Plain Speaker for Truth, Freedom, and Progress*, 5 January 1850, p. 1.
[64] *Reynolds's Political Instructor*, 5 January 1850.
[65] *Red Republican*, 22 June 1850, p. 1.

Even G.W.M. Reynolds, who continued to issue unqualified recommendations of universal manhood suffrage throughout 1849, had accepted this argument by 1850. 'With universal suffrage and social rights, all that is possible or desirable in Socialism would spontaneously arise from its natural and peaceable development', he informed his readers, 'it would have been so after the February Revolution, had the mass of the French people understood their social rights.'[66]

If French defeats supplied a new impetus for the integration of social issues and political agitation after 1848, they also suggested a means by which this integration could be effected. Evaluating the didactic potential of the revolutions for England in 1848, Bronterre O'Brien underlined the need for both an informed mass electorate and 'a uniform creed to bind them together in unity of object and action'.[67] To the extent that such a creed existed in England in the aftermath of 1848, it too was a legacy of the continental revolutions. Just as the collapse of the mass platform forced Chartist leaders to reassess their traditional radical agenda, the overwhelming electoral victory of Louis Napoleon in the presidential elections of 1848 compelled the French radical leadership to reassess the efficacy of the democratic franchise. In their efforts to revitalize the revolution in the face of conservative gains, French democrats and socialists alike came to embrace the ideology of the *république démocratique et sociale* adumbrated by the French Montagnards under the Provisional Government. Predicated upon the democratic franchise, this political vision was marked by its social imperative: the so-called *démoc-socs* were, in John Merriman's phrase, 'democrats who believed that universal suffrage was the foundation upon which the republic of social justice would be built'.[68]

In its original, French conception, the ideology of the democratic and social republic functioned as a middle ground upon which radicals of all descriptions could meet for political ends and yet preserve their divergent theories. Under the direction of the moderate republican leader Alexandre Ledru-Rollin, the effort achieved an instant, if ephemeral, success in France, with even the intransigent

---

[66] *Reynolds's Newspaper*, 9 June 1850, p. 4.
[67] *Social Reformer*, 29 September 1849, p. 57.
[68] Edward Berenson, *Populist Religion and Left-Wing Politics in France, 1830–1852* (Princeton, 1984), pp. 74–126; John M. Merriman, *The Agony of the Republic: The Repression of the Left in Revolutionary France, 1848–1851* (New Haven, 1978), p. xxi.

communist Etienne Cabet pledging his allegiance. 'I drink to the union of all democrats, even though I mean the union of all socialists', he announced at the inaugural banquet of the *démoc-soc* campaign in September 1848, 'because there are no real democrats who are not socialists and there are no real socialists who are not democrats and republicans.'[69] The utility of such arguments for English radicals was readily apparent to the leaders of late Chartism. Julian Harney had risen in defence of 'the Democratic and Social Republic, government of all, by all, *for all* – in short, the reign of justice', already in March 1849.[70] Other Chartist leaders soon followed Harney's lead. 'The social democrats of France, alarmed at the rapid progress of the counter-revolution, are bethinking themselves of a common ground upon which they may do battle together against the common enemy, without renouncing their distinctive opinions', Reynolds reported in August 1850, 'This salutary advice is not more applicable to France than England, and to every other country in which the struggle of the democratic party is broken into fragments and rendered powerless'.[71]

In England as in France, radical leaders embraced the concept of the democratic and social republic in an effort to construct an ideological platform from which both moderate and extreme reformers could articulate a shared democratic vision. But although the English adoption of the *démoc-soc* ideal was a tactical ploy developed by Chartist leaders in avowed emulation of prominent French revolutionaries, the fundamental beliefs that informed this ideology were rooted in the experiences and expectations of English labour. Neither imposed from above nor imported from outside English working-class life, the insistence upon the interrelation of social and political spheres and the conviction that political institutions could transform the character of economic relations spoke equally to new French conceptions of revolutionary sovereignty and English radical traditions that dated from the seventeenth and eighteenth centuries. Providing new ammunition for the skilled trades' battles with classical political economy, the rights of labour tapped a deep vein of trade union sentiment. The *Labour League*, journal of the National Association of United Trades for the Protection of Industry, was emphatic:

[69] Cited in Berenson, *Populist Religion*, p. 77.
[70] *Reasoner*, 21 March 1849, p. 187.
[71] *Reynolds's Weekly Newspaper*, 4 August 1850, p. 4.

The masses find themselves rapidly descending into the dreadful and dreary gulph of pauperism, without any chance of rescue, at the very same time when wealth of all description is multiplying to overflowing in the hands of the few ... The jargon of the political economists and the apostles of the gospel of profit has failed not only to convince, but even to silence the people ... The great question of the RIGHT TO LABOUR is manfully and earnestly mooted ...

It is the disregard of these fundamental principles of equitable distribution which has brought things to their present state in every country in Europe. This is ... why France is at this moment undergoing the throes of another revolution.[72]

Henry Mayhew's survey of the London poor, published in the *Morning Chronicle* from 1849 to 1850, revealed the currency of these ideals within the working population, exposing both patterns of chronic destitution and a persistent strain of working-class political argument that looked to the government for relief. Unionized shoemakers and hatters, Mayhew reported, were strongly protectionist, but so was a Spitalfields weaver recovering from the cholera. 'It's the competitive system; that's what the Government ought to put a stop to', he told Mayhew from his sickbed, 'the Government of my native land ought to interpose their powerful arm to put a stop to such things.' Outside the honourable trades, this argument was still evident. Detailing a lifetime of slopwork, casual prostitution, and frantic attempts to avoid separation from her children in the workhouse, a needlewoman concluded her history with the hope 'that public attention being now called to these matters, the oppressed will be oppressed no longer, and that the Parliament House even will interpose to protect them'.[73]

The adoption of *démoc-soc* ideals was successful in aligning Chartist leaders with the social and economic aspirations of unenfranchised workers for whom they claimed to speak, but it also served to embitter Chartist relations with middle-class reformers. In France bourgeois republicans such as Ledru-Rollin proved willing for a time to suppress their distaste for socialism and enter into the

[72] *Labour League: Or, Journal of the National Association of United Trades*, 11 November 1848, p. 113.
[73] Henry Mayhew, *The Unknown Mayhew: Selections from the Morning Chronicle 1849–1850*, ed. E.P. Thompson and Eileen Yeo (Harmondsworth, 1984), pp. 134–5, 283, 541, 211.

démoc-soc campaign against political reaction. But in England middle-class radicals would brook no *démoc-soc* alliance. Adherence to the tenets of the French Provisional Government, to their mind, rendered the working class and its radical leaders uneducable, and hence unfit to exercise the franchise. A choleric Francis Place, the artisanal radicalism of his youth long discarded for liberal alliances, recognized and condemned the implications of these beliefs for the new generation of working-class reformers in 1848. 'I hope you have not adopted the cant of party here and in Paris – in the use of the words "*the right to Labour*" ', he warned G.J. Holyoake in October. 'No one can regret more than I do the humbug – of the various *isms* – which have been and are the greatest impediment to the increase of knowledge among the working people and make them to a great extent unteachable in matters absolutely necessary to bettering of their condition as well physically as morally'.[74]

In the ensuing months, Place's strictures proved prescient, but unavailing. Throughout 1849, Holyoake's *Reasoner* served as a clearing-house for Chartist debates with liberal economists and their parliamentary allies. Repeatedly publicizing liberal critiques of French socialism, contributors to the *Reasoner* consistently refused to endorse them. Sir Robert Peel's parliamentary defence of Adam Smith against *démoc-soc* attacks was duly chronicled by the paper in April:

> With respect to social principles, I must say this, that I hope the working classes of this country will not be deluded by the doctrines that are held upon that subject which intimately concerns their labour and the wages of labour. If the doctrines that are held there [France] be true – if there be, indeed, an antagonism between capital and labour ... then all the experience and all the lights of the last 150 years have existed in vain. Let us burn the works of Turgot, Say, and Adam Smith.

But Peel's eloquent defence of the classical economists served only as an opening for Chartist testimonials on behalf of Louis Blanc. 'Competition', Holyoake insisted in defending the organization of labour, 'brings neither Justice, Harmony, nor Satisfaction, and it is on these accounts, and not on mere caprice, that such continental appeals are presented against it.'[75]

---

[74] Place to Holyoake, 8 October 1848, MCU, Holyoake Collection, item 285.
[75] *Reasoner*, 11 April 1849, pp. 231–2, 226–7.

Not content to confine their opposition to Tories such as Peel, these Chartist antagonists engaged in pointed attacks on interpretations of the French revolution that emanated from middle-class radical circles. Richard Cobden's efforts to tar parliamentary intervention in English economic life with the brush of French communism thus met with spirited Chartist resistance. When asked in July to consider limiting the hours worked by journeymen bakers, Cobden had responded that the proposal 'was communism', and that proposals 'of a precisely similar character' enacted by Louis Blanc had resulted in the June Days. Tracing the insurrection 'distinctly and directly ... to the socialist leaders', Cobden denounced democrats 'who taught the working men that a government can feed and employ the people, instead of teaching them as a fundamental condition of freedom, it is for the people to feed and clothe themselves, aye, and to support and pay government'.[76] W.J. Linton, responding to these charges in the *Reasoner*, offered a sustained defence of social politics. Himself chary of the communist schemes of Cabet and Saint-Simon, Linton yet denounced liberal economics as a class ideology antagonistic to the wider claims of the nation. Numbering Cobden among those who 'to keep up the market, seek *to divide the nation into two classes*', he urged 'that it is properly the business of Parliament to mediate between the disagreements of different classes of society, in all matters beyond the range of ordinary tribunals'. Holyoake's crafty positioning of this material exposed his readers to a double dose of social nationalism. An accompanying column reported a Chartist meeting chaired by Holyoake in Lambeth to support Hungarian independence. Participants at this event supplemented the resolution that the English government 'assist the Hungarians to regain their liberties by force of arms' with a motion that expressed 'sympathy for the social and political reformers of all countries, naming Louis Blanc, Proudhon, Rollin, Barbès'.[77]

Upheld by middle-class radicals as a corrective for class consciousness and socialist sympathies, nationalist sentiment figured in the Chartist critique of 1848 as an integument within which social conceptions of politics were enclosed and legitimated. The close association between politics and social reform defended by Chartist

[76] *Hansard's Parliamentary Debates*, 3rd ser., vol. CVII, col. 489, 17 July 1849.
[77] *Reasoner*, 11 April 1849, pp. 86–9, 96; 2 May 1849, p. 275.

leaders in the first two years after the continental revolutions was not entirely a product of 1848: middle-class observers believed from the outset of the movement that the political instruments of the Charter embodied a social revolution. What was distinct to the period after 1848 was the extent to which these pervasive fears were realized and entrenched by the evolving pattern of working-class political argument. For if the early Chartists saw the state chiefly in terms of an invasive force perpetuating aristocratic and industrial rule, late Chartism – inspired by the February revolution – articulated a vision of the state in which intervention in social and economic life was the essence of good government. Captured in the concept of the democratic and social republic, this shift in Chartist argument did not entail the wholesale abandonment of earlier radical traditions, but it did serve to polarize class alignments at mid-century to an extent that historians seldom appreciate. In doing so, as middle-class reformers discovered to their dismay, it impeded working-class liberalization and radical campaigns uniting the two classes. Gareth Stedman Jones argues persuasively that in the heyday of the Chartist movement its political and anti-aristocratic emphasis ensured that 'the spectrum of positions between moderate and extreme lay *within* radicalism, not *between* radicalism and something else'.[78] But liberals and radicals of the middle class found little cause for optimism in the spectrum of positions embraced by Chartists after 1848. Wedded to *démoc-soc* ideals, late Chartism lay outside both liberal economics and the exclusive patriotism of the early English radical tradition.

LIBERAL REFORMERS AND THE EXPERIENCE OF DEFEAT

... one of the peculiar features of the day is the assumption, on the part of the peoples, of a right to a choice of their rulers & of their countrymen. Hence the struggle of nationalities; hence the demand of Venice, Lombardy, Hungary, Poland, Germany, &c to be left to rule themselves according to their several likings ... These instincts may be thwarted for the day, but they are too

---

[78] Stedman Jones, 'Rethinking Chartism', in his *Languages of Class*, p. 110. For middle-class social interpretations of Chartism and the movement's depiction of the state as an aristocratic domain, see *ibid.*, pp. 90–3, 175–7.

deeply rooted in nature, & in usefulness, not to prevail in the end.[79]

For the bulk of the middle class, the state's success in suppressing Chartist protest removed England from the European tide of reform in the summer of 1848, effectively disproving the need for legislative change to meet the demands of popular unrest and consolidating support for established government institutions across party lines, economic divisions, and cultural boundaries. Robert Leader of the *Sheffield and Rotherham Independent* felt the impact of this reaction in June, when the Duke of Norfolk's private secretary wrote to apprise him that the duke, having 'taken alarm at your political opinions', wished to discontinue his subscription to the paper. Isaac Ironside sought to bolster Leader's flagging radicalism by citing John Stuart Mill and his qualified sympathy for French socialist experiments in the *Westminster Review*. But by 1849, Leader had retreated from his earlier French sympathies, and Ironside himself had abandoned his Chartist allies for liberal reformism.[80] This, as John Saville astutely concludes, 'was the significance of 1848: the closing of ranks among all those with a property stake in the country, however small that stake was'.[81]

Effectively alienating most propertied citizens from reform, the ideological expansion and tactical defeat of Chartism sharply curtailed middle-class radical efforts, but did not crush them entirely. As Ironside's reference to Mill suggests, pockets of Francophile sympathy endured in London among bourgeois radicals associated with the *Westminster Review*.[82] More substantial was the persistence of nationalist reform sentiment among Dissenters and the liberals of the Manchester School, men who – unlike the intellectuals of the *Westminster Review* – boasted considerable capital, organiza-

---

[79] Richard Cobden to Charles Sumner, 7 November 1849, BL, Cobden Papers, Add. MS 43, 676.

[80] Secretary of the Duke of Norfolk to Leader, 13 June 1848, and Isaac Ironside to Leader, 13 July 1848, University of Sheffield Library, A.J. Mundella Papers, 6P/85/1–2. For Ironside's subsequent reformism, see Gregory Claeys, 'Mazzini, Kossuth, and British Radicalism, 1848–1854', *Journal of British Studies*, vol. 28 (July 1989), pp. 225–61.

[81] Saville, *1848*, p. 227.

[82] For the persistence of French sympathy within the circle of the *Westminster Review*, see John C. Cairns, 'Introduction', in John Stuart Mill, *Collected Works of John Stuart Mill*, general ed. F.E.L. Priestley, 25 vols. (Toronto, 1963–86), vol.XX, pp. vii–xcii, esp. lxxxiii–xci, and Mill's 'Vindication of the French Revolution of February, 1848', in *ibid.*, pp. 319–63.

tional skill, and a popular following. The reform efforts of such middle-class liberals, dismissed somewhat peremptorily by Saville as 'scattered comments and gestures from a handful of romantics', bore no legislative fruit in the immediate aftermath of 1848.[83] But the occurrences of these months are nonetheless significant, for the obstacles encountered by middle-class radicals in this period, and the strategies with which they sought to surmount them, established the parameters that governed middle- and working-class radical interactions for a decade.

To John Bright, Richard Cobden, and their liberal disciples in the north, the Chartist riots were, in Bright's words, 'a two edged sword – they frighten some into inactivity, and they convince others that an unsafe uneasiness prevails among the people, which must have a remedy'.[84] Dependent upon manufacturers and merchants for contributions to sustain their agitations against corrupt government, Manchester School radicals relied upon the force of numbers to lend their reform incentives immediacy. In this context, as their provincial correspondence made abundantly clear to Bright and Cobden in London, neither Chartist collaboration nor defection from the radical ranks represented a viable political option. Bright's contacts in Liverpool and Rochdale reported radical communities sickened by aristocratic incompetence and 'ripe for reform'; in Stirling, the constituency of Bright's ally J.B. Smith, middle-class reformers – although intent to avoid connecting themselves 'with the disgraceful proceedings of those who pretend to lead the Chartists' – stood firmly behind universal manhood suffrage in May.[85] Cobden's correspondents, like Cobden himself, were more cautious. J.G. Marshall wrote to support household – not manhood – suffrage, 'founded on good practical & constitutional *reasons*, not on political theories'. And W.R. Greg, cotton manufacturer and veteran of the Anti-Corn Law campaign, warned Cobden against alienating his old allies in the League with unseemly radical fervour. 'They feel very strongly that all true friends of the People (while not seeking to deny

---

[83] Saville, *1848*, p. 227.
[84] Bright to George Wilson, 12 June 1848, MCRL, George Wilson Papers, M20/ 1848. Roland Quinault offers an excellent analysis of middle-class reform efforts in this context in '1848 and Parliamentary Reform', *Historical Journal*, vol. 31 (December 1988), pp. 831–51.
[85] Bright to Wilson, 18 April 1848, MCRL, Wilson Papers, M20/1848; John Christie to J.B. Smith, 8 April and 4 May 1848, MCRL, J.B. Smith Papers, 923.2.S.355, fols. 41, 43.

the existence of, or to shield, the many scandalous abuses which still remain) should teach them to look to *themselves* and not to legislation, for the improvements and reliefs of which their lot is susceptible', he cautioned in May.[86] Caught between the Scylla of radical finances and the Charybdis of popular pressure, Cobden was perplexed. 'The Charter has been so dragged in the mud, & so often thrust in our faces, at the point of the pike, that the middle class cannot be brought to look at it with calmness or toleration', he confided to a sympathizer. 'Yet out of doors it would be difficult to carry the masses for anything short of it'.[87]

Cobden optimistically predicted in his letter that 'a little time' would 'throw light upon this difficulty', but the passage of time only underlined the inherent contradictions of radical collaboration across deepening class lines. Despite the best efforts of the Manchester School, the call for reduced taxation and government retrenchment, long a rhetorical staple for Chartist and propertied radicals alike, failed to span the widening breach between the two classes. In July, the failure of Joseph Hume's moderate bill for household suffrage forced Cobden, Bright, and their parliamentary allies to confront the new realities of radical agitation. Together Hume and Cobden had laboured to convince the House that the bulk of the working class disdained to conflate social reform and politics. Hume emphasized that national expenditure would decrease by one third under household suffrage, a theme rehearsed by Cobden in defending the bill two weeks later:

> I believe that the householders, to whom the present proposition would give votes, would advocate a severe economy in the Government. I do not mean to say that a wide extension of the suffrage might not be accompanied by mistakes on some matters in the case of some of the voters; such mistakes would always occur; but I have a firm conviction that they would make no mistake in the matter of economy and retrenchment.[88]

Their colleagues were not convinced. Henry Drummond rose to attack Hume's bill and the argument that underpinned it by

[86] Marshall to Cobden, 4 May 1848, WSRO, Cobden Papers, vol. 2, fol. 104; W.R. Greg to Cobden, 11 May 1848, MCRL, Richard Cobden Papers, M87.4.2.
[87] Cobden to the Rev. Thomas Spencer, 20 April 1848, University of London Library, Herbert Spencer Collection, MS 791, fol. 6.
[88] *Hansard's Parliamentary Debates*, 3rd ser., XCIX, cols. 882–4, 20 June 1848: C, col., 185, 6 July 1848.

expressing 'regret that the hon. Member for Montrose should have used expressions in the course of his speech calculated to lead persons to imagine that there is any direct connection between the constitution of this House and relief from suffering of any kind which the public now endure'.[89] Roundly defeated, the bill lost by a majority of 267.

The following months saw continued middle-class efforts to capture working-class support for limited parliamentary reform and reduced government expenditure, but ultimately served to confirm liberal antagonism to Chartist social politics. John Bright, George Wilson, Sir Joshua Walmsley, Joseph Hume, and other affluent radicals formed a Parliamentary and Financial Reform Association in May 1849 to agitate for household suffrage, the ballot, triennial Parliaments, and equal electoral districts. Holding 223 meetings in the course of 1850, the Association won occasional, short-lived sympathy from individual Chartist leaders, but failed to generate either substantial grass-roots support or sustained co-operation from working-class radicals. As in the earlier Anti-Corn Law campaign, indeed, Chartist disturbances marred the conduct of public meetings called by these liberal reformers, shattering the central illusion of classless radical harmony cultivated by its leaders.[90]

The response elicited by J.B. Smith's reform speech at Dunfermline in January 1849 reveals the problems that plagued the Parliamentary and Financial Reform Association, clearly indicating the perils of courting popular support from an open audience in the divisive political climate generated by English reactions to 1848. Smith began on an optimistic note. Seeking to turn radical sympathy for the continental revolutions to the Association's advantage, he affirmed his continued commitment to the radical cause and conveniently traced the events of 1848 to the dual bugbears of all Parliamentary and Financial Reformers, 'over taxation and financial embarrassment'. But the presence of articulate non-electors in the audience rendered his pat analysis insufficient. One unenfran-

[89] *Ibid.*, CXIX, col. 906, 20 June 1848.
[90] Nicholas C. Edsall, 'A Failed National Movement: The Parliamentary and Financial Reform Association, 1848–54', *Bulletin of the Institute of Historical Research*, vol. 49 (May, 1976), pp. 108–31, provides a good discussion of the Association's genesis and activities, which are fully documented in the Francis Place Collection, BL, Add. MS 35, 151.

chised listener, initially overruled by the chair, rose to ask whether Smith would support a bill giving able-bodied workers the right to government relief when unemployed. When the chairman again ruled against the question, hissing, confusion, and uproar forced Smith to take a stand. 'Look at France, look at Ireland – where Government has demoralised the people by teaching them to depend on the state, and not on their own resources for support', he argued. Rehearsing arguments current in middle-class radical circles since the June Days, Smith was emphatic: 'as he was no Communist, and as the principle involved in the question was neither more nor less than Communism, he would answer it in one sentence – He would not'. His response met with both cheers and hisses, provoking further challenges from non-electors in the audience.[91]

In London, liberal efforts to inculcate correct notions of political economy under the aegis of popular radicalism met with similar attacks, as working-class crowds displayed their *démoc-soc* allegiance in disruptive spectacles of public protest. When in 1850 Hume, Cobden, and Bright organized a meeting to solicit contributions for a statue commemorating Peel's contributions to free trade their audience proved recalcitrant. Ignoring the financial support lavished on the Peel memorial by aristocratic and middle-class liberals seated on the platform beside him, Bright proclaimed that the assembly embodied a 'spontaneous disposition among the industrial classes'. But his claim that Peel's free trade measures made it 'more easy for an industrious man in this country to obtain a sufficiency of food' met with more spontaneous sentiment than he had intended. 'Cries of "No, No", followed by cheers, hisses, and other interruption' greeted his words, and set the stage for a Chartist counter-offensive. Egged on in part by Bronterre O'Brien, a man wearing a white hat – Henry Hunt's revered symbol of support for manhood suffrage – moved a Chartist amendment to Bright's resolution, inciting persons in the audience to force the liberals from the platform. In the ensuing uproar, Chartists and costermongers argued from the podium for government intervention in the labour market. 'They spoke exceedingly well for men of their stations', one paper recorded, 'and asked for something to be done for the protection of honest labour ... to enable hard-working men to get

---

[91] Newspaper Cutting, 11 January 1849, MCRL, Smith Papers, 923.2.S.335, fols. 49–50.

their living.' Only the arrival of the police restored order to the assembly hall.[92]

Repeated episodes of this character ensured that working-class commitment to social politics was understood by middle-class reformers as more than a rhetorical gesture affected by the Chartist leadership in the press. A lived experience that actively disrupted middle-class efforts to seize the aristocratic state, working-class antagonism to liberal economics took physical shape in opposition to radical movements that distinguished parliamentary reform from social and economic improvement. Frustration with working-class devotion to suffrage extension as the means to a social end pervaded middle-class reform circles after 1848, and encouraged bourgeois radicals to channel their energies into movements that eschewed electoral reform as a primary objective. Nationalist sentiment continued to inform these endeavours, providing both an ideological link to the masses and – if only in the middle-class imagination – a prophylactic against French socialist conceptions.

The spate of public meetings convened by middle-class reformers to promote English sympathy for Hungarian independence demonstrated this continued determination to tap popular radicalism with nationalist instruments. Hungarian sovereignty, although wrested from the Austrian government in the spring of 1848, captured the English radical imagination only in 1849, as confidence in France's revolutionary potential diminished. Led by the Protestant patriot Louis Kossuth, independent Hungary had pursued a radical path dear to the hearts of liberal and Chartist reformers alike, abolishing feudalism, expanding the franchise, establishing religious toleration, proclaiming free speech, and instituting trial by jury. Like Oliver Cromwell, with whom English radicals ceaselessly compared him, Kossuth assumed the burdens of both parliamentary and military leadership as Governor, attempting unsuccessfully to defeat the combined Austrian and Russian forces ranged against his nation in the summer of 1849.[93] From June to December, middle- and working-class English radicals in localities as diverse as Birmingham, Manchester, Liverpool, Sheffield, Southport, Nottingham, Sunderland, Stafford, Keighley, and Berry Edge organized public

---

[92] *Leader*, 10 August 1850, p. 489; *Daily News*, 8 August 1850, p. 6.
[93] Istvan Deák, *The Lawful Revolution: Louis Kossuth and the Hungarians, 1848–1849* (New York, 1979).

meetings and petitions to manifest their support for Kossuth and the cause of Hungarian sovereignty.[94]

George Dawson's speech at a Birmingham meeting succinctly conveyed the patriotic premises that underpinned this Anglo-Hungarian sentiment. 'Our present duty', he informed the assembled crowd, 'is to enable Kossuth to say: Hungarians, the English nation ... the men of Milton's isle cheer you on.'[95] Middle-class reformers found particular solace in the moderation of Hungarian expressions of patriotism, and their political emphasis. The success of 1848 in Hungary, the *Westminster Review* argued in language that evoked England's own radical traditions, derived from the circumstance that 'the patriotism of the nation enlarged its boundaries, admitting all classes of the people as free citizens of the Commonwealth'.[96] Couched in classless patriotic rhetoric, this liberal line of apologetic nonetheless served to advance bourgeois goals and values. The *Examiner*, having drawn a neat analogy between England's experience in 1688 and Hungary's revolution of 1848, proceeded to deploy Hungarian nationalism to buttress economic agendas foreign to the imagination of seventeenth-century English patriots. The paper was careful to indicate that the Hungarians' conception of sovereignty removed them 'far from the revolutionary excesses of Socialists and Communists', and celebrated the economic implications of Hungarian political virtue in terms that spoke directly to the interests of English manufacturers. In this view, the prosperity of the independent nation, 'fostered by liberal institutions, and by that spirit of free trade which the Hungarians have ever maintained, must afford an opening for English enterprise on a colossal scale'. Informed by their own tradition of national birthrights, it appeared, 14 million Hungarian patriots stood 'ready, nay anxious, to take from England her cottons and her hardware'.[97]

Like their attempts to reform corruption within the state, middle-class efforts to promote liberal economic interpretations of political nationalism required popular affirmation if they were to command

---

[94] *Northern Star*, 28 July 1849, p. 8; 11 August 1849, p. 5; 18 August 1849, p. 5; 18 August 1849, p. 5; 25 August 1849, p. 5; 1 September 1849, p. 5; 24 November 1849, p. 7. For a broader analysis of the Kossuth agitation, see my '" A Vent Which Has Conveyed Our Principles": English Radical Patriotism in the Aftermath of 1848', *Journal of Modern History*, vol. 64 (December 1992).

[95] *Northern Star*, 18 August 1849, p. 5.

[96] *Westminster Review*, vol. 51 (July 1849), p. 426.

[97] *Examiner*, 19 May 1849, pp. 306–7; 5 May 1849, p. 273.

the attention of an unregenerate Parliament dominated by aristocratic interests. Much touted by commentators of both classes, collaboration between middle- and working-class radicals was common and conspicuous at the Anglo-Hungarian public meetings. In July the contributors to a fund established to enable fifty-five Hungarians stranded in England to return to their embattled homeland included the Liberal lords Nugent and Dudley Stuart, the Liberal MPs Scholefield, Ewart, Milner-Gibson, and Duncombe, 'a few Chartists', 'a few Democrats', and 'almost every description of working men'.[98] At Exeter in August, a working man seconded the resolution, moved by a town councillor, supporting Hungarian independence; at Manchester, as the *Northern Star* reported with evident satisfaction, 'along with a large body of the working classes there were present many of the most respectable of the merchants and the public men of the borough'.[99] Encouraged by these precedents, reformers optimistically suggested that the shared international patriotism evinced by liberals and Chartists could lay new foundations for united reform efforts at home. When a tobacconist in Hamilton presided over a Hungarian sympathy meeting in October, inter-class collaboration offered a topic of radical self-congratulation. 'The middle classes were coming out liberally, and expressing a desire to join the working classes in an attempt to force the government into the adoption of measures of a progressionary nature', one orator explained to the crowd, and 'urged the working and middle classes of Hamilton to follow the example given them by those of London'.[100]

London precedents, notwithstanding the relentless patriotism of metropolitan gatherings, were, however, as illustrative of class conflict as they were exemplary of the virtues of inter-class collaboration. The diverging paths of Chartist and liberal nationalists at two related Anglo-Hungarian meetings in July revealed again the limitations imposed by economic differences upon middle- and working-class political cooperation. The first meeting, sponsored by Liberal MPs at the London Tavern on 23 July, used international patriotism to bring the unenfranchised masses, however briefly, within the ambit of parliamentary politics. In this the meeting succeeded, if perhaps too well. Liberal speakers, combining venerable political

[98] *Northern Star*, 14 July 1849, p. 5.   [99] *Ibid.*, 11 August 1849, p. 5.
[100] *Ibid.*, 13 October 1849, p. 4.

allegiances with more recent economic doctrines, appealed at once to seventeenth-century traditions and market forces. Cobden's speech celebrated laissez-faire in both the economic and diplomatic realms, urging non-intervention by the English government in Hungarian affairs as a natural corollary of liberal political economy at home. But when the Liberal MP Bernal Osborne sought to bolster his party's association with popular freedoms by adducing Lord John Russell as both a Hungarian sympathizer and the descendant of an English revolutionary martyr, his patriotic tactics backfired. For Russell, who like Cobden opposed diplomatic and military intervention in Hungary, failed to meet militant working-class standards of patriotism. Osborne's references to Russell's liberal ancestry met with cries of 'He is not worthy of it' and interrupted the meeting. Speeches by Julian Harney and G.W.M. Reynolds at the London Tavern and a second Chartist meeting at the John Street Institution the next evening left their audiences in no doubt as to the true nature of the nation's patriotic duty. Reynolds's speech at John Street 'concluded by calling upon the English in the names of Cromwell and Hampden', while Harney's barbed analysis of the two meetings ridiculed Cobden's efforts to promote economic and diplomatic laissez-faire.[101]

The troubling social and economic implications of nationalist conviction prefigured at John Street and the London Tavern unfolded more fully in the following weeks. Gatherings of radicals from London to Norwich displayed patriotism in its least cohesive aspect, as English defences of Hungarian sovereignty degenerated into increasingly shrill, partisan, and fictional interpretations of English and Hungarian history. At Marylebone, where Hume and J.B. Smith joined Harney and Henry Hetherington on the platform, constituents hissed and heckled Sir George de Lacy Evans – an MP who had abstained in the House on O'Connor's motion for universal manhood suffrage – when he attempted to speak in defence of Hungarian liberties. The Chartist Hetherington took pains to distance himself from this reception, delivering a speech which both linked the Hungarian cause to the Charter and underlined social differences. For Hetherington, as he noted at the outset, 'belonged to a class distinct from the gentlemen who had previously addressed

---

[101] *Examiner*, 28 July 1849, p. 466; *Northern Star*, 28 July 1849, pp. 8, 5; *Democratic Review* (August 1849), p. 83.

them. He was one of the workers.'[102] In the flurry of mutual recriminations that enveloped participants in the aftermath of the meeting, Julian Harney defended his militant stance from W.J. Fox's attacks in the *Nonconformist* by extending the purview of radical nationalism from the arena of civil and religious liberty to the domain of social freedom. 'I grounded my advocacy of the Hungarian cause on the fact that the Hungarian struggle was for social justice as well as national independence', he explained, 'and I closed my speech by advocating British support of Hungarian independence – if need be – by arms'.[103]

Diverse and at times contradictory, working-class radical responses to the continental revolutions acquire a striking coherence when juxtaposed with middle-class reactions to the events of 1848–9. Received notions of birthright and natural right, traditional conceptions of independence and sovereignty, informed late Chartist polemic and drew new sustenance from the brief success of nationalist uprisings in Hungary, Italy, and Germany. But these years also saw a significant extension of Chartist ideology, with the growing prominence of a cohort of radical leaders sympathetic to French socialism. As counterrevolution swept England and the continent from the summer of 1848, these Chartist internationalists, still committed to the concept of the radical nation, came to insist with new urgency on the imbrication of radical politics with the social and economic life of labour. In doing so, they rejected an exclusive allegiance to nations such as Hungary – which, in the words of one Chartist critic, 'march sooner under the banner of national independence than under the flag of the universal democratic and social republic'[104] – and looked increasingly to France.

For liberal and Dissenting radicals of the middle class, 1848 similarly marked a turning point and moment of awakening, firing bourgeois reformers with renewed enthusiasm for popular politics. But the insurrections of the June Days signalled a decisive restriction of middle-class radical vision, distancing liberals and Dissenters from French revolutionary events even as Chartists drew closer to

---

[102] *Northern Star*, 4 August 1849, p. 1; *Examiner*, 4 August 1849, p. 483. For Evans's relations with his constituents, see Edward M. Spiers, *Radical General: Sir George de Lacy Evans* (Manchester, 1983), pp. 135–6.
[103] *Northern Star*, 11 August 1849, p. 5.
[104] *People's Paper*, 3 May 1856, p. 4.

them. Unable to reconcile the competing claims of political economy and the *démoc-soc* ideal, middle-class radicals eschewed social politics and sought instead to soften the stark wisdom of liberal economics with appeals to nationalist sentiment. Recalling these Victorian values from the safe distance of the twentieth century, Goldwin Smith projected an image of benevolent compromise onto the liberal past. 'As to the limits of government, I am not aware that the Manchester School ever attempted to fix them', he asserted. 'What services Government should undertake, whether it should own the railways ... and the telegraph ... whether it should build in private yards or in yards of its own, is not a question of principle; nor am I aware that the Manchester School ever enunciated any dogma on the subject.'[105] The story told by 1848 is vastly different. Guided by pragmatic, dogmatic interpretations of Smith and Ricardo, liberal reformers were centrally concerned with the limitation of government. This preoccupation above all others governed the bourgeois reaction to 1848.

Chartist activists were fully alive to the basic contours of this middle-class response, which they continued to disparage for decades. G.J. Holyoake's critique of John Bright at the end of the century neatly captures the dominant and enduring tropes of Chartist and liberal antagonism after 1848:

> The patriots of Poland – of Hungary, of Italy, of France – never had help from his voice. He was for the extension of the suffrage, because it was a necessity – not because it was a right. With him the franchise was a means to an end, and that end was the creation of a popular force for the maintenance of Free Trade, international peace, and public economy.[106]

Constructed in the radical press, on the public platform, and through the experience of labour, the distinct patterns of national allegiance that liberal and Chartist radicals displayed in the wake of the continental revolutions moulded and entrenched perceptions of class in the decades after 1848. Running like a constant refrain through late Chartist polemic in myriad venues, regions, and agitations, *démoc-soc* opposition to liberal economics helped to map

---

[105] Goldwin Smith, *Reminiscences*, ed. Arnold Haultain (New York, 1910), pp. 230–1. But Smith, significantly, insisted that the Manchester School 'had nothing to do with Socialism, but on the contrary was always for the liberty to which Socialism would put an end'. *Ibid.*, p. 215.

[106] Holyoake, *Sixty Years of an Agitator's Life*, vol. I, p. 271.

the terrain within which contemporaries constructed class as a cultural and political category.

It did so not by destroying the English radical tradition's long-standing preoccupation with liberty but rather by changing its interpretation of the substance and meaning of freedom. Philosophers recognize that the term freedom encapsulates two competing conceptions of human independence, conceptions which they denominate positive and negative liberty. Negative liberty, as Isaiah Berlin has argued, is predicated on the absence of government action and gives primacy to individual freedoms (as opposed to social and economic needs). This construction of freedom strictly segregates the spheres of private life and public authority and is – notwithstanding the common assumption to the contrary – logically distinct from arguments for democratic government. Positive conceptions of liberty, in contrast, are grounded in the desire to act as a subject rather than an object and emphasize the role of the state as a guarantor of freedom. Linked semantically to negative notions of liberty by the rhetoric of freedom and independence, positive liberty has historically been opposed to the concept of negative freedom. It stands essentially outside the liberal tradition.[107] The recognition of this bivalence of the ideology of liberty was a commonplace of Victorian analyses of social relations after 1848. 'If I were asked which is the word most misused in our modern civilization, which has best served to disguise oppression, and to baffle the despair of its victims, I should answer Liberty', Louis Blanc explained to English radicals in 1851. Only under democratic socialism, he urged, would a true freedom govern economic relations, a freedom entailing 'neither the liberty of encroaching upon the rights of one's brethren ... nor that of monopolizing the instruments of labour'.[108]

To claim, as late Chartist leaders did repeatedly, that antagonism to the tenets of liberalism was axiomatic among the English working class is of course simplistic. Most workers declined to join Chartist protest in 1848, and many workers – as articulate artisans who did imbibe liberal principles were only too eager to argue – had little

---

[107] Isaiah Berlin, 'Two Concepts of Liberty', in his *Four Essays on Liberty* (Oxford, 1969), pp. 118–72, citation from p. 131. See also Ian Shapiro, *The Evolution of Rights in Liberal Theory* (Cambridge, 1986), pp. 276–9.
[108] *Leader*, 8 March 1851, pp. 228–9.

sympathy for French socialist conceptions.[109] But the cumulative effect of liberal and Chartist responses to the continental revolutions was to obscure this objective reality with ascriptions of partisan patriotism, ascriptions that located a line dividing middle- and working-class consciousness in competing conceptions of political economy and rival interpretations of freedom.[110] In the decades after 1848 this perceived distinction between the two classes was blurred but not erased. It is only by recognizing the persistence of this friction that the process and the extent of liberalization in the mid-Victorian period can be understood. For the trend toward class conciliation after Chartism was effected not by the triumph of bourgeois individualism, but rather through an ideological compromise in economic thinking mediated by the political idioms of the English radical nation.

[109] See for example 'A Working Man's Notions of Socialism', in Charles Manby Smith, *The Working Man's Way in the World* (London, 1857), pp. 337–47, in which Smith damns the February revolution and argues that most workers share his distaste, at least under favourable economic conditions. See also, Thomas Wright, *Our New Masters* (London, 1873), pp. 62–81.

[110] This represents the culmination of a process that had begun in the thirties, a point made by Thompson, *Making of the English Working Class*. esp. p. 727.

3 · *Working-class radical culture in the decade after 1848*

One Sunday morning in 1848, when I was barely nine years old, on coming home from chapel I saw two men washing the blood off their heads and faces at the pump opposite our house in Haggerston. I asked my father who had done this, and he replied that the police had beaten them ... because they had held a meeting to demand the vote ... Then I asked him if he had a vote, and he replied 'No' ... so I said, 'What do you call these men?' He replied, 'Chartists.' I at once said, 'Then I am a Chartist.' That was my first object lesson in politics ... My political education was further improved by reading a weekly Radical paper, the price of which was sixpence. My father and three others subscribed for it jointly, and it was passed from house to house.[1]

The events of 1848 delivered a voltaic shock to working-class radical culture in England, changing both its course and its complexion. Thwarted by state reprisals, leading Chartist agitators repudiated the mass platform, pledging themselves at the Ship Inn conference of November to continue the struggle for the Charter primarily through radical newspapers, tracts, and associations.[2] In this context, Chartist publications acquired new significance, and the newspaper press enjoyed a renaissance of influence in working-class radical circles. Providing Chartist thinkers with an opportunity to elaborate their *démoc-soc* ideals, the newspapers established in these years also drew new recruits to the radical cause in the face of sharply declining Chartist membership. Like Howard Evans, whose youthful Chartism laid the groundwork for later support of Garibaldi, the Reform League, and the Paris Commune, these radical recruits worked to sustain popular radicalism through decades of

[1] Howard Evans, *Radical Fights of Forty Years*, (London, 1913), p.19.
[2] Belchem, 'O'Connor and the Collapse of the Mass Platform', pp. 301–2.

decline.[3] Together with the Chartist stalwarts who had shaped the working-class response to 1848, they helped to construct radical enclaves that resisted liberal dominion throughout the fifties.

The ideas and actions of these radical agitators are not reflected in the radical press so much as they are enmeshed in it. Far more than an instrument for broadcasting the political vision of a radical élite, the battery of partisan papers and reviews that emerged in these years anchored arguments for change in the very fabric of working-class social life. Indeed, the pages of the oppositional press reveal a rich subculture of dissent, a distinct realm of thought and action inaccessible from the mainstream of the Victorian newspaper press. A sudden immersion in this radical medium, as a middle-class observer contemplating the temperance press found to his surprise, gave rise to 'feelings somewhat akin to those of our countrymen who the other day stumbled upon a well developed empire in Japan'. It was, as he admitted to the readers of a cosmopolitan weekly review, 'a world of which we have no conception'.[4]

THE LATE CHARTIST PRESS

The contours of the late Chartist press, like the characteristics of the wider movement in this period, remain largely unexplored by historians. Scholarly accounts of working-class journals typically stop short at mid-century, lending tacit credence to the common assumption that this medium declined abruptly with the demise of Chartism as a mass movement.[5] Yet it was at precisely this juncture that the press assumed an overriding significance in the annals of the Chartist movement. For Chartism as it persisted in the mid-Victorian period – and persist it did – took the form of interlocking local movements, often embattled and always exiguous, of radical education and propaganda. From its establishment in Leeds in 1837, Feargus O'Connor's *Northern Star* had integrated local manifes-

---

[3] Evans, *Radical Fights*, pp. 19–23, 113–15.
[4] *Saturday Review*, 25 December 1858, pp. 641–2. Cited by Brian Harrison, ' "A World of Which We Have No Conception": Liberalism and the English Temperance Press 1830–1872', *Victorian Studies* vol. 13 (December 1969), p. 125.
[5] Arthur Aspinall, *Politics and the Press, c. 1780–1850* (London, 1949); Donald Read, *Press and People, 1790–1850: Opinion in Three English Cities* (London, 1961); R.K. Webb, *The British Working-Class Reader 1790–1848* (London, 1955). For exceptions to this general rule, see esp. Richard Altick, *The English Common Reader: A Social History of the Mass Reading Public, 1800–1900* (Chicago, 1957), and Thompson, *The Chartists*, pp. 37–56, esp. pp. 44–5.

tations of Chartism into the national movement, and thereby secured its proprietor's ascendancy in the radical leadership. With the outbreak of revolution on the continent and O'Connor's gradual loss of mastery, the rival claimants to the Chartist leadership established a new series of proprietary newspapers designed to supplant O'Connor's journal as the focus of the movement. In key respects, these newspapers diverged from the O'Connorite editorial tradition. Concerned to maintain a broadly based agitation, O'Connor at the height of the Chartist movement displayed great tolerance with regard to the arguments expressed in his *Northern Star*.[6] In marked contrast, the editors of the late Chartist press sought to strengthen the partisan tendencies of the newspapers and periodicals to which they contributed. Their journals were launched less to endorse the basic precepts of the Charter than to expound particularistic strands of working-class radical argument that had evolved from it.

Despite this studied antagonism, the editors of the late Chartist press displayed remarkable unity on one issue of major importance. Almost without exception, they upheld the interrelation of English popular radicalism and continental politics. Here again they stood in opposition to O'Connor's editorial practice, for despite his general forbearance on domestic issues, O'Connor vehemently resisted the intrusion of continental politics into his paper. In a letter of January 1848 to Julian Harney, then chief editor of the *Northern Star*, he decreed that no more than one column each week concern foreign affairs, insisting that 'much & very just complaint is made of so much space being devoted to matters in which the *Star* readers and the English people take not the slightest interest'.[7] If the events of 1848 rendered O'Connor's directive ironic, the international sentiments of his rivals made his strictures ineffectual. In the decade after 1848, continental sympathies served a cohesive function in the networks of the Chartist press, linking rival factions, animating associational activities, and buttressing the organizational framework within which working-class radical argument was articulated and given substance.

No single newspaper dominated late Chartism as the *Northern*

---

[6] James A. Epstein, 'Feargus O'Connor and the *Northern Star*', *International Review of Social History*, vol. 21 (1976), pp. 88–9.
[7] O'Connor to Harney, 4 January 1848, in Frank G. Black and R.M. Black (eds.), *The Harney Papers* (Assen, 1969), pp. 61–2.

Star had earlier dominated the movement, but the multiplication of journals encouraged by the radical revival of 1848 enlarged the breadth of Chartist journalism dramatically in these years. A host of new Chartist newspapers surfaced in direct response to the revolutions: the *Cause of the People* (May–July 1848), the *Irish Felon* (June–July 1848), and the *Spirit of the Age: Journal of Political Education and Industrial Progress* (July 1848–March 1849) are characteristic of the genre. Although many of these journals proved as ephemeral as the revolutions that had inspired them, others survived for over a decade. Among the most successful, Holyoake's secularist *Reasoner* – transformed from the *Reasoner: And Utilitarian Record* to the *Reasoner: A Weekly Journal, Utilitarian, Republican, and Communist* in 1848 – endured until 1861, and Ernest Jones's *Notes to the People* (May 1851–May 1852) continued through 1858 as the *People's Paper*. *Reynolds's Newspaper*, an outgrowth of G.W.M. Reynolds's *Political Instructor* (November 1849–May 1850), ceased publication only in the twentieth century. Remaining under Reynolds's editorship until 1879, it became the most popular radical weekly in England. The history of even the most fleeting of these radical periodicals testifies to the persistence of radical protest: Julian Harney's monthly *Democratic Review* (June 1849–September 1850) gave place in rapid succession to his *Red Republican* (June–November 1850), *Friend of the People* (December 1850–June 1851, new series February–April 1852), *Star of Freedom* (May–November 1852), and *Vanguard* (January–March 1853).[8]

Circulation figures for such journals are elusive, but even the most short-lived London papers succeeded in reaching the provinces. Distribution records for Harney's *Red Republican* indicate a weekly readership of over 1,300 in Leicester in 1850, and analogous figures for the *Friend of the People* suggest a minimum readership of 5,000 in Manchester in 1851.[9] The *Reasoner* achieved a peak circulation of 5,000 copies per week in 1854, and the *People's Paper* advertised average weekly sales of 2,684 in the same year. *Reynolds's* weekly

8 Details of publication for these journals are recorded in Royden Harrison, Gillian Woolven, and Robert Duncan (eds.), *The Warwick Guide to British Labour Periodicals 1790–1970: A Checklist* (Brighton, 1977).
9 A. Temple Patterson, *Radical Leicester: A History of Leicester 1780–1850* (Leicester, 1954), p. 380; Altick, *English Common Reader*, p. 351. Readership is calculated here from a minimum of twenty readers per copy: Epstein, 'O'Connor and the *Northern Star*', notes that estimates for readers per copy of the Chartist press range from twenty to eighty.

enjoyed a circulation of 49,000 in 1855 and 60,000 in 1860.[10] Public readings brought this literature within the purview of even costermongers in London, where Mayhew's informants found illiterate pedlars eager to participate in the diffusion of Reynolds's tales:

> They are very fond of hearing anyone read aloud to them, and listen very attentively. One man often reads the Sunday paper of the beer-shop to them, and on a fine summer's evening a costermonger, or any neighbour who has the advantage of being 'a schollard', reads aloud to them in the courts they inhabit. What they love best to listen to – and, indeed, what they are most eager for – are Reynold's [*sic*] periodicals, especially the 'Mysteries of the Court'. 'They've got tired of Lloyd's blood-stained stories', said one man, who was in the habit of reading to them, 'and I'm satisfied that, of all London, Reynolds is the most popular man among them. They stuck by him in Trafalgar Square, and would again.'[11]

Continuing in the provinces into the 1870s, these public readings ensured that radical propaganda reached more than an affluent aristocracy of labour in these years.[12]

As Reynolds's popularity among the costers suggests, Chartist editors enhanced the popularity of their papers by supplementing political analysis with more literary appeals to their working-class audience. With the retreat from the mass platform, Chartist poetry and fiction enjoyed a period of expansion, as radical editors anxious to revive interest in the movement focused their attention on non-parliamentary political argument.[13] The subtitles that they selected to convey the dominant interests of their publications speak clearly to this trend. The first Chartist paper published by Julian Harney

---

[10] For the *Reasoner*, see Royle, *Victorian Infidels*, p. 303; Charles Mitchell, *The Newspaper Press Directory* (London, 1858), p. 117. Circulation for the *People's Paper* is derived from the stamp tax returns in Mitchell. Alvar Ellegård, *The Readership of the Periodical Press in Mid-Victorian Britain* (Götesborgs, 1957), p. 19, gives circulation figures for *Reynolds's*.

[11] Henry Mayhew, *London Labour and the London Poor*, 4 vols. (London, 1861–4), vol. I, p. 25. For Reynolds's successful combination of politics and literature, see Anne Humphries, 'G.W.M. Reynolds: Popular Literature and Popular Politics', *Victorian Periodicals Review*, vol. 16 (Fall and Winter 1983), pp. 78–89.

[12] Lucy Brown, *Victorian News and Newspapers* (Oxford, 1985), pp. 50–1.

[13] Martha Vicinus, 'Chartist Fiction and the Development of a Class-Based Tradition in Literature', in H. Gustav Klaus (ed.), *The Socialist Novel in Britain: Towards the Recovery of a Tradition* (Brighton, 1982), pp. 7–25, and *idem*, *The Industrial Muse: A Study of Nineteenth Century British Working Class Literature* (London, 1974), pp. 94–139.

was the *Democratic Review of British and Foreign Politics, History and Literature* (1849–50), and *Reynolds's Newspaper*, established as a 'Weekly Review of Democratic Progress and General Intelligence' in 1850, became a 'Weekly Journal of Politics, History, Literature, and General Intelligence' in 1851. Among the most prominent Chartist editors of this period, W.J. Linton, Ernest Jones, and Bronterre O'Brien were poets; Jones was, like Reynolds, a prolific novelist. As the titles of their works indicate, these Chartist activists deployed literature in a wide variety of democratic contexts. Ernest Jones published *De Brassier: A Democratic Romance* in the first volume of his weekly *Notes to the People* (1851–2) and *Women's Wrongs: A Novel in Four Books* in the second. 1854 saw the publication of his *Maid of Warsaw: Or, The Tyrant Czar, a Tale of the Last Polish Revolution*; his *Songs of the Lower Classes* and *Songs of Democracy* appeared two years later.

Literary pretensions, however, could not obscure the most salient characteristic of this body of work, its flagrant sensationalism. Regardless of its ideological content, working-class literature in Victorian England was preoccupied with violence, lust, death, and drama, an attribute that linked it closely with the street literature of broadsides and ballads.[14] Here again the titles of popular novels are revealing: Reynolds's works included *Wagner: The Were-Wolf, A Romance* (1846–7), *The Seamstress: Or, The White Slaves of London* (1850), *The Loves of the Harem: A Romance of Constantinople* (1855), and *The Empress Eugenie's Boudoir* (1857). Sensationalism suffused the overtly political journalism of late Chartist papers as well. Like popular novels, the writings of the working-class political press were steeped in violence and tinged with eroticism, a circumstance that contributed significantly to their sales.[15] Editors habi-

---

[14] Harold Perkin, 'The Origins of the Popular Press', in his *Structured Crowd: Essays in English Social History* (Brighton, 1981), pp. 47–56; Mayhew, *London Labour*, vol. I, pp. 213–23. Thomas Boyle explores the broader context of sensationalism in *Black Swine in the Sewers of Hampstead: Beneath the Surface of Victorian Sensationalism* (New York, 1989).

[15] For the commercial ramifications of sensationalism in the popular press, see Virginia Berridge, 'Popular Journalism and Working Class Attitudes, 1854–86: A Study of *Reynolds's Newspaper*, *Lloyd's Weekly Newspaper*, and the *Weekly Times*' (PhD thesis, University of London, 1976), pp. 184–9. At least one vein of early nineteenth-century radicalism was more closely tied to sensationalism, being directly linked to the pornographic press. See Iain McCalman, 'Unrespectable Radicalism: Infidels and Pornography in Early Nineteenth-Century London', *Past and Present*, no. 104 (August 1984), pp. 74–110.

tually interspersed items of lurid appeal among their columns of political commentary. A typical sample from *Reynolds's Newspaper* in 1856 ranges from a 'Glance at the Political Condition of Europe' and an enthusiastic appraisal of the revolutionary potential of Spain to the 'LATE FATAL ACCIDENT AT BRYN MALLY MINE', a 'SHOCKING CASE OF CHILD POISONING', a 'DREADFUL ATTEMPT AT MURDER AT LIVERPOOL', the 'OUTRAGE ON TWO EMIGRANT GIRLS IN NEW YORK', and a 'FRIGHTFUL DEATH BY A LION'.[16]

Sensationalism served more than an ancillary function in the late Chartist press: in writings focused on continental nationalism and its relevance for England, the attributes of popular sensational literature were fully integrated with the arguments of political radicalism. In launching a new series of the *Star of Freedom*, successor of O'Connor's *Northern Star*, Julian Harney incorporated sensational rhetoric into his pleas for international working-class solidarity, employing the language of melodrama to underscore the people's obligation to support the exiled revolutionaries of 1848. 'Looking from this Island over the face of Europe', he informed his readers, 'we see nations manacled, gagged, scourged, condemned to the relentless rule of the soldier and the executioner.' In this sensational context, the provision of funds for the refugees was both a patriotic duty and a strike against 'the ferocious Autocrat, the blood-stained Kaiser, the Prussian perjurer, the Neapolitan Vampire . . . by whom Europe is deluged by blood and tears'.[17]

If the literary devices of sensationalism provided a stylistic bond linking various papers of the late Chartist press, *démoc-soc* ideals served to unite these publications at the level of ideology. Endorsed emphatically in 1848, allegiance to radical reform as an instrument of social regeneration continued to inspire the programmes elaborated by working-class radicals in the 1850s. This commitment was conspicuous in the writings of both moderate and intransigent reformers. On the left, Julian Harney integrated the French republican conceptions with English cries for 'The Charter and Something

---

[16] *Reynolds's Newspaper*, 19 October 1856. These headlines should be compared with such popular ballads and broadsides as 'The Recent Murderers: A New Song', 'Execution of Alice Holt', 'Self Destruction of a Female', 'Fearful Colliery Explosion', and 'Shocking Rape and Murder of Two Lovers'. See W. Henderson (ed.), *Victorian Street Ballads: A Selection of Popular Ballads Sold in the Street in the Nineteenth Century* (London, 1937), pp. 26–7, 34–5, 43–4, 50–5.

[17] *Star of Freedom: Journal of Political Progress, Trades' Record and Co-operative Chronicle*, 14 August 1852.

More' in his *Red Republican* newspaper. In October 1850 he lambasted the limited radical vision of the Parliamentary and Financial Reform Association in 'The "Little Charter" *versus* "The Charter and Something More" ', asserting boldly that:

> The work of real Reformers is ... to establish the Sovereignty of the People expressed through the suffrage; and further, while seeking that great political revolution, to prepare the masses for a social revolution. The Charter, the means; and the Democratic and Social Republic – the end – such is the 'programme' of the *Red Republican*.[18]

This *démoc-soc* ideology was developed more fully in Harney's *Friend of the People*, and proved fully capable of accommodating English radical traditions while sustaining new social projects. Always weak on theory, Harney failed to elaborate a precise formulation of English life as it was to exist under the rule of the democratic and social republic, but his writings provide sufficient information to suggest the broad contours of the promised land. His democratic ideal was clearly socialist – in the context of his times – as well as social, and the rights of labour were of primary concern. Land redistribution orchestrated by the state, 'the right of all to live by free labour, on a free soil', was a necessary consequence of reform that was truly 'démocratique et sociale'.[19] Interwoven with these proposals were the shibboleths of the English radical tradition. It was:

> By the wrongs of your class and the miseries
> of your order throughout the world –
> By the blood of the martyrs, sacrificed on scaffold, barricade,
> and battle-field –
> By the sufferings of those thousands of patriots whose groans
> ascend daily from the Dungeons of Despotism

that Harney adjured his readers to associate with the continental émigrés and 'hasten the glorious time when ... the *Reign of Justice* shall be inaugurated to the jubilant cry of "*Vive la République Universelle, Démocratique, et Sociale*" '.[20]

The concept of the democratic and social republic found adher-

---

[18] *Red Republican*, 26 October 1850, pp. 145–6.
[19] *Friend of the People*, 25 January 1851, p. 50.   [20] *Ibid.*, 26 July 1851, p. 279.

ents in more moderate Chartist publications as well. In his *English Republic* (1851–5), W.J. Linton embraced *démoc-soc* ideals, but selectively emphasized their democratic and republican content. 'The Republic "democratic and social" is not a mere catch-phrase in our mouths', he insisted, 'the phrase "*democratic and* social" is indeed sufficient condemnation of all systems of mere socialism.'[21] Grounded in an idealized analysis of the institutions of the Tudor and Stuart state – Parliament and the Poor Law in particular – Linton's democratic vision pitted the combined forces of English and continental nationalism against the corrosive tenets of liberal economics. The issue posed to reformers in the fifties was clear:

> whether they believe with us that the faith of Milton should be to us an informing soul ... or with our opponents, that the strong hand of monarchical power should bind us in unity. This question of making England one, an united nation, held together by something more potent, and more sacred, than the poor myths of commercial correspondence – this is the question of no party, but the business of every honest Englishman; – of every honest Englishwoman too.[22]

It was to this end that the *English Republic* printed a series of 'Our Martyrs' ranging from Sir John Eliot and Sir Henry Vane to Marat and the Decembrists, and to this end that Linton championed Italian independence. For 'Milton himself, if living now, would take counsel of Mazzini.'[23]

Guided equally by *démoc-soc* and nationalist sentiment, Linton offered his own brand of 'republican socialism' in opposition to the theories of Cabet, Fourier, Saint-Simon, Blanc, and Owen. This vision of the democratic and social republic amalgamated republican individualism and socialist collectivism; under the *démoc-soc* banner, Linton upheld the tenets of the pre-industrial radical tradition and yet foreshadowed many of the features of the welfare state. Thus private property was to be strictly maintained, but the democratic operation of the republic would ensure that all citizens would acquire property. In its agrarian emphasis this programme smacked of the seventeenth century. Linton shunned state control of industry and industrial relations, but placed land redistribution – which he connected intimately with patriotism – second only to

[21] *English Republic*, vol. 2 (1852–3), p. 71. [22] *Ibid.*, p. 66.
[23] *Ibid.*, citation from vol. 3 (1854), pp. 1–2.

universal manhood suffrage on the agenda of republican priorities.[24] A partial list of 'what a republican government might do' included 'educate the rising generation; protect the republic from everything that would prevent the growth of individuals; furnish workmen with credit ... equalize the burthen of taxation; provide for the aged and infirm'.[25] An outgrowth of left-wing French politics and the English radical tradition, Linton's projected government was designed to ensure an opportunity for the reign of social justice to develop, but not to enforce its operation.

Sensationalism and *démoc-soc* ideals served to link the style and substance of the disparate papers of the late Chartist press, but the radical press network evinced more palpable bonds as well. Like the radical press of the eighteenth century – described by John Brewer as 'a press infrastructure, an interlocking complex of publications, engaging in frequent and blatant plagiarism, and generating controversy and polemic'[26] – the papers of late Chartism functioned in concert. Despite their recurrent hostilities, Chartist editors often combined forces to launch and sustain each other's publications. When illness prevented Julian Harney from producing the first issue of his *Friend of the People*, a cohort of radicals that included G.J. Holyoake and Ernest Jones united to ensure its publication. W.J. Linton engraved the revolutionary mastheads, sporting the French cap of liberty, that adorned both the *Friend of the People* and the *Red Republican*.[27]

An extended network of mutual endorsement consolidated these ties, linking readers of any one radical newspaper, through lengthy columns of advertisements and reviews, to an extended chain of other domestic and foreign publications. *Reynolds's Political Instructor* thus welcomed Harney's *Democratic Review* in 1849, and Harney's *Red Republican* extended greetings to *Reynolds's Weekly*

---

[24] *Ibid.*, vol. 1 (1851), pp. 89–91. Land redistribution and patriotism are intermingled in Linton's poem 'Patriotism': 'Where, my Country, are thy zealots? / Where thy freemen? echo saith: / Yonder crowds of famished helots / Have no country, have no faith. / What to them the deathless glory? / Can they lower sink than shame? / Give the serf a freeman's station, / Root him firmly in the soil, / He'll not then desert his nation, / Chary of his blood and toil.' In 'Prose and Verse: Written and Published in the Course of Fifty Years', 20 vols., a collection of writings by Linton in the BL, press mark 12269. g. 11, vol. X, p. 36. N.d., but *ca.* 1850.

[25] *English Republic*, vol. 2 (1852–3), p. 385.

[26] Brewer, *Party Ideology and Popular Politics*, pp. 137–67, citation from p. 16.

[27] *Friend of the People*, 7 December 1850.

Newspaper upon its appearance in 1850.[28] This pattern of endorsement extended from English journals to the newspapers of exiled continental revolutionaries. Chartist advertisements offered émigré works in translation, at prices well within the reach of an artisanal readership. Holyoake's Fleet Street Publishing House advertised the French weekly *L'Homme: Journal de la démocratie universelle* (1853–6) at 3d per copy in the *Reasoner*, and recommended an 'Address of the Workmen of France to Their Brethren, the Workmen of England', at 1/2d.[29] The 'Reformer's Library' compiled by Edward Truelove, the radical secularist who later served as publisher for the International Working Men's Association, offered Louis Blanc's *Right to Labour* (4d) and Lamennais's *Words of a Believer* ('Damned by the Pope', 3d).[30]

The exchange of political ideas among the myriad factions of English and continental radicalism, evident in the wholesale incorporation of competing radicals' tracts in each other's newspapers, further buttressed the international infrastructure of the late Chartist press. Bronterre O'Brien's *Rise, Progress, and Phases of Human Slavery: How It Came into the World, and How It Shall Be Made To Go Out* appeared in *Reynolds's Political Instructor* from 17 November 1849, and Harney serialized Louis Blanc's 'History of Socialism', extracted from Blanc's *Nouveau Monde* magazine, in the *Democratic Review*.[31] Chartist use of Giuseppe Mazzini's writings well illustrates the multiple layers of cooperation occasioned by the publication of émigré works. When Mazzini's 'Republic and Royalty in Italy' appeared in Harney's *Red Republican*, Linton's translation of George Sand's preface to the French edition provided the introduction. Ernest Jones similarly translated manifestos issued by Mazzini and his associates for Harney's *Friend of the People*. His own *People's Paper* printed extracts from Mazzini's *Parties in Italy: What Are They? What Have They Done?*, a tract published by Holyoake.[32]

Printing houses established to publish newspapers, pamphlets, and proclamations provided the final component of this press infrastructure. Among émigrés the Polish exile Zeno Świętosławski

[28] *Reynolds's Political Instructor*, 17 November and 22 December 1849; *Red Republican*, 24 August 1850.
[29] *Reasoner*, 14 September 1856, p. 84.
[30] *Investigator: A Journal of Secularism*, 15 April 1858, p. 28.
[31] *Democratic Review*, January and April 1850, pp. 296–301, 418–22.
[32] *Red Republican*, 29 June 1850, pp. 13–14; *Friend of the People*, 14 and 28 December 1850; *People's Paper*, 27 March 1858, p. 4.

was especially prominent, founding a printing house at St Hélier, Jersey in 1852 and publishing a broad range of occasional tracts in French, English, Polish, and Russian in addition to *L'Homme*. When expelled from Jersey in 1855, Świętosławski reestablished his Imprimerie Universelle in High Holborn, where he assumed responsibilities for a new edition of Alexander Herzen's works, originally entrusted to Nikolaus Trübner.[33] From 1857 Herzen commissioned Trübner, who was well known in radical circles for his acceptance of works rejected by conservative publishers, to supplement the efforts of the Vol'naia Russkaia Tipografia, Herzen's Free Russian Press. Herzen's press boasted a distinguished history of radical publication in its own right.[34]

Functioning together with these émigré printing concerns were the various publishing houses of the English radical leadership. W.J. Linton moved from London in 1849 to establish a printing press at Brantwood which issued Herzen's *Russian People and Their Socialism* (1855) in addition to Linton's *English Republic*.[35] In London itself, working-class leaders entrusted a large volume of Chartist material to James Watson, a publisher whose involvement in radical movements extended from the era of Richard Carlile's *Republican* through Owenism and Chartism to the English effort to support the Polish revolution of 1863. Watson's printing house at Queen's Head Passage, which Holyoake acquired upon Watson's retirement in 1853, provided the foundation of a wide-ranging publishing business that remained in operation at 147 Fleet Street until 1862.[36] The activities conducted at Fleet Street under Holyoake's direction encapsulate the myriad functions of the late Chartist press infrastructure. Supplied with assembly rooms, a library, and a bookshop, the Fleet Street House was a social, cultural, and political centre of the mid-Victorian radical movement.[37]

[33] Peter Brock, 'Zeno Świętosławski, A Polish Forerunner of the *Narodniki*', *American Slavic and East European Review*, vol. 13 (December 1954), pp. 566–7.
[34] Black and Black (eds.), *Harney Papers*, p. 115 fn. 2; M. Klevensky, 'Gertsen Izdatel' i ego sotrudniki' ['Herzen the Publisher and His Colleagues'], *Literaturnoe Nasledstvo* [*Literary Heritage*], nos. 41–2 (1941), p. 574; Alexander Herzen, *Desiatiletie Volnoi Russkoi Tipografi v Londone: 1853–1863* [*Ten Years of the Russian Free Press in London, 1853–1863*] (London, 1863).
[35] Smith, *Radical Artisan*, pp. 89–126.
[36] William James Linton, *James Watson: A Memoir* (New Haven, 1879); George Jacob Holyoake, *A History of the Fleet Street House* (London, 1856); Royle, *Victorian Infidels*, pp. 214–21.
[37] *Reasoner*, 1 January 1854, pp. 1–2.

It printed pamphlets and monographs by Louis Blanc, Giuseppe Mazzini, and Arnold Ruge; it published Holyoake's *Reasoner*; it served as the London distributor of *L'Homme*. It also sought to enrich the material culture of radical life, offering patrons 'Works of Art by Exiles and Others' which included portraits and busts of Milton, Cromwell, Saint-Just, Marat, Danton, Robespierre, Ledru-Rollin, and Garibaldi.[38] The existence of this institutional framework, and its close articulation with analogous émigré establishments, acted to sustain working-class internationalism in England beyond the failure of the O'Connorite movement and the continental revolutions of 1848.

SOCIAL AND CEREMONIAL LIFE IN RADICAL CIRCLES

Social and political theories represent only one aspect of English oppositional politics influenced by the international events of 1848, for ideology constitutes only one facet of the complex culture of mid-Victorian radicalism. From the early nineteenth century, local and national leaders of working-class radicalism had reinforced the intellectual appeal of their movements with the social attractions of family and community life. Appropriating the devices of the church, chapel, and public house, Chartist activists developed their own distinctive rites of radical passage, extending the domain of oppositional politics from the first to the last days of the radical life cycle. These rites, which culminated in the observance of elaborate funeral services to mark the passage of a lifetime of protest, were exercised from the baptismal font itself, where the children of radical parents were first impressed with the emblems of the oppositional tradition. One hapless infant emerged from a Chartist christening service as 'Feargus O'Connor Frost O'Brien McDouall Hunt Taylor'.[39]

The radical press network instrumental in mediating the English perception of continental ideologies also played an active role in the maintenance and expansion of this alternative culture in the decade

---

[38] *Ibid.*, 26 March 1854, pp. 213–14; 'Freethought Directory: A Catalogue of Works Produced by Holyoake & Co.', 1854, BI, George Jacob Holyoake Collection, Pamphlets, box 4, No. 168.

[39] Eileen Yeo, 'Robert Owen and Radical Culture', in Sidney Pollard and John Salt (eds.), *Robert Owen: Prophet of the Poor: Essays in Honour of the Two Hundredth Anniversary of His Birth* (London, 1971), pp. 84–114, citation from p. 105.

after 1848. Radical editors added events and figures from the continental revolutions to popular calendars and hagiographies in the oppositional press; radical activists gave life to these symbolic associations in public processions, anniversary celebrations, business partnerships, personal friendships, and family gatherings with émigré radicals from the continent. The resources of the radical press played a pivotal role in the development and coordination of these international activities. Radical memoirs consistently speak to this effect. 'The stirring events of Paris and the newer literature that began to be issued sent the young men of my age wild with excitement and enthusiasm', the radical compositor, editor, and activist W.E. Adams recalled of *Reynolds's Political Instructor*. 'I had previously read the "Rights of Man" and other political works of Thomas Paine ... and now I was fairly in the maelstrom.'[40] Similarly George Howell, an apprentice shoemaker in 1848, made his first acquaintance with radical internationalism through the newspaper press. 'I now heard about the Chartists, about the Revolutionary movements on the Continent, in France, Hungary, Poland ... and as my time was less valuable than my master's, or his lodgers', I often had to read to them while they were at work', Howell later noted. 'There would be discussions on the events, and I heard both sides of the question often put by different persons'.[41]

As the biographies of both Adams and Howell suggest, the radical function of the newspaper press was twofold. In addition to acquainting English workers with the concepts underlying continental political movements, the press introduced its readers to the associational life of the English radical movement. Adams became enmeshed in the radical cause through a sequence of events that extended directly from late Chartist newspapers to radical club life and camaraderie. A subscriber in succession to Julian Harney's *Democratic Review, Red Republican,* and *Friend of the People* newspapers, he joined the Cheltenham branch of the Fraternal Democrats in 1849. A letter to Harney on the affairs of this association then 'brought about an acquaintance which, becoming more and more intimate as the years advanced, lasted till his death'.[42] Howell's progress into radical politics followed a similar path and nicely captures the interrelation of English nationalism and

[40] W.E. Adams, *Memoirs of a Social Atom*, 2 vols. (London, 1903), vol. I, pp. 118–19.
[41] Howell MS Autobiography, BI, Howell Collection, vol. B, p. 27.
[42] Adams, *Memoirs of a Social Atom*, vol. I, p. 223.

internationalism at this time. By the early 1850s he had advanced from reading the continental news aloud to his workmates to joining a political debating society in Bristol, where he advocated republican government as 'a "Cromwellian", and a lover of Milton's prose works ... with the Revolution of 1848 fresh in my young mind'.[43]

Given substance in efforts to provide support for continental exiles who sought asylum in England, these international sympathies often served to underline class differences. Julian Harney, 'grieved to learn that the most shocking destitution prevails amongst a large number of refugees, particularly the Poles', offered the offices of his *Red Republican* as a collection point for funds in June 1850. 'As usual, the Refugees have found their best friends amongst the poor working men', he noted a year later, 'the rich men of Liverpool – including not a few *liberal politicians, financial reformers*, &c., – have treated the claims of the poor exiles with heartless indifference.'[44] Participants attending a soirée at London's John Street Institution in 1852 invoked both fraternal brotherhood and the right to labour in their efforts to raise funds for the refugees. Harney, the Chartist poet Gerald Massey, and Bronterre O'Brien – supported by letters from Mazzini and Ledru-Rollin – delivered speeches proclaiming 'All men are brothers.' Louis Blanc, who with Etienne Cabet and Pierre Leroux represented the French socialist emigration, expanded on this theme by conflating economic and national oppression. 'My fellow-countrymen have intelligence and courage; they ask only that right to lifelong labour which every human being ought to enjoy', he declared, 'and for the purpose of finding employment they rely on the fraternal sympathies of those who have suffered, because wherever the oppressed are born they are the sons of the same father – they are all of the same country.'[45]

A perennial shortage of funds linked the working-class public directly to the émigré community, encouraging the development of networks of sociability, services, and patronage that proved of mutual benefit. When a contingent of Polish exiles arrived at Nicholl's Temperance Hotel in Halifax, Benjamin Wilson and his

---

[43] Howell MS Autobiography, BI, Howell Collection, vol. B, p. 39. Howell also obtained a card of membership for the 'Friends of European Freedom', signed by Mazzini and Kossuth. See Leventhal, *Respectable Radical*, p. 223.

[44] *Red Republican*, 29 June 1850, p. 13; *Friend of the People*, 26 April 1851, p. 174. The same point was made by Linton in March 1851. See his 'Prose and Verse', vol. XI, pp. 5–6.

[45] *Reynolds's Newspaper*, 13 June 1852, p. 16.

fellow Chartists formed a committee to obtain employment for them, a process that soon led to the formation of friendships with the émigrés. 'The refugees were an intelligent class of men, and a few of us spent a great deal of time in their company', Wilson recalled in his autobiography.[46] Louis Kossuth sought to trade upon W.J. Linton's friendship and Hungarian sympathy in 1853 by securing a personal loan, but many of the ties that linked Chartists to their continental brethren helped to bolster English radical endeavour.[47] Having dined with Blanc and Caussidière, Harney secured their assistance with his *Democratic Review*, and sought to extend his partnership with Frederick Engels in the same manner.[48] G.J. Holyoake, who counted Louis Blanc among his social circle from December 1849, relied upon Blanc to provide him with material on French socialism.[49] Letters of recommendation from continental émigrés endorsing English radicals, like Chartist letters for refugees, were a commonplace of radical correspondence.[50]

An extended calendar of radical ceremonies lent structure to these partnerships between Chartist and émigré leaders, and extended their impact beyond the radical élite to sections of the larger working-class public. Shared ceremonial devices and revolutionary celebrations underpinned this aspect of late Chartist culture, mobilizing English and continental radicals in the face of substantial cultural barriers. The first French revolution provided an ideological point of departure for this common radical culture, offering symbols, martyrs, and catchwords that spoke at once to Chartists, nationalists, and socialists. Organizationally, however, these international celebrations owed as much to the associational traditions of friendly societies and trade unions as they did to revolutionary politics. Like the social activities of the friendly society and union, radical internationalist culture encompassed rites of passage, anniversary commemorations, music, marching, and general conviviality.

---

[46] 'Benjamin Wilson's Autobiography', in David Vincent (ed.), *Testaments of Radicalism: Memoirs of Working-Class Politicians 1790–1885* (London, 1977), pp. 213–14.
[47] Kossuth to Linton, 8 November 1853, Feltrinelli, Milan, Linton Papers, vol. 3, item 40.
[48] Harney to Engels, 1 May 1849, IISG, Marx-Engels Collection, L., Letters to Engels, item 2167.
[49] Holyoake Diary, 3 December 1848, BI, Holyoake Collection; Blanc to Holyoake, 21 August 1850, MCU, Holyoake Collection, item 382.
[50] See for example Black and Black (eds.), *Harney Papers*, pp. 12–13, 56–7, 97, 134–5.

Unlike the associational life of friendly societies, however, radical international activities were overtly political.[51] And unlike membership in trade unions, participation in radical international culture required neither possession of a particular skill nor employment in a specified trade. Rather, like the Chartist movement which had preceded it, the ceremonial life of mid-Victorian radical internationalism helped to generate an imagined community of labour, uniting disparate sectors of the working class behind a common political cause.

The ceremonies of late Chartist culture assumed a wide variety of forms but fell within two general categories of activity. On the one hand, a regular calendar of public commemorations of revolutionary figures and events established a predictable cycle of activities repeated at regular intervals; on the other, novel occurrences were marked by processions, banquets, and soirées tailored to suit the immediate needs of the occasion. Often these two varieties of celebration, spontaneous and ritualized, overlapped: during the Crimean War, Polish anniversary meetings expanded to reflect the new diplomatic realities and revolutionary expectations of the time. Regardless of their form and context, however, the international celebrations of the 1850s juxtaposed and blended the radical traditions of 1648, 1789, and 1848 to affirm the union of social and political reform maintained by English Chartists in response to the February revolution.

Chartist commemorations of Robespierre's birthday typified the annual events orchestrated by English radicals to underscore the strength and meaning of their international sympathies. Harney's Fraternal Democrats, joined by Bronterre O'Brien and G.W.M. Reynolds, initiated the custom in April 1850 with a 'Social Supper' attended by both English and émigré radical leaders. Participants listened to 'patriotic toasts, songs, and recitations' and sang an English version of the Marseillaise. The subjects chosen for the toasts at this event testified to the confluence of revolutionary traditions. They ranged from 'the memories of Paine and Washington', and the 'heroic and incorruptible Marat, Saint-Just, and

---

[51] For the associational life of friendly societies, and its apolitical character, see P.H.J.H. Gosden, *The Friendly Societies in England 1818–1875* (Manchester, 1961), pp. 11, 115–37. For trade union conviviality, see Thomas Wright, *Some Habits and Customs of the Working Classes: By a Journeyman Engineer* (London, 1867), pp. 67–82.

The Incorruptible
ROBESPIERRE.

A

TEA PARTY

AND

PUBLIC MEETING

WILL TAKE PLACE AT

THE NATIONAL HALL, HOLBORN,

On **WEDNESDAY, April 13th, 1853,**

IN COMMEMORATION OF THE ILLUSTRIOUS

ROBESPIERRE.

Messrs. **Louis Blanc, Nadaud,** and
G. W. M. Reynolds, have promised to attend·

Messrs. **Louis Kossuth, Ledru Rollin,
Saffi, Schoelcher, George Dawson, Gammage, G. J. Harney,** G. J. Holyoake,
Ernest Jones, Linton, Livingstone, and
Rd. Moore have been invited.

The Meeting is convened by the Council of The National Reform League, and the President

Mr. J. B. O'BRIEN, is appointed to preside.

TEA on the Tables at Six o'Clock.

Single Ticket (for Tea and Public Meeting) **1**s.
Double   do.   do.   do.   **1**s. **9**d.
Admission, after Tea, to Gallery **3**d.—Hall **2**d.

*Proceeds, after defraying expenses, will be applied to the
relief of our distressed Brethren—The Proscribed.*

Tickets may be obtained of Mr. MILLS, at The National Hall; of
Mr. ROGERS, The Eclectic Institute, 18a, Denmark Street, Soho; and
of Mr. GODDARD, Literary and Scientific Institution, John Street,
Tottenham Court Road.

[Samuel Bovingdon, Printer, 3' Sherrard Place, Golden Square.

2   Robespierre: tea party

Couthon', to 'the healths of John Mitchell, Thomas Meagher, Smith O'Brien, and all other true Irish patriots', the 'glorious Insurgents of June, 1848' and 'the Red Republicans of the Continent ... the speedy triumph of the Republic Universal, Democratic and Social'. Significantly, participants eulogized Robespierre himself in the new phraseology of 1848. His memory was honoured at the gathering in the hope that his example would inspire the audience 'with energy to the accomplishment of the good cause of Democratic and Social Equality, for which he lived, laboured, suffered, and died'.[52] Continued by Bronterre O'Brien and his associates, the celebration of Robespierre's birth was an annual event of London radical life, uniting émigré leaders each year with members of the major Chartist factions (Ill. 2).[53]

The annual celebrations of the Polish revolution of 1830 organized by émigrés in London evinced an equally high degree of international cooperation. First added to the English associational agenda in the early Chartist period, radical commemorations of the Polish uprising of 1830 gained new adherents from the enlarged émigré community in the aftermath of 1848.[54] The advent of the Crimean War – which the radical community hoped would encourage nationalist and social revolution in eastern Europe – further enhanced the political significance of these celebrations, a circumstance which the Polish émigré leadership was quick to appreciate. 'We intend, on the 29th, to prepare a showy anniversary, required by the close relation of the Turkish war with the cause of Poland', Stanislaus Worcell wrote to Linton in November 1853. 'It must be a manifestation of Poles, Italians, Frenchmen, Germans ... and Englishmen', he argued, 'without a rising of the oppressed peoples during the war, so as to extend it and defeat the views of diplomacy, the Turks can beat the Russians, but neither defeat them nor forward the cause of mankind.'[55]

Chaired by Worcell and attended by French, German, Hungarian, Italian, and Polish émigrés, the resulting anniversary celebration attracted both English working-class radicals and their wives.

[52] *Democratic Review*, May 1850, pp. 463–4.
[53] Holyoake Diary, April 1853, BI, Holyoake Collection. See also *Reynolds's Newspaper*, 11 and 17 April 1852, 11 April 1853, and *L'Homme*, 26 April 1854.
[54] Weisser, *British Working-Class Movements*, pp. 147–8.
[55] Stanislaus Worcell to W.J. Linton, 1 November 1853, Feltrinelli, Milan, Linton Papers, vol. 5, fol. 3.

Linton, Thomas Cooper, and James Watson delivered speeches, the latter stating 'that he represented the working classes, and that he stood there as an old Chartist prisoner'. Alexander Herzen successfully captured the spirit of 1848 when he 'alluded amid cheers to the cause of the *République démocratique et sociale*', while Linton interpreted contemporary international events and blasted liberal non-intervention in the light of the enduring English national tradition:

Mr Linton asked why an Englishman stood among refugees to speak for European freedom? Because, while there were men in England who held the faith of Milton and Cromwell, England would not be divorced from Europe . . . if they were to take Richard Cobden's word they would abandon their duty . . . there was an honest heart under the worst coat of English working men . . . Every patriot soul in England, he believed, was anxious for . . . war . . . it meant war against Austria and Prussia too, insurrection in Poland, Italy, and Hungary, convulsion in Europe, shattering the Czar and the Pope, and the imperial tyrants of every name – (great cheering) – the enfranchisement of all peoples. It meant a Polish nation . . . that France should be gloriously avenged for her present ignominy, that England should be worthy of what England was.

Couched in the rhetoric of both the Commonwealth and the *quarante-huitard* traditions, the resolutions of this meeting, the *Times* reported, were unanimously confirmed by participants.[56]

Because they were often designed to celebrate the distinctive merits of particularistic national or regional uprisings, émigré functions could include toasts, placards, and speeches incomprehensible to English radicals. Yet despite obvious linguistic barriers, activists of all European nations rallied to shared conceptions of radical patriotism and common traditions of revolutionary language, symbolism, and martyrology. The designation 'citizen', the singing of the Marseillaise, and the denunciation of governmental tyranny contributed to a rich body of ceremonial freighted with radical meaning in any social setting or political context. The decorations selected by organizers of a French meeting held in London to commemorate the third anniversary of the revolution of 1848 were thus national in emphasis but international in appeal. Meriting

[56] *Times*, 30 November 1853, p. 10. For more popular accounts, see *People's Paper*, 3 December 1853, p. 7; *Demokrata Polski*, 10 December 1853, pp. 97–100; *English Republic*, vol. 3 (1854), pp. 22–39.

detailed description in the late Chartist press, they required little elaboration for English readers:

> The immense room was beautifully decorated with true flags of liberty – the deep red; upon them were conspicuous many mottoes and devices. The names of the glorious martyrs fallen in the cause of liberty were suspended around the walls: and conspicuous among these were the immortal names of Robespierre and Marat. Black crepe was entwined upon the poles of the red flag, as emblematical of the dark cloud at present gathered over the liberties of the world. Caps of liberty ... were everywhere conspicuous; and the names of the different prisons at present filled with the patriots of France were inscribed on small stands surrounded by *imortelles*, placed in front of the tribune.[57]

In this manner, the associational life of radical circles gave body to abstract revolutionary ideals of international solidarity, reinforcing the arguments propounded in the radical press with the direct perception of and participation in international brotherhood.[58]

Invoked at regular intervals and often repeated in successive years with little innovation, the emblems of international opposition extended easily beyond prescribed annual functions to accommodate the immediate demands of the radical moment, and the claims of organized labour. In Birmingham, where strike activity and radical politics had joined sixteen crafts in the United Trades Union of 1830–35, the arrival of Hungary's revolutionary leader, Louis Kossuth, precipitated public demonstrations of labour and international solidarity in 1851. Among the many workers participating in the enormous Kossuth procession, shoemakers, tailors, builders, printers, and metal workers represented trades that had helped to form the backbone of the Chartist movement.[59] Wireworkers,

---

[57] *Reynolds's Newspaper*, 2 March 1851, p. 14. The use of black crepe to indicate adversity recalls the symbolism of the eighteenth-century food riots in which loaves of bread were draped in black.

[58] This is not to suggest that they invariably succeeded in promoting fraternity. Precisely because they gave voice and substance to emotive political convictions, the rituals of radical life could be divisive. Julian Harney, for example, suffered attacks from representatives of competing radical factions when he participated in the 1851 commemoration of the February revolution and the 1853 commemoration of the Polish revolution. See Schoyen, *Chartist Challenge*, pp. 213–16; Marx to Engels, 24 February 1851, *Marx, Engels: Collected Works*, vol. XXXVIII, p. 298; *People's Paper*, 3 December 1853, p. 7.

[59] Thompson, *The Chartists*, pp. 207–10, and Goodway, *London Chartism*, pp. 153–225, detail trade membership in Chartism.

pearl-button makers, japanners, coopers, carpenters, and joiners active in the Kossuth welcome belonged to precisely the crafts that had earlier established the United Trades Union.[60] Members of the procession bore trade flags aloft as they marched through the city, and banners proclaimed 'Associations, the interest of masters and men'. Printers operated a working press on a movable stage, printing poems by the Chartist Gerald Massey which they distributed to the crowd. But the unionized Flint Glass Makers arguably enjoyed pride of place. Their mounted marshals wore glass caps tinted with the Hungarian colours; their trade committee bore glass wands with streamers. Patriotism and French revolutionary sentiment equally informed their participation in the event. Extolling his 'patriotism and love of country', their testimonial to Kossuth ended by invoking 'Liberty! equality! fraternity!'.[61]

In the public welcome for John Frost organized by Ernest Jones and his associates from the *People's Paper* and the National Charter Association, ritualized conventions again lent dignity to an event that fell outside the annual radical cycle. Frost, transported to Australia in 1840 for his leadership of the Newport insurrection, figured in the radical press as both a Chartist and an exile upon his return to Britain in 1856. The latter designation promoted his depiction as a representative of the larger European revolutionary tradition, an association reified by the presence of perhaps five hundred émigré radicals from the continent in the welcome procession. As Jones's paper reported, 'there might be seen the flower of foreign democracy, the men who had fought at the barricades of Paris, Berlin, Vienna and Milan, or on the battlefields of Hungary, Italy, and Poland'.[62] Starting at noon from Finsbury Square, the main procession proceeded from Moorgate to Pall Mall, Regent Street, and Portland Place, ending at six o'clock with a public meeting at Primrose Hill. Headed by an open carriage-and-four bearing Frost and Jones, it boasted men on horseback wearing tri-

---

[60] Clive Behagg, *Politics and Production in the Early Nineteenth Century* (London, 1990), pp. 112–15, 248, discusses the United Trades Union.

[61] *Birmingham Mercury*, 'Extraordinary Kossuth Edition', 13 November 1851; *Birmingham Journal*, 15 November 1851, p. 7. The *Mercury* estimated 10,000 persons in the procession and a total of 250,000 persons at the event.

[62] For Frost, see David J.V. Jones, *The Last Rising: The Newport Insurrection of 1839* (Oxford, 1985). For his designation as an exile, see *People's Paper*, 10 May 1856, p. 8; 7 June 1856, p. 1; and 20 September 1856, p. 1. The quotation is from 20 September.

coloured silk scarves, marching bands 'pouring forth . . . the inspiring notes of the glorious Marseillaise hymn', men and women
holding flags and banners, and wagon-loads of women and children
at the rear.[63]

The ideological lessons inculcated by the leaders of this event
served to affirm the Chartist interpretation of 1848, and linked the
events of that year firmly to the English radical tradition. Legends
inscribed on the banners, which were often surmounted with a cap of
liberty, announced 'The Archangel is here; his name is Democracy'
and proclaimed 'Disobedience to a Tyrant is honour to God' while
upholding 'The Political Victims of 1848', the 'Alliance of the
peoples', and the 'Social and Democratic Republic'. National allegiances were integral to these broadly European sentiments, not
submerged by them. G.J. Holyoake, who decorated his Fleet Street
Publishing House for the passing of the procession, described the
event as 'an occasion on which an Englishman who either honoured
the people, or loved the constitution, could hardly fail to feel
serious'.[64] Holyoake's apposite comment clearly reflected Jones's
own intentions. Speaking to the crowd at Primrose Hill, variously
estimated at 20,000 by the *Times* and 'nearly one million' by the
People's Paper, Jones extolled Frost as 'A representative of a
principle which embodied the rights of labour'. But in 'The Workman's Song To the Rich', a democratic version of the national
anthem written by Jones and sung by the assembled participants to
conclude the celebration, the welcome for Frost invoked not 1848
but 1648:

> With bloodstained despots' shame
> You link our country's name
> and aid their crime;
> God! hear thy people pray
> If there's no other way,
> Give us one glorious day
> of Cromwell's time.[65]

Public celebrations such as the welcome for John Frost gave
whole families an opportunity to participate in oppositional politics,

[63] *People's Paper*, 20 September 1856, p. 1; *Times*, 16 September 1856, p. 10.
[64] *Reasoner*, 21 September 1856, p. 90. Frost, in fact, was Welsh.
[65] *Times*, 16 September 1856, p. 10; *People's Paper*, 20 September 1856, p. 1.

but it was the rites of radical passage prescribed by Chartist culture that brought women and children into the heart of a radical tradition otherwise dominated by men. The symbolism and rhetoric of these radical rites both politicized and internationalized the domestic and personal events of daily life. G.J. Holyoake, who named his own son Maximilien Robespierre in June 1848, blessed Edward Truelove's son with the name Mazzini in a secular baptismal ceremony at the John Street Institution in 1849, expressing the aspiration that the child 'in reverence of the name it bore, might preserve a loftier self-respect'.[66] Other children of Chartists bore the marks of their parents' international sympathies long after the demise of Chartism itself: G.W.M. Reynolds was survived at his death in 1879 by two sons, Kossuth Mazzini Reynolds and his brother, Ledru-Rollin.[67]

Marking future generations with the impress of 1848 offered one instrument for the expression of international solidarity, but deaths offered far more scope for ritualized internationalism than did births. The celebration of death preoccupied all classes of Victorian society: of £24 million invested in English savings banks in 1843, over £6 million was deposited to meet future funeral expenses.[68] Within the urban working class, membership in burial clubs was widespread, if not ubiquitous, an expression of cultural values in which the poor and the immiserated displayed an ethos of self-respect alien to middle-class notions of utilitarian thrift. Some especially cautious individuals were insured by as many as thirty burial clubs, and friendly societies customarily required attendance at the funerals of deceased members by their colleagues.[69]

Radical culture capitalized upon this obsession, encouraging elaborate funeral services that allowed the reiteration of fraternal concepts in the ultimate celebration of the radical international social calendar. Emigrés attended English radical funerals to demonstrate sorrow, respect, and sympathy for fallen comrades; commemorative volumes to honour the dead underscored their

---

[66] For the naming of Mazzini Truelove, see *Reasoner*, 14 November 1849, pp. 305–7. For Holyoake's choice of names for his own son, see Holyoake Diary, 7 June 1848, BI, Holyoake Collection.

[67] James and Saville, 'George William MacArthur Reynolds', p. 150.

[68] John Morley, *Death, Heaven and the Victorians* (London, 1971), p.12.

[69] Stedman Jones, 'Working-Class Culture and Working-Class Politics', in his *Languages of Class*, pp. 199–202. Morley, *Death and the Victorians*, p. 25, notes multiple membership in burial societies.

cooperation. When the Chartist Henry Hetherington died of cholera in 1849, fellow radicals at the John Street Institution undertook to conduct his funeral in what G.J. Holyoake described in a commemorative biography as 'quiet taste'. In the march to the grave site, 'mutes were superseded by pages with white and blue colored wands, and the officers of the John Street Institution, and various friends of the deceased, walked with similar wands on either side of the procession'. The undertakers bore maces. Among participants meriting mention in Holyoake's account were 'editors, lecturers, publishers, guardians of the poor, foreign socialists and politicians of note, who respected Hetherington, or had cooperated with him'.[70]

English participation in émigré funerals was no less devout. Descriptions of refugee burials are a commonplace in the radical press and memoir literature, and Chartists often figured in the commemorative volumes issued for the continental exile community. Julian Harney described his sense of loss upon the death of Philippe Faure in a volume to which Adèle and Victor Hugo, Aurelio Saffi, Blanc, Kossuth, Ledru-Rollin, and Herzen all contributed. 'He was more than a blood-brother to me', Harney wrote, 'he was a brother of the heart'.[71] At the funerals themselves, the full panoply of radical pageantry came into play. The Polish exile Albert Darasz was buried with great – but not unusual – ceremony at Highgate in 1852. The funeral car, arrayed with Darasz's sabre and Polish cap, preceded an estimated 1,200 mourners, led by Worcell, Mazzini, and Ledru-Rollin. 'Behind them came first the French Republicans in ranks of five abreast, bearing their red flag with the inscription "République démocratique et sociale"; the Italians with their tricolour; then the Germans; and last of all the Poles under their national flag, the white eagle on a sanguine field'.[72] Four years later Worcell was buried in the same grave with similar ceremony: Mazzini, Ledru-Rollin, and Herzen marched in the procession, accompanied by a band 'playing Polish and other national music'.[73] Worcell's funeral was frequently remembered in Chartist autobiographies, and a monument and commemorative volumes were soon

[70] George Jacob Holyoake, *The Life and Character of Henry Hetherington* (London, 1849).
[71] Phillippe Faure, *Journal d'un combattant de février* (Jersey, 1859), p. 20.
[72] William James Linton, *European Republicans: Recollections of Mazzini and His Friends* (London, 1893), p. 319.
[73] *Reasoner*, 22 February 1857, p. 30. There is a copy of the programme for the funeral in T&WAD, Cowen Collection, 634/A493.

under way, assisted by the efforts of the English radical leadership.[74] From the cradle to the grave, in annual commemorations and occasional celebrations, radical culture in England embraced and ritualized continental politics, fuelling the expansion of the national radical idiom effected by the events of 1848 and yet reinforcing patriotic notions of the English nation-state established in the seventeenth century. Caught between these interlocking trends, theories of class society were alternately underscored and undercut, confirmed and confounded.

CLUB LIFE AND INTERNATIONALISM

International ceremony and symbolism provided Chartist and émigré reformers with an effective lingua franca in the 1850s, but radical collaboration and activity relied upon an organizational framework for the creation of opportunities in which these fraternal sentiments could be expressed. Club life offered an important locus of oppositional culture in the decade after 1848, providing radical activists with a structured environment for education, organization, and protest. Although at times riven by faction, the clubs and associations of late Chartism, like the late Chartist press, functioned as a network in most contexts. Few working-class radicals belonged to only one club, and few frequented only a single debating hall or radical institute. Rather, they chose to participate in a wide range of interconnected associations that formed a central matrix for radical endeavour. Typically these organizations shared overlapping memberships, accommodations, and *démoc-soc* ideals.

Within the émigré community, the influx of exiles after the counterrevolutions of 1848–9 precipitated the formation of a number of radical associations, institutions designed to combat the economic and cultural disadvantages of refugee life. Isolated in a foreign environment, the continental exiles owed their primary allegiance to particularistic associations formed by their compatriots: among the most significant, the German Workers' Education Society, the Polish Democratic Society, and the French Société

---

[74] Anton Zabicki to Linton, 15 June 1857, Feltrinelli, Milan, Linton Papers, vol. 5, item 8. Herzen published a commemorative volume, *L'Etoile Polaire sur la mort de Stanislaus Worcell* (London, 1857). For autobiographical accounts, see Adams, *Memoirs of a Social Atom*, vol. II, pp. 324–5; and Linton, *European Republicans*, pp. 274, 337–8.

fraternelle des démocrates socialistes à Londres were organized along strictly national lines. Endowed with club and lecture rooms, libraries, and often a press and newspaper of their own, these institutions provided foci for the daily life of émigré communities and the organizational framework within which the ceremonial cycle of refugee radicalism took shape.[75]

Corresponding associations existed for native English radicals, offering their adherents an intensely radical education and milieu. At Brantwood, a Republican Association attracted three Cheltenham Chartists who worked with W.J. Linton to publish the *English Republic* and popularize the gospel of Mazzini.[76] More substantial were the clubs and associations that continued to propagate the Chartist message. A 'Democratic Conference' convened in August 1850 by a group of radicals that included Reynolds, Harney, Holyoake, Lloyd Jones, J.B. Leno, and Samuel Kydd resulted in the formation of the National Charter and Social Reform Association in October. Attracting representatives of various trades to their London meetings, these leaders briefly established correspondence with Chartists in Norwich, Bradford, Hull, Manchester, Birmingham, Brighton, and Halifax. Grounding their organization on the principle 'that all mankind are brethren', they advocated the six points of the Charter, land nationalization, and a national system of secular education. 'We feel ... that the time has come when the People may reach its hand and take possession of power', their declaration asserted. 'At the same time ... the state can be made to recognize the right of every man to labour, or to subsistence from the State, while bad laws fetter his labour and withhold him from the land to which he was born.'[77]

Ernest Jones's release from prison in July 1850 stimulated a revival of the fortunes of the National Charter Association, which had supplanted the National Charter and Social Reform Association

[75] For German émigré life, see Rosemary Ashton, *Little Germany: Exile and Asylum in Victorian England* (Oxford, 1986); for the Polish emigration, see Helena Rzadkowska, *Działalność Centralizacii Londyńskiej Towarzystwa Demokratycznego Polskiego 1850–1862* [*The Activities of the Centralization of the London Polish Democratic Society 1850–1862*] (Warsaw, 1971). The best source for the Société fraternelle is *L'Homme*, but see also Alvin Calman, *Ledru-Rollin après 1848 et les proscrits français en Angleterre* (Paris, 1921).
[76] Adams, *Memoirs of a Social Atom*, vol. I, pp. 267, 281.
[77] *Leader*, 24 August 1850, p. 509; 12 October 1850, p. 681; 19 October 1850, p. 706; 16 November 1850, p. 797; 7 December 1850, p. 858.

by December and continued to function until 1858.[78] Fifty-three Chartist localities and a hundred individuals cast votes for the Association's executive in December; Reynolds, Harney, Jones, O'Connor, Holyoake, and John Arnott placed at the top of the poll with over 1,000 votes each. Charging an annual subscription of twopence, the Association boasted 6,000 members by November 1851, but had meagre resources. Contributions received during one week in January amounted to only £12 7s 1d.[79] In keeping with the *démoc-soc* convictions evinced by members of the executive in 1848, the programme adopted by the National Charter Association in April 1851 called for land nationalization and underlined the duty of the state – not the parish – to provide remunerative employment, education, unemployment relief, and homes for the aged.[80]

These policies, although endorsed by the National Charter Association in the name of labour, did not win universal endorsement from working-class radicals and trade unionists. To the evident relief of John Bright – who declared in March that 'a portion of the Chartists are become rational' – Manchester's Chartist body declared its opposition to all efforts 'to attach a kind of mongrel Socialism to Chartism'. Denigrating notions 'borrowed from the Parisian school of philosophers', they broke with the National Charter Association and threw their support behind Bright's Parliamentary and Financial Reform Association in April.[81] Trade unions, which had initially joined in the late Chartist response to 1848, were also deeply divided by the Chartists' new social agenda and chose to retreat from the political arena for a decade rather than grapple with the divisive relations between parliamentary democracy and political economy.[82] Ernest Jones and his associates were unmoved by these defections and continued to insist upon the fundamental relation of social and political reform. In June 1853

---

[78] There is no definitive history of the association in this period, but some discussion of its activities can be found in R.G. Gammage, *History of the Chartist Movement: 1837–1854* (London, 1854); Saville, *Ernest Jones*, pp. 50–76; and John Belchem, *Industrialization and the Working Class: The English Experience, 1750–1900* (Aldershot, 1990), pp. 138–44.

[79] *Leader*, 21 December 1850, p. 916; 10 May 1851, p. 448; 22 November 1851, p. 1117; 18 January 1851, p. 54.

[80] *Ibid.*, 12 April 1851, pp. 350–1.

[81] Bright to George Wilson, 28 March 1851, MCRL, Wilson Papers, M20/1851; *Leader*, 17 May 1851, p. 459.

[82] John Belchem, 'Chartism and the Trades, 1848–1850', *English Historical Review*, vol. 98 (July 1983), pp. 558–87.

Jones addressed a meeting of 1,000 persons at Blackstone Edge; in August he spoke to 500 persons in London. His rationale for supporting the six points was clear and emphatic, for the Charter 'would do away with class legislation and give the People their Political and Social Rights'.[83]

Working-class radicals' allegiance to particularistic Chartist associations was supplemented by their eclectic sampling of coffee houses, halls, and institutes that combined a variety of radical creeds under a single roof. Although club loyalties were often strong, radical memoirs testify to the fluidity of associational life in the fifties. When W.E. Adams left Linton's republican community at Brantwood for London in 1855, he attended lectures by Thomas Cooper, Charles Bradlaugh, G.J. Holyoake, and Bronterre O'Brien – the latter speaking at a tavern in Shoe Lane decorated with oil paintings of Thomas Hardy and other 'famous Radicals'.[84] George Howell, introduced to London Chartism by the cabinetmaker Benjamin Lucraft and the plasterer Charles Bartlett, joined the Islington branch of Jones's National Charter Association but also associated with Cooper, O'Brien, Holyoake, Bradlaugh, and Edward Truelove before establishing his own Milton Club at a coffee house at Islington Green 'to make known Milton's Prose Political Writings'.[85]

The history of the venues that offered lecture halls and reading rooms to working-class radical associations in the fifties illustrates the extensive institutional overlap of divergent radical groups in these years. In London the National Hall, the Hall of Science, and the Cleveland Street Hall welcomed Chartist, socialist, theological, and temperance speakers; Highbury Barn, site of the French socialists' commemoration of the third anniversary of the February revolution, was also a common choice for the London printers' annual trade feast.[86] The Eclectic Institute at Denmark Street, established by Bronterre O'Brien's followers in 1851 and described

[83] Police Report of June 1853, HO 45/5128, item 256; Police Report of August 1853, HO 45/5128, item 357. Kate Tiller offers a fine analysis of the persistence of Chartism in this period in 'Late Chartism: Halifax, 1847–58', in Epstein and Thompson (eds.), *Chartist Experience*, pp. 311–44.
[84] Adams, *Memoirs of a Social Atom*, vol. II, pp. 313–18.
[85] Howell MS Autobiography, BI, Howell Collection, vol. A, part b4, chap. 7, pp. 62–7; part b5, pp. 1–22, esp. p. 16.
[86] *Ibid.*, vol A, part b5; *Leader*, 8 March 1851, pp. 228–9; Smith, *Working Man's Way in the World*, p. 305.

by O'Brien in 1857 as his 'sheet anchor', sponsored activities that ranged from lectures on 'Moral and Social Science', 'Home and Foreign Politics', and 'Parliamentary Representation for the Whole People' to evening language and science classes such as 'French for the Millions', admission twopence.[87] Its members included men whose participation in the radical movement extended without intermission from the early Chartist movement to the new socialism of the 1880s. Occupied by O'Brien's followers from 1849 to 1873, the Eclectic Hall that housed the Eclectic Institute provided a meeting place in London first for the O'Brienite National Reform League, later for the British section of the First International, and ultimately for a republican club established during the radical revival that followed the outbreak of the Paris Commune.[88]

London's John Street Institution, established in 1840 as an Owenite socialist base, similarly offered a haven for disparate radical speakers and associations. 'The platform was perfectly free', Adams later recalled, 'Chartism, Republicanism, Freethought, Socialism – all sorts and conditions of thought could be expounded' within its walls.[89] John Street provided a venue for public meetings convened by the National Charter Association, and was the location of O'Brien's Monday night Eclectic Lectures in 1857. The institution was instrumental in sustaining both Chartist agitation and working-class internationalist culture. It was at John Street that Harney's Fraternal Democrats held their annual New Year's Eve Festival in 1850, and at John Street that Holyoake named Edward Truelove's son Mazzini.[90]

Although English and émigré radicals enjoyed the use of shared lecture halls and club rooms, and joined in a common calendar of international celebrations, they rarely belonged to the same radical associations in the years immediately after 1848. Harney had established his Fraternal Democrats in 1846 with French, German, and Polish refugees, but the government's imposition of an Alien

[87] James Bronterre O'Brien to Matthews, 19 September 1857, National Labour History Museum and Labour Party Archives, Manchester, James Bronterre O'Brien Papers, OB.5, OB.10.
[88] Shipley, *Club Life and Socialism*, pp. 1–20.
[89] J.F.C. Harrison, *Robert Owen and the Owenites in Britain and America: The Quest for the New Moral World* (London, 1969), pp. 224–5; Adams, *Memoirs of a Social Atom*, vol. II, pp. 313–14.
[90] *Leader*, 18 January 1851, p. 52; National Labour History Museum and Labour Party Archives, Manchester, O'Brien Papers, OB.5; *Friend of the People*, 28 December 1850, p. 20; *Reasoner*, 14 November 1849, pp. 305–7.

Act in 1848 forced the organization to adopt an exclusively English membership in 1849.[91] With the formation of the International Committee (1854–6) and its successor, the International Association (1856–9), however, international fraternity again assumed sustained organizational form in working-class radical circles. Under the auspices of these successive associations, socialist propaganda effectively pre-empted nationalist agendas and conceptions of class vied with increasing stridency against English radicals' traditional preoccupations with aristocratic oppression.

The events leading to the formation of the International Committee and Association typify radical associational life in the 1850s. Informed in the autumn of 1854 that the imprisoned French revolutionary Armand Barbès had been pardoned by Louis Napoleon and hoping to stimulate renewed interest in radicalism in England, Ernest Jones and the National Charter Association established a 'Committee of Welcome' to encourage the French patriot to visit England and receive the accolades of the working-class radical community. When apprised soon thereafter that Louis Napoleon intended a trip to England, the group expanded its scope, becoming a 'Welcome and Protest Committee', which continued to meet through the winter. By January 1855 the committee had integrated its activities fully into the radical ceremonial cycle by preparing a banquet commemorating the seventh anniversary of the February revolution. When a deputation of French socialist émigrés requested admission to the committee 'for the purpose of co-operation in the union of Democracy in London with that on the Continent', the Chartists appointed a sub-committee to work with the French refugees and to test the wider émigré community's interest in an international association. In February the International Committee emerged from these deliberations. Headed by five English, five French, five Germans, and one Spanish representative, it reported the imminent allegiance of Polish and Italian delegations.[92]

In the historiography of the European labour movement, the International Committee and the International Association formally constituted by its members at the John Street Institution on 10 August 1856 figure as direct predecessors of the First International. The arguments of the association's historian are typical in asserting

[91] Weisser, *British Working-Class Movements*, pp. 134–49; *Red Republican*, 29 June 1850, p. 13.
[92] *People's Paper*, 21 October 1854, 20 January 1855.

that it must be 'regarded as the first international organization of a proletarian and socialist character, and forms the last and most important link in the series of international manifestations during the three decades prior to the foundation of the First International'.[93] From the perspective of English involvement in the two organizations, these claims are exaggerated, for no surviving records indicate the social composition of the English membership, which is more likely to have been artisanal than proletarian. But the complexion of English internationalism in this association is nonetheless significant. At the height of Chartist involvement, the tenor of working-class radical politics in London was both more strident and more sophisticated than it had been since 1848. If national idioms dominated much of English radicalism in the 1850s, Chartist activities in 1855 continued to cast the ascendancy of received radical traditions into doubt.

The public activities of the International Committee and Association chiefly consisted of the characteristic anniversary celebrations of the radical international calendar: they included a commemoration of the June Days of 1848 in June 1855, a celebration at John Street in December 1855 to mark the anniversary of the establishment of the first French republic, and a meeting to commemorate the Polish uprising of 1830 in December 1855.[94] Within these received radical parameters, Jones and his associates laboured to popularize a variety of Chartism that privileged socialist internationalism over particularistic, nationalistic reform, rather than merely combining the two strands of polemic together. At the initial meeting of the International Committee, James Finlen, a Chartist French polisher, objected on both tactical and patriotic grounds to the National Charter Association's formal affiliation with the international body. Acknowledging his 'great admiration for the refugees ... because they are democratic socialists', Finlen argued first that the Association would alienate moderate Chartists and then that

[93] Arthur Müller Lehning, *The International Association 1855–1859: A Contribution to the Preliminary History of the First International* (Leiden, 1938), p. 1. A similar line of analysis is followed in Theodore Rothstein, *From Chartism to Labourism: Historical Sketches of the English Working Class Movement* (London, 1929), pp. 166–81, and Julius Braunthal, *History of the International*, trans. Henry Collins and Kenneth Mitchell, 3 vols. (London, 1966), vol. I, pp. 74–83. Henry Collins and Chimen Abramsky offer a more balanced view in *Karl Marx and the British Labour Movement: Years of the First International* (London, 1965), pp. 11–14.

[94] *People's Paper*, 3 May 1856.

English radicals should be ashamed to rely upon help from other nationalities to effect their own reforms. Jones's rebuttal, ratified by the committee, turned the National Charter Association decisively 'towards the union of all peoples'. In describing the debates in the *People's Paper*, he employed not the language of early Chartism, but the idiom of 1848. 'Can we form an alliance with the men of France, of Germany, of Italy, of Hungary, of Poland, on the basis of England's Charter?', he asked rhetorically. 'No! we take the common ground of the wide world's Charter – the Republic, Democratic and Social.'[95]

In the following months, Chartists affiliated with the International Committee sought to distance English reformers from the shibboleths of the English radical tradition. Ernest Jones seized the opportunity afforded by the Chartists' new access of socialist sentiment to denigrate his chief rival in the press, G.W.M. Reynolds. Reynolds had retired from active participation in Chartist organizations in 1851, but his newspaper remained by far the most popular working-class radical weekly long after his departure from the leadership. As such, it drew readers away from Jones's *People's Paper*. When in March *Reynolds's* argued that 'to our aristocratic system is to be attributed *every political evil* which afflicts us, and *every social wrong* which the masses are compelled to endure', Jones was swift to take the offensive.[96] Asserting that aristocratic dominion represented 'a portion of the class curse, but it is the lesser portion of the two', he located the roots of contemporary economic exploitation in 'capitalist tyranny'. Warning his readers against alliances with 'designing, middle-class agitators and sham liberals', Jones characterized the battle against Old Corruption as 'an old exploded obsolete affair'. 'The war of the age is a SOCIAL war', he concluded. 'It is a war of labour against capital, of cooperation against monopoly, of the poor against the rich.'[97]

The International Committee's seventh anniversary celebration of 1848 further promoted this anti-capitalist agenda. Louis Blanc was naturally invited, and Alexander Herzen – rather wishfully described by Jones as the representative of Russia's 'proletarian millions' –

[95] *Ibid.*, 10 February 1856, p. 4.
[96] *Reynolds's Newspaper*, 25 February 1855. Significantly, Reynolds's anti-aristocratic sentiment, although moderate relative to Jones's anti-capitalist critique, still adhered to dominant Chartist principles – not middle-class reformism – in linking political and social spheres.
[97] *People's Paper*, 3 March 1856, p. 1.

delivered a socialist speech. After democratic choruses sung by German refugees, the men and women seated in the galleries of St Martin's Hall – decorated for the occasion with a red flag and festooned with crimson – listened to Jones's ringing oratory:

> Our ... duty is to restore the oppressed nations to independence. But what independence? I say *internal* as well as *external* ... For us, nation is *nothing*, man is *all*. For us the oppressed nationalities form but one: the universal poor of every land ... Let none misunderstand the tenor of this meeting: we begin tonight no mere crusade against the aristocracy ... We are against the tyranny of capital as well.

More moderate than Jones on this as on all occasions, G.J. Holyoake nonetheless affirmed the Chartists' *démoc-soc* aspirations in his speech to the assembled crowd:

> The term 'Republic' was the charmed word in politics ... it was the government in which justice was the indispensable policy, public intelligence a necessity, and moderation the condition of self-existence ... He (Mr. Holyoake) was glad to hear Mr. Finlen say he was a Chartist and also glad to find that he proved himself to be something more. The republic, democratic and social, in favour of which he spoke, was opening new ground ... No republic was secure that was not based also on social rights.[98]

These arguments fell far short of Marx's strictures against capitalist economics, but they also fell outside the national oppositional canon established by earlier generations of English radicals.[99] Viewed from this perspective, they testify to the dynamism – not the reformism – of English working-class culture after 1848.

Uniting English Chartists and continental socialists on a single radical platform in 1855 as it had united French revolutionaries in 1848, the *démoc-soc* banner suggested a different conception of international brotherhood than did the English patriotic idiom. But the tenure of the International Association was fleeting. Although émigré sections continued to meet until 1859, English involvement receded after 1855. Ernest Jones had essentially returned to single-minded adherence to the Charter by May 1856. 'I cannot see the

---

[98] *Ibid.*, p. 4.
[99] Marx, who had schooled Jones in materialism earlier in the decade, declined to join the International Association, in part because of Herzen's membership. See Marx to Engels, 2 and 13 February 1856, in *Marx, Engels: Collected Works*, vol. XXXIX, pp. 520–4.

utility of forming any new association', he wrote to Holyoake, 'it could only do mischief, as tending to divide that popular strength, which ought now more than ever to be united.'[100]

Conventionally ascribed to the immaturity of the English trade union movement in the 1850s,[101] the failure of the International Association to flourish in England is fully explicable only if placed in the broader context of its times. Although the organization's *démoc-soc* ideals spoke to longstanding Chartist convictions in urging the necessary relation between political structures and social conditions, the socialist formulation of these aspirations – however partial and innocuous it may appear in retrospect – clearly alienated sections of the working class itself. Finlen's reluctance to endorse the National Charter Association's affiliation with the International Committee was not, after all, alarmist: the Manchester Chartists had withdrawn from the body on precisely the issue of French socialism in 1851.[102] And whereas working-class Chartists content to decry the aristocratic jobbery of Old Corruption could point with relative ease – and middle-class accompaniment – to the conspicuous excrescences of the unreformed English state, *démoc-soc* Chartists could offer the public neither the example of a successful socialist nation nor a unified economic programme with which one might be created. For although each joined in supporting some form of land nationalization – a radical agenda that drew sustenance from anti-aristocratic, Spencean, and O'Connorite roots[103] – late Chartist leaders proved unable to generate a shared critique of industrial capitalism.

This failure, if often remarked, is hardly remarkable. The demands of the lecture circuit, the ceremonial claims of oppositional culture, the cut and thrust of Chartist rivalries, the paucity of radical patronage and financial reserves, all militated against the emergence of coherent and sustained economic theories in the late Chartist movement. Marx, whose research and writing were underwritten by Engels, could afford the luxury of a sophisticated critique of

---

[100] Ernest Jones to G.J. Holyoake, 7 May 1856, IISG, Eng. 2 File, Letters from Ernest Jones.

[101] See for example Collins and Abramsky, *Marx and the British Labour Movement*, p. 14.

[102] See above, p. 133.

[103] The popularity of proposals for land nationalization within the radical movement is detailed in Malcolm Chase, *'The People's Farm': English Radical Agrarianism 1775–1840* (Oxford, 1988), and Alice Mary Hadfield, *The Chartist Land Company* (Newton Abbot, 1970).

capitalism; Jones, Harney, Holyoake, and O'Brien could not. Constrained by the demands of the very culture that helped to sustain them, they were limited further by the class consequences of their *démoc-soc* allegiance. For unlike Engels, English middle-class radicals declined repeatedly to engage with socialist thought. The intransigence of the Chartist leadership on economic issues brought the full weight of middle-class displeasure down upon them, limiting the movement's financial base, depriving it of considerable experience and talent, and alienating many followers.[104]

It also served to sustain perceptions of class conflict and class consciousness after the demise of the mass platform. Confronted with the late Chartist leadership's seemingly ceaseless affirmation of the *démoc-soc* ideal – its processions, its soirées, its baptisms, and its burials – middle-class radical leaders came to identify Chartist opposition to liberal economics as a wider working-class phenomenon embedded in the culture of skilled artisans and the courts and alleys of Mayhew's London.[105] Historians in retrospect have emphasized the poverty of theory, the profound caesura of working-class radicalism in these years, but contemporary middle-class radicals were too consumed by efforts to negotiate the considerable obstacles placed in their path by late Chartist leaders to savour their apparent victory. In the successive reform campaigns with which these radicals wooed working-class support in the fifties, nationalism helped to foster alliances with the Chartists, but failed to secure their conversion to liberalism.

[104] A key exception to this general rule of middle-clas antagonism was the Newcastle radical Joseph Cowen, whose anonymous but generous support was crucial for many late Chartists. See Evan Rowland Jones, *The Life and Speeches of Joseph Cowen, M.P.* (London, 1885), and below, pp. 175–7.

[105] John Saville is one of the few historians to emphasize the significance of this divide. See his *Ernest Jones*, pp. 37–8.

4 · *Bourgeois radical nationalism and the working class, 1848–1858*

I too participate in the lively recollections of former times. . . . The French Revolution of 1848 brought us to nearly a stand still, and the apprehension which then seized nearly the whole of us above the common labourers is still to some extent upon us. What good things we should have achieved but for that apprehension it is impossible for me to conjecture but . . . I hope yet to live to see the completion of Free Trade, a vastly extended increase of knowledge and in sound Political Economy . . . and a very large portion of the working people capable of exercising, and discreetly exercising the right of suffrage under the ballot.[1]

Like Chartism, middle-class reform movements experienced fundamental changes in the decade after 1848, responding to the continental revolutions with both new enthusiasm for the nation and a heightened awareness of the social and economic implications of parliamentary reform. Like working-class radicalism, moreover, middle-class reform efforts in these years both built upon and served to entrench the radical traditions of earlier centuries, using received conceptions of the nation-state to buttress more recent theories of class relations. By emphasizing the fundamental continuities of the radical tradition over both time and social distance, these bourgeois agendas fostered collaboration between working- and middle-class reformers. As in the year of revolutions itself, however, the decade after 1848 saw radical culture deeply divided by fundamental differences of economic outlook. For even as Chartists responded to the revolutions with increased commitment to the economic uses of Parliament, middle-class radicals reacted by severely restricting the scope of their political vision.

[1] Francis Place to George Grote, 28 February 1850, BL, Place Collection, Add. MS 35, 151, fol. 40.

As Francis Place's reflections on the future course of radical action suggest, political economy and free trade figured centrally in this reconfigured radicalism of the middle class. In the context of radical agitation, indeed, otherwise disparate liberal economic doctrines and their political corollaries came to constitute a single ideological strand uniting otherwise antagonistic middle-class reformers in the fifties.[2] Scholars rightly underline the limits of liberal economic practice in the Victorian period, pointing to the massive expansion of bureaucratic and welfare structures in the nineteenth century.[3] But middle-class radicals who sought alliances with the working class remained essentially aloof from these developments. Often champions at the local level of improved sanitation or municipal lighting, they campaigned militantly against government centralization.[4] Acknowledging either the deficiencies of extant social relations or the inadequacies of existing political structures, they chose overwhelmingly to advocate either social or political reform at the national level, but not both. Far more than merely preaching the doctrine of separate spheres, the reform movements that they led in the course of the 1850s came to embody this division.

In elaborating their conceptions of nation, class, and political economy, bourgeois radicals drew upon a coherent, often sophisticated theory of society and a political vocabulary that diverged

[2] This is not at all to suggest that liberalism was inherently monolithic. For the varied texture of liberal politics and economics in these years, see Richard Bellamy (ed.), *Victorian Liberalism: Nineteenth-Century Political Thought and Practice* (London, 1990).

[3] William C. Lubenow, *The Politics of Government Growth: Early Victorian Attitudes toward State Intervention, 1833–1848* (London, 1971), and Oliver MacDonagh, *Early Victorian Government, 1830–1870* (London, 1977), offer detailed analyses of these complex issues. For excellent surveys of the wider literature, see Derek Fraser, *The Evolution of the British Welfare State: A History of Social Policy since the Industrial Revolution*, 2nd edn. (London, 1984), pp. 90–123, and Roy Macleod, 'Introduction', in Macleod (ed.), *Government and Expertise: Specialists, Administrators and Professionals, 1860–1919* (Cambridge, 1988), pp. 1–24.

[4] Joshua Toulmin Smith, discussed below pp. 147–8 and in W.H. Greenleaf, 'Toulmin Smith and the British Political Tradition', *Public Administration*, vol. 53 (Spring 1975), pp. 25–44, epitomizes this tendency, which is explored more fully in John Prest, *Liberty and Locality: Parliament, Permissive Legislation, and Ratepayers' Democracies in the Nineteenth Century* (Oxford, 1990). John Davis, *Reforming London: The London Government Problem 1855–1900* (Oxford, 1988), p. 10, notes that this revival of interest in parochial government 'was part of the broader mid-century movement of local self-determination that could be seen as a muted but lasting British response to European nationalism and the events of 1848'.

sharply from the characteristic political idioms of late Chartism. As in Chartist argument, the nation occupied a central position in the bourgeois worldview – Smith's concern for the 'Wealth of Nations' was significant. But whereas Chartists naturalized the political rights of both the nation and its male citizens, middle-class radicals naturalized the economic laws that governed the behaviour of individuals within a naturalized nation-state. The market, not the polity, served as the dominant metaphor in this vision of society, and provided the ultimate arbiter of its class relations.[5] This allegiance in turn entailed adherence to a cluster of linguistic turns that distinguished middle- from working-class radicalism. Intent to expand the freedom of the economic market but unwilling to admit all adult males to the political exchange of the electorate, middle-class radicals privileged pragmatism over theory, expediency over justice. In doing so they repeatedly invoked the bourgeois category of public opinion.[6] Evincing remarkable unanimity across otherwise deep social, cultural, and intellectual boundaries within their ranks, these radical responses to 1848 speak both to the maturity of class formation among the propertied and to the success with which a strident Chartist minority had articulated its claim to represent the English working class.

MIDDLE-CLASS CULTURE AND REFORM IN THE EARLY FIFTIES

If *démoc-soc* ideals underpinned Chartists' radical efforts in the decade after 1848, the broad body of thinking described by the term political economy laid the groundwork for middle-class political reform endeavour in these years. Far more than a putative science of market economics, political economy had from its origins in the

---

[5] These arguments are developed at greater length and with greater sophistication in Hall and Davidoff, *Family Fortunes*, pp. 229–71, 416–49; and in Theodore Koditschek, *Class Formation and Urban Industrial Society: Bradford, 1750–1850* (Cambridge, 1990), esp. pp. 228–347.

[6] The significance of public opinion as a bourgeois ideology and its relation to liberal and Enlightenment conceptions of politics and society are detailed by Jürgen Habermas, *The Structural Transformation of the Public Sphere: An Inquiry into a Category of Bourgeois Society*, trans. by Thomas Burger with the assistance of Frederick Lawrence (Cambridge, Mass., 1989), pp. 89–95, and J.A.W. Gunn, 'Public Spirit to Public Opinion', in his *Beyond Liberty and Property: The Process of Self-Recognition in Eighteenth-Century Political Thought* (Kingston and Montreal, 1983), pp. 260–315.

eighteenth century been intended to embody a systematic understanding of history and society. As Biancamaria Fontana's analysis
of the *Edinburgh Review* suggests, political economy constituted not
a monolith but a 'complex and internally differentiated' intellectual
construct, displaying 'complex relations to contemporary political
ideologies' rather than simple affiliations with either Whig or Liberal
party politics. But as Fontana also argues, the emergence of this
body of thought nonetheless marked 'a major theoretical divide'. In
the years following the first French revolution, the contributors to
the *Edinburgh Review*, like the wider middle-class audience to whom
they spoke, came to use adherence to the tenets of political economy
as a litmus test that distinguished their own, scientific approach to
political life from other, ostensibly theoretical – radical, conservative, or nostalgic – political allegiances. For these intellectuals, 'to
accept or reject the validity of political economy meant to accept or
to reject the heritage of an experimental science of man and society,
and the guidance of the laws and principles which it offered'.[7]
Middle- and upper-class social reformers inspired by paternalist
interpretations of Evangelical religion often subscribed to an alternative worldview, accepting intervention in economic relations as
the Christian duty of those favoured with wealth and status by a
deity whose own presence was manifest in interventionist acts of
particular Providence.[8] But these exponents of charitable social
reform were conspicuously absent from the radical ranks and
leadership, leaving the arena of middle-class political reform in the
hands of men committed to classical economics.

Hand in hand with the principles of political economy in the
middle-class radical analysis were the guiding precepts of national
identity. As Macaulay's *History of England* sought to demonstrate,
only free political institutions could secure the ordered economic
transition from an agrarian to a commercial society. Noted today
for its enunciation of the whig view of history, for its rejection of the
notion that commercial expansion had exacerbated social ills,
Macaulay's *History* was celebrated in his own time as a textbook of

[7] Biancamaria Fontana, *Rethinking the Politics of Commercial Society: The Edin-
    burgh Review 1802–1832* (Cambridge, 1985), pp. 9–10, 180.
[8] Boyd Hilton, 'The Role of Providence in Evangelical Social Thought', in Derek
    Beales and Geoffrey Best (eds.), *History, Society and the Churches: Essays in
    Honour of Owen Chadwick* (Cambridge, 1985), pp. 215–33, and *idem, The Age of
    Atonement: The Influence of Evangelicalism on Social and Economic Thought 1795–
    1865* (Oxford, 1988).

patriotism. An extended exposition on 'the peculiar feelings and habits of the English nation', his narrative laboured to excite 'hope in the breasts of all patriots'.[9] Hailed by the *Edinburgh Review* in 1849 as 'this great national work', the *History* did more than merely burnish the reputations of Pym, Hampden, and Cromwell, for its pragmatic justification of the seventeenth-century revolutions raised obvious comparisons with the French revolution of 1848. 'The people of England have always been of an eminently practical turn, especially in politics, – very little given to mere theory, and looking mainly to the immediate comforts and decencies of life, as the objects which they desire to secure', the review noted with satisfaction. This 'national peculiarity', it continued, offered 'a very striking contrast to those of their continental neighbours'.[10]

Enormously popular within the middle class from its first appearance in 1848, Macaulay's patriotic narrative both celebrated social harmony and provided an instrument for its extension. The publication of Thomas Carlyle's *Cromwell* had restored glory to the memory of England's heroes in 1846, but Macaulay repudiated Carlyle's pessimistic interpretation of the social and economic relations that had arisen on these patriotic foundations.[11] Readers were quick to recognize and act upon the class uses of this message. In Lancashire, one gentleman read the *History* aloud to his less affluent neighbours each evening in 1849, moving one listener to propose a vote of thanks to the author 'for having written a history which working men can understand'.[12]

Middle-class radicals intent to capture a working-class following appropriated and vulgarized this whig view of history and economy in their efforts to combat both Chartist and aristocratic influence in the political sphere. Richard Cobden, although reluctant to join fully with John Bright in the activities of the Parliamentary and Financial Reform Association, worked enthusiastically alongside

[9] Thomas Babington Macaulay, *History of England*, vol. I, in *The Works of Lord Macaulay*, 12 vols. (London, 1898), pp. 89, 61. On Macaulay's historical contributions, see J.W. Burrow, *A Liberal Descent: Victorian Historians and the English Past* (Cambridge, 1981), pp. 11–93.
[10] 'Macaulay's History of England', *Edinburgh Review*, vol. 90 (July 1849), pp. 281, 268.
[11] For Carlyle's popularization of the seventeenth-century patriots and its association with his dour social and economic outlook, see C.H. Firth, 'Introduction', in *Letters and Speches of Oliver Cromwell*, ed. Lomas, vol. I, pp. xxi–lii.
[12] Cited by Gertrude Himmelfarb, 'Who Now Reads Macaulay?', in her *New History and the Old*, p. 144.

the Birmingham barrister Joshua Toulmin Smith in a reform effort that wedded patriotism firmly to the precepts of political economy. Originating in an association established in Birmingham with Toulmin Smith's assistance, the Metropolitan and National Freehold Land Association offered an institutional framework within which unenfranchised men of small property could obtain a parliamentary vote without parliamentary reform: pooling the monthly subscriptions of their members, the societies bought tracts of land which, when subdivided at cost, qualified subscribers for the forty-shilling county franchise. This tactic, employed by the Anti-Corn Law League earlier in the 1840s to garner votes for free trade, enjoyed substantial economic – if only minimal political – success. Subscription rates were substantial: the Bradford Freehold Land Society, led by Titus Salt and W.E. Forster, required the payment of 1s 0d per share entry fee and an additional 1s 6d per week per share thereafter, effectively prohibiting participation by any but the more affluent of artisans.[13] But the National Society nonetheless boasted 30,000 members and nearly £150,000 in funds within its first year, and its London division had purchased fourteen estates with £62,000 by December 1850.[14]

Toulmin Smith's participation lent the Freehold Land Societies an association with the English radical tradition that extended from the historical privileges secured by early English patriots through the French revolution to the continental revolutions of 1848. A participant in the annual festivities in London with which Dissenters marked the anniversary of the acquittal of 'The Patriots of 1794' – Horne Tooke, Thomas Hardy, and John Thelwall – he was also a founder of the Hungarian Association, which expatiated upon the interdependence of the cause of 'free institutions' among the European nations.[15] The author of an extended tract on the *Parallels between the Constitution and Constitutional History of England and Hungary* (1849), Toulmin Smith grounded his support for suffrage

---

[13] Hinde, *Cobden*, pp. 196–8, discusses the origins of the movement. For Bradford's Society, see 'Votes for the People!! The Bradford Freehold Land Society, Established June 5th, 1849', West Yorkshire Archive Service, Bradford, Deed Box 17, case 12, no. 9, which notes that the average cost of an allotment was £19.

[14] *Leader*, 30 November 1850, pp. 842, 849.

[15] For the anniversary celebrations, in which the Unitarians W.J. Fox, William Shaen, and P.A. Taylor were also participants in 1850, see *ibid.*, 9 November 1850, pp. 771–2. The Hungarian Association is documented in the proof copy of 'Hungarian Association' pamphlet, 1849, Birmingham Reference Library, Joshua Toulmin Smith Collection, fol. 131.

extension not on natural rights but on constitutional law. Eschewing political abstractions, 'standing in the ancient ways of our Constitution', this approach to political reform appealed to Richard Cobden precisely because it avoided the excesses of 1848. 'Nobody can say that we are red republicans, or revolutionists', he told a London meeting of the Association in the tones of the Country Party tradition. 'Here we are, trying to bring back to the people the enjoyment of some of their ancient privileges.'[16]

The principle of voluntary association, central to middle-class efforts to advance reform without promoting dependence on government aid, served as a conduit for this radical offensive, but Cobden was careful to dissociate his version of voluntarism from Louis Blanc's subversive schemes of association.[17] In his many speeches in defence of the Freehold Land Societies, voluntarism and a patriotic conception of political privileges derived from property ownership flowed naturally into attacks on French socialism, attacks that selectively exempted the nationalist movements of Germany, Hungary, and Italy from censure. 'Let me not be considered as open to the charge of Communism, or Socialism: I am much more likely to be called a cold-blooded political economist', Cobden told an audience in Birmingham in 1850. 'It is ... for the benefit of society that the institution of property should be sacredly protected by all', he noted, emphasizing that 'habits of economy and self-denial' – not natural rights or government intervention – would secure workers the franchise.[18] In offering personal political economy as an alternative to physical force reform, Cobden distinguished scrupulously between the stage of historical development achieved by England and that of continental nations other than France, which might legitimately require violent revolutions to establish free institutions.

[16] Richard Cobden, *Speeches of Richard Cobden, Esq., M.P., on Peace, Financial Reform, and Other Subjects: Delivered during 1849* (London, 1849), pp. 170–1, 182–3.

[17] Voluntarism and its intercalation with market economics are discussed ably in Koditschek, *Class Formation*, pp. 252–319, and R.J. Morris, *Class, Sect and Party: The Making of the British Middle Class, Leeds 1820–1850* (Manchester, 1990), pp. 161–203. Kent, 'The Whittington Club', pp. 31–55, notes that visitors from the continent often described the English practice of voluntary association as socialism.

[18] *Leader*, 30 November 1852, p. 842. In the words of one of his most prominent disciples, 'the question whether it was proper to confer the franchise on the adult male population or on those who inhabited houses was one which Cobden argued not to be one of right, but of expediency, for he held that there was no natural right to the franchise, but merely a legal right'. James E. Thorold Rogers, *Cobden and Modern Political Opinion* (London, 1873), p. 279.

'Our ancestors did all that for us, and they were obliged to do it', he concluded. 'During the greater part of the seventeenth century, England presented a scene of commotion almost as great as that which has been witnessed in Hungary, Germany, and Italy; and to the great sacrifices then made, we owe almost all the liberties we possess at present.'[19]

Designed like the parallel Parliamentary and Financial Reform Association to curb 'the extravagant expenditure of the Government' by including small property owners within the franchise, the Freehold Land Societies failed to achieve their intended goal, producing instead a cluster of landowners noted for their political apathy.[20] Cobden's attention was, in any event, soon occupied by weightier issues. For the protectionist panic that attended the general election of 1852 provided middle-class liberals with new evidence of the economic heresies current in working-class radical circles, discouraging further efforts at political reform and reinforcing bourgeois notions of separate spheres. The Tories' avowed determination to dismantle liberal economic structures won by the Anti-Corn Law League in 1846 struck at the very heart of middle-class political consciousness, prompting a shared conviction that 'reform & everything else must be laid aside' until the election had been won for the forces of political economy. '*Let no other question be mixed up with ours*', Cobden wrote to George Wilson in February. 'The country will not entertain other reforms until our question is disposed of.'[21]

Swiftly reconstituting the structures of the Anti-Corn Law League to meet the Tory challenge, Manchester School liberals enjoyed enormous success in mustering their own class to the old cause. Under the deft leadership of its former president, George Wilson, the revived League won pledges for £27,500 from twenty-eight Manchester firms and fifty individuals in the first half-hour of its new existence.[22] But like the original League, it fared poorly with the Chartists. Just as the Manchester School liberals worked to use

[19] Richard Cobden, *Speeches on Questions of Public Policy by Richard Cobden, M.P.*, ed. John Bright and James E. Thorold Rogers (London, 1903), p. 554.
[20] For the movement's relation to the campaign against Old Corruption, see *ibid.*, p. 557, and *The Working Man's Friend*, 5 January 1850, p. 2, and 19 July 1851, pp. 57–60. Hinde, *Cobden*, p. 197, notes the political failure of the movement.
[21] George Hadfield to George Wilson, 24 February 1852, and Cobden to Wilson, 28 February 1852, MCRL, Wilson Papers, M20/1852.
[22] *Daily News*, 3 March 1852, p. 4.

the election campaign to demonstrate the nation's allegiance to free trade, late Chartist leaders sought to force liberal candidates to recognize the rights of English labour or face ejection from the House of Commons.

In London, the presence of the National Charter Association ensured that this tension between the radical factions was evident, and recognized as an aspect of class conflict. In March Chartists repeatedly disrupted a public conference convened by the Parliamentary and Financial Reform Association, articulating an opposition to liberal measures that would soon lead them into Tory alliances for the duration of the campaign. Sir Joshua Walmsley opened the event with a speech that called for 'not only cheap bread but cheap government . . . the perpetual blessings of free trade, and a general amelioration of existing burdens' and declared that only pragmatic considerations prevented his support of the Charter. Chartists in the audience, under the leadership of Ernest Jones, rose to urge the six points and claimed that the convention 'did not represent the feelings of the working classes'. Having succeeded in disrupting the meeting, they forced its adjournment to the following day, when all but members of the Parliamentary and Financial Reform Association were barred from participation.[23] One vociferous Chartist from Clerkenwell nonetheless succeeded in articulating his opposition to liberal economics. 'The millowners of Manchester had obtained free trade, but it was a delusion, and the wish of the working classes was to have protection for every British interest', he insisted, amid cries of both 'Hear, hear' and 'Time'. 'If he was saying what was unpopular in that assembly', he concluded, 'he knew he was speaking the sentiments of the people outside.'[24]

Given this antagonism, the election of 1852 threatened to revitalize working-class adherence to the tory radicalism that had informed the struggle for the Factory Acts and against the New Poor Law in the 1830s and 1840s. Already in 1851 Bronterre O'Brien, Samuel Kydd, and other Chartist stalwarts had joined with the Tory MP G.F. Young to this end. At a public meeting of workers in the Tower Hamlets, Chartist speaker after Chartist speaker rose to affirm O'Brien's assertion that 'the universal cheapness sought in the policy falsely called Free Trade, necessarily includes cheapness of labour, and must, therefore, by whatever

---

[23] *Leader*, 6 March 1852, pp. 214–16.   [24] *Daily News*, 3 March 1852, p. 2.

means obtained, be injurious to the labouring classes'.[25] Although the tory National Association for the Promotion of British Industry sponsored the event, conservative political principles suffered Chartist attacks alongside the liberal economic principles of middle-class radicals. 'He had no faith in the rich Protectionist who would not give the working man a share in the representation of the House of Commons', one working-class speaker asserted. 'For his own part, he wished to free and deliver the people from the Free-traders, and to protect them from the Protectionists. (Cheers).'[26]

By the spring of 1852, Chartist strategists had begun to translate these sentiments into increasingly partisan political tactics that struck selectively at Liberal candidates. The *Leader* newspaper, under the Chartist influence of G.J. Holyoake and Thornton Hunt, had little quarrel with free trade in corn, but warned in April that middle-class radicals' liberal attitude to labour would propel workers into the arms of Tory protection:

> The most obvious and most urgent question of the day . . . is this Labour question, yet the Liberal constituencies flinch from entertaining it! It is the Ministerial, the Protectionist, the Tory candidates, that allude to it in their electoral addresses, with a desire to facilitate the advance toward a solution. Liberal candidates prune their talk of Reform to a 'moderate' measure, which shall not alarm the middle class with fear of being swamped . . . Political impotency is the retribution for that result of utilitarian philosophy.[27]

In the provinces, Chartists made the import of these arguments palpably evident to Liberal candidates. Paired with a Tory, Ernest Jones stood for Halifax. Here he was supported by the West Riding Chartist Executive's reminder to its 'Brother Chartists' that 'the example of France fully teaches us that working men alone are capable of representing labour'. Defining labour relations under free competition as 'a deliberate cheat on the part of the employer', Jones handily won an unofficial show of hands from an audience of 20,000, although he lost badly in the official poll of a thousand-odd electors

25 *Stockport Advertiser*, 24 October 1851, p. 4.
26 *Liverpool Mercury*, 21 October 1851, p. 836; *Stockport Advertiser*, 24 October 1851, p. 4. The limits of tory radicalism as a political strategy (and as a historiographical category) are detailed by Cecil Driver, *Tory Radical: The Life of Richard Oastler* (New York, 1946), and Stewart Angas Weaver, *John Fielden and the Politics of Popular Radicalism 1832–1847* (Oxford, 1987).
27 *Leader*, 3 April 1852, p. 322.

on the following day.[28] In Oldham, the same pattern of radical allegiance was evident. The joint manifesto of Tories and working-class radicals supported a shorter, ten-hour working day and pledged the candidates 'to protect the labouring classes against the machinations of a false political economy'.[29]

The ensuing Tory victory, although shortlived, illustrated at the national level the consequences of radical leaders' divisions over economic policy. G.J. Holyoake's analysis was perceptive. Denigrating the Liberals' determination to establish economic opportunity only by dismantling economic protection, Holyoake emphasized the distinction between positive and negative conceptions of liberty. 'A country which has long consented to be hoodwinked by Whig negatives is naturally at the mercy of any more positive party that will boldly relieve it or boldly deceive it', he suggested. 'Such a party have now attained to power.'[30] Middle-class radicals were fully alive to this division. 'We the so called Manchester party have a sickening fate before us in the House', Cobden confided to Bright in October:

> Hated by the old Tories, dreaded by the Whigs, suspected by the Peelites, we have no hopes from any existing party, & in any attempt, if we should be foolish enough to make it, to set up for ourselves, we should become the objects of the envy hatred & malice of the kid-glove democrats, the unscientific radicals of the Finsbury school, & everybody else, with the exception of 25 earnest Free traders and financial reformers.[31]

The formation of the Aberdeen coalition – a government described by Cobden as 'a fair representation of the state of public opinion ... on agreement upon free trade, and [with] no decided views upon any other question' – brought some relief in 1853, but could not dispel the gloom that surrounded liberals on the eve of the Crimean War.[32] For the burden of radical ideology and activity in the early fifties had served to underscore, not obliterate, the middle-class reaction in 1848.

Boasting substantial financial resources, commanding – thanks to

[28] Tiller, 'Late Chartism', pp. 321–6. Jones polled 38 votes, the Liberal candidates 596 and 573, the Tory 521.
[29] Cited by Foster, *Class Struggle and the Industrial Revolution*, p. 210.
[30] *Leader*, 10 July 1852, p. 661.
[31] Cobden to Bright, BL, Cobden Papers, Add. MS 43,649, fols. 247–48.
[32] Cobden to Sir Joshua Walmsley, WSRO, Cobden Papers, Add. MS 37,108, fol. 8. Chartists, clearly, did not constitute a part of public opinion.

the Anti-Corn Law campaign – allegiance from the wider middle class, and represented in Parliament by a small but vociferous cadre of committed MPs, adherents of the Manchester School were by far the most prominent and influential bourgeois radicals to pursue reform activities in the early fifties. But their political liberalism represented only one of many disparate efforts by middle-class reformers to wean workers from Chartism by rebuilding their radicalism upon the twin principles of patriotism and political economy. At the opposite end of the middle-class radical spectrum from the Manchester School and yet ultimately compatible with it, the Christian Socialists of 1848–54 demonstrate at once the variety of middle-class reform culture and its fundamental unity. Standing virtually alone among the bourgeois reformers, they sought to adapt the cooperative labour schemes of Louis Blanc – albeit in a truncated form – to English needs. The movement's leaders, more-over, made much of their distinctive radical genealogy. Oxbridge educated F.D. Maurice and – to a lesser extent – Charles Kingsley traced their philosophy not to Adam Smith but to a tradition of romantic conservatism distilled from the Greek classics by Coleridge and Southey. Even the group's more radical wing, led by J.M.F. Ludlow, Edward Vansittart Neale, and Thomas Hughes, was avow-edly hostile to the perceived hegemony of Manchester economics in English society.[33]

Despite these claims to distinction, the Christian Socialists' patriotic convictions brought their movement within the intellectual ambit of the English radical tradition. Maurice's treatise on *The Kingdom of Christ* (1838) had denounced Catholicism as an un-patriotic religion, upholding nationality as an integral component of the creator's divine scheme for man.[34] Ten years later, in the immediate aftermath of the June Days, the Christian Socialists' *Politics for the People* urged restive Chartists to love and obey the English law 'for this single reason – that it is *ours*. It is our birthright.'[35] In Kingsley's writings, this message expanded to embrace the revolutionary patriots of the seventeenth century,

---

[33] Philip N. Backstrom, 'The Practical Side of Christian Socialism in Victorian England', *Victorian Studies*, vol. 6 (June 1963), pp. 304–24, and Edward Norman, *The Victorian Christian Socialists* (Cambridge, 1987), pp. 14–97, trace the group's intellectual ancestry.

[34] R.J. Smith, *The Gothic Bequest: Medieval Institutions in British Thought, 1688–1863* (Cambridge, 1987), pp. 181–2, develops this argument.

[35] *Politics for the People*, no. 17, extra supplement for July 1848, p. 275.

whose Protestant conviction the Anglican clergyman was careful to underscore. 'Who delivered England from the Pope?', he asked the readers of *Alton Locke* rhetorically in 1850. England's early Protestant martyrs, with their patriotic synthesis of radical religion and reform, he concluded in response to his own question, represented only 'a few great and striking manifestations of an influence which has been ... at work for ages ... and which is now on the eve of Christianising democracy, as it did Medieval Feudalism, Tudor Nationalism, Whig Constitutionalism'.[36]

Although it meshed neatly with received conceptions of the historic birthrights of the English nation, the Christian Socialists' patriotic message proved problematic. In Kingsley's fiction, Chartist dissidents fell rapidly under the sway of Christian nationalist sentiment, but in the producers' cooperatives established by the Christian Socialists, working-class patriotism was often a divisive force. Subsidized and overseen by Anglican gentlemen, the eight original associations of boot and shoemakers, tailors, printers, bakers, and builders sought 'to beat down & moralise competition by competition itself'.[37] Nationality was as central to these ventures as it was to the historical vision of their middle-class patrons. 'For Socialism', as Ludlow explained to the readers of the *Christian Socialist* in 1851, 'as it starts from the Person, and seeks to give him full development according to his individual needs and faculties, so it recognises the Nation, and strives to give it that organic fullness of life whereby alone it shall play its individual part in the great Brotherhood of nations.'[38]

Sympathy for the Hungarian exile Louis Kossuth, in this view, was a logical extension of Christian Socialism, for Kossuth was a patriot of the same complexion as the 'patriots we had in England two centuries ago' – before the advent of 'political economists'.[39] But when the members of the Pimlico Working Builders' Association themselves sought to link Christian Socialism and patriotic sentiment with an address to Kossuth, their middle-class leaders responded with outrage. Rehearsing received bourgeois notions of the separate spheres constituted by social and political life, they reminded the builders sharply that participation in a Christian

[36] Kingsley, *Alton Locke*, chap. 40.
[37] J.M.F. Ludlow, MS Autobiography, Cambridge University Library, Ludlow Correspondence and Papers, Add. MS 7348, p. 426. Charles E. Raven, *Christian Socialism 1848–1854* (London, 1920), pp. 194–214, provides background on the various cooperative associations.
[38] *Christian Socialist*, 18 October 1851, p. 242.   [39] *Ibid.*, p. 241.

Socialist association specifically prohibited the cooperative's connection with political agitation.[40] The builders' response was disingenuous, and drew renewed criticism from their patrons. Proclaiming that their address 'was a social, and not a political one', the Pimlico workers warned that future developments could easily force them to become 'instruments or agents of a political agitation'.[41]

Central to the Christian Socialists' antipathy for radical political agitation was a rejection of state intervention in labour relations that ultimately served to unite them with wider middle-class conceptions of political economy. For despite their professed distaste for the doctrines of the Manchester School and their bold adoption of 'socialism', the Christian Socialists offered producers' associations as a charitable palliative to the existing economic framework, not as a political alternative to economic liberalism itself. 'The State . . . is by nature and law Conservative of individual rights, individual possessions', Maurice cautioned Ludlow in 1849. 'To uphold them it may be compelled (it must be) to recognise another principle than that of individual rights and property; but only by accident; only by going out of its own sphere, as it so rightly did in the case of the factory children.'[42] Adult workers, in sharp contrast, were to elevate themselves by restraining their passions. Ludlow's *Labour and the Poor* (1850) urged workers to eschew reliance upon 'the mere husks and shells' of 'this or that political or social system'. Vansittart Neale's homily to the striking Amalgamated Society of Engineers in 1852 similarly paid lip service to 'the social theories which have so long and so earnestly been discussed in France' only to insist that it lay within the workers' own powers to rise above subjection to capital.[43] Louis Blanc, much beloved of the late Chartist leadership, spoke at one early Christian Socialist meeting, but even Ludlow – the most ardent Francophile in the group – 'never "grew intimate" with him, as he seemed to me stuck up, if not in himself yet in a certain narrow circle of ideas which had become himself'.[44]

[40] *Ibid.*, 22 November 1851, pp. 331–2.   [41] *Ibid.*, 20 December 1851, p. 399.
[42] Maurice to Ludlow, 25 August 1849, in Frederick Maurice (ed.), *The Life of Frederick Denison Maurice: Chiefly Told in His Own Letters*, 2 vols. (London, 1884), vol. II, p. 8.
[43] John Malcolm Forbes Ludlow, *Labour and the Poor*, 2nd edn (London, 1852), p. 24; Edward Vansittart Neale, *May I Not Do What I Will with My Own?: Considerations on the Present Contest between the Operative Engineers and Their Employers* (London, 1852), esp. pp. 44–7.
[44] Raven, *Christian Socialism*, p. 140 fn. 2; Ludlow, MS Autobiography, Cambridge University Library, Ludlow Correspondence and Papers, chap. 23.

Designed to circumvent, not disprove, the economic laws preached by Cobden and his school, the tenets of Christian Socialism appealed even to staunch adherents of economic laissez-faire. Blanc's insistence 'that "competition" invariably leads to the degradation and wretchedness of the working classes', rendered French socialism anathema to the Manchester manufacturer Salis Schwabe. But the Christian Socialists, as he patiently explained to a female correspondent, were not:

> I willingly admit that it is a laudable effort on the part of Mr Maurice and of other benevolent persons to get up such a scheme on behalf of such tailors and needlewomen as are distressed by the competition that their large numbers create . . . On a limited scale, such an attempt is likely to succeed, since it is started, and will be supported by the hand of charity. But when it is proposed that the Association principle is to be carried out in every branch of trade, and that Competition is to be put an end to, I must say that, in my opinion, nothing more absurd could have been conceived.[45]

Christian Socialist leaders were themselves eager to cultivate liberal support, and swift to argue that the hand of charity would only complement the invisible hand of market economics. When the *Edinburgh Review* attacked the movement for reviling political economy, Kingsley rebutted the charge vociferously, ascribing opposition to economic laws instead to 'working men, whose prejudice against political economists is extremely strong'.[46]

Late Chartist responses to Christian Socialism ranged from guarded enthusiasm to overt hostility. Ernest Jones launched an extended campaign against the movement upon his release from prison, deriding its failure to recognize 'the *connecting link* between POLITICAL POWER AND SOCIAL REFORM'.[47] Julian Harney contracted with the Working Printers' Association to produce the *Red Republican* in 1850, but found to his fury that 'the gentlemen who had advanced the capital' could not countenance the cooperative's publication of a paper 'so ultra in principle'.[48] Public meetings propelled this conflict beyond the control of the Christian Socialist leadership. When Vansittart Neale chaired an open meeting to promote the formation of voluntary cooperative associations, he

[45] Salis Schwabe to Mrs Rich, 14 March 1850, in Julia Salis Schwabe (ed.), *Reminiscences of Richard Cobden* (London, 1895), pp. 89–90.
[46] *Leader*, 1 February 1851, p. 100.   [47] *Northern Star*, 10 August 1850.
[48] *Red Republican*, 10 August 1850, p. 58.

met the same fate at the hands of the Chartists as did the Parliamentary and Financial Reform Association. Disputing the liberal voluntarism of the official speakers, working men interrupted the proceedings to insist that 'as society is the result of legislative enactments, no permanent remedy can be appointed until a thorough change has been effected in our representative system'.[49]

The behaviour of those working-class radicals who did embrace Christian Socialism was equally revealing. Both the Chartist poet Gerald Massey and the fustian cutter Patrick Lloyd Jones joined Christian Socialist societies, lending credence to middle-class assertions that voluntary associations would disarm both political radicalism and popular opposition to liberal political economy. A closer analysis reveals significant fissures in this interpretation, for Massey's political conduct testified more to his facility with the rules that governed social and political role playing than to his conversion to the laws of supply and demand. At Vansittart Neale's public meeting, Massey extolled the 'sublime old truism that "God helps those who help themselves" ', but in Harney's *Red Rupublican* he continued to expound a Chartist vision which broke from liberal norms in celebrating the achievements of the June Days. Departing from the classical precepts that inspired Maurice, Massey celebrated 'not the Democracy of ancient Athens, with its hereditary helotage for the masses ... but the Democracy of Socialism ... which shall eternalize the doctrine of Christ's equality' and thus alleviate social problems. 'This is the Democracy which is coming', he proclaimed, 'it burst forth in June, 1848, that was the real revolution, not the revolution in February.'[50] Forced by the leaders of the movement to choose between Christian Socialism and Chartism, Massey chose subterfuge. When prohibited by his employers from contributing to Harney's journal, he simply adopted a series of pseudonyms and continued his polemical campaigns.[51]

These tensions between the Christian Socialist workers and their patrons helped to precipitate the collapse of the producers' cooperatives in 1854. Ludlow's recognition of the problem, and its potential

[49] *Leader*, 3 August 1850, p. 442.
[50] *Red Republican*, 22 June 1850, p. 6.
[51] 'The Reminiscences of Robert Crowe: The Octogenarian Tailor', in *Chartist Biographies and Autobiographies* (London, 1986), p. 14. These tactics fit with the pattern of working-class manipulation of 'respectability' detailed by Bailey, 'Will the Real Bill Banks Please Stand Up', discussed above, p. 4.

solution, was perceptive, but unavailing. As he wrote to Maurice already in 1852:

> my quarrel with you about Democracy is certainly this at bottom, that you will . . . look at it thro' Greek or Roman, & not thro' a Xn [Christian] medium, & borrow a pair of spectacles 'from Aristophanes . . . instead of using your own English eyes as a man of the 19th century . . . the experience of the past two years has brought me round to the value of the principle of democracy, for the safe practice of that art of partnership which we call Socialism. I am sure all our friends . . . are very good Socialists, insofar as they feel that they have a common interest with others, & seek to promote that common interest as far as they can. But they do it, and I have done it, – each one after his own fashion . . . so that if I were in France again, I am afraid I should be much more of a . . . republican than before, & 'go the entire animal' for 'la république démocratique et sociale'.[52]

Always repelled by the commercial aspect of the Working Men's Associations, Maurice ultimately responded to the challenge posed in Ludlow's letter by abandoning cooperative production for working-class education, while Ludlow, Vansittart Neale, and Hughes were active in the secular cooperative movement and in labour relations, but remained aloof from working-class politics until the 1860s.[53] By 1854, the group had severed its formal affiliation with the cooperative associations, and with it a potential channel for *démoc-soc* reform under the aegis of the middle class. Despite their conspicuous lack of success in Christianizing the heathen masses, Anglican social workers continued to pursue mission work among the poor throughout the century, but such work – entrusted largely to women – rested securely in the social sphere that the bourgeois imagination had separated from the intractable realm of politics.[54]

Embraced by otherwise antagonistic middle-class reformers, the line of argument articulated by Christian Socialists and Manchester liberals alike inverted the reasoning employed by the late Chartist leadership. Increasingly, Chartists urged that the state must intervene to improve the quality of life of its citizens; increasingly,

[52] J.M.F. Ludlow to F.D. Maurice, 13 September 1852, Cambridge University Library, Ludlow Correspondence and Papers, 7348/17, fol. 3.
[53] Raven, *Christian Socialism*, pp. 302–16.
[54] See esp. Martha Vicinus, *Independent Women: Work and Community for Single Women, 1850–1920* (Chicago, 1985), pp. 211–46.

middle-class radicals argued that only a prior reformation of individuals by individuals would permit a reform of the institutions of the state. If the theories of history and economics that informed this middle-class individualism were often varied and sophisticated, the form that they assumed in encounters with the working class was not. In *Eliza Cook's Journal*, broadly representative of the vast hortatory literature directed at labour in this period, the whig view of history and economics was overwhelmingly stark. 'Notwithstanding the reports of distress among the working classes ... and the intense competition to which all must submit who depend upon their labour for their subsistence – the weak going to the wall, while the strong and skillful keep the crown of the highway', Cook proclaimed cheerily in 1850, 'there is yet sufficient reason to believe that the condition of working classes generally does not deteriorate, but is gradually and steadily improving'.[55] This philosophy, popularized in the tracts of Samuel Smiles, caricatured in the works of Charles Dickens, and reluctantly embraced in the novels of Elizabeth Gaskell, swelled the ranks of local voluntary societies, but did little to advance the reform aims of middle-class radicals. Like the Chartists with whom they contended for the allegiance of labour, many committed bourgeois radicals turned from this disheartening prospect to find consolation in a distinctive radical subculture that drew sustenance from international patriotism.

BOURGEOIS RADICAL CULTURE AND THE CONTINENTAL EMIGRES

Just as participants in the late Chartist movement created a rich network of institutions, rituals, and mutual assistance to sustain their aspirations, middle-class radicals constructed a reticulation of venues, organizations, patronage, and alliances that nurtured their nationalist and internationalist aspirations in the decade after 1848. Providing points of intersection between middle- and working-class radical culture, these structures also served to delimit contact between the classes. For although some radical efforts linked bourgeois reformers to workers and their avowed leaders, the characteristic social activities of middle-class radicals diverged sharply from the norms of working-class culture. While late Char-

---

[55] *Eliza Cook's Journal*, 22 June 1850, pp. 113–15.

tism drew its social and cultural attributes from newspaper networks, radical institutes, friendly societies, and the public platform, middle-class radical culture centred on family life, private houses, Nonconformist chapels, and liberal salons.

Houses and the home lay at the heart of bourgeois radical culture, just as they constituted the centre of social life within the wider middle class. Conceived as both a physical and symbolic barrier against the disruptive forces of poverty and passion, disease and death, private houses also embodied a separate social sphere, distinct from middle-class endeavour in politics and economics.[56] Although bourgeois radicals upheld the ideology of separate social and political spheres vigorously in their writings and oratory, the practice of mixing politics and social life through nationalist activity was pervasive in middle-class reform circles. In Newcastle, Joseph Cowen's Stella House was a centre of radical activity, providing respite and hospitality for a variety of itinerant nationalist leaders. The cluster of men and women connected with the solicitor W.H. Ashurst, whose house at Muswell Hill had welcomed patriots such as Mazzini since 1844, formed one node of this radical network in London; John Chapman's evening parties, which brought nationalist émigrés into contact with the luminaries of the *Westminster Review*, formed another.[57] P.A. Taylor's home in London, Aubrey House, emerged under his wife Mentia's supervision as a locus of support for Italian unity in the sixties, its walls appropriately graced with a portrait of Cromwell refusing the crown.[58] At the pinnacle of this nationalist salon culture, Sarah Milner-Gibson, as befitted the wife of a prominent Manchester MP, was 'a staunch Liberal, her house a centre and place of rendezvous for Liberals, a firm friend of Mazzini and Italian freedom'.[59]

Women, indeed, who were rarely conspicuous in working-class radical circles in this period, figured prominently in the social life of middle-class radical culture. Educated, affluent, and leisured, they

---

[56] Hall and Davidoff, *Family Fortunes*, pp. 357–96, explore these themes in greater depth.
[57] For the Muswell Hill connection, see Giuseppe Mazzini, *Mazzini's Letters to an English Family: 1844–1872*, ed. E.F. Richards, 3 vols. (London, 1920–2), esp. vol. I, pp. 20–6; for Chapman's circle, see Gordon S. Haight, *George Eliot: A Biography* (Oxford, 1968), pp. 98–100.
[58] Moncure Daniel Conway, *Autobiography: Memoirs and Experiences*, 2 vols. (Boston, 1904), vol. II, pp. 57–69.
[59] Linton, *Threescore and Ten Years*, p. 169.

embraced the cause of continental nationalism with enthusiasm, and one suspects relief. The spirituality of Mazzini's creed, which he referred to as his 'apostolate', appealed particularly to women dissatisfied with Protestant conventions. Emilie Ashurst, whose sister Caroline Stansfeld had named her only son after Mazzini, responded 'I am a Mazzinian' when asked to name her religion. Mrs Hamilton King, on a spiritual quest that eventually led her from the Anglican fold to Catholicism, found solace in the fifties and sixties in Mazzinian nationalism.[60] More concretely, support for nationalist agitations brought middle-class women opportunities for activity and employment denied them in more conventional circles. Unable to secure admission to medical training in England because of her sex, Jessie Meriton White found her vocation (and her future husband) serving in Italy as a nurse for Garibaldi's troops.[61]

If English radical women benefited from the opportunities provided by nationalist agitations, exiled continental leaders benefited substantially from the educational and financial resources commanded by middle-class radical men. Enjoying an amphibious existence at the interface of working- and middle-class radical culture, émigré patriots succeeded in tapping both Chartist and liberal patronage networks in the decade after 1848. George Dawson helped to advise Louis Kossuth on his children's religious instruction, and Francis Newman supervised the education of Kossuth's son at the University of London.[62] Kossuth recommended a fellow Hungarian exile to Cobden as 'worthy of any patronage' that he might bestow in 1852; the following year saw Cobden negotiate generous credit for Kossuth with his own banker.[63]

Themselves men of bourgeois (or aristocratic) tastes and education, the French republican and socialist leaders of the continental emigration participated in this radical milieu along with émigré

---

[60] Mrs Hamilton King, *Letters and Recollections of Mazzini* (London, 1912), pp. 113, 139.

[61] Elizabeth Adams Daniels, *Jessie White Mario: Risorgimento Revolutionary* (Athens, Ohio, 1972), pp. 36, 41, 103. For prominent feminists influenced by Garibaldi's cause, see *Josephine E. Butler: An Autobiographical Memoir*, ed. G.W. and L.A. Johnson (London, 1928), pp. 26, 28, and Millicent Garrett Fawcett, *What I Remember* (London, 1924), p. 42.

[62] Kossuth to Dawson, 16 August [1850s], Birmingham Reference Library, Dawson Collection, vol. 9, fol. 116; Newman to Kossuth, 13 November 1863, University College, London, Francis Newman Papers, MS Add. 170, item 66.

[63] Kossuth to Cobden, 23 June 1852 and 23 July 1853, WSRO, Cobden Papers, vol. 20, fols. 299, 301.

national leaders, but the easy interchange between nationalist and socialist sympathy that obtained in Chartist circles was absent from middle-class radical culture. Herzen attended Sarah Milner-Gibson's soirées, and Ledru-Rollin's mementos of his exile in England included both Julian Harney's picture and an autographed photograph of Thackeray.[64] But the catholicity of even Milner-Gibson's purely social functions was suspect to liberal purists. John Bright described a party at her home in 1851 as 'a curious medley' when it included both Mazzini and Louis Blanc as guests.[65] Goldwin Smith, who reported seeing 'a good deal' of Blanc in society in this period, hastened to underline his preference for the nationalist émigrés. 'I took to the Italian exiles, Mazzini, Saffi, and Arrivabene, whose cause, that of Italian independence, was perfectly pure', he recalled. 'To Mazzini, whose acquaintance I formed at the house of Sir James Stansfeld, I took very much.'[66] When faced with a choice between associating with nationalist or *démoc-soc* émigré politicians, English middle-class radicals did not hesitate. 'Poor L.B.', Stansfeld wrote of Blanc in 1860, '17 years ago he and M[azzini] had a quarrel ... and ... (though still and always friendly when we chance to meet in society), we had at that time to choose between two friendships, as far as intimacy was concerned, and ... he has not entered any house of ours ... since.'[67]

Guided by these discriminating tastes, middle-class radical culture stood essentially apart from the social life of Chartist politics in the aftermath of 1848. Herzen's social gatherings incorporated W.J. Linton, the Polish republicans, and the French *démoc-socs*, but largely excluded middle-class English radicals.[68] Taylor and Stansfeld attended the funerals of the Polish exiles Albert Darasz and Stanislaus Worcell,[69] but like other bourgeois internationalists they

---

[64] Monica Partridge, 'Alexandr Gertsen i ego angliiskie sviazi' ['Alexander Herzen and His English Ties'], in V.P. Volzin (ed.), *Problemi izucheniia Gertsena [Problems in the Study of Herzen]* (Moscow, 1963), pp. 348–69; Bibliothèque Historique de la Ville de Paris, Papiers Ledru-Rollin, Manuscrits divers, vol. 14, items 461, 465.
[65] *The Diaries of John Bright*, ed. R.A.J. Walling (New York, 1931), p. 126.
[66] Smith, *Reminiscences*, p. 155.
[67] James Stansfeld to G.J. Holyoake, 30 June 1860, MCU, Holyoake Collection, item 1181. Stansfeld misdated the altercation between the two exiles, which is discussed below, pp. 170–1.
[68] For Herzen's social circle, see Malwida von Meysenbug, *Memoiren einer Idealistin*, 2 vols. (Stuttgart, 1922), vol. I, pp. 386–403, and N.A. Tuchkova-Ogareva, *Vospominaniia [Reminiscences]*, ed. V.A. Putintseva (Leningrad, 1929), pp. 102, 109.
[69] *Reasoner*, 20 October 1852, p. 295; *ibid.*, 22 February 1857, p. 30; Adams, *Memoirs of a Social Atom*, vol. II, p. 325.

were conspicuously absent from the great body of public ceremony that surrounded Chartist social and political life, most notably the annual celebrations of the French revolution of 1848. Nor could even those few Chartist leaders who gained admittance to the private dwellings of middle-class radicals hope to respond with invitations to their own homes. G.J. Holyoake was welcomed by the Ashursts, the Stansfelds, and the Taylors, but the toll of poverty and radical activity upon his own family life prohibited reciprocal relations. 'My home has long been broken up', he informed John Stuart Mill in 1871. 'My wife wore herself out, as the best women do, by devotion to duties to her family in long years of small means, and is now dying, like Gerald Massey's wife, of Drink Madness.'[70]

Clubs and institutes established by middle-class reformers provided a more accommodating environment for radical interaction between the classes. Although radical men of property largely avoided events at venues such as the Eclectic Institute and the Shoe Lane Tavern, they did not inevitably exclude working-class radicals from their own venues of reform. Holyoake, Linton, and other self-improving artisans were welcome at the Whittington Club in London, which occupied the old Crown and Anchor Tavern, earlier the location of a famous Hampden Club.[71] But the Unitarians' South Place Chapel enjoyed pride of place among middle-class radical institutes in London. Descended from an eighteenth-century society of Philadelphians, South Place flourished under the leadership of W.J. Fox from 1819 to 1852. Enjoying the patronage of affluent liberal Unitarians such as P.A. Taylor, who served as its treasurer in the 1850s, South Place was also frequented by radical artisans, attracted to the chapel by its members' devotion to advanced politics and the freedom of continental nations.[72]

Like the Chartists, middle-class radicals tapped the resources of their social networks and their associations to raise funds for the exiles of 1848. Declining on the whole to treat with the French

[70] Holyoake to Mill, 25 March 1871, BLPES, John Stuart Mill–Harriet Taylor Collection, vol. 2, item 170.
[71] Holyoake, *Sixty Years of an Agitator's Life*, vol. I, pp. 185, 238; Bamford, *Passages in the Life of a Radical*, vol. I, p. 15. It had also housed the People's International League in 1847. See Linton, *Threescore and Ten Years*, pp. 99–100.
[72] *A Short History of South Place Ethical Society and an Urgent Appeal* (London, 1927), pp. 5–6; South Place Ethical Society, London, Minute Book of South Place Chapel, 25 January 1852–28 March 1862, vol. 9; Francis Soutter, *Recollections of a Labour Pioneer* (London, 1923), p. 23.

republicans and socialists, they focused their efforts on the nationalists, whose struggle for civil and religious liberties appeared to replicate the seventeenth-century English experience. In Liverpool, a committed cohort of supporters sought to obtain employment for the Polish troops who had fought for Kossuth in Hungary. 'Since the political struggles of France, Italy, and more especially those of *Hungary* and *Poland*, the word Patriotism has been employed ... to express ... a desire for the emancipation of the whole human race from the thraldom of despotism, *whether civil or religious*', their *Refugee Circular* proclaimed in 1851.[73] Ignoring the issue of economic exploitation, this selective, charitable approach to international patriotism exercised a wide appeal among the bourgeoisie. Eliza Cook contributed to a fund for wounded Italian patriots in 1849, and the Italian Refugee Committee of that year garnered contributions from the Manchester School liberals Thomas Milner-Gibson, Joseph Hume, and Richard Cobden as well as South Place's W.J. Fox.[74]

In Newcastle, the rhetoric of middle-class sympathizers demonstrated the compatibility of Christian charity, liberal economic apologetic, international brotherhood, and English radical traditions. Here the arrival in 1851 of twelve Polish soldiers from the Hungarian campaign thrust the young industrialist Joseph Cowen into the patriotic arena. Cowen engaged the Christian Socialist Working Tailors' Association to provide clothes for the refugees, and had loaned Newcastle's Polish Hungarian Relief Committee over £40 by June 1852.[75] But he and his associates were quick to defend the émigré Poles from the charges of sloth and intemperance perpetually levelled against English workers by middle-class reformers, using the refugees instead to provide an object lesson in individual political economy:

It has been falsely urged that they would rather remain in a state of pauperism, than by manly industry and self-reliance support themselves. To this unfounded and malicious statement we give the most unequivocal and unqualified contradiction. The only complaint of the men is, that they are the forced recipients of

---

[73] *Refugee Circular*, 26 April 1851, T&WAD, Cowen Collection, 634/A 26, pp. 6–7.
[74] *Jerrold's Weekly News*, 2 June 1849, p. 703; Emilia Morelli, *L'Inghilterra di Mazzini* (Rome, 1965), p. 101.
[75] Receipt from the Working Tailors to the Polish–Hungarian Refugee Committee, and Polish–Hungarian Committee Cash Book, T&WAD, Cowen Collection, 634/A120 and 634/A42.

charity; and they are willing to accept any kind of labour by which they can earn a livelihood. We have upwards of eighty testimonials from different parties in Liverpool, Manchester, Sheffield, Padham, Burnley, Leicester, Paisley, and other places where the refugees have been employed, and they attest that the men whom they have with them (the companions of those in Newcastle) are steady, sober, industrious, and highly intelligent and virtuous.

An appeal to English national sentiment nicely rounded out this paean to industry and self-reliance. 'Remember, these men were not engaged in a servile war – in a war of aggression', Cowen urged his townsmen. 'They were merely doing for their country what our own Cromwell and his colleagues did for England.'[76]

Couched in such patriotic terms, appeals for refugee aid could link Chartists with middle-class radical activists. In Halifax, the arrival of a contingent of Polish–Hungarian soldiers led the Chartist Benjamin Wilson to seek aid from Judge Stansfeld, whose son James was already active in the Hungarian cause in London.[77] In 1852, Thomas Cooper, G.J. Holyoake, W. J. Linton, and James Watson joined with Joseph Cowen, George Dawson, W.H. Ashurst, Edward Miall, James Stansfeld, and other middle-class radicals to launch a Shilling Subscription for European Freedom. This project raised funds for Kossuth and Mazzini to use in their nationalist struggles, rallying both anti-Catholic and anti-pacifist sentiment in the name of European democracy, but hesitating to include France among the radical nations. Its directors, determined to elicit funds from all classes, wisely abstained from projecting partisan interpretations of liberty on to the continental cause. The subscription, they insisted, was not limited to 'any particular form of freedom which we may think best fitted for such a time or place; but for such freedom as the Nations themselves may choose'.[78] Guided by these elastic principles, the effort succeeded in gathering 2,400 shilling subscriptions by April 1853. Contributors included workmen at the Bowling Dye Works in Bradford, a few journeyman comb-makers in Sheffield, and six members of the Medley family of London – which boasted four women and the young Alfred Kossuth Medley.[79]

[76] Printed Broadsheet signed by Cowen for the Committee, 19 May 1851, T&WAD, Cowen Collection, 634/A41.
[77] Wilson, 'Autobiography', in Vincent (ed.), *Testaments of Radicalism*, pp. 213–14.
[78] *Reasoner*, 25 February 1852, pp. 230–1; 10 November 1852, pp. 346–7.
[79] *Ibid.*, 26 April 1853, p. 270; 15 September 1852, p. 214; 26 April 1853, p. 270.

By far the most popular beneficiary of these radical efforts was
Giuseppe Mazzini. Mazzini's nationalist ideology spoke powerfully
to dominant middle-class concerns, denouncing at one and the same
time the conflictual social relations that contemporaries perceived to
mark their age and the economic alternatives proposed by radical
socialists. A philosophy that emphasized the primacy of duties over
rights, Mazzinian nationalism nonetheless appealed to radical artisans by advancing the nation's collective claims alongside (and at
times above) those of the individual, who figured in Mazzini's
thinking less as an autonomous agent than as a component of the
Commonwealth.[80] The Friends of Italy, established by Mazzini and
his English allies in May 1851, lent social and institutional form to
these patriotic sentiments. A national organization with representatives in Halifax, Leeds, Norwich, Liverpool, Manchester, Birmingham, Derby, Coventry, Exeter, and London, the Friends of Italy
sought to advance the cause of civil and religious liberty by
broadcasting Mazzinian propaganda in liberal and radical circles.
The association spanned a broad sector of the progressive middle
class, but was especially successful in attracting proponents of free
trade and parliamentary reform, Dissenters, and the figures of
Victorian literary bohemia. Douglas Jerrold, G.H. Lewes, Leigh
Hunt, and Walter Savage Landor were members of the Society, as
were several reformers who had supported William Lovett's Peo-
ple's League in 1848. Among adherents, W.E. Forster, George
Dawson, Francis Newman, Edward Miall, John Epps, and Joseph
Cowen were Nonconformists or sceptics; William Shaen, James
Stansfeld, Samuel Courtauld, and P.A. Taylor were Unitarians.[81]
Financial contributions to the cause were substantial: most initial
subscriptions were in the range of £5, and the Society ultimately
contributed over £12,800 to Mazzini and Garibaldi.[82] Although
Chartists largely avoided the Society, Linton, Holyoake, and the

[80] For Mazzini's development of these themes, see his treatise *On the Duties of Man*,
in Emilie A. Venturi (ed.), *Joseph Mazzini: A Memoir* (London, 1875), pp.
259–402.
[81] Lists of members are found in T&WAD, Cowen Collection, 634/A53, and Morelli,
L'Inghilterra di Mazzini, pp. 113–14. Friends of Italy who had previously belonged
to Lovett's association include Miall, Epps, Shaen, and Stansfeld. See Birmingham
Reference Library, Lovett Collection, fol. 289.
[82] 'Friends of Italy', T&WAD, Cowen Collection, 634/A53; Norbert J. Gossman,
'British Aid to Polish, Italian, and Hungarian Exiles 1830–1870', *South Atlantic
Quarterly*, vol. 68 (Spring 1969), p. 241.

members of W.E. Adams's Cheltenham Republican Association all supported the Friends of Italy, which proclaimed in its prospectus its intention to deploy 'a truly national enthusiasm' to guard the Society against 'all that is sectarian or exclusive'.[83]

Launched in the midst of the Papal Aggression controversy of 1851, the Friends of Italy appealed to Dissenters and secularists alike by underlining Mazzini's spiritual and political opposition to the church in Rome. P.A. Taylor and other Dissenters naturally equated this international struggle against Catholicism, corruption, censorship, and political reaction with the national struggles of their seventeenth-century progenitors. Extolling freedom of speech as 'a great principle fought for by our forefathers, world-wide in interest, – a principle struggled for in this country for three centuries past . . . on the tented field', Taylor urged an audience at a Mechanics' Institute later in the decade to uphold 'the principle of progress against priestcraft . . . of Protestantism against Popery'.[84] These sentiments were widely shared by working-class radicals and offered an ideological link to the late Chartist movement. Ernest Jones responded to Papal Aggression by calling upon 'Democrats and Dissenters' to unite against the serried forces of Rome, 'thirsting for the blood of Garibaldi and Mazzini'.[85]

Like the Chartists, moreover, the most vocal Dissenters within the Friends of Italy recognized class conflict as a consequence of free trade and industrial expansion, and sought to use nationalism as an instrument of reconciliation. The Unitarians, who formed the backbone of the Society, came from a religious tradition wedded to liberal economics: as John Seed has argued of their eighteenth-century predecessors, 'the conviction that the state's involvement in social life should be minimal did not have to await the *Wealth of Nations* . . . to enter consciousness – laissez-faire was inscribed within the very "structure of feeling" of rational dissent'.[86] But nineteenth-century Unitarian reformers who experienced direct contact with the urban labouring poor had found the strictures of

[83] Morelli, *L'Inghilterra di Mazzini*, pp. 113–14; Adams, *Memoirs of a Social Atom*, vol. I, pp. 273–4; *Leader*, 26 July 1851, p. 697.
[84] Peter Alfred Taylor, *Burning a Theological Book: Libraries and Mechanics' Institutes: Should They Be Free, or Subject to Theological Censorship?* (London, 1858), p. 6.
[85] *Friend of the People*, 15 March 1851, p. 107.
[86] John Seed, 'Gentlemen Dissenters: The Social and Political Meaning of Rational Dissent in the 1770s and 1780s', *Historical Journal*, vol. 28 (June 1985), p. 316.

classical political economy increasingly difficult to apply, legitimate, and accept in the 1830s and 1840s.[87] Unitarian involvement in the Friends of Italy testifies both to their desire to locate an alternative formulation of social and economic relations, and their ultimate inability to do so.

George Dawson, whose spiritual path from his Congregationalist origins led him into increasing contact with the Unitarians, expressed these conflicting aspirations in his many public lectures. Fully committed to individual freedoms, he groped in 1850 for a force that would associate citizens without obliterating their distinct identities. 'I am not going to blaspheme individualism, because I count that to be the greatest achievement of modern times', he told an audience in 1850 before cautioning them to acknowledge that 'the cry of Europe now is that the overwrought individualism of modern times wants checking'. The binding affinities of the nation, in this view, would serve to overcome the atomization of citizens in liberal society. 'Thus a nation has, as it were, a life and being in but higher than, the individuals', Dawson concluded, 'it was a truer symbol, Britannia, seated with her spear and helmet, on the penny-piece, than to hold that a nation should be but a mere bundle of individuals'.[88]

Dawson participated vigorously in the social and political life of the Friends of Italy, developing these arguments further into a critique of liberal pacifism that cast aspersions on the Manchester School's obsession with peace and free trade – without, however, questioning liberal economic mechanisms themselves. At the second public *conversazione* of the Friends of Italy in 1852, Dawson 'longed for a re-action to ... some of those emotions which Manchester decided to be follies', for 'cosmopolitanism was a good thing; but to real cosmopolitanism nationalism was necessary'. Affirming the duty of all true English patriots to aid Italy in its armed struggle, Dawson 'utterly and heartily despised the sniffling non-intervention doctrines that were current'.[89] In a speech of the same year delivered

[87] *Idem*, 'Unitarianism, Political Economy and the Antinomies of Liberal Culture in Manchester, 1830–50', *Social History*, vol. 7 (January 1982), pp. 1–25. W.J. Linton astutely suggested that Mazzini's spirituality appealed to the Unitarians by its contrast to 'the cold dead formalism' of their creed. Linton, *European Republicans*, p. 340.
[88] 'Old Times and Old Ways', [1850], Birmingham Reference Library, Dawson Collection, vol. 11, fols. 520–5.
[89] 'Newspaper Clipping on Second *Conversazione*', Birmingham Reference Library, Dawson Collection, vol. 19, fol. 29.

to Birmingham's Flint Glass Makers' union, he linked these sentiments to the Protestant patriotism of Cromwell's age, an age in which 'the word Englishman' had struck terror in the hearts of continental despots and made the Pope 'look for the coming of the Avenging Angel'. Despite these rhetorical skirmishes with the Manchester School, Dawson's ultimate allegiance clearly lay with liberal economics. He ended his speech to the Flint Glass Makers by exhorting them to endorse only candidates 'favourable to Free Trade' in the impending election.[90]

Anti-Popery and concern for the impact of extreme individualism on social relations united Chartists and the Friends of Italy, but here as in the radical campaigns of other middle-class reformers distinct patterns of allegiance to economic ideologies drove middle- and working-class radicals increasingly apart as they sought to use partisan nationalist sentiments to unite disparate, class interpretations of the radical tradition. Like the Christian Socialists, Mazzini decried economic exploitation and endorsed voluntary cooperative schemes; like Christian Socialists and the liberals of the Manchester School, he rejected state intervention and French socialism as appropriate responses to the social and economic ills of his age. His speech at the first *conversazione* of the society played upon middle-class economic fears and underlined his fundamental commitment to liberal ideals:

> Work for all, fairly apportioned for all; idleness or starvation for none. This, I say, is the summed-up social creed of all those who, in the present age, love and know. To this creed we belong ... But beyond that we cannot go; we shall never go. The wild, absurd, immoral dream of communism – the abolition of property, that is, of individuality asserting itself in the material universe – the abolition of liberty by systems of social organization suddenly, forcibly, and universally applied – the suppression of capital ... the materialist notion that 'life is the seeking of physical welfare', the problem of the kitchen of humanity substituted for the problem of humanity ... are not and never shall be ours.[91]

Less prosaic in its manner of expression than the scientific diatribes of the Manchester economists, Mazzini's defence of liberal freedoms

---

[90] 'The Glassmakers' Presentation to Mr George Dawson', Birmingham Reference Library, Dawson Collection, vol. 19, fol. 31.
[91] Giuseppe Mazzini, *M. Mazzini's Lecture, Delivered at the First Conversazione of the Friends of Italy* (London, 1852), pp. 2, 9.

nonetheless smacked of Samuel Smiles – who was, appropriately, a Friend of Italy.

Couched in these terms, Mazzini's nationalist message provoked a series of rebuttals from Louis Blanc, which Mazzini in turn attacked repeatedly. Blanc's defence of French socialism was ingenious, adopting an English nationalist genealogy to legitimate the *démoc-soc* ideal. Allying French scepticism, which Mazzini had censured, with Protestantism, he underlined the international patriotism of the Jacobins by noting that they had placed a bust of Richard Price beside that of Rousseau, a bust of Sidney beside that of Mably, in their hall. He proceeded, predictably, to blast laissez-faire, uphold the workers of the June Days, endorse the economic role of 'the bond of interests – that is, the STATE', and link socialist economics to political liberties.[92] Mazzini, counselling English workers to 'combat not the bourgeoisie, but egotism, wherever you find it – under the blouse, or under the broad-cloth', was hard pressed to respond with concrete measures for the alleviation of economic distress. He retreated behind the defences of negative freedom, accusing the socialists of 'giving positive solutions to the problem of human life'.[93]

Confronted with this breach between their continental idols, Chartist leaders responded by defending Blanc and the French patriots. Harney, although at odds with Holyoake on Chartist strategy, offered the more moderate radical the columns of his *Star of Freedom* for a defence of the French *démoc-socs*.[94] Holyoake, friend and publisher of both Blanc and Mazzini, responded to the liberal nationalist challenge to his loyalties not by abandoning Blanc for Mazzini but by claiming Mazzini for the socialist camp:

> Louis Blanc has replied [to Mazzini] in a series of letters in the *Leader* – letters as eloquent and as brilliant as any he has produced . . . We dissent very much from Mr Mazzini's strictures on socialism . . . It is some imaginary system which he attacks . . .

---

[92] *Leader*, 21 February 1852, pp. 171–2; 14 February 1852, pp. 146–8; 28 February 1852, pp. 194–5.

[93] *Ibid.*, 27 March 1852, pp. 290–2; 10 April 1852, pp. 340–1.

[94] Harney to Holyoake, 30 September 1852, MCU, Holyoake Collection, item 526. W.J. Linton, no longer formally affiliated with Chartism, responded by attacking both French socialism and English laissez–faire and expanding the associational elements of Mazzini's creed. See *English Republic*, vol. II (1852–3), pp. 121–4, 279–99.

With theories of Industrialism as understood among us, and sought to be realised by our French neighbours, Mr Mazzini seems to us to agree. He has written himself on association and unity, in a manner which socialists generally would accept. Indeed, we would not know that Mr Mazzini was not a socialist, if he did not take the precaution of saying so.[95]

Marring middle-class relations with Holyoake's followers, Mazzini's individualist creed clearly dampened enthusiasm among working-class radicals for middle-class efforts to promote the Italian cause through the Shilling Subscription. James Stansfeld was baffled and irritated by this intransigence. 'What does it matter whether Mazzini does or does not understand socialism & is or is not just to socialists', he asked Holyoake in October, dismayed by the low level of contributions from Holyoake's allies. 'Do they wish to help freedom in chainbound Europe', he concluded. 'If they do, Mazzini is the man for that.'[96]

Established to unite middle- and working-class patriots behind the common cause of the nation, the Friends of Italy succeeded rather in exposing the basic ideological fissures of the English radical movement. As in the other radical efforts of these years, the distinction between market economics and economic intervention divided bourgeois reformers from Chartist internationalists, who wilfully conflated Italian nationalism with French socialism. But the activities of the Friends of Italy also revealed divisions within the middle class itself. For if bourgeois radicals were united in disclaiming domestic economic intervention by the English state, they were divided on the issue of intervention in foreign policy. In the decade after 1848, the enthusiasm with which many Dissenters endorsed English intervention abroad – a policy which united them with Chartists – served to distinguish them from the Manchester School. Already in 1850, Cobden sadly attributed Sarah Milner-Gibson's refusal to participate in a Peace Bazaar to her Mazzinian tendencies.[97] By 1852, the Friends of Italy had deepened this divide, and with it Cobden's antagonism to English radical sympathy for continental nationalism. 'As for the liberties of *Europe*', he confided to Henry Ashworth in October, 'if 150 millions of people on the

[95] *Reasoner*, 14 April 1852, p. 337.
[96] Stansfeld to Holyoake, 9 October 1852, MCU, Holyoake Collection, item 528.
[97] Cobden to Henry Richard, [9 December 1850], BL, Cobden Papers, Add. MS 43,657, fol. 67.

Continent could be saved from oppression by 40,000 English soldiers, they were not worth saving.'[98] Fully consistent with middle-class radicals' obsession with cheap government, this opposition to military intervention nonetheless provoked divisive opposition from within the liberal phalanx of middle-class radicalism in the course of the Crimean War.

POPULAR PROTEST, WARFARE, AND THE RULE OF LAW

If the formation of the Aberdeen coalition in 1852 acted to allay liberal fears for domestic free trade, the advent of the Crimean War served to illuminate the obstacles that continued to prohibit the creation of a united patriotic front in English radical politics. War in itself was a problematic consequence of nationalist fervour, as Cobden's growing antagonism to the Mazzinian cause had demonstrated early in the fifties. Ostensibly a contest with Russia over the protection of Christian shrines in the Ottoman empire, the Crimean War of 1854–6 brought Britain's government into a diplomatic alliance with Napoleonic France. The late Chartists initially greeted the hostilities as a force which would advance the cause of continental nationality by weakening Russian absolutism; as it progressed, the war came to figure as an emblem of aristocratic corruption when governmental incompetence delayed a swift British victory. The years that followed the outbreak of this struggle saw the activities of England's continental émigré community further complicate these radical responses, bringing new alliances into being under the unifying influence of the rule of law in 1855 and again in 1858. Allowing both middle- and working-class radicals to appear together on public platforms, the incidents of popular protest that marked these years left both the fundamental divide between Chartist and liberal economics and the antagonism within liberalism between militant and pacifist radicals essentially intact. But they did help to weaken the purchase of partisan patriotism in some radical circles, and thereby laid the groundwork for further collaboration between working- and middle-class radicals in the sixties.

Despite widespread hopes and expectations that the conduct of

---

[98] Cobden to Ashworth, 16 October 1852, BL, Cobden Papers, Add. MS 43,653, fols. 205–7.

war would unite disparate classes in an access of patriotism, class tensions and political differences escalated in the course of the Crimean campaign.[99] For Cobden, Bright, and the wider Manchester School, the war served both to deepen their suspicion of the political judgement of the masses and to dash their belief in the growing accessibility of the governing élite to Manchester principles. Aberdeen's coalition, although it included no members of Cobden and Bright's immediate circle, had drawn the Manchester School radicals to a position much closer to the inner corridors of power than they had hitherto imagined they could acquire in a state governed by the landed interest. Cobden and Bright now became – to their evident surprise and delight – frequent guests at aristocratic dinner parties; Joseph Sturge contrasted Aberdeen most favourably to Melbourne upon meeting the new premier as a member of a peace delegation in 1853.[100] The onset of war failed to dash this optimism entirely, for the prospect of a campaign waged by an aristocratic government for indeterminate ends appeared to promise new hope for radical action. J.B. Smith predicted in January 1854 that the impending war would soon bring decreased trade and increased taxation, and thereby breed new enthusiasm for parliamentary reform.[101]

Public response to the war effort dimmed these hopes in the ensuing months. Most disturbing was the failure of Manchester's own liberal community to rally in a body to the Manchester School's calls for peace. 'What brutal ignorance prevails in Manchester, even after all our labours', Bright wrote to George Wilson in December. 'We may ask with Milton's Sampson, "How we are to make *outward* free of *inward* slaves?"'[102] Liberals previously staunch in their adherence to the leaders of the Anti-Corn Law League now adduced patriotism to explain their antagonism to liberal pacifism. Mark Philips, writing to Wilson in January 1855 to decline an invitation to a liberal soirée, objected vehemently as a liberal proponent of the

[99] Olive Anderson, *A Liberal State at War: English Politics and Economics during the Crimean War* (London, 1967), pp. 101–28, analyses the central tensions of these years.
[100] Bright to Elizabeth Bright, 3 March 1853, University College, London, John Bright Papers, Ogden MS 65; Bright to George Wilson, 24 February 1853, MCRL, Wilson Papers, M20/1853; Sturge to Wilson, 28 February 1853, MCRL, Wilson Papers, M20/1853.
[101] Smith to Cobden, 10 January 1854, WSRO, Cobden Papers, vol. 4, fol. 2B.
[102] Bright to Wilson, 10 December 1854, MCRL, Wilson Papers, M20/1854.

war to 'what I consider the anti-national policy of the two Members for Manchester'.[103] J.B. Smith, travelling from Lancaster to Leamington, was pained to see his earlier predictions of heightened reform sentiment unrealized. Far from finding opposition to increased taxation and military expenditure, Smith perceived everywhere a 'nation ... prepared to make any sacrifice to preserve their liberties' against Russian despotism at home or abroad. 'John Bull and Mrs Jellaby are kindred spirits', he concluded sadly.[104] Cobden and Bright, spurned by many of their former allies, turned for solace to petulant denunciations of the government that had exposed to ridicule their claim to represent the public opinion of the nation. 'Our Govt. will have to eat dirt, & just now, the more dirt the better', Bright wrote to Smith in November.[105]

Chartist and artisanal radical responses to the war exacerbated this antagonism, for even working-class radicals eager to increase collaboration with middle-class liberals repudiated pacifism. W.J. Linton, convinced already in 1851 that 'non-intervention between states is the same as laissez-faire between individuals – the right of ruffianism', responded to the Crimean War with a compilation of 'War Cries' urging vigorous prosecution of the military campaign. 'Cromwell's Sword', sung to the tune of the Marseillaise, linked the war effort against Russia to the realization of Polish nationality.[106] Widely current in radical circles, this theme extended to less overtly political sectors of the working-class population as well. Street ballads offered jingoistic analyses of the war effort that linked English, Polish, and Hungarian national aspiration into a single ideological unit. 'John Bull and the Russians', sung to the tune of the 'King of the Cannibal Islands', was characteristic:

> The Russian's pride must be brought down, in
>   spite of his imperial crown,
> For England fears no tyrant's frown, her sons
>   are born to freedom.

[103] Philips to Wilson, 10 January 1855, MCRL, Wilson Papers, M20/1855.
[104] Smith to Bright, 9 October 1855, BL, John Bright Papers, Add. MS 43,388, fol. 142.
[105] Bright to Smith, 4 November 1855, MCRL, Smith Papers, MS 923.2.5.344, fol. 19.
[106] *English Republic*, vol. 1 (1851), p. 31; Linton, 'Prose and Works', vol. XV. Pacifism was essentially a middle-class movement in this period, a circumstance discussed in Eric W. Sager, 'The Social Origins of Victorian Pacifism', *Victorian Studies*, vol. 23 (Winter 1980), pp. 211–36.

He robbed poor Poland of her rights, though
    she sustained a hundred fights,
Now let him try his boasted might against our
    British cannon.
The Hungarians felt the tyrant's screw, when he
    pinched the aged nobles through,
And flogged the backs of women, too, but
    now . . . he'll pay the piper.[107]

In Newcastle Joseph Cowen, assisted by Julian Harney and James
Watson, demonstrated the ability of militant nationalism to unite
liberal and Chartist radicals. Active from September 1854 in efforts
to encourage 'a more vigorous and hearty prosecution of the war',
Cowen invoked 'the *national will*' in defence of his actions. The
Newcastle upon Tyne Foreign Affairs Committee, which Cowen,
Harney, and Watson established in November, sought to broadcast
the claims of the continental nationalities suppressed by Russia and
Austria while inciting domestic reform.[108] This radical association
tapped a broad spectrum of English oppositional ideologies, drawing elements of its appeal from the popular Russophobia cultivated
by the conservative agitator David Urquhart.[109] The committee
agreed with the Manchester School that the government's incompetent war effort was a clear mandate for radical reform, but
departed from liberal pieties both in calling for universal manhood
suffrage and in embracing, with increasing ardour, French republican alliances.[110]

The nexus of affiliations encompassed by the Foreign Affairs

[107] 'John Bull and the Russians', BODL, John Johnson Collection, Street Ballads,
Box 4, item 529.
[108] Circular on the War, 4 September 1854, T&WAD, Cowen Collection, 634/A230;
Minute Book of the Newcastle upon Tyne Foreign Affairs Committee, 28
February 1855, T&WAD, Cowen Collection, 634/A247.
[109] For Urquhart, whose opposition to democratic politics and to nationalist leaders
such as Mazzini and Kossuth – who he insisted were Russian spies – placed him
essentially outside the radical tradition discussed here, see Miles Taylor, 'The Old
Radicalism and the New: David Urquhart and the Politics of Opposition, 1832–
1867', in Eugenio F. Biagini and Alastair J. Reid (eds.), *Currents of Radicalism:
Popular Radicalism, Organised Labour and Party Politics in Britain, 1850–1914*
(Cambridge, 1991), pp. 23–43.
[110] Resolutions of the Newcastle Foreign Affairs Committee, 28 March 1855,
T&WAD, Cowen Collection, 634/A330. Middle-class efforts to channel opposition to the war into agitation for decreased government expenditure drew little
support from working-class radicals. See Olive Anderson, 'The Janus Face of Mid-
Nineteenth-Century English Radicalism: The Administrative Reform Association
of 1855', *Victorian Studies*, vol. 8 (March 1965), pp. 231–70.

Committee, indeed, represents a midpoint between Chartist and liberal political aspiration, and testifies as much to Cowen's radicalization by his association with former Chartist leaders as to their growing moderation under the influence of nationalism. The minutes of December 1854 indicate the group's intent to associate with middle-class radicals, recording correspondence with P.A. Taylor and the Friends of Italy, which vowed to assist Poland in its nationalist efforts against Russia. But they also testify to enduring Chartist sympathies with France. Harney moved a vote of thanks to Kossuth, who had formed an alliance for the duration of the war not only with Mazzini and Italian nationalism but with the moderate French republican Ledru-Rollin.[111] Falling far short of full-blown *démoc-soc* allegiance, Kossuth's alliance – like that of the Foreign Affairs Committee – nonetheless violated the rigid demarcation of French and nationalist aspiration maintained by middle-class English radicals since 1848. Francis Newman, a bourgeois patriot who – unlike Cowen – avoided political entanglements with working-class radicals, condemned this alliance out of hand. '*To ally the hopes of Hungary with the hopes of republican France, seems to me so fatal*', he warned Kossuth's advisor Francis Pulszky, '*that I should [not] wish any other section of patriotic Hungarians to support Kossuth if he makes this desperate alliance.*'[112]

Refusing to bow to such pressures, Cowen, Holyoake, Harney, and other militant radicals formed the Republican Brotherhood in January 1855, an association that underscored their allegiance to French republican ideals and entered into a correspondence with Louis Blanc. Like late Chartist associations, the Republican Brotherhood drew much of its inspiration from the events of 1789. Cowen and Harney thus invited Holyoake to become an honorary member in a letter 'done at the Republican Palace, Blaydon . . . in the year of the Republic I'.[113] While welcoming England's military alliance with France, their association decried the complexion of the govern-

[111] Minutes of the Foreign Affairs Committee, 7 December 1854, T&WAD, Cowen Collection, 634/A330. For Kossuth's alliance, see Louis Kossuth, Alexandre Ledru-Rollin, and Giuseppe Mazzini, *Manifesto of the Republican Party* (London, 1855).

[112] Newman to Pulszky, 2 December 1854, University College, London, Newman Papers, Add. MS 170, item 8. Blanc attacked Kossuth's republican alliance for its failure to deal with social problems in his *Observations on the Recent Manifesto of Kossuth, Ledru-Rollin, and Mazzini* (London, 1855).

[113] Cowen and Harney to Holyoake, 21 January [1855], MCU, Holyoake Collection, item 728.

ments that had negotiated it, endorsing not aristocratic diplomacy but 'the alliance of free nations'. Appeals to seventeenth-century English precedents naturally legitimized their international patriotism. When Louis Napoleon made an official visit to Queen Victoria in April, the Republican Brotherhood denounced 'his very presence, poisoning the air and contaminating the soil of England – the native land of Milton, Hampden, Sidney, and others who, in better days, made the name of England the glory of the world'.[114]

The so-called Jersey coup d'état of the ensuing months built upon these sympathies, and briefly united a broad array of liberal and Chartist reformers behind a shared patriotic front. The origins of this incident lay in the dictates of foreign policy. The French government, long galled by Britain's willingness to provide a safe haven for foreign political dissidents, pressed with new urgency for the expulsion of French émigrés as the Crimean War progressed. The French refugee community in Jersey, engaged in a ceaseless round of denunciations of their emperor, became a point of particular contention between the two allies, as French officials called repeatedly for their removal and Palmerston repeatedly refused to comply.[115] In October, a speech by Félix Pyat – a central figure in the French branch of the socialist International Association – finally forced Palmerston's hand. Speaking at an anniversary celebration in London that marked the establishment of the first French republic, Pyat criticized Queen Victoria for exchanging ceremonial kisses with Louis Napoleon to signify the Anglo-French alliance. In the government's translation, Pyat's speech offended both bourgeois moral and political sensibilities, casting aspersions on the queen's virtue only to raise the spectre of the red republic. 'Yes, *you have sacrificed ALL . . . ALL* – EVEN CHASTITY! – *for the sake of that Ally!*', it proclaimed. 'Long life to Marianne (the guillotine). Long life to the Democratic, Social, and Universal Republic.'[116] A public indignation meeting of native residents of Jersey, orchestrated by the British Lieutenant-Governor, led promptly to the expulsion from the island of a French republican émigré whose newspaper had published Pyat's speech.

[114] Broadsheet, 'A Welcome to Emperor Bonaparte', April 1855, T&WAD, Cowen Collection, 634/A335.
[115] Porter, *Refugee Question*, pp. 122–4, 164–9, offers an excellent narrative of this incident and analysis of its official implications.
[116] Broadside, 'To the British Residents in Jersey and All not Conversant with the French Language, Translation of the Insulting Letter Addressed to the Queen of England', [1855], HO 45/6188.

A group of thirty-six émigrés, including Victor Hugo, protested the expulsion and were themselves expelled from Jersey in consequence.[117]

Radical responses to the expulsions were predictable, interweaving expectations of international popular solidarity and insurrection raised by the war with the manly, constitutional idiom of the English patriotic tradition and the sensationalist tropes of the late Chartist press. Little love was lost on Louis Napoleon, and little credence given to Pyat's purported attacks on the queen. Employing a less damning translation of 'pudeur' than the government's 'chastity', English radicals simultaneously defended the queen's personal honour, denounced her political alliance with Louis Napoleon, and upheld received stereotypes of acceptable feminine behaviour. Chartists used a neat distinction between the queen's two bodies in their defence of Pyat's speech, carefully separating Victoria the monarch from Victoria the woman. 'The most ardent republican, while denying her public utility', Harney asserted, 'will readily warmly acknowledge her womanly virtues.'[118] This Chartist commentary was of a piece with liberal analysis. The *Manchester Examiner* underlined 'the unsullied virtue of our beloved Sovereign', but characterized the offending ceremonial kisses as 'compliments which, interchanged with such a person as LOUIS NAPOLEON, violate morality and sully the conscience'.[119]

Public meetings to protest the expulsions succeeded in uniting liberal and Chartist, pacifist and militant radicals, bringing middle-class reformers on to platforms occupied by working-class leaders with whom they rarely associated to defend French refugees whose political beliefs they deplored. The Manchester School's efforts to use the Jersey coup d'état to bolster its campaign for pacifism and political economy proved unavailing in this context, for the expulsion strengthened both middle- and working-class radical antagonism to Louis Napoleon's despotic rule in France. At a meeting in November chaired by Edward Miall, Cobden's attempt to argue that Palmerston's behaviour to the refugees 'ought to open the eyes of at least that part of the public which is supporting the war from a sympathy with liberalism abroad' met with 'marks of disapproba-

---

[117] Porter, *Refugee Question*, pp. 122–4, 164–9.
[118] *Reasoner*, 23 December 1855, p. 309. Ernest Jones offered essentially the same analysis in *People's Paper*, 20 October 1855, p. 1.
[119] *Manchester Examiner and Times*, 18 October 1855, p. 2.

tion'. Ernest Jones's speech, greeted with 'loud and general cheering', was in sharp contrast a masterpiece of partisan patriotism, conflating at once the English radical tradition, continental nationality, and the French revolutionary cause. 'While on the one hand they did not go to war with Louis Napoleon, on the other they should not make war on their own history and their own honour', he reminded the crowd. 'Let them seek less to ally themselves with Francis Joseph, and more with Kossuth; less with Bomba and more with Mazzini; less with Louis Napoleon and more with the . . . exiles who had never tarnished their fame.'[120]

Seventeenth-century precedent was integral to this response, enabling radical leaders to rouse English popular radicalism while denouncing both British and foreign government. 'In our very midst, suspicion, calumny, Lynch-law, and proscription, have been invoked against . . . men who as patriots, and exiles for Freedom's sake, had a double claim on our protection', Harney lamented. 'Alas! the land of Hampden, Milton, and Sydney, is still far, very far, from being, in reality, "the ark of liberty, the home of the free".'[121] Far from being masked or disavowed, the English radical tradition was glorified in this context. Adduced in the radical press as an instructive parable for absolutist tyrants, the course of English history conveniently exemplified the virtues of constitutional government as well. The balance struck in one liberal newspaper's description of the fates of the two kings Charles was delicate, but telling. 'LOUIS NAPOLEON, in the sunny days of some future republic, is to be dealt with after the fashion of CHARLES I or LOUIS XVI', it predicted. 'The scaffold is to be his doom; his accursed remains are not to pollute the French soil, but are, we suppose, to be hung in chains, in the same way as CHARLES II, of blessed memory, dealt with the mouldering relics of regicides.'[122]

Ultimately, however, adherence to the shibboleths of the English radical tradition precluded effective protest against the Jersey coup d'état. Advocates of the émigrés located the outrage inflicted upon them in the absence of due process, in the violation of principles of national government forged with the early modern state, in prosecution 'without any indictment, without a trial, without any appeal

[120] Report of a Meeting in London, 15 November 1855, T&WAD, Cowen Collection, 634/A404; *Glasgow Sentinel*, 17 November 1855, p. 1.
[121] *Reasoner*, 16 December 1855, p. 301.
[122] *Manchester Daily Examiner and Times*, 18 October 1855, p. 2.

to a jury, but by the mere will of the executive'. As a constitutional monarch, they argued, the queen was barred by her own laws from summary action, 'the very point against which our forefathers battled in the days of the TUDORS and STUARTS'.[123] But Victoria's government knew otherwise. Whatever its legality if conducted in England, the expulsion, as Palmerston had been careful to ascertain beforehand, was permissible in Jersey without recourse to the courts or the jury system. Radical internationalists inspired by the venerable traditions of legal resistance to arbitrary government were thus effectively paralysed, their arguments undercut by the very institutions that lent their cause its legitimacy. Public meetings held in London, Paisley, Newcastle, and Glasgow were poorly attended, and ineffectual: when Parliament reconvened in January, liberals sought no inquiry into the expulsion.[124] Lacking a shared conception of natural rights and committed to opposing interpretations of contemporary nationality, middle- and working-class radicals turned to a common conviction in the letter of the English law only to be constrained by its national limitations.

To dismiss the rule of law as a bankrupt radical instrument would, however, be misguided, for events soon demonstrated that popular belief in the institutions of the state could strengthen alliances between middle- and working-class radicals. Although ineffectual in 1855, the legal system continued to serve as a vehicle of popular political expression beyond the age of John Wilkes. W.E. Adams dwelt in his memoirs on the humiliation of seeing the émigré republicans expelled 'without warrant and without trial', but by 1858 Adams was himself at the centre of a protest movement in which middle- and working-class reformers used the rule of law triumphantly to vindicate both English and continental radical convictions.[125] Precipitated by the Italian exile Felice Orsini's attempted assassination of Louis Napoleon, this radical agitation offered a successful counterpoint to the Jersey coup d'état. In forcing middle-class radicals to accept and embrace the Chartists' time-honoured practice of subsuming French democratic socialism under a nationalist banner, the Orsini affair marked a significant moment of radical rapprochement. Without obliterating differences in social and economic ideology, it encouraged Chartists and liberals to pursue shared goals through national institutions.

---

[123] *Ibid.*, 6 November 1855, p. 2.   [124] Porter, *Refugee Question*, pp. 164, 123.
[125] Adams, *Memoirs of a Social Atom*, vol. II, p. 350.

An effort engineered by Italian and French émigrés who had sought asylum in England and involving bombs manufactured in Birmingham, Orsini's attempt to assassinate Louis Napoleon renewed the French emperor's determination to rid Britain of continental political refugees. Palmerston's ministry, under great pressure from the French government, responded in February by framing a Conspiracy to Murder Bill designed to convert conspiracy to murder from a misdemeanour to a felony. The bill explicitly included conspiracy to murder abroad within the compass of the English law, and was thus an obvious strike against the continental émigré community. The initial vote in the House was ominous, with the government commanding a majority of 200. But political infighting and widespread public protest against the bill quickly eroded the government's advantage.[126]

Radicals in Sheffield, Newcastle, and London organized public meetings to protest the bill, which drew fire from the full range of liberal and Chartist agitators. Together W.J. Fox, Sir George de Lacy Evans, John Bright, and Richard Cobden supported a meeting at the Freemason's Hall in February at which Ernest Jones was a featured speaker.[127] For the Manchester School, the event offered an opportunity to rehabilitate reputations badly damaged by opposition to the Crimean War and the ensuing Liberal losses in the election of 1857. Cobden and Bright, worried throughout 1856 and 1857 by their 'constant mortification and opposition from war people and Chartists', sought in opposing the Conspiracy Bill to reverse their reputation 'as anti-national' politicians, and thereby bring their principles into closer line with 'public opinion'.[128] In this they were unsuccessful, for Bright's letter, which urged English radicals to eschew continental politics and attend instead to domestic reform, was hissed by the audience. Ernest Jones, introduced by the chair as 'one who has suffered in the cause of the people', proved more acceptable. His speech was a paean to the French republic of 1848, destroyed in 1852 by Louis Napoleon but soon to 'rise again in glory from its ashes'. Washington Wilkes's speech rounded the event

[126] Porter, *Refugee Question*, pp. 170–8; *Manchester Weekly Times*, 27 February 1858, p. 1.
[127] 'Proceedings at a Meeting Convened for the Purpose of Taking into Consideration Lord Palmerston's Conspiracy Bill', 15 February 1858, MEPO, 2/68, pp. 2–3.
[128] J.B. Smith to Cobden, 25 April 1857, WSRO, Cobden Papers, vol. 5, fol. 92; Bright to Cobden, 19 June 1857, BL, Bright Papers, Add. MS 43,384, fol. 108; Bright to Cobden, 16 April 1857, BL, Bright Papers, Add. MS 43,384, fol. 92.

out nicely, linking English freedom to continental nationality. It appealed to the audience 'not only in the name of our ancestral pride and independence, not only in the name of that liberty enshrined in our common law, not only in the name of our own country but in the name of brother nations' such as Italy and Hungary.[129]

When defeated in the House of Commons, the Conspiracy to Murder Bill brought down Palmerston's ministry, and inaugurated the second stage of the Orsini affair. Radical attention now shifted to the prosecution of Simon Bernard, the French *démoc-soc* exile accused of assembling Orsini's bombs. Bernard, arrested in February for conspiracy, stood trial in April for accessory to murder, a crime bearing the death penalty. In this episode – unlike the Jersey coup d'état – the full panoply of the rule of law came into play, with prosecution and defence alike intent to exploit the public theatre of trial by jury. English officials were determined to restore the credibility of strong government both at home and abroad and disbursed over £5,000 to procure seventy-three witnesses to testify against Bernard – a sum which the Treasury itself thought excessive.[130] Equally determined to acquit the accused exile, middle- and working-class English radicals rushed to his aid. The radical press discharged volley after volley of polemic on his behalf, ranging in content from legalistic abuse of the prosecution to calls upon the patriotism of the English public to assure Bernard's release. The *Manchester Examiner and Times* questioned the government's adherence to due process, reporting that Bernard had been locked in Scotland Yard for twenty-four hours without access to legal advice and querying the extended length of time that had elapsed between his arrest and prosecution.[131] G.W.M. Reynolds played upon the patriotic aspects of the case, counselling his readers that the jury had 'not only to try the prisoner, but to vindicate their country'. The nationalist legacy of earlier centuries was explicit in his synopsis of their charge: 'whether, in short, we are to remain a free and independent nation, or to become a department of the French empire – whether the many principles of Milton and Knox . . . are to animate our politics and mould our institutions – must, to a great and alarming extent, depend upon the courage, veracity, and

---

[129] 'Proceedings at a Meeting', MEPO 2/68, pp. 48–62.
[130] Porter, *Refugee Question*, p. 190; Appeal of A.B. Richards, 12 June 1858, T&WAD, Cowen Collection, 634/A617.
[131] *Manchester Examiner and Times*, 27 March 1858, p. 4.

incorruptibility of the twelve Englishmen who have to try the French Republican Bernard'.[132]

Packed with spectators, Bernard's trial in April was calculated to fulfil the patriotic expectations raised by the radical press. An alien committed to Fourier's system of socialism, the French republican employed a defence strategy crafted to exploit English national sentiment to the full. As a non-national, Bernard enjoyed the option of a jury composed of six foreigners and six Englishmen. But when ranged against the forces of order – the Lord Chief Justice, the Lord Chief Baron, the Lord Mayor, and several aldermen attended the trial in state – Bernard 'in a firm voice, said "I trust my case to a jury of Englishmen"'.[133] His advocate's counsel to the jury was a case-study in the partisan application of the rule of law, redolent with the patriotic idiom of the Country Party tradition:

> Be not intimidated into giving a verdict which you may hereafter regret, and with which your children hereafter may upbraid you. He, at whose instigation this prosecution was undertaken, little knows the firmness, the attachment to the law, the regard for mercy, and the unconquerable love of liberty which animates the breasts of the English people ... Tell him that the jury box is the sanctuary of English liberty ... Tell him that on this very spot your predecessors have not quailed before arbitrary power of the Crown, backed by the influence of Crown-serving and time-serving judges. Tell him that under every difficulty and danger, your predecessors have maintained inviolate the liberties of the people.[134]

Despite an official synopsis of the case which the presiding judge himself acknowledged 'summed up strongly for a conviction', the jury returned a verdict of not guilty after less than two hours of deliberation.[135] The crowd's exultant response to his acquittal was fully affirmed in Bernard's panegyric to bystanders. 'I do declare that this verdict is the truth, and it proves that in England there will always be liberty to crush tyranny', he cried. 'All honour to an English Jury.'[136]

[132] *Reynolds's Newspaper*, 11 April 1858, p. 1.
[133] George Jacob Holyoake, *Life of Dr. Bernard: With Portrait and Judgment of the Press on His Trial* (London, 1858), pp. 10–11.
[134] *Ibid.*, p. 12; *State Trials* (London, 1898), n.s., vol. VIII, col. 1024.
[135] Cited by Porter, *Refugee Question*, p. 192.
[136] Holyoake, *Life of Dr. Bernard*, p. 12.

Radical responses to the acquittal enshrined Bernard securely within the framework of England's national tradition, without renouncing the significance of his actions for the wider European radical movement. Writing as 'Cromwell' in the *Glasgow Sentinel*, Patrick Lloyd Jones informed his readers that the jury had acted justly in its proceedings. 'It would be foolish to insist that Dr Bernard did not plot with Orsini and his confederates', the erstwhile Christian Socialist reported, 'no doubt he did, and no doubt he had a perfect right to do so.'[137] Holyoake's pamphlet made both the English and the continental relevance of Bernard's actions obvious: 'in working out the problem of liberty, it was a sad necessity to compass the deaths of our Charles I., and the French Louis XVI.: but the other alternative might have brought upon the world a series of eventualities, not only more unpleasant, but of more fearful consequence'.[138] Ernest Jones noted that 'the struggle of the two elements of freedom and oppression' assumed constitutional forms in some nations and physical forms in others, but that 'nevertheless, the war will be waged for kindred objects and guided for kindred ends'. 'We are not wrong, then, in ascribing a European importance to the verdict of the jury on Bernard', he argued. 'Through them the honour of England has been vindicated, the liberty of Europe has been saved.'[139]

With Bernard's acquittal, radical argument and agitation entered the third phase of the Orsini affair, the defence of Edward Truelove and Stanislaus Tchorzewski. Truelove, a secularist and former Owenite socialist whose publishing house formed an integral part of the late Chartist press network, was charged in 1858 with printing and distributing W.E. Adams's pamphlet, *Tyrannicide: Is It Justifiable?.*[140] Tchorzewski, an émigré Pole, was arrested for publishing and selling the *Letter to the Parliament and the Press*, a defence of Bernard written by Félix Pyat's Committee of the Revolutionary Commune. Fusing French republicanism to continental nationalism,

[137] *Glasgow Sentinel*, 24 April 1858, p. 4.
[138] Holyoake, *Life of Dr. Bernard*, p. 3.   [139] *People's Paper*, 1 May 1858, p. 4.
[140] The best index of Truelove's radical commitment is the *Catalogue of Books, Pamphlets, Tracts, Etc., Chiefly Political and Controversial, from the Library of the Late Edward Truelove* (London, 1900), in BODL, Johnson Collection, 'Religion:25'. It includes works by or about Algernon Sidney, Cromwell, Bolingbroke, Cartwright, the London Corresponding Society, Babeuf, Mazzini, Owen, Harney, Linton, O'Brien and Jones as well as the Reverend W.M. Cooper's *Flagellation and the Flagellants: The History of the Rod in All Countries.*

these works briefly harnessed middle-class English radicals to the *démoc-soc* tradition of 1848.

Adams's *Tyrannicide* deftly interwove the various strands of national and international argument current in working-class circles in the 1850s to underline the perceived interrelation of the English and continental radical traditions. Richly Mazzinian in tone, the work reflected Adams's earlier radical activity as a compositor for the republican association at Brantwood that produced Linton's *English Republic*. The opening sentences glorified life as sacred, but Adams soon distinguished true life from mere existence, and elevated national life over the life of the individual. 'For a nation to be great and holy', he argued, 'it is necessary for a nation to live, fulfilling in life the special mission God has given it.' This national life in turn required the autonomy of individual citizens, for 'in the slave there can be neither virtue when he does well from necessity, nor vice when he does ill from compulsion'.[141] Enslaved by the tyranny of the French government, Italy and Orsini were thus exculpated from wrongdoing in attempting to assassinate Louis Napoleon. The analogy with England's own revolutionary past was obvious and explicit. 'If the falseness of Charles I left England no other safety but in his death, was he not himself responsible for all his falseness occasioned?', Adams asked rhetorically. 'If the perfidy, the atrocities, the mad despotism of an adventurer leave France no other hope but in his destruction, does he not himself invoke the avenging dagger?'[142]

Pyat's pamphlet made essentially the same point. An extended diatribe against Louis Napoleon as the murderer of both the French and Roman republics, it invoked the precedent of Cromwell alongside that of Charlotte Corday. '*We will no longer discuss the right of regicide*', it soon concluded. 'In the country of Charles I it would be superfluous.' Couched in these terms, the pamphlet appealed to even convinced liberal opinion. Francis Newman, who

---

[141] Extracts from the tract are reprinted in the *Glasgow Sentinel*, 27 February 1858, p. 4. Adams's argument recalls the rhetoric of the elect nation, but was most directly derived from Mazzinian nationalism. Linton's *English Republic*, vol. 1 (1851), for example, reprinted a Mazzinian tract which asked, 'Do the people live today? . . . Above all things, and before all things, they must be recalled to life and action. The highways of liberty must be opened to them. In order that the noble and great thoughts may arise in their hearts, the shameful sign of servitude must be effaced from their brows.'

[142] *Glasgow Sentinel*, 27 February 1858, p. 4.

had stood opposed to Kossuth's alliance with moderate republicans in 1855, now supported the pamphlet of committed socialists. Holyoake's edition of the tract displayed Newman's endorsement prominently on the title page.[143]

Support within the radical community for the prosecuted publishers was widespread, and quickly crossed class boundaries. The Truelove Defence Fund, established in March with Newman as chairman, Charles Bradlaugh as honorary secretary, and James Watson as treasurer, expanded in April to raise funds for Tchorzewski's trial as well. Its appeals, broadcast in Ernest Jones's *People's Paper* and Holyoake's *Reasoner*, immediately inspired a national audience. The *Reasoner* reported subscriptions totalling over £96 in the first three weeks of the collection from locations as various as Lincoln, Derby, Bristol, Reading, Berwick, Coventry, and Oldham. Contributors included the Unitarians Fox, Taylor, and Stansfeld, Joseph Cowen, John Stuart Mill, 'A Few Members of the City Bootmakers' Society', and 'Three Working Men'. The subscriptions of forty-seven patriots from Barnstaple, Devon, conveyed the dominant tenor of the proceedings. Emphasizing their allegiance to 'national character', the subscribers made their contributions 'feeling our British spirit roused'.[144]

Faced with this publicity, and the probability of a second and third verdict of not guilty from sympathetic juries, the government capitulated, withdrawing its prosecution in June. Regarded as great popular victories in radical circles, the press prosecutions, the trial of Bernard, and the defeat of the Conspiracy to Murder Bill served to affirm received beliefs in the impartiality of the institutions of the state, in a legal system responsive to the just claims of the disadvantaged against the ruling élite, and in a parliamentary system capable of registering the decrees of the people even in an unreformed state. In this manner, the national idiom of Victorian radicalism undercut the language of class, encouraging collaboration between liberals and Chartists by underscoring their shared ancestry in a radical tradition that predated industrial capitalism. But as the pattern of

---

[143] Félix Pyat, A. Besson, and Alexandre Talandier, *Letter to the Parliament and the Press* (London, 1858), pp. 7, 9.

[144] *Reasoner*, 12 May 1858, p. 151. Subscriptions for the first three weeks are calculated from *ibid.*, 31 March, 7 April, and 14 April 1858, pp. 103, 110, and 118. Adams, *Memoirs of a Social Atom*, vol. II, p. 362; *Glasgow Sentinel*, 27 March 1858, p. 4. Mill's liberal justification for his support is detailed in his *On Liberty*, chap. 2.

radical activism in the fifties also suggests, this allegiance to the nation was multivalent. Fully capable of expanding to encompass new economic ideologies – whether liberal or socialist – English national identity both reflected class differences and helped radical leaders to articulate and perpetuate them.

Recent scholarship has done much to amend our understanding of the class-conscious bourgeoisie so confidently delineated by Asa Briggs in 1956. Reduced to a congeries of sub-groups possessed of conflicting economic interests and fissiparous political tendencies, the Victorian middle class emerges from this newer literature less as a social formation than as an historical fiction created by Karl Marx and perpetuated by the heirs to his historical imagination.[145] The history of English radical politics in the 1850s reminds us, however, that Marx's contemporaries, while immune to his materialist analysis, were fully alive to the conflict between classes that he described. For if the historiography of the mid-Victorian period is a historiography of liberalization, the history of liberal, radical, and Chartist relations in the fifties was a history of tumultuous dissent. Manchester liberals, Christian Socialists, and ardent Unitarian radicals displayed diverse and often mutually antagonistic responses to commerce, industry, war, and religion, but they enjoyed a common worldview nonetheless. In the decade after 1848, late Chartist responses to their shared liberal patriotism, their shared demarcation of social and political spheres, assured that men of the middle class were acutely aware of this common identity, and the limitations that it imposed on radical reform. The following decade saw the proponents of nationalist sentiment mediate a gradual elision of Chartist and liberal thought without destroying perceptions of labour's distinctive political and economic vision. For as working-class radicals moved to the centre, middle-class liberals moved to the left, first questioning and then discarding the rigid adherence to received dogmas of political economy that had crystallized in English responses to the continental revolutions of 1848.

[145] Asa Briggs, 'Middle-Class Consciousness in English Politics, 1780–1846', *Past and Present*, no. 9 (April 1956), pp. 65–74. For analyses that emphasize internal divisions within the middle class, see esp. Geoffrey Crossick, 'The Petite Bourgeoisie in Nineteenth-Century Britain: The Urban and Liberal Case', in Geoffrey Crossick and Heinz-Gerhard Haupt (eds.), *Shopkeepers and Master Artisans in Nineteenth-Century Europe* (London, 1984), pp. 62–94.

5 · Nationalist fervour and class relations 1858–1864

England has retrograded greatly during the last 100 years – I attribute this to our wars & intermingling with the Continent, since the American war of independence, which have all been in the interest of legitimacy & privilege; but which our self-conceited people have been persuaded have been for the promotion of 'civil & religious liberty all over the world'. These wars & intrigues have distracted public attention from domestic questions.[1]

Like 1848, 1858 marked a watershed in English radical politics. For middle-class radicalism, the significance of the decade after 1858 lay in a gradual expansion of the middle-class radical vision, in a reintegration of the political and social spheres earlier disassociated in bourgeois radical conviction. Inspired by sympathy for nationalist agitation in Italy and Poland and determined to increase contact between the classes within their own nation, the cohort of radical leaders that emerged from these years expanded the horizons of middle-class radicalism beyond Old Corruption and the Manchester School. For working-class radicalism, the legacy of 1858 was more complex. At one extreme, this year witnessed the demise of the National Charter Association, and Ernest Jones's acceptance of the need for class collaboration to advance radical reform. Yet the same decade also saw a resurgence of labour militancy, the politicization of skilled unionized workers, and English participation in the formation of the First International. Here as in middle-class radical culture, nationalist sentiment was of central importance. Participating together in campaigns to advance continental nationalism, middle- and working-class radical leaders established patterns of both discourse and organizational co-

[1] Richard Cobden to J.E. Thorold Rogers, 9 January 1865, BODL, J.E. Thorold Rogers Papers, Box. 1.

operation that laid the foundations for effective political reform activities in 1867.

This new trend toward cooperation and the forms that it assumed were not without critics in the Victorian period, nor have they escaped the strictures of twentieth-century historians. Cobden and Bright constantly bewailed radicals' preoccupation with continental freedom, arguing – like many historians after them – that it functioned to divert significant reform activity away from domestic politics.[2] Farther to the left of the radical movement, John H. Mackay, general secretary in 1858 of the exiguous International Association, equated cooperation between the classes with defeat of the workers' cause, pitting Italian sympathy and bourgeois demands 'that the democracy should shelve their social opinions' inexorably against class conflict and the *démoc-soc* ideal.[3] Fully consonant with schools of analysis that portray nationalist sentiment as the antithesis of working-class consciousness, this line of reasoning fails, however, to capture the historical function of nationalist sentiment in the English radical experience. In the decade after 1858, sympathy for Italy and Poland provided a common ideological hub from which the spokes of middle- and working-class opposition radiated, often in opposing directions. Acting as a vehicle for the expression of both shared and antagonistic political beliefs, nationalism mediated not a capitulation by either class but rather a renegotiation of political roles, values, and expectations in which each class both made concessions to and exacted concessions from the other.[4]

THE EXPANSION OF THE RADICAL LEADERSHIP

For moderate artisanal radicals, Chartist efforts to form alliances with middle-class reform leaders in 1858 were a welcome, if belated,

---

[2] Simon Maccoby, *English Radicalism 1853–1886* (London, 1938), pp. 20–1, G.M. Trevelyan, *Garibaldi and the Thousand* (London, 1909), pp. 22–3, and Christopher Kent, *Brains and Numbers: Elitism, Comptism, and Democracy in Mid-Victorian England* (Toronto, 1978), p. 26, illustrate the argument that interest in foreign relations substituted for action in domestic reform. Harvie, *Lights of Liberalism*, pp. 97–8, however, recognizes the instrumentality of these sentiments in forging effective ideologies and alliances for reform.

[3] *Reynolds's Newspaper*, 2 January 1859, p. 9.

[4] For broader discussions of class negotiation, see esp. Crossick, *Artisan Elite*, and Gray, *Labour Aristocracy in Victorian Edinburgh*. Both ultimately emphasize the success of the liberalization process.

development that promised to lend the cause of labour new funds of capital, organizational talent, parliamentary influence, and respectability. G.J. Holyoake, now an established publisher with rising social aspirations, championed the cause of union in his *Reasoner*, and illustrated in his own life the palpable benefits of class collaboration. A beneficiary of patronage, gifts, and loans from W.H. Ashurst, Joseph Cowen, and John Stuart Mill, Holyoake had by 1857 made a tentative, if disingenuous, peace with liberal politics that was to deepen in the coming years.[5] Although he continued to uphold French social ideals, Holyoake was increasingly swayed by Mill's arguments for a limited franchise. He basked in the new opportunities presented by the diminution of radical conflict, enjoying a role as an intermediary between working- and middle-class radical leaders throughout the 1860s.

Less moderate working-class radicals, however, faced wrenching political decisions in 1858–9. Ernest Jones's decision to engage the National Charter Association in middle-class alliances, first mooted in 1857, precipitated defections and acrimonious backbiting in 1858. G.W.M. Reynolds, himself unwilling – unlike Jones – to participate in the organization of working-class protest, resisted cooperative efforts vociferously in his paper, enmeshing Jones in a protracted, libellous spate of infighting that forced him to sell the *People's Paper* in June.[6] If economic necessity and political realism encouraged Jones to seek middle-class cooperation in these months, the Orsini affair served as an emollient in the process of reconciliation. The defeat of Palmerston's Conspiracy to Murder Bill and the acquittal of Simon Bernard offered an obvious opportunity for building alliances with middle-class radicals without renouncing distinctive working-class ideals. 'Who, then, saved England's honour?', 'that which you won under a Cromwell', Jones asked his readers rhetorically in reviewing 'the indignant outburst of the nation's voice'

---

[5] See *Reasoner*, 17 February 1858, pp. 49–50, for his support of collaboration with the middle class. John Stuart Mill repeatedly rescued the *Reasoner* from financial ruin and helped to locate additional middle-class funding for the paper. See Holyoake to Mill, 26 March and 2 April 1856, and Mill to Holyoake, 1 and 5 April 1856, BLPES, Mill–Taylor Collection, vol. 1, fols. 101–6. Holyoake cast his first vote, for the liberal Lord John Russell, in 1858. See his *The Workman and the Suffrage: Letters to the Right Honourable Lord John Russell, M.P., and to the 'Daily News'* (London, 1859), p. 3.

[6] Saville, *Ernest Jones*, pp. 63–73, provides an excellent synopsis of these developments.

against Bernard's prosecution. 'The People did. The Middle Classes did. The Working Classes did. The . . . poverty of London's streets, and the middle-class wealth of London's jury box.'[7]

By autumn, the *People's Paper* had given way to Jones's *Cabinet Newspaper: The Union of Classes, and the Liberty of Man* (1858–9). This journal, which traced England's woes to aristocratic rule imposed by the Norman Yoke, both supported and was supported by the middle-class leadership of radical Dissent. 'Too much praise' could not be accorded by Jones's paper to the reform efforts of the Newcastle radical Joseph Cowen, while James Stansfeld – like Cowen a former Friend of Italy – supported the newspaper by advertising the ales and porter of his Swan Brewery in its pages.[8] Championship of Italian unification flowed naturally from such associations. By 1859 Jones had adopted Italy as the 'true and holy watchword . . . needed now to counteract the infamy into which the nations of the earth are sinking'.[9] He continued to resist middle-class efforts to restrict the suffrage to property owners, but failed either to create an enduring reform agitation under the dual aegis of Chartism and the middle class in this period, or to recruit the finances of his radical movement. Returning to the practice of the law late in 1859, he moved to Manchester in 1861.[10] Chartism, although it left an indelible mark on the politics of the ensuing decade, was an enduring radical legacy after 1858, not an active organization for social and political reform.

Throughout the 1860s, internationalist traditions elaborated in the aftermath of 1848 helped to preserve Chartist aspirations, and to distinguish working-class radical culture from the social and political activities of middle-class reformers. In 1862, Bronterre O'Brien's radical followers celebrated the 102nd anniversary of the birth of 'the incorruptible Robespierre', Louis Blanc addressed an English audience gathered to mark Robert Owen's birthday, and English radicals joined with representatives of the émigré community to profess their enduring allegiance to 'La République, Démocratique et Sociale' at the funeral of Simon Bernard.[11] Patriotism and the

[7] *London News*, 9 May 1858, p. 1.
[8] *Cabinet Newspaper*, 27 November 1858, p. 1; 4 December 1858, p. 1; 25 December 1858, p. 8.
[9] *Ibid.*, 29 January 1859, p. 4.   [10] Saville, *Ernest Jones*, pp. 73, 77.
[11] *The Working Man: A Political and Social Advocate of the Rights of Labour, and a Monthly Record of Co-operative Progress*, 1 May 1862; *The Secular World: And Social Economist*, 17 May 1862, p. 19; *The National Reformer*, 6 December 1862, p. 5; 13 December 1862, pp. 2–3.

revolutions of 1848 continued to figure prominently in the annual cycle of working-class radical celebrations in these years. London radicals participated with German socialists in a public commemoration of the June Days in 1865; in 1869, the Clerkenwell Patriotic Society celebrated the 39th anniversary of the second Polish revolution.[12]

What distinguished working-class radical efforts in this period from the activities of late Chartism was not so much the ideological content of protest as the reinvigoration of the radical ranks by members of the new model unions. With the onset of the London Builders' Strike in 1859, the formation of the London Trades Council in 1860, and the establishment of the *Bee-Hive* newspaper in 1861, trade unions reentered the public arena and came to dominate public perceptions of working-class radical aspiration. Determined to build national unions with deep financial resources, the trades most active in this renaissance of organized labour were generally loath to engage in wildcat strikes and jealous of their privileged status as skilled male craftsmen. Labour aristocrats in the parlance of their own time, they figure in twentieth-century historiography as a liberal, reformist élite determined above all else to raise their own economic status through institutions 'constituted in such a way as to shut out the vast majority of workmen.'[13] A recognition of the élitism inherent in the economic outlook of skilled labour is indeed central to an understanding of trade unions' economic strategies in the 1860s, but the history of radical politics suggests that it is dangerous to extrapolate from the economic exclusivity of organized labour to its putative liberal political convictions. Heirs to Chartist traditions predicated on universal rights and patriotic identities, unionized craftsmen – like generations of middle- and upper-class radicals before them – were often forced by the logic of their own rhetoric to expand their conception of the political nation beyond the pale of property and skill.

Among the unions most prominent in the radical struggles of the sixties, boot and shoemakers, compositors, and the building trades –

---

[12] *The Miner and Workman's Advocate*, 8 July 1865, p. 5; *National Reformer*, 7 November 1869, p. 301.

[13] Harrison, *Before the Socialists*, p. 32. The debate on the labour aristocracy is discussed above, pp. 2–4.

carpenters and joiners, brickmakers and bricklayers, masons, painters, and plasterers – boasted strong affiliations with the early Chartist movement. For many individuals within these trades, late Chartism had continued to offer a source of political inspiration and radical camaraderie. George Howell, inducted into radical circles in London by a cabinet-maker and a plasterer, served a political apprenticeship in the Islington branch of the National Charter Association before rising to prominence within the Operative Brick-layers; the bootcloser Charles Murray, a vociferous critic of liberal economics after 1848, was sustained by Bronterre O'Brien's Soho Chartist association before he joined the ranks of the First International.[14] The final months of Chartist agitation in 1858 elicited participation from unions and unionists at the forefront of strike and organizational activity. William Allan and William Newton of the Amalgamated Engineers attended Jones's conference on cooperation with the middle class in February alongside delegates dispatched by the unionized London painters, plasterers, and masons.[15]

The newspapers and trade circulars that replaced the late Chartist network in these years continued to articulate social, political, and economic arguments developed by their Chartist predecessors. George Potter's *Beehive*, edited by the former Chartist compositor Robert Hartwell, rejected middle-class reformers' separation of spheres from the outset, proclaiming support in its prospectus at one and the same time for social, political, and economic reform under the aegis of trade unionism (Ill. 3). And if George Howell is now remembered as a trade unionist intent to ingratiate himself with the liberal leadership, his early editorials in the *Operative Bricklayers' Circular* consistently violated the conventional liberal wisdom of his day. The first issue of the paper struck a militant note, proclaiming that 'every trades' unionist is a missionary, and wherever he goes he preaches a crusade against the tyranny of capital and the oppression of employers.' Subsequent issues were careful to locate the English working class within a broadly European context that specifically included France. In October 1861 the circular advocated an 'Organization of Labour' to effect political and economic reform,

---

[14] For Howell, see above, pp. 119–20. Shipley, *Club Life and Socialism*, pp. 4–6, discusses Murray's career.
[15] Saville, *Ernest Jones*, pp. 68–9.

NOTICE TO THE WORKING CLASSES.

Will be Published on Saturday, October 19th, 1861,

By the " Trades' Newspaper Company," (Limited,)

AT

2, BOUVERIE STREET, FLEET STREET, E.C.

PRICE TWO-PENCE.

"THE BEE-HIVE:"

A Weekly Newspaper,

Containing 16 Pages (of the size of the Illustrated News.)

The BEE-HIVE will be a general Newspaper, comprising a carefully prepared digest of intelligence, and is designed—

To Claim for the Working Classes a complete REFORM IN PARLIAMENT.

To Advocate a REDUCTION IN THE HOURS OF LABOUR.

To Promote the application of the CO-OPERATIVE SYSTEM to Industrial Movements.

To support all requisite measures of SANITARY REFORM.

To notice all Financial and Monetary Projects adapted to ameliorate the conditions of the industrial classes, including TRADES' UNIONS, BENEFIT SOCIETIES, BUILDING AND LAND SOCIETIES, AND INSURANCE ASSOCIATIONS.

Orders can be received by any Newsagent, and by

GEO. POTTER, MANAGER,

On behalf of the Company,

2, BOUVERIE STREET, FLEET STREET, E.C,

TO WHOM COMMUNICATIONS MAY BE FORWARDED.

and vowed to pursue correspondence with workers from France, Italy, Belgium, Holland, Hungary, and Poland to this end.[16] *The Workman's Advocate*, a product of the Industrial Newspaper Company over which George Odger of the West End Ladies' Shoemakers presided, similarly listed 'international fellowship' as the first of its principles.[17]

Assuming more material form in financial support extended to striking workers, these sentiments served to unite members of individual trades with men dispersed in widely disparate crafts, regions, and nations. Scholars rightly emphasize the particularism and exclusivity of mid-Victorian unions, but the minutes and quarterly reports of labour organizations also testify to skilled artisans' ability to conceptualize labour as a national, and international, phenomenon with shared interests and claims against capital. The London Compositors provided funds for the Builders' Strike that galvanized organized labour in 1859–61, but they also contributed £70 to striking cork-cutters and, in 1862, offered their 'Parisian Brothers' a loan of £400 to sustain their Typographical Society against encroaching masters.[18] Provincial unions, although commanding fewer resources and removed from the immediate orbit of the London Trades Council, often evinced the same sense of solidarity. Sheffield's Saw Makers' Society sent the Builders £5 in January 1860 and dispatched an additional £2 10s in August towards expenses incurred by the National Association of Trades of London in 'contending for the rights of Labour'.[19] Wolverhampton's Tin Plate Workers' Society, which took the *Bee-Hive* from June 1867, was both eclectic and international in its support for the cause of labour. Having voted funds for both tailors and bootmakers striking in London in 1867, they contributed £5 to Liverpool Brickmakers in 1868, offered a Society of Co-operative Locksmiths additional time to repay a loan of £50 in 1869, dispatched £10 to aid

[16] *The Operative Bricklayers' Society Trade Circular and General Reporter*, 1 September 1861, p. 2; 1 October 1861, pp. 9–10, 18–19.
[17] *Workman's Advocate*, 9 September 1865, p. 4. Stephen Coltham, 'George Potter, the Junta, and the *Bee-Hive*', *International Review of Social History*, vols. 9 and 10 (1964–5), pp. 391–432, 23–65, provides the best introduction to the labour press of this period.
[18] London Society of Compositors, Quarterly Reports, 2 April 1859, 31 January 1860, and August 1862, Modern Records Centre, University of Warwick, MSS 28/CO/1/1/6/5; MSS 28/CO/1/8/6/10; MSS 28/CO/1/8/7/8.
[19] Saw Makers' Protection Society Minute Book 1860–96, 11 January and 1 August 1860, Sheffield City Archives, L.D. 1446 (1).

soldiers suffering in the Franco-Prussian War in 1870, and gave £20 to striking agricultural workers in 1874.[20]

Opposition to liberal economics ran like a refrain through the literature and protest generated by organized labour in these years, lending force to earlier, Chartist arguments that the working class – in England as in France – stood united in its opposition to the laws of political economy. Canny strategists within the unions were fully capable of using classical economics to their own ends, but the burden of union rhetoric in the midst of strike activity flatly denied the legitimacy of market mechanisms.[21] The manifesto of the Northamptonshire Boot and Shoemakers' Mutual Protection Society protested the masters' intentions to 'dictate their own terms to the workmen, & the carrying out of their favorite dogma of unrestricted competition' in 1859; Coventry silk weavers marched through town in the strike of 1860–1 singing songs against 'Political Economy'.[22] Far from distancing themselves from these arguments, London's new model unionists embraced them with enthusiasm. George Howell blasted political economy as a 'fiction' and a 'farce' in which workers had no faith. Robert Applegarth's union, the Amalgamated Carpenters and Joiners, advanced labour organizations as a cause that would 'sound the trumpet of liberty', correct 'the defective working of our political system', and provide the worker with 'that bread of which political economy deprives him'.[23]

Although the early years of the London Trades Council and the

[20] Wolverhampton Tin Plate Workers' Society, Minute Book, 1867–84, 13 March and 11 June 1867, 4 September 1868, 10 March 1869, 14 September 1870, and 11 June 1874, National Labour History Museum and Labour Party Archives, Manchester.

[21] Harrison, *Before the Socialists*, pp. 16–17, notes the variety and fluidity of workers' attitudes towards political economy. Eugenio Biagini, 'British Trade Unions and Popular Political Economy, 1860–1880', *Historical Journal*, vol. 30 (December 1987), pp. 811–40, emphasizes labour's ability to deploy liberal economics to its own ends, while R.V. Clements, 'British Trade Unions and Popular Political Economy, 1850–1875', *Economic History Review*, 2nd ser., vol. 14 (August 1961), pp. 93–104, emphasizes labour's outright rejection of market mechanisms.

[22] Northamptonshire Boot & Shoemakers' Manifesto, 1859, BLPES, Webb Trade Union Collection, part A, vol. xxv, fol. 78; Chancellor (ed.), *Master and Artisan*, pp. 180–1.

[23] *Operative Bricklayers' Circular*, 1 December 1861, p. 33; Amalgamated Society of Carpenters and Joiners, Financial Reports and Minutes, Modern Records Centre, University of Warwick, MSS 78/ASC&J/4/1/5–6.

Bee-Hive newspaper were marked by significant tension both within and among the skilled trades, the broad success of the new model unions in these years lent organized labour an appearance of radical unanimity and vigour conspicuously absent from middle-class radical circles. In retrospect, the liberal accord reached in Willis's Rooms in 1859, the formation of the Social Science Association, and the tentative stirrings of liberal discontent with classical economics appear to have laid foundations in the late fifties upon which a large degree of consensus between liberal and radical opinion would later be achieved, but few reform-minded liberals could regard their prospects with particular enthusiasm in this period.[24] In the north, Joseph Cowen sustained parliamentary reform agitation with his Northern Reform Union, a body constituted with the assistance of former Chartists at Newcastle's Chartist Hall in December 1857 and pledged to manhood suffrage, the ballot, and the abolition of property qualifications for MPs. Its members welcomed an alliance with Ernest Jones in 1858, and addressed eighty meetings with over 60,000 participants in 1858–9, establishing support for suffrage reform upon which the Reform League would capitalize in the mid-sixties.[25] But the Northern Reform Union was an anomaly within the wider middle-class reform movement and failed to rally liberal opinion behind manhood suffrage. John Bright enjoyed some success in uniting his followers behind household suffrage in 1858, but even this relatively moderate proposal swiftly alienated significant portions of Manchester opinion as a threat to cheap government. E.H. Greg, scion of the extensive Greg cotton dynasty, would support no candidate who advocated a rental franchise for fear that urban operatives would obtain the vote and

---

[24] For liberal political organization and the Liberal party's limited incorporation of popular radicalism, see John Vincent, *The Formation of the British Liberal Party, 1857–1868* (London, 1966); for the Social Science Association and its role in mediating relations between labour and the middle class, see Lawrence Goldman, 'The Social Science Association 1857–1886: A Context for Mid-Victorian Liberalism', *English Historical Review*, vol. 101 (January 1986), pp. 95–134. Ellen Frankel Paul, *Moral Revolution and Economic Science: The Demise of Laissez-Faire in Nineteenth-Century British Political Economy* (Westport, Conn., 1979), esp. pp. 119–209, discusses many of the intellectual forces that challenged classical economics in this period.

[25] Northern Reform Union Minute Book, 27 December 1857 – 26 December 1859, T&WAD, Cowen Collection, 634/C6; Ernest Jones to Cowen, 3 October 1858, T&WAD, Cowen Collection, 634/C197; R.B. Reed to G.J. Holyoake, 1 February 1860, MCU, Holyoake Collection, item 1182.

favour candidates allied in sentiment to the 'rank ultra Chartist' Abel Heywood. 'If enfranchised, workers will shift taxes from their shoulders to ours in the shape of income tax, for things like paid members', he warned. 'This will be, among other things, a threat to property.'[26]

Manchester radicalism was both unable to match the organizational success of the new model unions and threatened economically by the American Civil War, but it nonetheless enjoyed an infusion of new liberal talent in these years that expanded the potential for political reform alongside the working class. For the older generation of the Manchester School represented by Cobden, Bright, Smith, and Wilson – a generation denounced by labour leaders for its narrow allegiance to political economy and distrusted by both Chartist and liberal militants for its opposition to the Crimean War – now benefited from the emergence of a cohort of university-educated liberals dedicated to reform. The Oxford radicals J.E. Thorold Rogers and Goldwin Smith championed Cobdenite free trade and the progress of democracy, but also evinced a concern for the persistence of poverty in England and the cause of national freedom abroad that distinguished them from the elder statesmen from whom they drew their inspiration. At Cambridge, Henry Fawcett combined fierce anti-aristocratic sentiment, staunch adherence to political economy, and a devotion to representative government that extended even to women with tentative support for the growing trade union movement. Culturally, economically, and geographically removed from the industrial heartland, these academic radicals helped to expand the horizons and burnish the image of radical liberalism through scholarship, journalism, and political debate.[27]

Most significant for the course of middle-class radicalism in the early sixties was the emergence within liberal academic circles of the English Positivists. Early English enthusiasts for the principles of

[26] E.H. Greg to George Melly, 28 April [1859?], LCL, George Melly Papers, 920 MEL, 5/vol. 1, fol. 336. For the Greg family's political and economic background, see Mary B. Rose, *The Gregs of Quarry Bank Mill: The Rise and Decline of a Family Firm, 1750–1914* (Cambridge, 1986).

[27] Harvie, *Lights of Liberalism*, details the emergence and impact of this generation, and its allegiance to nationalist causes. On Fawcett, see Lawrence Goldman (ed.), *The Blind Victorian: Henry Fawcett and British Liberalism* (Cambridge, 1989). For Thorold Rogers, see Alon Kadish, *Historians, Economists, and Economic History* (London, 1989), pp. 3–34.

Auguste Comte had included G.H. Lewes, Harriet Martineau, and John Stuart Mill, but it was Richard Congreve of Wadham College who introduced the Oxford radicals Frederic Harrison, E.S. Beesly, and J.H. Bridges to the positive philosophy. A disciple early in his life of Saint-Simon, Comte – like the disciples of Adam Smith – sought to reshape society through science, historical understanding, and ordered industrial progress. But he departed sharply from the liberal tradition in privileging social solidarity and collective groups over the self-interest of the individual. Comte's positive philosophy offered a cohort of influential Anglicans perplexed by the relationship between faith and science a new 'Religion of Humanity', but it also provided economic arguments that justified the role of trade unions and helped to wean middle-class radicals from classical economics.[28] Successful in encouraging the English Positivists to form alliances with labour leaders, Comte's religion of humanity failed quite spectacularly to win converts among the working class.[29] In this context, patriotic traditions proved of central importance. For if Positivist religion had little appeal for labour unionists, the English Positivists' enthusiasm for French social theory and continental nationalism allied their radical vision with the political ideals of the labour movement and working-class radical tradition.

Frederic Harrison's intellectual development reveals both the instrumental role of nationalism in forming middle-class contacts with labour and the tension generated within middle-class radical culture by French social and economic theory. Still only a schoolboy in 1848, Harrison was impressed by the continental revolutions but not politicized by them: he later recalled the Chartist procession of 10 April as 'a school holiday and day of fun', a 'picnic' not a political protest. At Oxford, however, he came under the influence of the exile Aurelio Saffi, a triumvir with Mazzini in 1849 of the Roman republic. Employed as an instructor of Italian language and culture at the Taylor Institute, Saffi introduced a generation of young

---

[28] There are several excellent studies of the English Positivists. T.R. Wright, *The Religion of Humanity: The Impact of Comtean Positivism on Victorian Britain* (Cambridge, 1986), and Martha S. Vogeler, *Frederic Harrison: The Vocations of a Positivist* (Oxford, 1984), are strongest on Positivism and middle-class culture; Harrison, *Before the Socialists* and Kent, *Brains and Numbers* are the best sources on the Positivists' relations with labour.

[29] Harrison, *Before the Socialists*, pp. 319–20.

Oxford liberals to Mazzinian nationalism: James Bryce, engaged as
an undergraduate in 'constant arguments on the character of Oliver
Cromwell, whom of course I entirely admire and love', studied
Italian with Saffi in 1858.[30] Harrison, although politically and
religiously orthodox when he matriculated, left Oxford 'a Republican, a democrat, and a Free thinker' under the combined influence
of Saffi, Mazzini, Francis Newman, Cobden, and the Christian
Socialists.[31]

Travel in France and the Crimean War both expanded Harrison's
radical horizons and rendered them increasingly problematic.
Comte's positive philosophy disdained the purely negative freedoms
of liberal individualism, encouraging Harrison to develop allegiances to radical ideals that lay outside the conventional wisdom
of the Manchester School. A visit to France in 1852 elicited a burst
of enthusiasm for 'the République démocratique et sociale' and an
extended meditation on the perils of unalloyed liberty. 'It is true that
Liberty is a mockery in France, but those other two, Equality and
Fraternity are not a mockery, but living realities, those two without
which liberty loses half its sweetness, & with which servitude loses
half its pain', he confided to Beesly. 'That is I do think that a man is
better & happier in Paris though a dragoon stops him at every street,
than he is in London under the tyranny of our present state of
society which wounds him worse than steel.'[32] Commitment to the
cause of Italian and Hungarian freedom further weakened his
allegiance to the Manchester School in the course of the Crimean
War, leading Harrison to discount the efficacy of liberal pacifism in a
world governed by despotic rulers. 'Anything like rational European
policy must stand over until the respective governments become
liberal', he rationalized. 'In the meantime I am rather for Elizabeth's
and Cromwell's policy than for Cobden's – that is throwing the
whole of our moral weight backed by vigorous action into the free
scale.'[33]

These radical sentiments, confined to his private correspondence
and circle of friends from Oxford throughout the Crimean War,

[30] Frederic Harrison, *Autobiographic Memoirs*, 2 vols. (London, 1911), vol. I, pp. 55 and 96; James Bryce 'D' Diary, BODL, James Bryce Uncatalogued Papers, fols. 1–4.
[31] Harrison, *Autobiographic Memoirs*, vol. I, pp. 95–7, 106.
[32] Harrison to Beesly, 5 October and 20 September 1852, BLPES, Frederic Harrison Collection, 1/3/13 and 1/3/18.
[33] Harrison to Beesly, [1856], BLPES, Harrison Collection, 1/4/31–2.

gained public expression in 1858–9 when Harrison began to support both parliamentary reform and Italian independence in the *Daily News* and the *Morning Post*. Becoming 'a furious Radical in the days when Reform of Parliament was opened by Bright', he soon found that adherence to Bright's programme was an impediment to contact with the workers on whose behalf he wished reform to be carried.[34] Like the middle-class reformers whose efforts he championed in this period, Harrison rested his arguments for reform on expediency rather than abstract conceptions of justice. Anxious to see 'men like ... Holyoake' in the House of Commons, Harrison intended 'to give the artizan a vote not because I think it is his right, but because I think he will get some good indirectly by having it'. But middle-class liberals' refusal to sustain these reform efforts convinced Harrison of the need to 'go & make friends with the hard hands & rough tongues' of the working class, and this development in turn exposed the economic antinomies of English radical culture.[35] Commenting to Beesly that antagonism to French ideals was 'prevalent in England – (*though not among the proletariat remember*)', Harrison made his first tentative soundings of working-class radical opinion and identified Bright's insular foreign policy and dogged adherence to negative freedom as serious obstacles to class collaboration. Working men in both London and the north 'want manhood suffrage & they dislike & fear Bright & his class', he concluded. 'They have never forgiven him for the 10 hours' bill opposition.'[36]

The ensuing months saw Harrison 'repudiate Political Economy and all that stuff' and establish his first close contacts with the workers whose interest he now believed himself to represent. His initial encounters, as a lecturer at F.D. Maurice's Working Men's College, were disappointing. Here Harrison taught seventeenth-century history 'pitching into the Pope', to 'working men of the first class (£2 a week)' whom he found to have 'no political opinions – or

---

[34] Harrison, *Autobiographic Memoirs*, vol. I, pp. 169–70, 184–96. 'He has alienated the rich & he has not gained the poor', Harrison wrote to Beesly of Bright in 1859. 'Besides being without a foreign policy he is hampered.' BLPES, Harrison Collection, 1/6/34.

[35] Harrison to Beesly, [1857–8], BLPES, Harrison Collection, 1/4/84, 1/4/91–2.

[36] Harrison to Beesly, [1858], BLPES, Harrison Collection, 1/5/35 and 1/5/21–4; [1859], 1/6/32. 'There is no disguising it – there is no coherence [or] union or sympathy in anything but the negative ... Let us reject the negative & work silently for a sound comprehensive positive basis.' Harrison to Beesly, [1858], 1/5/23.

views at all'.[37] Lectures at the Freethought Hall, Cleveland Street, where Holyoake and Truelove provided him with an entrée, introduced Harrison to workers more to his tastes, and involvement with the striking building trades consolidated his working-class alliances. By 1863 he had become both an intimate of the London unions and a frequent contributor on foreign affairs to the *Bee-Hive*.[38] Armed with introductions from Holyoake, Francis Newman, and the secretaries of the unionized building trades, Harrison struck out for the provinces, where travels through Lancashire and Yorkshire in 1863 confirmed his Positivist conviction that the working class was the repository of social and political forces that could revitalize English culture. Many of his working-class contacts boasted venerable radical records. In Manchester, C. Turpic was a 'news vendor, secularist, leader of Chartists, &c' and J. Taylor was a Chartist cotton operative; in Ancoats J.E. Edwards, a former engineer who managed a cooperative store, was an 'out & out Chartist'. Nationalist sympathies clearly informed and bolstered these political observations: the best of the English workers, Harrison recalled, reminded him of Italians.[39]

The lone venture of an idiosyncratic individual, Harrison's intellectual odyssey is nonetheless significant, for it prefigured many of the developments that were to mark English radical culture in the sixties. Although even Harrison's friend and confidant E.S. Beesly declined to share his synthetic radical vision in the fifties, the following decade saw the gradual emergence within middle-class radical circles of sympathy for the integrated reform of parliamentary structures and labour relations. Nationalist sentiment did not create this new ideological departure, which was rooted in the maturation of capitalist production, the resurgence of organized labour, and the persistence of aristocratic government.[40] But nationalist idioms did mediate radicals' negotiation of this crucial juncture, and in so doing shaped the contours of Victorian class relations.

[37] Harrison to Beesly, [1862], BLPES, Harrison Collection, 1/9/41–2, and Harrison to Beesly, [1860],1/7/31–4.
[38] Harrison, *Autobiographic Memoirs*, vol. I, pp. 250–1, 265, 285.
[39] 'Diary of Journey through Lancashire', 1863, BLPES, Harrison Collection, 2/1; Harrison, *Autobiographic Memoirs*, vol. I, pp. 255, 258.
[40] Harrison, *Before the Socialists*, pp. 37–9, and Joyce, *Work, Society and Politics*, pp. 50–89, discuss the underlying economic forces that combined to create this juncture.

ENGLISH RADICALS, ITALIAN NATIONALISM, AND POLISH FREEDOM

Eclectic sympathy for the independence of all European nations characterized the international outlook of English labour in the sixties, but it was Polish and Italian nationalist campaigns that guided radical politics in the early years of this decade. Garibaldi's successful Sicilian venture in 1860, his failure at Aspromonte in 1862, and the abortive efforts of Polish revolutionaries to wrest independence from Russia in 1863 provided the backdrop against which radical leaders of both classes sought to coordinate their efforts. The web of committees, organizations, and contacts established in these campaigns helped to integrate the leaders of the new labour movement into radical politics without forcing them to repudiate individual unions' rules against collective involvement in political agitation. Liberal parliamentary candidates sought to capitalize on this wave of nationalist enthusiasm in the election of 1862, but found, like an earlier generation of middle-class politicians, that nationalist ideology was a political force with multiple meanings and troubling consequences.

Just as Mazzinian nationalism had attracted English proponents of both laissez-faire and the democratic and social republic in the 1850s, Garibaldi's nationalist exploits appealed broadly to different classes in the 1860s. Few reformers, indeed, sought to distinguish between the aims and philosophies of the two Italian patriots: radical iconography typically portrayed Garibaldi as the military embodiment of the Mazzinian nationalist spirit. 'While we look upon Garibaldi as the sword, we . . . look upon Mazzini as the pen of Italian emancipation', Reynolds argued characteristically. 'The one is the head which conceives, the other the hand which executes.'[41] Continental émigrés worked to reinforce this perception of Italian nationalist unity, and to integrate their own national preoccupations with the Italian cause. Louis Kossuth informed the Glasgow patriot John McAdam that 'all you do for Italy of course serves Hungary too indirectly', a judgement confirmed by Aurelio Saffi. Louis Blanc, preparing in 1860 for a northern lecture tour on cooperative production, was equally anxious to ally his name with Italian

---

[41] *Reynolds's Newspaper*, 13 April 1862, p. 4. For the ideological divisions of Italian nationalism which English radicals largely discounted, see Clara M. Lovett, *The Democratic Movement in Italy 1830–1876* (Cambridge, Mass., 1982).

freedom, seeking 'to know beforehand in what way and to what extent you think it expedient that I should blend the name of Garibaldi with the subject of my lectures'.[42]

Spanning otherwise significant ideological barriers to national unity, Garibaldi's campaigns proved less divisive for English radicals than support for the North in the American Civil War, a cause which generated considerable tension within labour circles until 1864.[43] But Garibaldian sympathy nonetheless reflected, and exacerbated, fundamental divisions within Victorian society. Anti-Popery, a persistent strand of the radical tradition since the seventeenth century, figured prominently in English radical responses to the invasion of the Two Sicilies, uniting infidels, Anglicans, and Nonconformists, but dividing these groups from the Catholic population in both England and Ireland. Francis Newman, a lapsed Anglican hostile to denominational Protestantism, observed in October that 'all sides of English society except Roman Catholics are jubilant at Garibaldi's success', and linked the creation of an Italian nation to broad-ranging ecclesiastical reform with 'momentous consequences to all the Christian churches of Europe'.[44] Convinced Protestant opinion was less discreet. The *Illustrated London News* detailed the anti-Catholic elements of a domestic scene from Garibaldi's home at Capri with obvious relish. 'Major Stagnatti (anything but a good Catholic) lovingly hugs "Pio Nono" ', the paper commented, 'a shaggy, quiet, and even for a donkey unintelligent-looking animal, that has been christened in compliment to his holiness.'[45]

Like religious differences, class distinctions were evident beneath the wave of patriotism that greeted Garibaldi's feats. For members

[42] Kossuth to John McAdam, 22 December 1859, Saffi to McAdam, 20 January 1860, and Blanc to McAdam, 14 September 1860, all in John McAdam Collection, Bedlay Castle, Chryston, by Glasgow.
[43] For labour's attitude toward the American Civil War, see Royden Harrison, 'British Labour and the Confederacy', *International Review of Social History*, vol. 2 (1957), pp. 78–105, and Coltham, 'Potter and the *Bee-Hive*', pp. 393–4. Harrison, *Before the Socialists*, p. 69, argues that the Civil War was a more decisive influence on the expansion of labour's political vision than was Italian and Polish nationalism, but the perspective of the 1850s suggests that the latter movements, through their late Chartist association with the February revolution, were of greater significance for perceptions of class relations in this period.
[44] Francis Newman to Francis Pulszky, 5 October and 12 November 1860, University College, London, Newman Papers, Add. MS 170, fols. 29, 31.
[45] *Illustrated London News*, 26 January 1861, p. 73.

of the upper class, the Italian cause was redolent of classical civilization, the Grand Tour, and the literary high culture that distinguished an educated gentleman from lesser mortals.[46] In contrast, middle-class admirers imbued Garibaldi with all the traits of a successful businessman. Frugal, sober, and industrious – 'tilling the scanty patch of ground which by dint of great labour has been made sufficiently fertile to produce the small stock of vegetables consumed on the farm' – he was a natural exemplar of the virtues of political economy, and thus a caution to the improvident proletariat.[47] Working-class partisans neatly reversed the inflection of these arguments in their own analysis of Garibaldi's significance. G.W.M. Reynolds, who claimed that 'all the peers of the kingdom are engaged against Garibaldi, and would hail the news of his being shot or hanged with rapturous delight', described the general as 'something more than the deliverer of Italy' in 1860:

> He is even now the emancipator of the manhood of Europe from the soul-crushing tyranny of mechanisation and routine. In our time, machinery has attained to such importance, invading and taking possession of almost every department of human endeavour, as to have established a general belief in its omnipotency. In point of fact, machinery has become the great god of the age ... It has become one of the missions of Garibaldi to destroy this faith – to teach men that a good deal may be accomplished without machinery, which ... is inferior and subordinate to the souls of true men. The whole of the public life of the Italian hero has been the working out of this problem: given the minimum of means to achieve the maximum of results.

Employing only 'old-fashioned muskets' against the very 'latest and best ... weapons of war' wielded by his opponents, Garibaldi in this analysis represented not the *bonne bourgeoisie* but the spirit of the common people.[48]

The mobilization of these disparate conceptions of Italian unity required radicals to suppress or sublimate their partisan patriotisms, a process aided considerably by their shared aversion to Catholic

---

[46] G.M. Trevelyan, 'Englishmen and Italians: Some Aspects of Their Relations Past and Present', in his *Clio, a Muse: And Other Essays* (Freeport, N.Y., 1968), pp. 104–23; John Pemble, *The Mediterranean Passion* (Oxford, 1987); Rudman, *Italian Nationalism and English Letters*.

[47] *Illustrated London News*, 26 January 1861, p. 73.

[48] *Reynolds's Newspaper*, 27 May 1860, 9 September 1860, p. 8.

religion. Concerted English efforts to provide supplies and soldiers for Garibaldi's Sicilian campaigns in 1860 capitalized on this potential, a living legacy of earlier centuries of radical patriotism. Agents for the Pope began recruiting Irish volunteers for the Papal army in March, and by autumn had succeeded in raising 1,000–1,500 Irish soldiers to fight against the nationalist insurgents; English and Scottish secularists, Nonconformists, and republicans countered by equipping a 'British Legion' of between 600 and 800 British volunteers for Garibaldi's army.[49] Although hampered by legal restrictions and plagued by embezzlement, the Central Committee of the Garibaldi Fund, which administered the British Legion, demonstrated the vitality of nationalist belief in English popular politics. Recruitment of volunteers in England, illegal under the Foreign Enlistment Act, suffered a temporary setback when mayor Crawshay of Gateshead – a follower of David Urquhart – applied for a warrant against the publisher of the *Newcastle Daily Chronicle*, who had permitted open appeals for recruits to appear in the newspaper's August issues. But Crawshay's efforts proved unsuccessful. Dismissed by the Court of Queen's Bench in November, his attempt to block recruitment in England altered the language of advertisements for volunteers, but not their substance.[50] Significantly, the Liberal government itself invoked the nationalist tradition to countenance the formation of the British Legion. Lord John Russell, defending his failure to prosecute the recruiters, justified the Legion to the House of Commons by equating Garibaldi's mission with William III's military exploits in the Glorious Revolution.[51]

The flow of capital into the Garibaldian Fund was substantial, testifying to both the persistence of old Chartist sympathies and a new largesse on the part of middle-class radicals. The Central Committee's most assiduous members were W.J. Linton and G.J.

[49] For the Irish volunteers, see Benedict Ramos, 'Recruitment to Italy in 1860' (MA thesis, Birkbeck College, University of London, 1984), and Anthony P. Campanella, *La Legione Britanica nell' Italia Meridionale con Garibaldi nel 1860* (Palermo, [1964]). Estimates of the number of British volunteers are found in G.M. Trevelyan, *Garibaldi and the Making of Italy* (London, 1911), p. 260, and Smith, *Radical Artisan*, p.137.

[50] Garibaldi's British Legion, T&WAD, Cowen Collection, 634/A663. Advertisements issued in September described the Legion as 'a Select Party of English Excursionists' intent to 'visit' Italy, and noted that the Excursionists would be armed, 'as the country is somewhat unsettled', *Reasoner*, 2 September 1860, p. 286.

[51] *Hansard's Parliamentary Debates*, 3rd ser., vol. CLVIII, cols. 1405–16, 17 May 1860.

Holyoake, whose fundraising efforts were evident in the £50 raised by October from small subscriptions to the *Reasoner*'s Garibaldi Fund.[52] But these modest funds, typical of working-class radical campaigns of the fifties, were dwarfed in the sixties by contributions from London tradesmen and magnates – reassured, perhaps, by the presence on the committee of a City solicitor and a Liberal MP. Although the volume of recruits far outstripped contributions for their provisions and passage, forcing the committee in September to limit enrolment to volunteers willing to provide for themselves, the sums at its disposal were impressive. Scottish sympathizers sent the treasurer £2,050 at the end of August, and T. Durrel Hodge of Great Portland Street – signing himself 'a friend of Orsini' – contributed £1,000 for arms in mid-September, more than compensating for £500 lost to an unscrupulous arms dealer earlier in the month.[53] Lancashire liberals who had stood opposed to the Manchester School's 'anti-national' pacifism in the Crimean War years also embraced the Garibaldian cause. Mark Philips signed appeals for aid for the Italian troops, while R.P. Greg supported Garibaldi as an Italian 'Cromwell' whose rebellion against tyranny would be 'a great blessing to the nation'.[54]

From a military standpoint the contribution of the British Legion, which sailed for Sicily in September, saw action on the Volturno later in the autumn, and returned to England in February, was minimal.[55] The significance of the Legion, like that of nationalist sentiment itself, lay rather in the creation of a political framework within which rapprochement between classes was possible, but not inevitable. Like the Volunteer Force established in 1859 to protect Britain from foreign invasion, Garibaldi's British Legion armed workers alongside men of the middle class and the aristocracy. Unlike the Volunteer Force, however, the Garibaldi movement

[52] For attendance at meetings, see the Minutes of the Central Committee of the Garibaldi Special Fund, BI, Holyoake Collection, Garibaldi carton. For the *Reasoner* subscription, see Royle, *Victorian Infidels*, p. 255.

[53] Minutes of the Central Committee, BI, Holyoake Collection, 3, 12, 13, and 18 September 1860; John McAdam to R.B. Reed, 1 September 1860, in John McAdam, *The Autobiography of John McAdam (1806–1883): With Selected Letters*, ed. Janet Fife (Edinburgh, 1980), pp. 132–3.

[54] John Buxton, *English Aid to Garibaldi, On His Invasion of the Sicilies: Is It Lawful and Just? Correspondence between the Manchester Foreign Affairs Association and Mark Philips, esq. and also between the Former and R.P. Greg* (Manchester, [1860]), pp. 5, 13–14. For Philips and the Crimean War, see above, pp. 173–4.

[55] Trevelyan, *Garibaldi and the Making of Italy*, p. 260.

lacked a dominant class ideology.[56] Indeed, its strength derived from the variety of arguments that it could accommodate. For if men of wealth dominated the finances of the Central Committee, they failed to control the discourse that it generated within the wider Anglo-Italian movement in the following years.

Garibaldi's injury and capture at Aspromonte on 27 August 1862 further consolidated the pattern of pragmatic cooperation and ideological independence adumbrated in English responses to the Sicilian campaigns in 1860. Eliciting sympathy and mobilizing financial resources across a broad social spectrum, this incident again offered English radicals an opportunity to participate directly in continental politics. Upon learning of Garibaldi's condition, the Garibaldian Italian Unity Committee promptly organized a public subscription for the Italian patriot and his followers. This committee, an outgrowth of the British Legion's executive council modelled on the Friends of Italy, included four liberal MPs, as well as W.H. Ashurst, Joseph Cowen, W.J. Linton, William Shaen, P.A. Taylor, and James Stansfeld.[57] Under its aegis, Taylor and Stansfeld dispatched an English surgeon – paid over £600 for his services – to tend to Garibaldi's wounds, and travelled to Italy themselves to ensure full and frequent reports of the invalid's progress. Garibaldi, nothing loathe to enter into the theatre of English radical politics, promptly issued a manifesto of thanks from his sickbed, denouncing the 'immoral monstrosity which is called the Papacy' and exalting 'the sacred soil of Albion', home of the continental exiles of 1848.[58]

Reports issued by the Italian Unity Committee appeared in working-class, Nonconformist, and secularist publications, but Garibaldi also found adherents among the Anglican élite. At Cambridge, undergraduates debated the merits of his cause at the Union; in Bristol, an Anglican dean delivered 'a very telling speech' in

---

[56] On the Volunteer movement and its class uses, see Hugh Cunningham, *The Volunteer Force: A Social and Political History, 1859–1908* (Hamden, Conn., 1975). The Central Committee held its meetings at the St James Volunteer Service Club, included a number of members of the club, and actively solicited members of the Volunteer Rifle Corps for Garibaldi's British Legion.

[57] For the formation of the Italian Unity Committee, see P.A. Taylor to G.J. Holyoake, 15 March 1861, MCU, Holyoake Collection, item 1297, and Taylor's circular of 4 April 1861 in T&WAD, Cowen Collection, 634/A663.

[58] James Stansfeld Jr to James Stansfeld Sr, 21 September 1861, in Mazzini, *Mazzini's Letters to an English Family*, ed. Richards, Vol. III, p. 39; 'Garibaldi's Letter to the People of England', 22 September [1862], BL, Karl Blind Papers, Add. MS 40, 124, fols. 259–60.

Garibaldi's defence at a public sympathy meeting.[59] Middle-class radicals laboured to underscore this national appeal, and to downplay the political implications of their aid. In October the *Nonconformist*, blithely ignoring the fact that support for Garibaldi's followers necessarily entailed opposition to the established governments against which he battled, noted with approval that any surplus from the Italian Unity Committee's surgical fund would 'not be appropriated to political objects, but spent upon Garibaldi's wounded followers'.[60] The participation of women in efforts to aid Garibaldi lent support to this apolitical interpretation of Italian nationalism, and assisted middle-class radical efforts to advance liberal principles under the guise of patriotism. Public and private subscriptions for Garibaldi and his wounded soldiers nicely demonstrated the efficacy of the voluntary principle, suggesting that charity and individual initiative – not government intervention – offered the key to national progress at home and abroad. Julia Salis Schwabe's justification for her contribution to a fund for the poor of Turin – a cause endorsed by Garibaldi in 1861 – derived from her conviction 'that individual efforts of private associations bring often better results than public institutions'.[61] Members of the Italian Unity Committee emphasized the same cluster of liberal principles. Supporting liberal nationalism as a vehicle of 'peace and progress', committee members claimed that their contributions to Garibaldi's cause would 'moralize' the principle of non-intervention.[62]

Liberal parliamentary candidates who sought to channel this access of voluntarist Italian sympathy into electoral victories were, however, forced to confront the conflicting (and conflictual) political potentials of English patriotism. The unsuccessful campaign waged by the Liverpool merchant George Melly was instructive in this

---

[59] Charles Dilke to Sir Charles Wentworth Dilke, 5 November 1862, BL, Sir Charles Dilke Papers, Add. MS 43,899, fol. 43; *Nonconformist*, 1 October 1862, p. 841.

[60] *Nonconformist*, 1 October 1862, p. 841.

[61] Julia Salis Schwabe to Edwin Chadwick, September 1861, University College, London, Edwin Chadwick Collection, 1761/1–2. English women also contributed to the Italian cause as volunteer nurses for Garibaldi's troops, a role that laid foundations for their future collaboration in reform efforts such as opposition to the Contagious Diseases Acts. See Jessie White Mario to Barbara Bodichon, 15 September 1877, Istituto per la Storica del Risorgimento, Rome, Jessie White Mario Collection, vol. 110, no. 50, fol. 6.

[62] Printed Circular from P.A. Taylor, 4 April 1861, T&WAD, Cowen Collection, 634/A683; James Stansfeld, *The Italian Movement and Italian Parties* (London, 1862), esp. pp. 4, 6–7.

respect. A Unitarian related to the Manchester Gregs, Melly fitted the classic profile of a liberal bourgeois patriot. Active in charities such as Liverpool's Discharged Prisoners' Aid Society and in the Social Science Association, he opposed Palmerston's Conspiracy to Murder Bill and helped to raise funds for distressed exiles in 1858. Liberal in his economic convictions, Melly identified 'self-government, self-reliance, and independence' as the basic tenets of 'every Englishman'. 'We do not want our work cut out for us by the State', he exhorted a working-class audience in 1858. 'We do not want a government which pretends to fix what should be the price of labour.'[63] Like many liberal Nonconformists, however, Melly repudiated the 'peace at any price school', a decision that earned him a promise of support from G.J. Holyoake, who was by 1859 active in promoting radical candidates for popular constituencies.[64] Standing for Preston in the spring of 1862, Melly declared his allegiance to Garibaldi and Italian independence in a bid to garner liberal votes with the ideological instruments of the English radical tradition. Every man, 'if he is an Englishman', Melly declared in a campaign speech, 'must feel that if any people ... wish to be governed otherwise than they now are, that people have a right to turn those governments, be they whom they may, to the right about, and to assert their right to choose the rule under which they will live'.[65] This tactic succeeded in winning Melly the endorsement of the *Preston Chronicle* as a proponent of 'civil and religious freedom', but it failed to gain him a Liberal seat in a constituency that boasted a significant Irish population. Articulate Preston Catholics opposed his candidacy vigorously, warning electors that support for Garibaldi constituted a direct threat to the Papacy. Both the *Preston Chronicle* and Melly's correspondents attributed his loss to a Tory candidate to his alienation of the Catholic vote.[66]

The participation of labour leaders in the Garibaldi sympathy campaigns of 1862 lent partisan perceptions of the movement additional force. While providing members of trade unions with a

[63] Newspaper Cuttings on 'Political Refugees in England', and on 'Society of Friends of Foreigners in Distress', 22 February and 8 December 1858, LCL, Melly Papers, 920 MEL, vol. 37, fols. 43 and 81; 'The Working Classes: Their Duty to Themselves', 26 November 1858, in LCL, Melly Papers, H 825 MEL, fols. 4–5.
[64] Percy Greg to Melly, 14 December 1859, LCL, Melly Papers, 5/vol. 1, fol. 474.
[65] *Preston Chronicle*, Supplement to 29 March 1862, p. 1.
[66] *Ibid.*, 26 March 1862, p. 2; 29 March 1862, p. 2; George Rusort to Melly, 5 April 1862, LCL, Melly Papers, 920 MEL, 11/vol. 7, fol. 1780.

public platform shared with middle-class radicals, it ultimately undercut liberal efforts to claim Italian unity as a patriotic arena devoid of class or political meaning. The demands of the Builders' Strike of 1859–61 limited the trades' involvement in the early phases of the Garibaldian effort, but by 1862 London labour leaders were free to declare their Italian sympathies. Determined to demonstrate the strength of support for Garibaldi in the labouring population, a Workingmen's Garibaldian Committee met in London to organize weekly sympathy meetings in Hyde Park from 28 September. Chaired by the O'Brienite bootcloser Charles Murray and supported by Charles Bradlaugh, Holyoake's successor to the leadership of the secularist movement, the Garibaldian Committee's opening meeting attracted 10,000–20,000 participants. Not all, however, were English workers or secularists: 500 Irish labourers, abetted by their wives and daughters, attended the meeting intent to uphold the Catholic cause. Singing 'God and Rome' amidst the speaker's panegyric to the patriot Garibaldi, they were soon in conflict with the English crowd. Rain dispersed the ensuing hour-long riot, but weeks of intermittent violence followed, with crowds estimated at 20,000–60,000 gathering in Hyde Park despite a massive mobilization of the Metropolitan Police.[67]

Liberal analyses of the Garibaldi riots deployed nationalist argument against the international language of class, bolstering images of inter-class harmony habitually encountered in patriotic rhetoric. The *Daily News* was careful to distinguish between English workmen and their Irish compeers, for it was 'not seemly that our intelligent artisans should be matched with LOONEY, ROONEY, and MOONEY' in discussions of the Garibaldi riots.[68] Representatives of both the secularist movement and organized labour capitalized on such stereotypes in their own analysis of the riots' significance. Charles Bradlaugh spoke to fears that had pervaded the radical tradition since the seventeenth century in his denunciation of Irish Catholics.'Papists have so little regard for public liberty', he noted, 'that they are prepared ... to bury in ruin and disorder the rights and liberties which the best and bravest of our countrymen have

[67] For the initial meeting, see *British Miner and General Newsman*, 4 October 1862, and Richard Mayne to H. Waddington, 6 October 1862, HO 45/6794. The riots and their context are discussed at greater length by Sheridan Gilley, 'The Garibaldi Riots of 1862', *Historical Journal*, vol. 16 (December 1973), pp. 697–732.

[68] *Daily News*, 1 October 1862, cited by Gilley, 'Garibaldi Riots', p. 707.

laboured and suffered to establish.'[69] The *British Miner and General Newsman* was equally strident. Denouncing 'the scum of the Irish who inhabit the dirtiest dens of London', it called upon 'the authorities' to prevent the tyrannization of London working men 'by a mob of vagabonds fit for nothing but to lower the labour market, fight for hire, and fill police cells'.[70]

Not all interpretations of Garibaldi's significance, however, promoted harmony between English labour and the middle class. Police reports associated the Garibaldi riots with the spectre of republicanism and socialism, reviving perceptions of working-class nationalism earlier established by Chartists. Richard Mayne used the opportunity of the Garibaldi riots to inform the government that speakers in Hyde Park were denouncing 'the disgraceful conduct of the Queen in keeping Buckingham Palace empty when so many Lancashire weavers were houseless', and expounding the 'doctrines of Chartism, Socialism, and infidelity'.[71] Leaders of the labour movement, while declining to elaborate a socialist interpretation of Garibaldi's patriotic activities, refused to subscribe to liberal interpretations of nationalism. The Trades' Garibaldian Demonstration Committee, founded in October by six members of the London Trades Council to prepare a working-class reception for the Italian patriot in the event that he visited England, echoed middle-class radicals in commending the 'pure and disinterested patriotism' of Garibaldi's character.[72] But the masons, joiners, and shoemakers of the Trades' Committee extolled their hero in the international language of the democratic and social republic, rather than in the liberal nationalist idiom. 'Fellow workmen, General Garibaldi is not only a patriotic citizen ... but a social reformer', they proclaimed in an address to the trade unions and friendly societies of London.

[69] *National Reformer*, 25 October 1862, p. 2.
[70] *British Miner and General Newsman*, 11 October 1862, p. 3. These characterizations were common even in internationalist radical circles: Louis Blanc asserted that 'the Papacy is represented in London by a mob of brutalized Irishmen, who even in the dens where the scum of the population boils over, form the scum of that scum'. See 'A Battle in Hyde Park', in his *Letters on England*, 2 vols. (London, 1866), vol. II, pp. 159–63. D.G. Paz explores the prevalence of such stereotypes in 'Anti-Catholicism, Anti-Irish Stereotyping, and Anti-Celtic Racism in Mid-Victorian Working-Class Periodicals', *Albion*, vol. 18 (Winter 1986), pp. 601–17.
[71] Richard Mayne to H. Waddington, 6 October 1862, HO 45/6794.
[72] *Bee-Hive*, 25 October 1862, p. 1; 1 November 1862, p. 1. Members included W.R. Cremer, George Odger, George Potter, and Robert Hartwell.

The elevation of the toiling masses is one of the principles he has ever maintained, his voice and influence has [*sic*] always been exercised in favour of lifting up labour from its present downtrodden position; he is the friend of, and beloved by, our Italian fellow workmen, and therefore must be the friend of, and beloved by, the brotherhood of labour in all countries.[73]

Confined in Italy, Garibaldi was unable to reinforce these patriotic arguments in person until 1864, but Polish nationality served to sustain English international patriotism in the interim. English responses to the Polish revolution of 1863 relied on many of the radical networks and rehearsed many of the patriotic themes evident in radical nationalist movements since the fifties, but also signalled a significant expansion in the scope of inter-class radical activity. Cobden and Bright stood aloof from this phase of radical activity, and thereby allowed a cohort of liberals favourable to English intervention abroad to capitalize on working-class enthusiasm for the continental cause. Bright was unable to 'feel deeply about English or European subjects' until American politics stabilized, and Cobden dismissed the Poles (an aristocratic nation) as 'bad citizens' incapable of self-government, but scores of provincial merchants and manufacturers organized public meetings in northern towns to demonstrate English support for the Polish patriots.[74] In Preston, George Melly's political strategist advised the aspiring Liberal candidate to nurse his constituency by speaking in favour of the Polish revolution, 'an apparently accidental method of bringing your friends together, without displaying any political design on the surface'.[75] Anxious to recoup ground lost in the election of 1862 by advancing a cause that would appeal to radical liberals without antagonizing Catholics, Melly rose to the occasion in May with a stirring speech on behalf of Polish nationality. In this Melly dismissed conservative assertions that support for the Polish revolution emanated from French revolutionary principles,

---

[73] Printed Circular, 'Trades Garibaldi Demonstration: To the Trade and Friendly Societies of London', 15 November 1862, BI, Holyoake Collection, Garibaldi carton.

[74] Bright to Elizabeth Bright, 22 June 1863, University College, London, Bright Papers, Ogden MS 65; Cobden to Charles Sumner, 7 August 1863, cited by John F. Kutolowski, 'Victorian Provincial Businessmen and Foreign Affairs: The Case of the Polish Insurrection, 1863–1864', *Northern History*, vol. 21 (1985), p. 247. Kutolowski provides an excellent overview of the provincial response to the Polish insurrection.

[75] Edward Ambler to Melly, 4 May 1863, LCL, Melly Papers, 920 MEL, 11/vol. 7, fol. 1622.

and adduced Macaulay as his guiding light on international patriotism. Militant Protestantism inspired his calls for England to intervene in Poland if other nations failed to maintain neutrality. 'When that dread hour approaches', he told the assembled crowd, 'we will appeal to the God of battles under a banner beneath which we have fought many victories, and with a war cry under which we shall always conquer – "Civil and Religious liberty all over the world." '[76]

In London, support for Polish freedom mobilized both former Chartists and emerging labour leaders alongside middle-class radical activists. The Central Committee of Friends of Poland united W.J. Linton, James Watson, and W.E. Adams with Francis Newman, Joseph Cowen, James Stansfeld, P.A. Taylor, and John Stuart Mill in efforts to raise funds for the Polish revolutionaries.[77] Frederic Harrison, breaking decisively with his earlier radical idol, John Bright, advocated English intervention on behalf of Poland in the *Bee-Hive* 'as an ardent Nationalist'.[78] Shared patriotic rhetoric allowed labour leaders to enter into this collaboration without relinquishing their claims to represent a distinct class within the nation. When London liberals convened a public sympathy meeting for Poland in July, George Odger, a shoemaker active in the London Trades Council and the Trades' Garibaldi Committee, captured the spirit of the occasion in a speech both redolent of the radical tradition and conscious of the new role of labour in the English nation. 'He stood before them as one representative of . . . workmen of England; and they were of the opinion that when a power had broken the Constitution it ought to be amenable to the highest law of the land', Odger proclaimed. 'If our government did not move in the matter, it was for the working people of the country to call upon them to take an active part in the question, and to tell them, in the event of their not doing so, they would lose the confidence of the nation.'[79] Liberal patriots cited such sentiments as evidence that England was ripe for democratic reform. When a deputation of working men from the Tower Hamlets encouraged Palmerston to wage war with Russia to support 'oppressed nationality' in Poland,

[76] *Preston Chronicle*, 9 May 1863, p. 7: 'Our Responsibilities to Poland', 7 May 1863, LCL, Melly Papers, H 825 MEL, vol. 1, fol. 31.
[77] Adams, *Memoirs of a Social Atom*, vol. II, pp. 442–9; *Secular World*, 1 May 1863, p. 227; *National Reformer*, 28 May 1863, pp. 1–2.
[78] *Bee-Hive*, 27 June 1863, p. 4; Harrison, *Autobiographic Memoirs*, vol. I, pp. 184–96, 285–8.
[79] *Bee-Hive*, 25 July 1863, pp. 5–6.

the *Times* used the incident to belittle the political judgement of workers, but the *Preston Chronicle* disagreed. 'Now, with respect to the readiness of the working classes to draw the sword for Poland, we think that so far from it being a just ground of accusation against democracy it exhibits the collective Demos at its most elevated and favourable light', the paper asserted. 'Who ever heard of an aristocracy stimulating a war in favour of an oppressed nationality?'[80]

Drawing strength from received anti-aristocratic sentiments, the radical response to the Polish revolution also moved beyond them. With the formation of the National League for the Independence of Poland, London radicals created an organization that contained both middle-class members and labour leaders, and a programme that embraced both continental nationalism and French conceptions of social relations. Upper-class adherents included the Marquis Townshend, but the participation of the barrister Edmond Beales, who presided over the National League, was most significant. Beales's radical credentials were extensive, and impeccably liberal until 1863. An advocate of Polish independence since the fifties, he had contributed with Cowen, Dawson, Shaen, Stansfeld, and Taylor to the Emancipation of Italy Fund in 1858, and joined the Garibaldi Italian Unity Committee in 1861.[81] Participation in the National League expanded both the social range of his radical contacts and the democratic content of his nationalist arguments. Radical artisans in trades such as carpentry, shoemaking, and book binding formed the backbone of the association, which actively cultivated a working-class following. Middle-class nationalist organizations typically demanded subscriptions of over a shilling, but the National League sold its membership cards for sixpence, 'so as to bring them within the reach of all working men'.[82]

Ideological breadth complemented the wide social range of the National League for the Independence of Poland and further distinguished it from earlier organizations headed by middle-class radicals. Three political characteristics of the National League were particularly noteworthy: its democratic procedures, its Francophilia, and its repudiation of the doctrine of non-intervention. A

[80] *Preston Chronicle*, 21 March 1863, p. 2.
[81] For his earlier involvement in the Polish cause, see the *Report of the Twenty-Third Annual Meeting of the Literary Association of the Friends of Poland* (London, 1855), p. 2. His Italian activities are documented in T&WAD, Cowen Collection, 634/A692, 634/A478, and 634/B38.
[82] *Bee-Hive*, 8 August 1863, p. 4.

touchstone of working-class radicalism since 1848, the combination of these attributes prefigured a more extensive attenuation of bourgeois radicals' doctrinaire liberalism over which Beales would preside later in the decade. Middle-class leaders of the National League were at pains to underline the working-class provenance and implications of these characteristics of the association. Beales wrote in the *Bee-Hive* that, while individuals of the aristocracy and the middle class supported the Polish movement, members of the working class 'alone, as a body, have thrown themselves heartily and unreservedly into the cause ... and have refused to perplex themselves with the much-misunderstood and grievously-applied doctrine of non-intervention'.[83] Peter Fox underscored the working-class presence in the League and emphasized the fact that its deliberations were 'formed on the most democratic basis' – all members were welcome to attend and participate at League meetings. Fox, significantly, traced the League's intellectual origins to 'a small section of the Liberal party – that section which adheres to the principles of 1789 and which proclaims its undying friendship for the nation which gave them birth – and the urban working classes, who were utterly discontented with the turn given to events by the English aristocracy and bourgeoisie'.[84]

National League activities substantiated these abstract international sympathies, and elaborated upon their particular significance for labour. When a deputation of French workmen travelled to England to attend a demonstration in support of Polish independence, Beales read their proclamation to a League meeting and pronounced it 'an admirable address in every respect, reflecting credit on those who had drawn it up'. The working-class supporters of the organization, however, went beyond mere commendation in their address to the French workmen. Starting from the premise that an international gathering of representatives from England, France, Germany, Italy, and Poland would promote 'the good of mankind', the working-class sub-committee proceeded to link the claims of internationalism to those of the working class. 'A fraternity of peoples is highly necessary for the cause of labour', they argued:

> for we find that whenever we attempt to better our social condition by reducing the hours of toil, or by raising the price of labour, our employers threaten us with bringing over Frenchmen,

[83] *Ibid.*, 11 July 1863, p.4.   [84] *National Reformer*, 13 February 1864, pp. 6–7.

Germans, Belgians, and others to do our work at reduced rate, and we are sorry to say that this has been done, though not from any desire on the part of our continental brethren to injure us, but through a want of regular and systematic communication between the industrious classes of all countries.[85]

Assiduously defending the principle of nationality, labour leaders who interpreted the meaning of this interaction for the larger union membership were careful to include France within the fraternity of nations. 'We were proud to welcome the representatives of the liberty-loving French people, who came forward to initiate, what has been too long delayed, a grand fraternity of peoples', a member of a committee composed of a painter, a joiner, a book binder, a carpenter, and a shoemaker told the bricklayers, before proceeding to expatiate upon the achievements of Garibaldi.[86]

Describing internationalism as a vehicle for the protection and improvement of labour's position within the independent nation rather than as an instrument for the overthrow of the state, the League's address anticipated the arguments advanced by English labour leaders in support of the First International. This correspondence was not fortuitous, for it was a call by working-class members of the National League in December 1863 to organize an international gathering which produced the preliminary meeting of the First International in September 1864.[87] In the interim, a revival of Garibaldian enthusiasm revitalized the Garibaldi Trades Committee – most of whom were also members of the National League – and mobilized both liberal Nonconformists and Positivists against aristocratic government. Setting the stage for the formation of the First International, this nationalist revival also paved the way for renewed radical agitation for universal manhood suffrage and the social and economic rights that working-class patriots insisted the franchise necessarily entailed.

GARIBALDI AND REFORM

Garibaldi's visit to England in the spring of 1864, eagerly awaited by liberal and radical leaders active in the Italian cause, permitted a ceremonial enactment of the patriotic and political idioms

---

[85] *Bee-Hive*, 5 December 1863, p. 1.
[86] *Operative Bricklayers' Circular*, 1 January 1864, pp. 238–9.
[87] See below, p. 229.

218   *After Chartism*

expounded in reform circles from 1860 to 1863. But it also demonstrated the dangers of accepting nationalist ideology at face value, illustrating the pitfalls inherent in efforts to translate shared patriotic rhetoric into shared patriotic activities. From his arrival at the Isle of Wight in April, Garibaldi became a source of contention among rival political factions intent to bend his patriotic image to their own ends. Enmeshed in a struggle for symbolic mastery of the English nation, anxious to raise sufficient funds to purchase a warship, and advised by his English host to avoid political pronouncements that 'would soon make him the guest of a small party instead of the guest of a great nation', Garibaldi sought to curry favour with all sympathetic interests.[88] This tactic, which dismayed his radical partisans, failed to prevent the illusions of social harmony purveyed in patriotic rhetoric from fracturing to reveal the limits of national unity. The resolution of these tensions in the following years enhanced the popular appeal of Liberal party politics, but it did so only by expanding the established parameters of liberal economics.

Within the tide of Garibaldian enthusiasm that swept England from March to April, three currents of nationalist argument – reflecting the three perceived class divisions of English society – contended for dominance. At the apex of the social structure, Palmerston encouraged representatives of the social and political élite to ensure that Garibaldi was 'taken up by the aristocracy, and . . . not [left] . . . in the hands of agitators who would . . . use him for their own purposes'. Contained by the nobility, Palmerston explained to the queen, Garibaldi's visit would afford 'great pleasure to the bulk of the nation, as a proof of the community of feeling among all classes of the nation'.[89] Middle-class enthusiasts were at one with the aristocracy in advancing Garibaldian nationalism as a corrective to class, but they departed from the aristocratic analysis in ascribing liberal political motives to the Italian patriot. The *Illustrated London News* found 'a talismanic influence of unprecedented potency' in the Garibaldian sympathies harboured 'in the

---

[88] Giuseppe Mazzini to Joseph Cowen, 12 April 1864, and M.E. Chambers to Cowen, 16 April 1864, T&WAD, Cowen Collection, 634/A766, 634/A786.
[89] Lord Palmerston to Queen Victoria, 17 April 1864, in George E. Buckle (ed.), *The Letters of Queen Victoria*, 2nd ser., 3 vols. (New York, 1926), vol. I, p. 173. For a fine discussion of the dynamics of this encounter, see Derek Beales, 'Garibaldi in England: The Politics of Enthusiasm', in John A. Davis and Paul Ginsborg (eds.), *Society and Politics in the Age of the Risorgimento* (Cambridge, 1991), pp. 184–216.

bosoms of the nobility, the middle classes, and the toiling millions', but attributed these sentiments to Garibaldi's function as 'the popular symbol of national unity, independence, and liberty', a symbol 'sure to exert a liberalising influence upon public opinion abroad'.[90] In sharp contrast, the working-class press was at pains to disavow any connection between Garibaldi and the ruling classes. 'He is not a butterfly of fashion, but a man of the people', Reynolds insisted. 'He has no reverence for sovereignty, excepting that which belongs to the people.'[91]

Alarmed by the ardour of aristocratic responses to the news of Garibaldi's visit, middle- and working-class radical leaders united in an effort to remove the general from the 'doubtful hands and surroundings' of élite culture. P.A. Taylor, William Ashurst, and G.J. Holyoake convinced Joseph Cowen to meet the Italian patriot at the Isle of Wight and attempt to convince him to begin his tour through England in the robust radical circles of the provinces.[92] Although representatives of the Manchester School remained aloof from these activities, Manchester's wider radical community joined in the popular efforts to appropriate the Italian hero. Ernest Jones joined Manchester's Garibaldi Reception Committee – which included five aldermen and six town councillors – to invite Garibaldi to visit the industrial north.[93] When Cowen's efforts to launch Garibaldi in the provinces proved unsuccessful, the focus of radical activity shifted to London, where middle- and working-class activists hoped to loosen the aristocracy's patriotic stranglehold by combining forces. The City Reception Committee, composed of tradesmen, merchants, and common councilmen, united middle-class liberal radicals under the leadership of Edmond Beales, Samuel Morley, and P.A. Taylor, but it was careful to invite delegates of the London trades to its deliberations.[94]

Labour leaders cultivated these alliances, inviting delegates from the City Reception Committee to attend the meetings of the revived Garibaldi Trades Committee, which met at the Whittington Club.

[90] *Illustrated London News*, 23 April 1864, p. 382.
[91] *Reynolds's Newspaper*, 27 March 1864, p. 4.
[92] P.A. Taylor to Joseph Cowen, 22 March 1864, W.H. Ashurst to Cowen, and G.J. Holyoake to Cowen, 22 and 23 March and 10 April 1864, T&WAD, Cowen Collection, 634/A730, 634/A734, 634/A740. The quotation is from Taylor's letter.
[93] Printed Notice, 'Garibaldi Reception Committee', 26 March 1864, MCRL, Wilson Papers, M20/1864.
[94] *Bee-Hive*, 26 March 1865, p. 1; 2 April 1864, p. 1.

But their collaboration with liberal patriots at a liberal venue did not signal a capitulation to liberal insistence that national freedom encompassed only civil and religious freedoms. Headed by a shoemaker, a bricklayer, a painter, a compositor, a tin-plate worker, and four carpenters and joiners, the Trades Committee sent representatives to the meetings of the City Reception Committee, but claimed Garibaldi as a particular representative of the working class. Extending 'a hearty English welcome' to Garibaldi as a soldier 'for his country and freedom', its address called upon the labouring masses to hold the Italian nationalist leader in especial veneration 'as the interests of that class have ever been his guiding star'.[95] Editorials in the *Bee-Hive* reinforced this line of reasoning, privileging the claim of English labour to identify with oppressed nationalities by identifying Garibaldi as a representative of 'the sons of toil and industry, the poor, and the oppressed; not alone those of his own nation, but those of the world at large'.[96] Provincial working-class organizations echoed these themes as they prepared to send delegations to London for the Garibaldi reception. The Manchester and Salford Equitable Co-operative Society conflated Garibaldi's 'services to the sacred cause of freedom' with their own efforts to assert 'the just claims and fair rewards of labour'.[97]

Orchestrated by upper-class parliamentarians, Garibaldi's ceremonial entry into London in mid-April was a celebration of social cohesion. Hundreds of thousands of spectators lined roads decorated with banners upholding at one and the same time the queen, the constitution, and Garibaldi – 'The Pure Patriot!', 'The Hero of Italy!', 'The Man of the People!'. Held on a Monday – the day, as one member of the Garibaldi Trades Committee commented, on which 'the working men were most at liberty' – the Garibaldi demonstration saw 'Saint Monday ... kept as it was never kept before'. At the Nine Elms station, festooned with patriotic banners and bunting, George Potter shared the platform with P.A.Taylor, Samuel Morley, Edmond Beales, Lord Shaftesbury, and Lord and Lady Kinsale. Deputations from both the City Reception Committee and the Garibaldi Trades Committee presented the Italian patriot with addresses. Later, an hour-long procession of trade

[95] *Ibid.*, 26 March 1864, p. 1.   [96] *Ibid.*, p.4.
[97] Manchester and Salford Equitable Co-operative Society Minute and Attendance Book, 13 April 1864, MCRL, M473/1/1/183–6.

union representatives, friendly societies, and gentlemen's private carriages filed by the reception platform, which was graced strategically by a duke and a marquis.[98]

As in earlier manifestations of support for Italian unity, contemporary analyses of the significance of Garibaldi's London debut revealed class differences beneath a shared patriotic carapace. Lord Granville, responding to the queen's querulous accusation that Garibaldi had received lavish honours 'usually reserved for Royalty' from members of the government, underlined the advantages of aristocratic intervention in popular politics. 'The joining of the aristocracy, including some Conservative leaders, in demonstrations in his favour, although making the affair more offensive and more ridiculous to foreign nations, has been of great use', he assured Victoria. 'It has taken the democratic sting (as to this country) out of the affair.'[99] Middle-class publications also downplayed the perceived democratic content of the Garibaldi reception, and minimized its significance to the labour movement. The *Illustrated London News* reported with approval that 'there were no political banners and few relating to trades, the bulk of the devices exhibited belonging to friendly societies, Odd Fellows, Foresters, and Teetotalers'[100] – the least threatening of working-class associations.

Labour publications, conversely, underscored the presence of trade union deputations at the reception and reiterated Garibaldi's identification with the working class. Garibaldi's speech to the trades' deputation praised the efforts of 'that class I have the honour to belong to', sentiments that the *Miner and Workman's Advocate* claimed received 'immense applause, exceeding any of the outbursts ... preceding it'.[101] Democratic reasoning flowed naturally from this analysis. Reynolds railed against middle- and upper-class assertions that 'however much the people of this country may admire Garibaldi's character, they cannot possibly sympathise with him in his aspirations, inasmuch as Englishmen are not exposed to such grievances as those of which he has been the great redeemer'. Claiming that the warmth of the welcome resulted from Garibaldi's

[98] *Manchester Daily Examiner and Times*, 6 and 12 April 1864, pp. 3, 5; *Miner and Workman's Advocate*, 16 April 1864, p. 2; *Bee-Hive*, 16 April 1864, p. 1.

[99] Queen Victoria to Lord Granville, 21 April 1864, and Lord Granville to Queen Victoria, 21 April 1864, in Buckle (ed.), *Letters of Queen Victoria*, vol. I, pp. 174–6.

[100] *Illustrated London News*, 16 April 1864, p. 374.

[101] *Miner and Workman's Advocate*, 16 April 1864, p. 3.

significance as 'the most effectual champion of European democracy', he proffered an analysis in which only universal manhood suffrage could correct the social and political grievances of the working class.[102]

Conservative observers of this working-class response to Garibaldi's visit seized upon the social and economic meanings encoded in labour leaders' patriotic appeals to liberty, democracy, and the nation. The pamphlet literature generated by Garibaldi's visit to England is significant in this respect, revealing the enduring force of perceived class differences forged in 1848. Jerym Cooper's conservative denunciation of the working-class Garibaldians was typical. Beginning with a quotation from the address presented at Nine Elms station by the Garibaldian Trades Committee, Cooper proceeded to conflate Garibaldi's cause first with the French revolution of 1789, then with the French republican and socialist cause of 1848, and finally with English aspiration for universal manhood suffrage.[103] Henry Edward Manning rendered a similar portrait of radical, nationalist, and socialist complicity in anatomizing English Garibaldian sentiment. Underlining Garibaldi's commitment to French revolutionary ideals, Manning claimed that the Italian patriot 'invites the English people to assume the mission and office held by France in 1789 ... that is, of stimulating and assisting the seditious and socialist revolutions which at this moment threaten every government, absolute or constitutional, throughout Europe'. Wilfully confusing nationalist and socialist reform, Manning's analysis was of a piece with working-class radical polemic since 1848. His derision of men of property and status who dabbled in revolutionary patriotic movements was both clear and emphatic. 'The sympathy of America and the patriotic effusions of the Fenians were old stock', Manning expostulated, 'but who would have hoped for the enthusiastic nationalism of the English aristocracy and of the City of London?'[104]

Although the Garibaldi reception at Nine Elms had allowed middle- and upper-class observers to celebrate class comity within

[102] *Reynolds's Newspaper*, 17 April 1864, p. 1. For trade union participation in the welcome, see *Bee-Hive*, 16 April 1864, p. 1.

[103] Jerym Cooper, *Three Letters to the Conservatives of England, and through Them to the People of England, on the Subject of Garibaldi and Revolution* (London, 1864), pp. 7, 13, 19.

[104] Henry Edward Manning, *The Visit of Garibaldi to England: A Letter to the Right Honourable Edward Cardwell, M.P.* (London, 1864), pp. 13, 21.

the nation, the conduct of the political élite after Garibaldi's arrival forced middle-class radicals into a closer alliance with the labour movement. For once secured in London, Garibaldi was effectively captured by aristocratic liberals and their followers. He attended a private gathering of English radicals and continental émigrés at Herzen's London residence and delighted middle-class radicals gathered at the Taylors' Aubrey House by praising Oliver Cromwell's refusal to accept the crown, but the Duke of Sutherland, Garibaldi's official host in London, supervised his public appearances closely.[105] Determined to contain the democratic potential of Garibaldian nationalism, Sutherland exhibited Garibaldi to select audiences at the Opera and Stafford House, but acted in concert with Palmerston and W.E. Gladstone to thwart Garibaldi's projected six-week tour of thirty towns and cities in the provinces, convincing the general to return to Capri instead.[106] These élite liberal supporters were unwilling to endorse Garibaldi's political programme openly by providing funds for a warship, but sought to soften the impact of his departure by bolstering his personal finances. A 'preliminary meeting of a few friends of General Garibaldi' held at Sutherland's London residence generated over £1,900, a sum offered as a token of 'the profound admiration felt by all classes throughout the United Kingdom for his unselfish patriotism and disinterested services to the cause of liberty'.[107]

Intended by the government to attenuate the force of English popular politics, Garibaldi's premature departure served instead to precipitate agitation for domestic political reform. Gladstone badly mismanaged his part in the affair, claiming in the face of all the evidence that medical rather than political considerations had shortened Garibaldi's visit.[108] Members of the Trades' and City Reception Committees, assisted by Frederic Harrison and E.S. Beesly, pooled their communication networks to discover the cause

[105] For Herzen's reception, see Linton, *European Republicans*, pp. 277–9. Moncure Daniel Conway noted that at the Taylors', Garibaldi 'saw with delight for the first time a portrait of Cromwell. It represented the Protector refusing the crown, and Garibaldi knew English enough to exclaim, "Noble fellow, noble fellow – not to accept it!"' Conway, *Autobiography*, vol. II, p. 59.

[106] The high politics of the incident are detailed in Richard Shannon, *Gladstone: 1809–1865* (London, 1982), pp. 501–4.

[107] *Reynolds's Newspaper*, 24 April 1864, p. 2.

[108] *Hansard's Parliamentary Debates*, 3rd ser., vol. CLXXIV, col. 1422–6, 26 April 1864; *The Gladstone Diaries: 1861–1868*, ed. H.C.G. Matthew (Oxford, 1978), pp. 268–9.

of Garibaldi's departure.[109] They were soon dissatisfied with official responses to their inquiries and turned to the masses for support. In late April, Edmond Beales, Frederic Harrison, and London labour leaders joined forces to co-opt a meeting of the Workingmen's Shakespeare Tercentenary Committee at Primrose Hill, where they denounced the government's role in the expulsion to an audience of 50,000 until police intervention dispersed the crowd.[110] Agitation for an expanded franchise was a logical corollary of these circumstances, calculated to bring government policy and national sentiment into closer accord. By late May, Beales had established a suffrage reform association in London.[111]

John Bright, preoccupied by his own efforts to revive franchise reform with an agitation for household suffrage, contemplated the Garibaldi agitation and despaired of mounting an effective radical campaign in England. Cobden, who shared his pessimism, detailed their mutual concern to T.B. Potter in May:

> When will the masses of this country begin to think of home politics? Our friend Bright observed, as he gazed from a window in Parliament Street on the tens of thousands that cheered the Italian, 'If the people would only make a few such demonstrations for themselves, we could do something for them.' But nothing except foreign patriots seems to occupy the attention of the people, press, or parliament.[112]

Bright's lament fits easily with received historical arguments that nationalism functions to displace class conflict, but it was surpassed in its own day by events. Far from impeding political reform in the 1860s, nationalist sentiment proved central to the emergence of effective radical organizations capable both of expressing class interests and of bridging them. The rise to prominence with the Garibaldian agitation of radicals such as Beales, Cowen, Harrison, Stansfeld, and Taylor, who boasted parliamentary influence or

[109] Frederic Harrison to E.S. Beesly, 21 April [1864] and [1864], BLPES, Harrison Collection, 1/11/50–2 and 1/11/105–6; E.S. Beesly to G.J. Holyoake, 21 May 1864, MCU, Holyoake Collection, item 1544. Beesly, encouraged by Taylor and Shaen, sought information from Holyoake on Garibaldi's expulsion; Harrison worked with Cremer and Odger to mobilize workers to protest Garibaldi's departure.

[110] *Bee-Hive*, 23 April 1864, p. 1; 30 April 1864, p. 4; Philip T. Smith, 'The London Metropolitan Police and the Public Law and Security, 1850–1868' (PhD thesis, Columbia University, 1975), pp. 249–50.

[111] *Bee-Hive*, 28 May 1864, p. 1.

[112] Richard Cobden to T.B. Potter, in John Morley, *The Life of Richard Cobden*, 2 vols. (London, 1905), vol. II, p. 911.

ambitions, was of particular significance. Liberal interventionists in foreign policy, these men helped to moderate middle-class radicalism's relentless commitment to laissez-faire, providing interpretations of the meaning of liberalism that contrasted sharply with the unpopular dogmatism of the Manchester School.[113] Tolerant of trade unionism, these men acted with working-class leaders to mobilize organized labour in movements sympathetic to continental nationalism under the aegis of English patriotism. While middle-class opinion of this period consistently depicted patriotism as an axiomatic force above class and party, labour leaders repeatedly deployed it to gain admittance to the public sphere of politics and economics.

[113] Radical antagonism to Manchester School pacifism continued to fester long after the Crimean War. William Maccall's 'England the Coward', *National Reformer*, 13 August 1864, lampooned this aspect of liberal policy in the aftermath of the Garibaldi expulsion: 'I am feeble and fat, saith old John Bull, / I cannot afford to play the fool; / I sit content on my money bags, / And I love the world to go to rags. / Danes may be murdered and Poles may die, / Circassians may utter an anguished cry . . . / The Manchester preachers are now my priests, / I am not fond of the nasty beasts; / But they gorge me with cotton, and cant, and cash, / And keep me clear of the general smash.'

6 · The Reform League, the Reform Union, and the First International

... in all times men have been prone to believe that their happiness and well-being were to be secured by means of institutions rather than by their own conduct. Hence the value of legislation as an agent in human advancement has always been greatly over-estimated. To constitute a millionth part of a legislature, by voting for one or two men once in three or five years, however conscientiously this duty may be performed, can exercise but little active influence upon any man's life and character. Moreover, it is every day becoming more clearly understood, that the function of government is negative and restrictive, rather than positive and active ...

National progress is the sum of individual industry, energy, and uprightness. If this view be correct, then it follows that the highest patriotism and philanthropy consist, not so much in altering laws and modifying institutions, as in helping and stimulating men to elevate and improve themselves by their own force and independent action.[1]

Notions of sovereignty lay at the heart of English nationalist sentiment in the first two decades after 1848, but sovereignty assumed myriad forms in the patriotic rhetoric and activities of liberal and radical activists in these years. In the radical revival of the early sixties, trade union leaders – drawing variously from the Commonwealth, French revolutionary, and Chartist traditions – equated national sovereignty at once with democratic and social reform, the rights of labour and the rights of man. Exploiting liberal enthusiasm for Italian and Polish independence to create a space within the public political sphere for social and economic organiza-

---

[1] Samuel Smiles, *Self-Help: With Illustrations of Character and Conduct*, 2nd edn (Boston, 1866), pp. 15–17.

226

tions, labour leaders underlined the collective nature of sovereignty, and its class meaning. Liberal patriots such as Samuel Smiles, in contrast, seized upon national sentiment as a means with which to limit or assail both class identity and political activity. Locating national regeneration in the advance of self-improvement and self-restraint among individual citizens, exponents of classical economics prized the individual's sovereignty over his own passions, convictions, and economic activities, discounting the citizen's contribution to the collective sovereignty of the political nation.

Just as two strands of political argument, liberal and social democratic, vied for dominance in the Garibaldi and Polish movements of 1860–4, two paths of radical activity, liberal and socialist, issued from the nationalist agitations of these years. On the one hand, the Reform League and the Reform Union orchestrated working- and middle-class participation in suffrage reform and ultimately underpinned the creation of a viable Liberal party in England; on the other, the International Working Men's Association ostensibly sought to establish the foundations for class-based social revolution throughout Europe. Yet the separation of these two strands of development – however valid conceptually – is misleading, for these years saw a gradual melding of class and liberal idioms within English radical culture rather than their increasing divergence. Therein lies the significance of these years. In the decade after 1848, radical responses to continental politics helped to reinforce perceptions of class difference in English society, but nationalist and internationalist endeavour in the sixties ultimately helped to reconcile liberals to labour. The working-class Reform League failed to achieve universal manhood suffrage and the First International failed to forge a class-conscious revolutionary proletariat, but together these two organizations worked to mediate the recasting of liberal nationalism in a social democratic mould.

NATION AND CLASS IN THE FIRST INTERNATIONAL

Established on 28 September 1864, the International Working Men's Association figures in the orthodox history of Marxism as the 'first international proletarian mass organization [which] paved the way for the world communist movement of today', a movement whose 'immense significance ... was due to the notable part played in it by Karl Marx and Frederick Engels'.[2] Viewed from the perspective of English labour radicalism, these claims are exaggerated, but also significant. Constituted by labour aristocrats and artisans in trades largely untouched by mechanization rather than by operatives in the cotton or steel industries, the First International expressed the longstanding radical traditions of skilled craftsmen. The significance of labour involvement in the organization derived not from the triumph of proletarianization but from the ability of men affiliated with exclusive trade unions to see beyond the particularistic claims of their crafts to the wider needs and claims of the working class, from the willingness – to borrow Ber Borochov's terminology – of working-class radical patriots to acknowledge the importance of relations of production alongside that of conditions of production.[3] The influence exerted by Marx and Engels on English members of the International was, similarly, less extensive than the orthodox Marxist interpretation would suggest. Engels's residence in Manchester limited his participation until 1870, and illness prevented Marx from assuming a key role in the International during the first two years of its existence.[4] Yet if it is facile to ascribe a new revolutionary class consciousness to English workers under the influence of the First International, it is also simplistic to dismiss the organization's impact out of hand. Like other middle-class radicals of their generation – Edmond Beales, E. S. Beesly, Frederic Harrison, and J. S. Mill – Marx and Engels had remained largely aloof from active involvement in English working-class politics in the decade after 1848. Their new willingness to engage in the politics of labour from the mid-sixties both expanded the potential impact of radical culture and encouraged rival middle-class reformers to widen the horizons of their political vision by advocating democratic instruments of social reform.

Marx's involvement in the First International marked a new departure for the English labour movement, but the ideological and organizational ties that linked the International to indigenous (and continental) radical traditions were substantial. Uniting class argu-

---

[2] 'Preface', *The General Council of the First International: 1864–1872*, 5 vols. (Moscow, 1964), vol. I, p. 11.

[3] See above, pp. 31–2.

[4] Collins and Abramsky, *Marx and the British Labour Movement*, offer a balanced analysis of both the composition of the movement and Marx's and Engels's impact upon it. See esp. pp. 30, 76.

ments with fervent nationalist sentiments, the association's genesis
reflected the characteristic preoccupations and modes of working-
class international culture that had evolved in the aftermath of the
revolutions of 1848–9. Its origins derived from the Garibaldi Trades
Committee and the National League for the Independence of
Poland, which in April 1864 sponsored a visit to London by a
deputation of French workmen sympathetic to the Polish cause.[5]
This deputation, calling on English labour to join in an effort to
create a congress of European working men, laid the groundwork
for a conference at St Martin's Hall in September, which established
the International Working Men's Association along broad lines
encompassing both nationalist aspiration and the international
solidarity of labour. Marx's inaugural address and provisional rules
catered to established working-class radical tastes and traditions,
denouncing classical economics and upholding the integration of
social, economic, and political spheres. Hailing the passage of the
Ten Hours' Act as 'the first time that . . . the political economy of the
middle class succumbed to the political economy of the working
class', his inaugural address asserted – like the *démoc-soc* manifestos
of the late Chartist movement – that 'the economical emancipation
of the working class is . . . the great end to which every political
movement ought to be subordinate as a means'. His provisional
rules built upon both the French revolutionary tradition of 1789 and
the sentiments inscribed in Mazzini's popular *Duties of Man* (1862).
Urging each member to pursue 'the abolition of all class rule' by
claiming 'the rights of man and a citizen, not only for himself, but
for every man who does his duty', the rules lent new, class inflections
to Mazzini's adage, 'no rights without duties, no duties without
rights'.[6] Within English branches of the International, these rhetorical traditions proved especially enduring. The principle advanced by the British section of the International in 1872 was 'The
Abolition of all Class Rule'; the mottoes inscribed on its membership cards were 'No Rights without Duties', 'No Duties without
Rights', and Louis Blanc's 'The Right to Live by Labour'.[7]
  Largely peripheral to Marx's critique of political economy, the

[5] *Ibid.*, p. 26, and above, p. 217.
[6] 'Inaugural Address' and 'Provisional Rules', in *General Council Minutes*, vol. I, pp. 284, 288–9.
[7] 'Membership Card of the British Section of the International Working Men's Association', IISG, Hermann Jung Collection, C. 193.

nationalist and social democratic arguments of working-class radicalism were central to the appeal of the International in English labour circles. Patterns of activity and meaning established in the decade after 1848 recur throughout the ceremonial life of the organization, consolidating the distinctive working-class interpretations of labour's relation to the nation first elaborated by Chartists in their efforts to counter liberal reactions to 1848. Like the Chartists before them, English members of the International participated in the émigré community's annual celebrations of the June Days and the February revolution to advance *démoc-soc* ideals. When in 1868 English members joined their French colleagues for the twentieth anniversary of the February revolution, they concluded their celebration, like countless others in the two preceding decades, not by denouncing the sway of industrial capital but rather with 'loud cries of "Vive la République, Démocratique et Sociale" . . . followed by prolonged and enthusiastic cheering'.[8] The associational life of the First International itself perpetuated these traditions. George Odger, shoemaker, secretary of the London Trades Council, and president of the International's General Council, intertwined the cause of England, France, and Poland in a speech at the conference that marked the culmination of the International's first year of activities. Recalling that French and English workmen had laid the organization's foundations in efforts to support the Polish nation, he insisted that labour's sympathy for this 'the very type of oppressed nations' rested equally upon the rights of nationality and the imperative of 'reestablishing that country on a Social and Democratic basis'.[9]

Tea parties, soirées, and public meetings sponsored or endorsed by the International reinforced this confluence of class and nationalist conviction with internationalist symbolism and interventionist argument. The programme of songs for the tea party and public meeting held to commemorate the fourth anniversary of the Polish revolution of 1863 spoke to the martial tendencies of labour internationalism, offering participants the enjoyment of the Polish National Hymn, Garibaldi's Air, and the Marseillaise.[10] Eschewing

[8]   *Bee-Hive*, 20 February 1868, p. 1.
[9]   'Minutes of the Sitting of the Congress', 27 September 1865, IISG, Jung Collection, A. 5.
[10] 'Programme for the Tea-Party and Public Meeting', 22 January 1867, *General Council Minutes*, vol. II, p. 277.

liberal pacifism and liberal market mechanisms, English members of the International, like working-class radicals in the years of the Crimean War, deployed Polish nationalist sympathies to justify political intervention – in foreign relations as in labour relations – against Manchester economics. Speaking at the International's third anniversary commemoration of the Polish revolution, W. R. Cremer of the Amalgamated Society of Carpenters and Joiners 'said he stood there as a British working man to repudiate the non-intervention policy preached by a certain school in Great Britain'. Regardless of the national provenance of oppression, he argued, 'whether it was the black population of America, their ill-used sable brethren in Jamaica, or their gallant but oppressed friends, the Poles ... it was our duty to interfere and use every exertion on behalf of liberty and justice'.[11] Engels endorsed this line of argument and asserted, somewhat grandiloquently, that 'the working men of Europe unanimously proclaim the restoration of Poland as part and parcel of their political programme'. Tracing international labour's Polish sympathies to the Chartist movement, he asserted that workers 'mean intervention, not non-intervention; they mean war with Russia while Russia meddles with Poland'.[12]

Continuity of personnel underpinned these ideological links between the First International and the Chartist movement, testifying at once to the endurance of earlier radical traditions and their persistent evolution. Among the English members of the General Council, George Harris, the mechanic Martin James Boon, the tailor George Milner, and the bootcloser Charles Murray were disciples of Bronterre O'Brien, while Benjamin Lucraft and George Howell were former followers of Ernest Jones. Jones himself, although prevented by his residence in Manchester from involvement in the General Council's activities in London, joined the International in 1865 and worked to extend its influence in Lancashire.[13] Press coverage of meetings and publications of the International's manifestos similarly benefited from the resources of

[11] *Workman's Advocate*, 27 January 1866, p. 5.
[12] *Commonwealth*, 24 March 1866, p. 5.
[13] Brief but useful synopses of the biographies of members of the International are compiled in the index at the end of each volume of the *General Council Minutes*. For Jones's participation, see Jones to Marx, 15 February and 3 March 1865, IISG, Marx–Engels Collection, D., Letters to Marx, items 2506 and 2508.

working-class radical networks developed in the decade after 1848. Under the guidance of J. B. Leno, a compositor and former Chartist internationalist, the Industrial Newspaper Company's *Workman's Advocate* proved willing to report and publicize the International's activities when infighting among labour leaders prevented the *Bee-Hive*, its official organ, from doing so. Edward Truelove's contributions were equally significant. Publisher of the organization's manifestos, he also offered his premises for the International's meetings.[14] Although especially conspicuous among the leaders of the International, this pattern of radical continuity extended as well to the ranks of the general membership. A letter written by John Smith of Whitechurch, Dorsetshire, in 1868 was revealing. 'The principles of the Association were not new to him', Smith explained in requesting admittance, for 'he had joined the Chartists in 1838, and the Fraternal Democrats in 1846 and thought any society must be good to which the name Odger was attached'.[15]

If substantial overlap of ideology and commitment obtained between working-class radical movements of the fifties and the sixties, the First International nonetheless signalled a decisive departure from the patterns of radical allegiance that had marked late Chartism. Adherents of both movements derived overwhelmingly from crafts and trades in which mechanization had not yet transformed the production process, but the scale of formal trade union involvement in the International distinguished it sharply from late Chartism. As in the Garibaldi and Polish agitations of the early sixties, the building trades were especially prominent, providing over 40 per cent of the members of the first General Council.[16] But the organization represented a striking diversity of crafts, winning the affiliation of trades whose resources had scarcely been tapped in earlier manifestations of labour internationalism after 1848. Two years after its foundation, the International could boast a membership of over 25,000 men – shoemakers, bricklayers, carpenters, ribbon weavers, packing case makers, cabinet-makers, coopers, tailors, bookbinders, plumbers' brass finishers, cigar makers, organ

[14] For Leno, see his volume of poetry, *The Aftermath: With Autobiography of the Author* (London, 1892), esp. pp. 28, 61; for Truelove, see Truelove to Marx, 15 June and 9 August 1871, IISG, Marx–Engels Collection, part D., Letters to Marx, items 4323 and 4328, and Collins and Abramsky, *Marx and the British Labour Movement*, p. 235.

[15] *General Council Minutes*, vol. III, p. 98.

[16] Collins and Abramsky, *Marx and the British Labour Movement*, p. 15.

builders, and saddle and harness makers.[17] By 1867, bootmakers, basket makers, block printers, coach builders, coach trimmers, elastic web weavers, excavators, French polishers, pattern drawers, and curriers had joined the ranks, and extended the influence of the International from London to Coventry, Darlington, Nottingham, Kendal, and Lancashire.[18]

Marx's manifestos and the ritualized celebrations of the European revolutions offered members of these trade societies exposure to an array of sophisticated internationalist argument and popular fraternal symbolism that helped to expand their political vision beyond their individual craft and nation. But more mundane economic considerations typically precipitated union membership in the International. Enjoying considerable success, the General Council's policy of using the lines of communication established among the organization's various national sections to prevent English employers from replacing their workers with continental blacklegs lent the International considerable appeal to trades engaged in strikes in an era of escalating industrial conflict. Thus by using internationalist structures to regulate national markets, the Council earned the gratitude and allegiance of the London Basketmakers' Society in 1866, successfully dispatching their representatives to convince eight Belgian workers – brought to London by employers determined to break a strike – to return to their homeland.[19]

Far from exerting a universal appeal within organized labour, activities such as this alienated unions whose rules prohibited corporate involvement in political issues. Citing tactical (not philosophical) objections to the integration of social and political agitation within unions, the executive council of the London Society of Compositors adduced the International's support for the Polish cause and its efforts to coordinate labour strategies across Europe as justification for its decision to set aside an earlier delegate meeting's

[17] 'List of Societies that have already joined the International Working Men's Association' (1866), London Society of Compositors, Quarterly Reports, Modern Records Centre, University of Warwick, MSS 28/CO/1/8/9/1. The distribution of trades was as follows: cordwainers (9,227); bricklayers (3,289); carpenters (554); ribbon weavers (200); packing case makers (600); cabinetmakers (1,570); coopers (120); tailors (7,062); bookbinders (600); plumbers' brass finishers (500); cigar makers (1,100); organ builders (350); and saddle and harness makers (400).
[18] *General Council Minutes*, vol. II, pp. 301–2.
[19] *Ibid.*, pp. 63–4.

vote to join the organization in 1866.[20] But the burden of labour activity in the later sixties was to limit the force of these tactical distinctions. As middle- and working-class reformers joined to revive large-scale agitation for extension of the suffrage, perceptions of the political potential of labour unions gained new significance, and tentative acceptance. Moving beyond the more defensive economic practices of the International to attack the defective political institutions of the state, working-class radicals sought through the Reform League of 1865–9 to amalgamate social and political issues within the public sphere. They also worked to wrest acceptance of this amalgamation from middle-class radicals and the wider political nation.

THE REFORM UNION, THE REFORM LEAGUE, AND THE REFORM AGITATION

Episodic and ineffectual in the aftermath of 1848, middle-class reform efforts gained new coherence and force from the spring of 1864. Just as the confluence of English trade unionism and continental nationalism encouraged reform initiatives by the working-class radicals of the First International in London, the perceived stabilization of industrial relations in cotton combined with sympathy for foreign movements of emancipation to encourage reform activity among middle-class radicals in Lancashire. Concern for the impact of the American Civil War on labour and profits had dampened John Bright's enthusiasm for reform in 1863, but the orderly behaviour of unemployed cotton operatives during the American hostilities and their willingness to endorse the Northern cause despite its devastating economic consequences had by 1864 revived middle-class confidence in the mythic, innate liberalism of the working class. As James Moir commented in contemplating reform in April, there could be 'no expectation that real economy in the management of our national affairs will

---

[20] 'Seventy-fifth Quarterly Report' (1866), London Society of Compositors, Quarterly Reports, Modern Records Centre, University of Warwick, MSS 28/CO/1/8/9/ 1. Their opposition did not rest upon a belief that social issues constituted a category distinct from politics, but rather upon the consideration that 'in our ranks will be found men of all shades of politics; and were we to make it a practice to entertain questions of that character we are satisfied that the primary object for which we associate might be lost sight of in the tumult of political passions, and the very existence of our Society threatened'.

ever be attended to till the representations [*sic*] of the poor meet along with those of the rich'.[21] Garibaldi's arrival in England and the government's cancellation of his projected provincial tour both raised these bourgeois radical expectations and helped to direct reform activity into domestic channels: of the forty-two men who constituted Manchester's Garibaldi Reception Committee in March, twenty-five supported household suffrage under the aegis of the National Reform Union, established in Manchester on 20 April.[22]

Presided over – like the Anti-Corn Law League to which its adherents traced their ideological roots – by George Wilson, the National Reform Union sought to revive large-scale political agitation behind household suffrage, the ballot, equal electoral districts, and triennial Parliaments – a programme that essentially recapitulated the earlier reform incentives pursued by Bright, Cobden, and Hume. Drawing the bulk of its members from industrial Manchester, Leeds, Oldham, Rochdale, Stockport, and Bradford, the Reform Union served to broadcast the economic convictions of the Manchester School, upholding capitalist growth, liberal individualism, and the politics of peace, retrenchment, and reform. Wilson's opening remarks at the organization's first public meeting in the autumn rehearsed the familiar themes of Cobdenite liberalism, applying the laws of supply and demand to the dynamics of parliamentary reform in an extended series of analogies which compared the administration of government policies and the manufacture of cotton textiles.[23] Hostile to organized labour, the Manchester liberals who provided the Union's central core of leaders predictably urged workers to abandon combination in restraint of trade for political cooperation with the middle class. The *Manchester Examiner and Times*, edited by the Reform Unionist Alexander Ireland, upheld such concerted political activity as a form of 'enlightened patriotism'. But it decried the 'delusive and unjust plea of protecting labour' with which trade unionists sought to 'assail the inherent right which every man has to make the most of the capacities and talents which God has given him, and reduce the

[21] James Moir to George Wilson, 18 April 1864, MCRL, Wilson Papers, M20/1864.
[22] Printed Notices, 'Garibaldi Reception Committee', and 'National Reform Union', 26 March and April 1864, MCRL, Wilson Papers, M20/1864.
[23] *Manchester Examiner and Times*, 26 October 1864, p. 3.

cleverest and most industrious to a level with the incompetent and idle'.[24]

Endorsed repeatedly by the leaders of the middle-class reform movement, the tenets of Manchester liberalism pervaded Reform Union rhetoric, but failed to dominate it entirely. For although the Union drew its initial inspiration from Cobden, Bright, and Wilson, it also embraced middle-class reformers whose association with labour unions and international politics had expanded their interpretation of liberalism beyond the negative definition of freedom propounded by the Manchester School. Nonconformists such as Cowen, Dawson, Stansfeld, and Taylor who had opposed liberal pacifism vigorously in the fifties joined the Reform Union in 1864 without renouncing their earlier refusal to apply the principle of non-intervention to international politics. The adherence of academic liberals such as Henry Fawcett and J. E. Thorold Rogers reinforced these ranks of militant Dissent with liberal thinkers reconciled to trade union intervention in market relations. Grounded in conventional radical conceptions of liberty and oppression, Fawcett's speeches on behalf of household suffrage invoked arguments for international intervention both to deprecate class differences within the nation and to encourage political reform of the state. Speaking at the Free Trade Hall in April 1864, Fawcett detailed a liberal platform that condemned the evils of extensive taxation, upheld the need 'to emancipate our commerce from its remaining thraldom', and underlined the sharp contrast that divided the corruption of the aristocratic court from the proverbial patriotism of the wider English nation.[25] At Brighton the following September, Fawcett expanded this radical framework beyond the limits of Manchester liberalism. Dismissing class consciousness as a political chimera, he rested his arguments for extension of the suffrage on cotton operatives' sympathy for the Northern cause, labour's warm reception of Garibaldi in April, and working-class enthusiasm for an English war on behalf of the Polish nation. In this view, labour's ability to look beyond its narrow class interests in the English economy – and thus its qualification for the franchise – was

---

[24] *Ibid.*, 21 February 1865, p. 4. John Bright, speaking at Birmingham in January 1865, combined calls for household suffrage with sharp criticism of proposals to extend the Factory Acts. See *Manchester Weekly Times*, 14 and 21 January 1865, pp. 5, 3.

[25] *Manchester Examiner and Times*, 21 April 1865, p. 3.

manifest in its willingness to see beyond England's immediate national interests in matters of foreign policy.[26]

If the tenor of Fawcett's speeches suggested a new willingness on the part of middle-class reformers to entertain or endorse working-class radical sentiments, the associational ties that linked the Reform Union and the Reform League demonstrated their willingness to lend these new sympathies practical force. Under the leadership of Edmond Beales, the Reform League established in London in February 1865 to promote manhood suffrage and the ballot attracted an estimated 65,000 members to over 600 local branches, becoming by far the largest working-class political movement in Britain since Chartism.[27] Radicals earlier active as leaders of the Chartist agitation flocked eagerly to the cause: of this older generation, Harney, Holyoake, and Reynolds served essentially symbolic roles, while Ernest Jones campaigned actively for the League both in Manchester and throughout the wider nation. A younger cohort of working-class radicals associated with the new unions, the London Trades Council, and the First International dominated the daily management of the League's activities. George Howell, the League's secretary, George Odger, J. B. Leno, W. R. Cremer, Robert Applegarth, and Benjamin Lucraft were especially prominent.[28] No less significant – and far more surprising – was the allegiance of middle-class reformers who accepted honorific titles as vice-presidents within the League's administration. Christian Socialists such as Thomas Hughes, paternalist employers such as Samuel Morley, Dissenters such as P. A. Taylor, and academics such as J. E. Cairnes played little part in the day to day activities of the Reform League, but their nominal affiliation significantly enhanced the League's

---

[26] *Ibid.*, 15 September 1864, p. 3. This was not an isolated line of argument. Ludlow, writing with the former Owenite Chartist Lloyd Jones, argued to the same effect in 1867. 'Surely a class which can appreciate the simple manhood of a Garibaldi has risen itself to a true, wise manhood', they argued. 'Surely the men who can take so genuine an interest in the destinies of foreign nations are fit henceforth to share in ruling their own.' John Malcolm Forbes Ludlow and Patrick Lloyd Jones, *Progress of the Working Class, 1832–1867* (London, 1867), p. 288.

[27] The best general surveys of the Reform League are Harrison, *Before the Socialists*, pp. 78–209, and Leventhal, *Respectable Radical*, pp. 43–116. For the estimated membership, see James Hinton, *Labour and Socialism: A History of the British Labour Movement 1867–1974* (Brighton, 1983), p. 11.

[28] Reform League Council Minute Book, 16 June 1865, 17 November 1865, and 7 September 1866, BI, Howell Collection, documents the support of old Chartists; Abramsky and Collins, *Marx and the British Labour Movement*, pp. 60–5, note the role of trade unionists associated with the International.

public profile, status, and resources. The financial contributions offered by men such as these were crucial to the League's sustained activities: Morley alone contributed one tenth of the League's recorded income for 1865–8.[29]

In the historiography of the mid-Victorian labour movement, the character and extent of these relations between middle- and working-class reformers serve to confirm the liberalization and labour aristocracy theses by illustrating the essential unity of the bourgeois and popular radical traditions, and hence revealing the relative insignificance of class consciousness in social and political relations after Chartism. 'Behind Chartism lay boundless, if inchoate dreams of social reconstruction', Royden Harrison argues characteristically, 'behind the Reform League lay little more than the expectation of "rising in the social scale".'[30] This analysis contains essential elements of truth, rightly emphasizing the relative moderation that distinguished working-class radicalism in the sixties from the tension and acrimony that had marked the two previous decades of reform endeavour. Chartist leaders had disdained to treat with Manchester School liberals, but the Reform League's first minutes record a unanimous resolution lamenting Cobden's premature death. And whereas Chartists persistently disrupted liberal reformers' public meetings, members of the League pledged from the outset to work 'without hostility' alongside adherents of the Union.[31] From March to July 1866, moreover, the League bowed to sustained pressure from members of the Reform Union and agreed to promote the Liberal government's bill for limited parliamentary reform alongside their programme of manhood suffrage and the ballot.[32] A capitulation to longstanding middle-class demands that working-class radicals sacrifice principles for expediency, this aspect of the League's activities promotes the common depiction of the League's

[29] Aldon D. Bell, 'Administration and Finance of the Reform League, 1865–67', *International Review of Social History*, vol. 10, pt 3 (1965), pp. 385–409, offers an excellent survey of middle-class contributions to the League. Bell estimates that Morley contributed at least £425 of the League's budget of £4,420 in its first two and a half years (pp. 401–3).

[30] Harrison, *Before the Socialists*, pp. 80–1. Essentially the same line of argument is advanced by Bell, 'Administration and Finance', p. 409.

[31] Reform League Council Minute Book, 15 April 1865, 22 May 1865, BI, Howell Collection.

[32] *Ibid.*, 16 and 22 March 1866. The failure of the Liberal bill, and the fall of the Liberal government in July returned the League to its original programme, a policy officially underlined by the Council on 5 October.

leaders as representatives of a labour élite anxious to gain the franchise at the expense of the wider working class.

But although liberalization and labour aristocracy theories illuminate the tactical developments that distinguished early labourism from late Chartism, undue adherence to these lines of analysis can obscure the concessions exacted from middle-class reformers who constructed alliances with working-class radicals. It conceals, moreover, the significance of ideological differences that continued to divide liberal and labour interests within the new tactical parameters of reform. For just as labour leaders moderated their claims to maintain liberal support, middle-class radicals were compelled to temper their convictions and alter their practices to sustain large-scale popular enthusiasm for the reform of aristocratic government. Organizers of the Reform Union's initial conference thus invited Ernest Jones – anathema to Manchester School liberals since 1848 – to address their meeting, an effort to bridge the gap dividing labour from liberal radicalism. Here Jones rehearsed familiar Chartist arguments for manhood suffrage, repeatedly invoking 'principle' against 'an unwise expediency' and concluding his speech with the claim that 'all the moneyed interest wanted was to be placed on an equality with the landed interest, and the working classes must not look for help from them'. Despite these antagonistic sentiments, Union members sought, unsuccessfully, to convince Jones to accept an honorary vice-presidency within their association.[33]

Middle-class participation in the Reform League similarly testified to the changed temper of liberal conviction required by class collaboration. Samuel Morley's obvious preference for a limited measure of reform – manifest in his significantly more generous contributions to the Union than to the League – is easily adduced as evidence that Reform League leaders allied themselves with class enemies hostile to working-class aspiration. But an understanding of the course of radical interaction in the decade after 1848 suggests that this emphasis is in part misplaced. First recruited to political reform through Cobden's Freehold Land Society campaign in 1849, Morley belonged to the self-help school of liberal reformers committed to political emancipation through economic probity.[34] In this

---

[33] *Manchester Examiner and Times*, 20 and 21 April 1864, pp. 3, 3.
[34] For Morley's contributions to the Union, see Bell, 'Administration and Finance'. His participation in the Freehold Land Society is noted in Cobden, *Speeches of Richard Cobden on Peace*, p. 176.

context, his new willingness to contribute to an association that upheld manhood suffrage as a right is perhaps more telling than his ultimate preference for a middle-class organization dedicated to the property franchise. The refusal of prominent liberal intellectuals within the Reform Union to follow Morley's example underlined the extent of his concession, illustrating the degree to which perceived class differences continued to inform radical relations in the sixties. Bright, Ludlow, Mill, and Goldwin Smith all declined to join the League, citing arguments that echoed the dominant themes of the middle-class response to 1848. Mill's refusal was especially revealing, for although increasingly willing to discard the trammels of classical economics Mill yet retained the characteristic social fears of his class. 'I cannot join with you (glad as I shd be to do so) in thinking that the wages-receiving class, if universally enfranchised, would have no class feeling or class opinions as such', he wrote to John Boyd Kinnear in August 1865. 'The *vertical* divisions of opinion which you speak of seem to me to belong to the past, & to be almost wholly the effect of bad laws, now mostly removed', Mill continued in September. 'But the division between labourers & employers of labour seems to me to be increasing in importance & gradually swallowing up all others.'[35]

Reform League activists cultivated these middle-class perceptions of class difference with considerable determination, even as they courted the patronage of bourgeois liberals. Retaining the characteristic discursive tropes of late Chartism, the League's orators and publicists consistently defied conventional liberal wisdom to uphold the fundamental unity of social and democratic reform. Radical artisans schooled in the Chartist tradition were especially vociferous in urging this connection. 'Let no man believe ... any social reform possible until the House of Commons is rescued ... through the enfranchisement of the adult males of the population', Bronterre O'Brien's disciple James Murray urged in 1866. 'Anything short of this is a fraud, a delusion, and a snare.'[36] Contributors to Leno's *Workman's Advocate* laboured to impress members of the new

[35] Leventhal, *Respectable Radical*, pp. 63–4, notes the unwillingness of leading middle-class radicals to unite with the League. Ludlow's refusal, which repeatedly emphasized that the timing of manhood suffrage was a matter of 'expediency', not principle, is in Ludlow to Howell, 26 June 1865, BI, Howell Collection, Reform League Correspondence (1865). Mill's letters of 19 August and 25 September 1865 are printed in his *Collected Works*, vol. XVI, pp. 1093–4, 1103.
[36] *Commonwealth*, 22 September 1866, p. 5.

model unions with the same emblems of their political heritage. Warning workers against the blandishments of 'those who desire to be called the friends of the working classes, and who have obtained a smattering of political economy', they advanced manhood suffrage and the ballot as mechanisms for obtaining 'those social rights for which Trades' Unions are continually struggling.' The liberal ideology of separate spheres had no place in this working-class analysis. For as Parliament's refusal to repeal class-based laws such as the Master and Servants Act made manifestly evident, 'the "labour" question is eminently political, bound up and interwoven with every other question affecting land, finance, and free trade'.[37]

Like earlier representatives of working-class radical aspiration, proponents of the Reform League interwove appeals to nationalist sentiment with their social democratic lines of argument. A tactic employed in part to legitimate the leadership to their working-class followers, the invocation of nationalist themes also helped to secure the League an ideological space within the established framework of political discourse by reformulating its class goals in terms of the interests of the wider nation. Edmond Beales, a barrister and a relative newcomer in working-class radical circles, sustained his credentials as the League's president with recurrent references to his role in advancing Italian nationality. At Cubitt Town in 1865, class and nationalist interests were conflated by the speaker who introduced Beales to workers as a patriot 'whose name was found in connection with all questions concerning their interests ... especially, with the Garibaldi funds'.[38] At Cambridge in 1867, Beales recalled his visit with Garibaldi at Monte Rotondo; at the League's largest demonstration in London, he estimated that 'the numbers present ... were greater than, I believe, ever gathered together, and the enthusiasm was greater than was ever before exhibited, except only at the welcome of Garibaldi'.[39] Garibaldi himself entered into these efforts to assimilate English parliamentary reform with continental nationalist politics, dispatching letters to the League to cheer

[37] *Workman's Advocate*, 11 November 1865, p. 4. As in the fifties, a rejection of classical political economy was central to this repudiation of separate spheres. 'These instructors of the people', the paper noted of liberal reformers, 'forget that the pet science of which they are the assumed expounders is itself called "Political Economy".'

[38] *Ibid.*, 23 September 1865, p. 2.

[39] *National Reformer*, 24 November 1867, p. 327; *Commonwealth*, 16 February 1867, p. 5.

its members on, soliciting funds for his own campaigns from English reformers, and accepting the title of honorary president of the League.[40] Cited by Reform League activists as evidence that a broadly European consensus underpinned their demand for manhood suffrage, Garibaldi's patronage by no means confined the League to the more anodyne liberal sentiments favoured by his middle-class English proponents. At Clerkenwell Square, French symbols of revolution – the red flag and caps of liberty of the Holborn branch of the Reform League – established the ideological parameters within which speakers couched their appeals to nationality. Here League members framed references to Garibaldi with an O'Brienite speech by Charles Murray on capital and labour and a defence of the Fenians by James Finlen, who demanded that the government must not be permitted 'to crush out the patriotism and nationality of a poor down trodden people'.[41]

As in earlier working-class radical campaigns, the multivalence of the patriotic idiom was central to these efforts to mediate between class interests by referring to the wider claims of the nation. Patriotic rhetoric employed by members of the League to critique the reign of capital served to advance particularistic social and economic goals through claims to national political rights. George Odger illustrated this working-class manipulation of the politics of nationalism in explaining the Industrial Newspaper Company's decision to change the title of the *Workman's Advocate* to the *Commonwealth*. 'As justice is the rightful heritage of all, we have deemed it expedient to indicate by our new title that we are in pursuit, not of exclusive advantages on behalf of any section of the people, but of the "Common weal" ', he began, invoking seventeenth- and eighteenth-century notions of rights before elaborating a programme that privileged the contemporary interests of labour. Arguing from the premise 'that Government is invested with authority by the people ... for the protection of the people's interests', Odger advocated manhood suffrage as a means to effect parliamentary redistribution of the land, reduction of the hours of labour, and the protection of 'Political, International, and Trade Associations, and all similar efforts for raising the position and bettering the circumstances of the

[40] *Commonwealth*, 1 June 1867, p. 1; Printed Circular from John McAdam to James Smith, 17 October 1867, Bedlay Castle, Chryston, by Glasgow, McAdam Papers.
[41] Report of Reform Meeting at Clerkenwell Square, 27 May 1867, HO 45/7854.

working class'.[42] The pronouncements made from Reform League platforms were of a piece with this analysis. 'Reform had come to this position, that they had to decide – the people at large had to decide – whether the upper ten thousand were the nation, and should rule the country', Ernest Jones told a Birmingham audience. 'No class should rule', he concluded, 'but all classes, conjointly, should look after their own interests.'[43]

Running parallel to this appeal to national political rights as a mechanism of social emancipation was the Reform League's tactical deployment of the nation as an instrument at once of class fear and of class reconciliation. Edmond Beales used this rhetorical device to particular effect in his speeches, alternately underlining the nation's primacy over the claims of class and veiling threats of class conflict in a tissue of nationalist sentiment. 'I have denounced the system of class legislation ... as unjust and oppressive', he told workmen at Birmingham in 1866. 'You are as much members of the State and of the great country as you are members of any trades' union or any benefit or building society to which you belong', he concluded, seeking to subsume the interests of both labour and capital within the concept of the English nation.[44] Unlike the middle-class radicals of the fifties, however, Beales proved willing to supplement this interpretation of the nation's overriding interest with warnings that the ruling class's failure to respond to the call for manhood suffrage would unleash a social revolution. The League, in his analysis, sought by 'equalizing to every just and rational extent those rights which lie at the very heart and root of our existence as a free nation' to supply 'the only effectual precaution and safeguard against violence, anarchy ... revolution' – forces palpably evident, he noted, in the recent history of Italy and France.[45]

Used in concert at the public meetings convened by the League, these varied interpretations of the meaning of the nation created a gradient of political argument that ascended from a patriotic base to an apex of class expression. League demonstrations often began by advancing patriotism as an alternative to class sentiment, only to conclude by invoking the nation to express perceived class differ-

---

[42] *Commonwealth*, 10 February 1866, p. 1. The new title was also redolent of the perceived seventeenth-century origins of the radical tradition.
[43] *Ibid.*, 16 February 1867, p. 5.   [44] *Ibid.*, 1 September 1866, p. 8.
[45] *Workman's Advocate*, 7 October 1865, p. 2.

ences. A meeting held to establish a local branch of the Reform League in Uxbridge in 1865 was characteristic. Beales, although unable to attend the demonstration in person, sought to establish the branch on broadly nationalist foundations. His letter to the assembled radicals described the League's goals as 'objects which ought to be dear to every true patriot ... as tending to give *all* their just rights, bring about union and harmony amongst all classes in the state, and remove a fruitful source of ill-will and disunion'. The arguments of the League's speakers struck a distinctly different note. 'We have wasted too much time already upon this question', Leno – an Uxbridge Chartist in his youth – exclaimed. 'It is the great barrier to our social progress, and must be removed.' The refusal of capital to unite with labour behind manhood suffrage, in his analysis, confirmed that 'the middle classes are interested in a restricted suffrage', for 'class representation produces class legislation'.[46]

If the League's decision to agitate on behalf of the Liberal bill from March to June 1866 was one logical consequence of that strand of its rhetoric which privileged the interests of the nation to the claims of class, the League's activities and fortunes from the fall of the Liberal government in June illustrated the radical potential of its parallel claims to embody the national rights of labour against an oligarchic ruling class. Propelled by the course of high politics, the trajectory of the League's relations with the Reform Union from July helped to transform both liberal attitudes toward labour and the nature of working-class involvement in politics itself. For with the resignation of Russell's government and the formation of Derby's Conservative ministry, middle-class liberals were forced to court the working classes in an effort to wrest the initiative of reform from the Tories.[47] Already in July, Bright had begun to urge the League to ignore the government's restrictions on public meetings in Hyde Park, and offered funds to support League members if prosecuted for so doing. By January E. S. Beesly, who in March had counselled the League to accept limited reform, offered to speak at League meetings and advised members to block all reform efforts

---

[46] *Ibid.*, 16 September 1865, p. 2.
[47] For the high politics of this transition, see Francis B. Smith, *The Making of the Second Reform Bill* (Cambridge, 1966), pp. 111–33, and Maurice Cowling, *1867, Disraeli, Gladstone and Revolution: The Passing of the Second Reform Bill* (Cambridge, 1967).

that fell short of manhood suffrage.[48] In the process of seeking to mobilize labour in this manner against the Tory government, middle-class liberals engaged in a gradual, public rapprochement with working-class conceptions of the fundamental interrelation that obtained between the spheres of social life, politics, and economics.

Central to this transformation of middle- and working-class radical relations was the decisive politicization of trade unions that marked 1866–7. From the outset, members of the Reform League had been anxious to secure trade union support for their activities, appointing a sub-committee in April 1865 which instructed Howell 'to use every means to induce the active and leading members of these Unions to join our movement'.[49] But progress to this end was painfully slow. The League succeeded in gaining its first union affiliation, the Finsbury branch of the Amalgamated Cordwainers, only in August 1865, and made little additional progress on this front in the remainder of its first year.[50] Spurred on, however, by the conjuncture of economic depression, a rising tide of strike activity, and the insult delivered to their political aspirations by the Conservatives' rejection of the Liberal reform bill, unionized workers began to shed their political lethargy. In July and August the Birmingham Trades Council joined forces with the Reform League, and urged Birmingham unionists to embrace political agitation; in September both the Hanley hollow ware pressers and the Manchester branch of the Amalgamated Society of Carpenters and Joiners brought men to reform demonstrations under union banners.[51] The *Times*, surveying the rise of labour activism in November, saw not the triumph of liberal values perceived by twentieth-century historians but rather an effort to subvert the laws of 'political economy'

[48] Bright to George Howell, 19 and 31 July 1866, BI, Howell Collection, Reform League Correspondence (1866); *Commonwealth*, 24 March 1866, p. 7; Beesly to Howell, 14 January 1867, BI, Howell Collection, Reform League Correspondence (1867).

[49] Reform League Council Minute Book, 15 April 1865, BI, Howell Collection.

[50] *Ibid.*, 18 August 1865, 23 February 1866.

[51] For the activities of the Birmingham branch of the Reform League and the Birmingham Trades Council see W. Hamish Fraser, *Trade Unions and Society: The Struggle for Acceptance 1850–1880* (London, 1974), p. 130. For the potters, carpenters, and joiners, see 'Extracts from Hollow Ware Pressers, Hanley Lodge Minute Book', September 1866, BLPES, Webb Trade Union Collection part A, vol. xliv, p. 376, and Amalgamated Society of Carpenters and Joiners, Financial Reports and Minutes, 22 September 1866, Modern Records Centre, University of Warwick, MSS 78/ASC&J/6/1/12/1.

and institute in England the 'organization of labour' attempted by revolutionary France in 1848.[52]

In December this process of politicization accelerated, when George Potter of the *Bee-Hive* succeeded in mobilizing a broad array of trades behind manhood suffrage in a mass demonstration in London that saw 20,000–25,000 workers march from Pall Mall to the Beaufort House grounds via Piccadilly and Knightsbridge.[53] Here labour aristocrats joined with members of trades and occupations that boasted little status and security, and calls for labour to support liberal leaders elided with allusions to labour's solidarity with the French revolutionary tradition. Among nearly fifty different trades that participated, the boilermakers, engineers, and iron-moulders represented the élite of unionized labour, while the presence of French polishers and common seamen spoke to the presence of reform sentiments within less privileged strata of the labouring population.[54]

The symbols employed by trades in this demonstration encompassed liberal aspirations, but were not constrained by liberal precepts. Thus the tallow-chandlers' motto, 'Bright and Light', recognized the contributions made to reform endeavour by the Manchester School, while the glassworkers who marched with specimens of their handiwork played upon the full range of meanings

[52] *Times*, 27 November 1866, p. 8.
[53] *Ibid.*, 29 November 1866, p. 12 and Fraser, *Trade Unions and Society*, pp. 129–30. Potter's acrimonious relations with the 'Junta' had earlier led him to break with the Reform League and establish his own London Working Men's Association to promote reform. Although the latter organization sponsored the demonstration of 3 December, deputations from the Reform League also participated in the event.
[54] The ironmoulders, with a long history of organization and trade agitation, had barred 'political discourse' and 'seditious sentiments or songs' from their meetings since 1809, but now came to petition Parliament for manhood suffrage (not a property franchise for the labour élite). London's French polishers were, in contrast, poorly unionized, with only twenty members and only a single benefit (for burial) in 1871. See BLPES, Webb Trade Union Collection, part A, vol. xix, pp. 162, 176, and part A, vol. xxii, p. 62. The programme for the demonstration printed in the *Times* of 29 November 1866, p. 12, lists the following trades as participants: farriers, tallow-chandlers, hatters, coopers, glassworkers, stonemasons, coach body makers, coach lace weavers, ropemakers, seamen, tailors, bricklayers, painters, plasterers, corkcutters, saddlers, ironmoulders, smiths, carpenters and joiners, boilermakers and iron shipbuilders, silver trades, wheelwrights, carvers and gilders, bookbinders, horse collar makers, organ builders, French polishers, musical instrument makers, cabinetmakers, engineers, machinists, pattern makers, millwrights, garment dyers, shipwrights, lightermen and watermen, brass moulders and finishers, paper-hangers, leather trades, wireworkers and wireweavers, tinplate and zinc workers, boot and shoemakers, bakers, and the silk trades.

contained within the patriotic radical idiom, carrying ornamental crowns alongside glasswork rifles, bayonets, and a sword. Most telling (from a middle-class perspective) was the conspicuous presence of French revolutionary imagery. Reform League members participating in the demonstration carried tricolours and three silk red flags, each surmounted by a cap of liberty. 'The Reform League may be innocent of levelling designs', the *Times* noted in a dry comment that testified to the social meanings with which French political imagery was freighted in England, 'but if its object were to proclaim such tendencies openly, it could hardly have chosen more significant emblems.'[55]

Potter's initiative forced the hand of the union leaders associated with the London Trades Council, who now brought their unions and the Trades Council itself into formal alliance with the League. At an executive council meeting of 5 December, William Allan – secretary of the Amalgamated Engineers and earlier an adherent of Jones's National Charter Association – decried the 'treachery' of the House in rejecting the Liberal bill, upheld the cause of 'the working classes of this kingdom, now unjustly excluded by class laws, made by class-elected Parliaments', and pledged his union's support for the principles of the League. Applegarth of the Amalgamated Society of Carpenters and Joiners, Coulson of the Operative Bricklayers, and George Odger – representing 9,000 cordwainers – swiftly followed suit.[56] The London Trades Council's official endorsement of the Reform League's programme in January lent these actions of individual unions added force, and offered working-class radical spokesmen an opportunity to reiterate labour's rejection of bourgeois notions of separate spheres. 'Trade organizations have repeatedly shown the fallacy of the argument, for their members have continually taken action against and also in favour of political measures affecting their interests, not only as workmen, but as citizens', the *Commonwealth* instructed its readers. 'Social and political Reform are so intimately interwoven, that it is extremely difficult to distinguish the one from the other, and hence we have heard men object to being called politicians, while their entire action proved them to be political rather than social Reformers.'[57]

Preparations for the mass demonstration held in London in mid-

[55] *Times*, 4 December 1866, p. 8.
[56] Reform League Council Minute Book, 5 December 1866, BI, Howell Collection.
[57] *Commonwealth*, 12 January 1867, p. 4.

February underlined these convictions. Speakers at a meeting of
trade union delegates in January resolved to support 'the efforts of
the Reform League to emancipate the working man from class
legislation' and insisted that workers 'would never have succeeded to
the extent they had if they had not backed up their trade unions with
the elements of political power'. At the demonstration itself, the
tricolour and French caps of liberty accompanied banners that
proclaimed 'Liberty, Equality, Fraternity' and 'The Voice of the
People Can't be Opposed with Safety to a Nation'.[58] Provincial
workers further swelled the League's ranks in a series of demonstrations that drew hundreds of thousands into the reform agitation.
These months saw 25,000 workers march under League banners in
Newcastle, and smiths, moulders, plumbers, tinmen, tailors, hatters,
cordwainers, bricklayers, plasterers, brushmakers, corkcutters,
masons, joiners, cabinetmakers, house painters, and general
labourers demonstrate in favour of League principles in Exeter.[59]
By May, the escalation of activities had created a crisis of public
order, as League members defied with impunity government proclamations that closed public parks to political agitators. London
vestries were forced to call repeatedly for the creation of special
constables to preserve the peace; the Horse Guards, the Coldstream
Guards, the Life Guards, and the Metropolitan Police charged 'the
mob' with increasing fear and reluctance as spring gave way to
summer.[60]

In sharp contrast to Chartist attempts to wrest political power
from the governing élite in 1848, the Reform League's campaigns of
1866–7 met with increasing support from middle-class liberals even
as the tenor of labour radicalism grew more strident. Whig and
conservative commentators sought to contain public opinion within
the pragmatic parameters established by statesmen of both parties in
response to the June Days, conflating the League with Chartism and
Chartism at once with abstract political principles and utopian
social experiments. In the press, the *Times* was anxious that readers
recall the dangers of 'radical Reform' unleashed by the February
revolution and disdained to 'encourage theories which have no

[58] *Ibid.*, 19 January 1867, pp. 4–5, 16 February 1867, p. 4.
[59] *Ibid.*, 12 January 1867, p. 1, and 2 February 1867, p. 5; *Newcastle Weekly Chronicle*, 2 February 1867.
[60] Police reports and vestry petitions, 4 May–25 July 1867, HO 45/7854/2, HO 45/7554/17–18. Harrison, *Before the Socialists*, pp. 78–136, documents and analyses in greater detail the collapse of government authority in this period.

foundation'; in the House of Commons, critics of the League cautioned that universal suffrage would force Parliament to entertain the socialist schemes concocted by Fourier, Saint-Simon, and Louis Blanc in France.[61] But middle-class radicals who in 1848 had joined in the construction of this fearful interpretation of the Chartist challenge now worked to associate the liberal cause with the perceived political aspirations of the working class. Fears of rising class consciousness were central to this development. 'There is a danger that the struggle may in the end cease to be one between parties in Parliament and become one between classes – the class represented by the House of Commons on one side and the class represented by the trades' unions on the other', the *Nonconformist* warned in July 1866. 'A true statesman would almost rather drag the working men within the pale of the Constitution by force than suffer them thus to organize themselves into a separate community outside it.'[62] Determined both to pre-empt the escalation of class sentiment incited by Reform League speakers and to seize the initiative of reform from the Tory government, bourgeois liberals now offered working-class radicals new varieties of liberal argument that conceded, albeit reluctantly, the legitimacy of abstract political rights alongside historical birthrights, the efficacy of trade unions as political agents, and the power of parliamentary institutions as instruments of social reform.

The new trajectory of John Bright's radical rhetoric brought this liberal transformation to the heart of middle-class radical culture, and assured liberal polemic on the relations between class and national allegiance a prominent place within the broader political discourse generated by the reform agitation. Faced with the Conservatives' refusal to work alongside liberal reformers, Bright recognized the need to bolster the Reform Union's forces with the radical trade unionists who formed the backbone of the League. 'The Tories care little for a middle-class call for reform', he wrote to George Wilson in June 1866. 'It is only numbers, and the aspect of force that will influence them.'[63] Becoming a frequent speaker alongside the orators of the Reform League at provincial demonstrations, Bright now came to adopt the League's characteristic rhetorical strategies

[61] *Times*, 7 January 1867, p. 6, and 14 January 1867, p. 6; Harrison, *Before the Socialists*, p. 124.
[62] *Nonconformist*, 25 July 1866, p. 598.
[63] Bright to Wilson, 27 June 1866, MCRL, Wilson Papers, M20/1866.

and influences, using appeals to the English nation as an ideological platform upon which he expounded new and increasingly militant liberal political visions. Speaking to a crowd of 5,000 at Manchester in September, Bright supplemented obligatory liberal references to the glories of the Anti-Corn Law League and the evils of government expenditure with patriotic pleas that the political nation avert class warfare by embracing political reform. 'I charge Lord Derby and his friends with this . . . that they have brought class into conflict with class', Bright expostulated. 'I say that they have done much to separate Parliament from the nation', he concluded, pointing to the reformers' need 'to make a desperate fight for it, just as though they were wresting it not from their countrymen and brothers, but from the representatives of a conquering nation.'[64]

Standing upon this patriotic edifice, Bright now flirted with universal suffrage, toyed with 'abstract principles', and laboured to distance himself from 'the peace at any price school' of liberal pacifism. 'I believe that however much any of us may have thought that political questions in our country should never again be settled by force', he told Manchester reformers, 'there is something in the constitution of our nature that when evils are allowed to run on beyond a certain period unredressed, the most peace-loving of men are unable to keep the peace.'[65] At Leeds in October, Bright described workers as 'the great nation excluded' and counselled them that 'if the nation is to be split into two parts, and there is to be a wide gulf between them, there is nothing for the future but subjection or violence, for without this you are powerless to attain your ends'.[66] Far from diminishing with the rise of trade union militance, Bright's calls for the politicization of labour grew apace. A detractor throughout the previous decade of trade union organization, Bright in December proclaimed himself an early supporter of union involvement in political campaigns.[67]

Fully consistent with the preceding two decades of working-class radical agitation, these lines of patriotic argument marked a new departure for the middle-class reform movement, a public breach with the liberal tradition of the 1840s and 1850s. Most significant

---

[64] John Bright, *Speeches on Parliamentary Reform, &c., by John Bright, Esq., M.P.* (Manchester, [1866]), pp. 11, 16.
[65] *Ibid.*, p. 20.   [66] *Ibid.*, p. 26.
[67] *Ibid.*, p. 69. The speech in which he did so was, significantly, delivered in London on the day following Potter's massive trade demonstration.

was Bright's new acceptance of a fundamental relationship between social and political reform and his use of appeals to the nation to legitimate this capitulation to working-class radical argument. Speaking to a reform meeting at Glasgow in October, he touched traditional chords of Manchester liberalism in denouncing the aristocracy and the increase of naval expenditure while lauding free trade in corn, the omnipotence of God, and the charitable instincts of British womanhood. But Bright's analysis broke new ground – in bourgeois radical politics – by justifying democratic reform as an agent of social change:

> Now look, I beg of you, to this mass of misery. It is so great a mass that benevolence cannot reach it. If benevolence could do it, there would be no pauperism in England, for in no country do I believe that there is more benevolence than there is in the United Kingdom ... There does not exist among created beings, beneath the angelic ranks, those who are more kind and charitable than the women of the United Kingdom. But benevolence can touch scarcely the fringe of this vast disorder. There is another virtue we could add, and that virtue and that quality is justice ... But justice is impossible from a class. It is most certain and easy from a nation; and I believe we can only reach the depths of ignorance and misery and crime in this country by an appeal to the justice, the intelligence, and the virtues of the entire people.

Convinced now that 'just laws ... would change the face of the country', creating an English 'Eden', Bright concluded 'if class has failed, let us try the nation. That is our faith, that is our purpose, that is our cry – let us try the nation.'[68]

Bright's liberal conversion was representative of a broader ideological development within middle-class radical circles, a development that extended beyond the oratory of national leaders to the rhetorical devices employed at the local level by parliamentary aspirants associated with the Reform Union. The evolving liberal rhetoric of George Melly, the Unitarian merchant who had contested Preston unsuccessfully under Garibaldian and Polish nationalist banners earlier in the decade, illustrates this wider trend within the radical wing of middle-class liberalism. A self-described 'Radical' and 'advocate for "civil and religious liberty" in the largest sense of the term', Melly joined the Reform Union as a proponent of the

[68] John Bright, *Speeches on Questions of Public Policy by the Right Honourable John Bright, M.P.*, ed. James E. Thorold Rogers (London, 1880), pp. 281–2, 284.

extension of voting rights to £6 householders and as an antagonist – if only in his speeches – of 'the bribery, corruption, and undue influence' that pervaded aristocratic government.[69] A deep commitment to classical political economy – and a correspondingly intense distaste for trade unions – underpinned his philosophy of social, economic, and political relations in 1864. 'I will pass over the subject of Trades' Unions and the shop rules which emanate from them, with the object they pretend to have of protecting labour and the effects they so often have of placing, aye and of keeping, the idle and stupid workmen on the same level as the sober and industrious one', Melly told Liverpool workers in December. 'The time will come when the working classes will find out as the merchant and the manufacturer has found out, aye, and even as the farmer has at last discovered, that freedom in labour would be as beneficial to him as freedom in trade has proved itself to be.'[70]

By the spring of 1866, the imminent threat of a Tory rejection of the Liberal reform bill had forced Melly to reconsider his opposition to trade union organization. Informing a crowd at Hanley that 'the leaders and members of the trades unions were all radicals', Melly applauded labour's earlier refusal to engage in political activities only to suggest that the time had now come for a politicization of the unions which would counter the pernicious effects of aristocratic combination.[71] In agitating for the Reform Union during the next months, Melly – like Bright – came both to endorse the use of political instruments to achieve social reforms and to admit labour's right to contest the received wisdom of the political economists. Speaking at Hanley, Melly acknowledged that democratic reform would bring 'questions of social Reform and Education touching the welfare of the masses' to the forefront of national consciousness. 'As the aristocracy were best fitted to lead us into battle, and the middle classes to extend our trade and commerce', he asserted, 'so from a Reform Parliament in which the working men have a larger share of

---

[69] 'To the Electors and Non-Electors of the Borough of Stoke-upon-Trent', 14 February 1865, LCL, Melly Papers, 920 MEL, 15/vol. 10, fol. 2408. His persistent attacks on electoral corruption notwithstanding, Melly was himself deeply enmeshed in efforts to purchase political support in Preston, a circumstance of his early political career documented in great detail in his correspondence with his agent, Edward Ambler, in LCL, Melly Papers, 920 MEL, 11/vol. 7 and 13/vol. 9, pt 1.

[70] George Melly, *Self-Help: The Future of the Working Classes* (Liverpool, 1864), p. 5.

[71] 'Parliamentary Reform Speeches', Easter 1866, LCL, Melly Papers, H 825 MEL, *Stray Leaves*, vol. 2, n.p.

power and influence we may fairly expect a searching consideration and courageous Legislation on the questions which so nearly touch them.'[72] By the spring of 1867, the transformation of Melly's liberal vision was complete. Now anxious that liberal politicians encompass labour's aspirations, he couched his capitulation to the perceived working-class interests of the trade unions in the patriotic rhetoric of the national interest. 'If they are wrong; if their ideas of political economy, of the laws which rule labour and regulate the price of wages is at fault; if their class notions are mistaken; if they are ignorant, self-deluded men, buoyed up by a thirst for popularity, or notoriety', he proclaimed at a town meeting in Longton, 'let them go before the grand inquest of the nation, where they will find their level.'[73]

Viewed from within the broad context of liberal antagonism to social politics in the aftermath of 1848, the radicalization of Reform Union spokesmen such as Melly and Bright in the face of rising labour militance in 1866–7 is especially significant. In sharp contrast to the contraction of middle-class radical aspiration precipitated by the divisive tactics of late Chartism, the escalation of class consciousness under the aegis of the Reform League in these years encouraged an efflorescence of bourgeois radical agitation in which left-wing liberals endorsed lines of political argument that they had earlier denounced as socialist delusions of the working class. Nationalist sentiment played a central role in this process of political negotiation between the two classes. Serving in previous decades as a repository for distinct systems of political values which contemporaries understood to possess distinctive class meanings, nationalism served in the later sixties as an ideological instrument that eased and legitimated the incorporation of working-class aspirations into the existing parliamentary system. This process of rapprochement saw class interests inform the construction of national identities even as radical patriots advanced the nation as a force that transcended class differences. To describe these developments as the liberalization of the working class is at once perceptive and fundamentally misleading. For if the reform agitation of 1864–7 brought new working-class electors to the Liberal rolls, it did so in part by forcing a redefinition of the radical meaning of liberalism. Wedded to negative

[72] *Ibid.*
[73] 'Speech on the Reform Question', 3 April 1867, LCL, Melly Papers, H 825 MEL, *Stray Leaves*, vol. 3, fol. 150.

conceptions of freedom since the French revolution of 1848, middle-class radicals now reached tentatively for positive liberties associated since the Chartist era with the radical convictions of the working class.

THE NEW LIBERALISM

In the short term, Tory machinations effectively deprived the Liberal party of the popular benefit of this expanding liberal vision, for the Reform Act passed in the summer of 1867 was a radical measure orchestrated by a Conservative – not a Liberal – government. Doubling the electorate and enfranchising the artisanal sector of the urban working class, Disraeli's reform legislation undercut the Liberals' exclusive claim to represent the interests of the wider nation in a Parliament dominated by a narrow aristocratic class. Stopping short of manhood suffrage but extending well beyond the demands of the Liberals' earlier bill, the act served as a brake on broad-based middle-class reform agitations for over a decade. The Reform Union, which suspended its activities in June 1868, found its hitherto generous patrons loath to contribute to the liquidation of its debt in 1869.[74]

But although Disraeli's political manoeuvres pre-empted the Liberals' claim to constitute the party of parliamentary reform, the passage of the Second Reform Act failed to stem entirely the development of social democratic argument within liberal political thought. The continued activities of working- and middle-class radicals associated with the Reform League and the First International were central to this development, encouraging liberal spokesmen and candidates with radical inclinations to court constituents by engaging with working-class interpretations of labour relations. Samuel Morley, who gained a seat for Bristol in the election of 1868, kept his name before the working class in 1867 by defending this new line of liberal argument. In November, Morley presided over a Reform League lecture on 'Trades' Unions & Strikes' by Ernest Jones, the latter still, in the words of Morley's biographer, 'a leper – socially' (Ill. 4).[75] Here Jones, as the *Times* noted with great

---

[74] Thomas Thomasson to the guarantors of the National Reform Union, 16 June 1868, and Mark Price to George Wilson, 15 March 1869, MCRL, Wilson Papers, M20/1868, M20/1869.
[75] Edwin Hodder, *The Life of Samuel Morley*, 2nd edn (London, 1887), p. 250.

TRADES' UNIONS & STRIKES

Their Causes and Remedies.

A LECTURE

Will be delivered on the above subject (under the auspices
of the REFORM LEAGUE) by

ERNEST JONES,

ESQ., (BARRISTER-AT-LAW,)

On Thursday Evening, Nov. 14,

AT

ST. JAMES'S HALL,

PICCADILLY.

Doors open at Seven—Chair to be taken Eight o'clock precisely, by

SAMUEL MORLEY, ESQ.

ADMISSION.

Platform and Reserved Seats, 1s.   Balconies, 6d.
Body of Hall and Gallery, **Free.**

Tickets to be had of the local Secretaries of the London Branches of
the League, of Trades' Union Secretaries, at St. James's Hall, and of
the Secretary of the Reform League.

By Order of the Council,

8, Adelphi Terrace, Strand, W.C.   GEO. HOWELL, *Sec.*

4 'Trades' Unions and Strikes'

disdain, 'began his remarks by an attack on political economy',
praised the achievements of trade unionism, disparaged voluntarist
principles as mere palliatives, and endorsed 'the unmeaning phrase,
"a fair day's wages for a fair day's work"', which is never heard from

the lips of any one who has mastered the elements of economic science'.[76] When the *Times* and the *Pall Mall Gazette* sought to tar Morley with the brush of working-class socialism for his participation in the event, Morley stood intransigent:

> I am brought into contact directly and indirectly with working men, have opportunities of observing the condition of the people, and am overwhelmed by a fear, not that communism will proceed to universal confiscation (I have no fear of this), but lest wealthy ... educated Englishmen may not promptly and faithfully devote themselves to solve the problems of how the poverty, disease, and vice of so many of our own flesh and blood can be diminished and removed.

Upholding the ability of laws to shape 'the character of the people', Morley distanced himself from his earlier adherence to negative freedoms. 'If we can succeed in maintaining legislation on right principles', he concluded, 'we shall, I believe, overtake, and in the end master and destroy, some of the enormous evils which are now only partially alleviated by public and private charity.'[77]

The election of 1868 saw Liberal candidates integrate these arguments with more traditional veins of radical argument in efforts to capture the new working-class electors of borough constituencies. Edmond Beales, who stood unsuccessfully for the Tower Hamlets, was at the forefront of this development. 'In labouring to obtain the Parliamentary franchise ... for as large a number as possible ... I have been actuated by the principle of improving and elevating their political condition as the necessary means to improving and elevating their social and material welfare', he told electors in October, 'and by the conviction that the main object of good government should be to secure the substantial happiness and contentment of the millions who are, after all, the real source and support of the national wealth and power.'[78] George Melly, whose prolonged quest for a Liberal seat now met with success at Stoke, was equally determined to assert the fundamental interrelation of the social and political spheres. His address to electors in February predicted that 'social topics' would now preoccupy Parliament; in August he appealed to his constituents with the conviction 'that the new Parliament will at once earnestly devote itself to the solution of the

---

[76] *Times*, 16 November 1867, p. 8.
[77] Cited by Hodder, *Life of Morley*, pp. 250–1.
[78] *Eastern Post*, 18 October 1868, p. 1.

important questions of social progress and reform, which have been so long neglected or overlooked'.[79] Upon winning the election in the autumn, Melly bolstered these novel claims by returning to the established traditions of the radical nation. 'In the name of my Puritan forefathers', he told Stoke electors, 'in the name of civil and religious freedom, in the name of freedom of religious thought, I thank you.'[80]

Within Positivist circles, these years also saw a growing willingness to acknowledge the political functions of labour, as Frederic Harrison and E. S. Beesly began to play an increasingly prominent, public role in radical efforts to represent the working class in a social democratic light. Harrison, speaking to workers at the request of the London Trades Council in 1868, was anxious that enfranchised workers assume their proper role in the reformed polity. 'I would sum up in a word, the element which it is your part to bring into English politics – it is the Revolutionary element', he told his audience, identifying Cromwell as 'our true type of a revolutionary statesman'. Revolutionary government, in this view, clearly required workers to articulate the need for new, positive conceptions of the state. 'You who have had practical experience of its results are not likely to be caught by the cant which is so dear to the commercial . . . class, the cant about self-government and non-legislation', he urged them. 'Fear not over-legislation.'[81]

E. S. Beesly, unwilling to share Harrison's social democratic vision of national liberalism in the later 1850s, had largely accepted it by 1868. The pattern of his political development in these years is instructive, indicating at once the substantial obstacles to middle-class acceptance of working-class radicalism and the significant diminution of these barriers in the wake of the nationalist agitations of the 1860s. Like Harrison, Beesly first encountered continental nationalism as a student of Aurelio Saffi at Oxford early in the 1850s. But despite Harrison's encouragement, Beesly in 1858 refused an offer to become the paid secretary of the 'International League

[79] 'To the Electors and Non-Electors of Stoke-upon-Trent', February 1868, and 'To the Householders in the Parliamentary Borough of Stoke-upon-Trent', 9 August 1867, LCL, Melly Papers, 920 MEL, 18 and 19/vol. 13, fols. 3294 and 3360.
[80] 'Stoke-upon-Trent Election', 1868, LCL, Melly Papers, H 825 MEL, *Stray Leaves*, vol. 3, fols. 64–5.
[81] Frederic Harrison, *The Political Function of the Working Classes: A Lecture Delivered at the Cleveland Street Institution, on March 25, 1868* (London, 1868), pp. 12, 18, 14.

Association', a body projected by Saffi, Stansfeld, and P. A. Taylor in an effort to combat aristocratic intrigue against the 'oppressed nations' of the continent. 'I was too much a follower of Bright to accept their offer', he later recalled.[82] Becoming active, with Harrison, in trade union activities in the years of the London Builders' Strike, Beesly yet remained enamoured of Manchester School radicalism. He recommended Cobden and Bright to the bricklayers in 1862 as 'honest men, and the best leaders you can follow at present'; Harrison, looking forward to Beesly's publication of an article on trade issues in 1864, feared 'it will show the cloven foot of polit[ical] econ[omy]'.[83]

Drawn into active political involvement with both labour leaders and Nonconformist radicals over Garibaldi's expulsion in April 1864, Beesly still hesitated to commit himself fully to a life of work alongside trade unionists and radicals. Perceptions of social class were central to his dilemma, for Beesly feared that an association with working-class politics would taint his standing in society and ruin his prospects for an acceptable marriage. Harrison, in an extended effort to overcome these objections, remained fully alive to their force. Feeling himself 'certain of being forcibly expelled' from genteel social circles, he cautioned that Beesly 'might any day get into an affair [i.e., a political agitation] which might place you in the position (in the eyes of respectable people) of Mr. Holyoake or Ernest Jones'. Admitting that 'the matrimonial case [is] a very substantial one', Harrison tempered the consequences of radical involvement by suggesting that Beesly would never feel 'quite justified in making any woman your wife whose nerves could not stand a good deal of social snubbing hazing & screaming'.[84]

Beesly, who became a friend and correspondent of Louis Blanc in 1864,[85] began to discard his Manchester convictions as middle-class radical culture grew more tolerant of working-class radical endeavour. He fell under the sway of the Reform League with the defeat of

[82] Aurelio Saffi to E.S. Beesly, 28 May 1858, University College, London, E.S. Beesly Papers, 4/3–5; Frederic Harrison to E.S. Beesly, [1858], BLPES, Harrison Collection, 1/136–43. Beesly's undated explanation for his refusal is written at the bottom of the letter from Saffi.

[83] *Operative Bricklayers' Circular*, 1 December 1862, p. 137; Harrison to Beesly, [February 1864], BLPES, Harrison Collection, 1/11/117.

[84] Harrison to Beesly, [1864], BLPES, Harrison Collection, 1/11/69–86.

[85] Louis Blanc to Beesly, 10 May 1864 and 21 February 1866, University College, London, Beesly Papers, 4/8, and 4/13–14. The two exchanged material on French and English trade unions and on socialism.

the Liberals' bill in 1866, and emerged as a friend of Karl Marx and a middle-class spokesman for the First International at the end of the decade.[86] His speech to a meeting of trade unionists in May 1868 made Beesly's breach with his earlier radical idols emphatically clear. Still unwilling to endorse state socialism, he nonetheless celebrated the role played by French workers in advancing the cause of labour in the June Days of 1848. Denigrating the cooperative movement as an effort on the part of capitalists to expand the capitalist class, Beesly located the source of future advance by workers in the growth of unionized labour. Here his reasoning neatly inverted the logic of Cobden, Bright, and the self-help school of liberals – of which he had earlier been a partisan. Cooperative schemes, he asserted, erred precisely in assisting the most able workers, while rejecting 'the less energetic . . . the men who take life easily'. Identifying the latter group as 'just the men we want to elevate, for they form the bulk of the working-class', Beesley was now determined to defend the indolent and unable from their detractors. 'They are in very bad odour with the preachers of the Manchester School, the apostles of self-help', he noted caustically. 'To my mind there is not a more degrading cant than that which incessantly pours from the lips and pens of these wretched instructors.'[87]

Scholars of later Victorian and Edwardian England trace the development of socially conscious liberal thought committed to government intervention in the economy – the so-called 'New Liberalism' – to the later 1880s and the 1890s. Freed from the trammels of classical economics and diversionary political theatre by the decline and death of W. E. Gladstone, appalled by the deteriorating social conditions exposed by early sociological investigations, and threatened by the rise of organized socialism, they argue, a new generation of middle-class reformers replaced the classical liberalism of earlier decades with a new creed of social democracy. This new school of liberal thought, counting R. B. Haldane, H. H. Asquith, Arthur Acland, and Sir Edward Grey among its parliamentary exponents and L. T. Hobhouse, J. L. and Barbara Hammond, Graham Wallas, and J. A. Hobson among its political theorists,

---

[86] See above, pp. 244–5 and below, pp. 289–90.
[87] Edward Spencer Beesly, *The Social Future of the Working Class: A Lecture Delivered to a Meeting of Trades' Unionists, May 7, 1868* (London, 1869), pp. 6, 9–10, and 15.

triumphed in the Education Act (Provision of School Meals) of 1906, the People's Budget of 1909, and the National Insurance Act of 1911.[88] Strengthened by the Idealist philosophy of T.H. Green, it lent a new theoretical framework to the politics of liberal citizenship and offered an appealing alternative to class-based socialism for the unenfranchised worker.[89]

An understanding of the evolving pattern of liberal and radical thought from the mid-Victorian perspective suggests, however, that the provenance of liberal social democracy in Britain lies in an earlier period than the last two decades of the nineteenth century. Born of the nationalist struggles that dominated popular politics from late Chartism, the radicalization of the middle class dates from the reform movement of the 1860s. This trend to the left within the middle class was not monolithic: significant sectors of the bourgeoisie continued to uphold ideals of liberal individualism that minimized state intervention, a circumstance reflected in the early history of the Charity Organisation Society, founded in 1869.[90] But the shifting emphasis of radical liberalism is striking nonetheless. Even before liberal economists such as W. Stanley Jevons and J.E. Cairnes initiated their intellectual onslaught on classical economics,[91] middle-class radicals active in parliamentary and popular politics began to elaborate a new, pragmatic liberal viewpoint far removed from the teachings of the Manchester School. That they did so in collaboration with the radical artisans of the labour aristocracy is hardly surprising. To the veterans of late Chartism and the nationalist agitations of the sixties, new liberalism was old hat.

Not all radical artisans greeted the new liberalism of this period with enthusiasm. Rather, the significance of these years lies in the emergence of clusters of working-class political allegiance within

---

[88] Peter Clarke, *Lancashire and the New Liberalism* (Cambridge, 1971); *idem, Liberals and Social Democrats* (Cambridge, 1978); Michael Freeden, *The New Liberalism: An Ideology of Social Reform* (Oxford, 1978); and Peter Weiler, *The New Liberalism: Liberal Social Theory in Great Britain 1889–1914* (New York, 1982).

[89] Andrew Vincent and Raymond Plant, *Philosophy, Politics and Citizenship: The Life and Thought of the British Idealists* (Oxford, 1984).

[90] Gareth Stedman Jones, *Outcast London: A Study in the Relationship between Classes in Victorian Society* (Oxford, 1971), esp. pp. 241–80.

[91] For the changing contours of economic thought in this period, see Maurice Dobb, *Theories of Value and Distribution since Adam Smith: Ideology and Economic Theory* (Cambridge, 1973), pp. 166–210, and John W. Mason, 'Political Economy and the Response to Socialism in Britain, 1870–1914', *Historical Journal*, vol. 23 (September 1980), pp. 565–87.

larger constellations of political activity that spanned the political spectrum from the right to the far left. Once enfranchised, one third of the working class proved susceptible to Tory party appeals, a circumstance that middle- and upper-class conservatives were increasingly anxious to exploit as the century advanced.[92] For the remaining two-thirds of the working-class electorate, the political landscape now consisted not of two discrete islands of political sentiment, one described by middle-class visions of political economy and the other informed by *démoc-soc* ideals upheld by the working class, but rather in a complex array of political creeds patronized by middle-class leaders whose sympathies ranged from the teachings of the Manchester School to those of the First International. Sketched with tentative strokes in the nationalist and internationalist events of the sixties, the lineaments of this new liberal politics were to find new sources of strength in English radical responses to the Paris Commune of 1871.

[92] Robert McKenzie and Allan Silver, *Angels in Marble: Working Class Conservatives in Urban England* (Chicago, 1968); Martin Pugh, *The Tories and the People: 1880–1935* (Oxford, 1985).

7 · Republican revival: Liberals, radicals, and social politics, 1870–1874

The fact is that there are no sacred rights of property of any kind: all rights are conferred by the State by process of law, and are defended by the State under certain conditions, these being regulated by Acts of Parliament, which are altered nearly every session it meets ... Hence it is manifest that Parliament has the same power now as it had in 1659 when, on November 21st, by a majority of two, it altered entirely the conditions upon which the land was held then, and had been held for six hundred years before that time. To make any Act of Parliament binding on the conscience of the nation, it should have a majority of votes in its favour, not only in the House, but in the country also ... It is quite possible that a Parliament elected in such a manner would reverse the Act of 1659, and abolish landowning altogether.[1]

The passage of the Second Reform Act and the Liberal electoral victory of 1868 acted to undercut national radical activity in England, temporarily exhausting the financial resources, political imperatives, and funds of enthusiasm that had sustained middle- and working-class efforts to expand the franchise through Reform League and Reform Union agitation.[2] But although the immediate aftermath of the reform campaign saw a diminution of radical ardour, these years nonetheless witnessed crucial developments in the evolution of English radical culture. First manifest in attempts to

[1] Charles C. Cattell, *The Land: How to Make It Feed the People and Pay the Taxes. Second Edition with Reply to the Rt. Hon. John Bright, M.P.* (Birmingham, [1879]), p. 4.

[2] See esp. Royden Harrison, 'The British Working Class and the General Election of 1868', *International Review of Social History*, vols. 5 and 6 (1960–1), pp. 424–55, 74–109.

explore land tenure reform – long a staple working-class radical argument – the tentative radical efforts of the late sixties gave way in the following decade to a strident, if shortlived, republican movement that tied the fortunes of English radicals again to the course of French revolutionary politics. Guided by their relations with the working-class radicals who had orchestrated the Garibaldi agitations, the activities of the Reform League, and the First International, radical leaders of the middle class greeted the Franco-Prussian War and the Paris Commune of 1870–1 with a new liberal conscience. Increasingly troubled by social conditions and progressively sceptical of the classical economists' ability to dispatch with them, these men of the middle class evinced a new tolerance of government intervention in the economy. In sharp contrast to bourgeois radicals in the aftermath of 1848, the new liberals of this era came to expound a radical vision that emphasized the necessary interrelation of the social, economic and political spheres.

The broad contours of this transition within English liberalism are well illustrated by the radical progress of Richard Marsden Pankhurst, husband and father to the notorious Edwardian suffragettes. Educated at Owens College in the 1850s, the young Pankhurst evinced sympathies with working-class radical causes, but remained committed to the liberal teachings of the Manchester School. A member of the Social Science Association, a critic – in collaboration with George Odger – of the labour laws that hobbled trade unions, and a personal friend of Ernest Jones, Pankhurst in the sixties nonetheless claimed John Bright as his political leader, choosing to join the Reform Union rather than the League.[3] Yet the following decade saw this liberal reformer break with Bright and the Manchester School. For like his future wife – converted to radicalism at a Paris boarding school by her roommate, the daughter of the French republican Henri Rochefort – Pankhurst proved susceptible to French revolutionary influences in the seventies.[4] Middle-class radicals of an earlier generation had elected to disavow French radicals in response to the revolution of 1848, but Pankhurst and an

[3] Printed Leaflet, 'Independent Labour Party: Gorton Parliamentary Division. Dr. Pankhurst', [1895], IISG, Pankhurst Family Collection, Volumes of Newspaper Clippings, vol. 4 (93), p. 90.
[4] For Mrs Pankhurst's radical conversion, see Sylvia Pankhurst, 'Synopsis of Autobiography', IISG, Pankhurst Collection, Correspondence etc., folder 194, fol. 3.

increasingly vocal cohort of middle-class politicians chose to abandon John Bright rather than to denounce French radical traditions
in the aftermath of the Paris Commune.

Patriotic sentiments were conspicuously evident in this radicalization of liberal thought. In defending his new political principles in
1873, Pankhurst reiterated Bright's plea, voiced at a Glasgow reform
meeting in 1866, for government by the 'nation' rather than by class
interests. He then proceeded to dismiss his former leader – an
antagonist of the Commune – as a 'captive to the Philistines of
hereditary influences ... grinding in the Conservative mill'.
Informed by avowedly 'patriotic' motives, Pankhurst and the Manchester Republican Club now sought to revive English politics by
paying tribute to 'the perpetual monument' of the French republic.
The political significance of the French revolution, Pankhurst
emphasized in his inaugural address, derived from its demonstration
of 'the principle of the supremacy of the good of the whole people as
the object and end of government'. 'As to our own English revolution', he concluded, 'the general principles which it reveals decisively
point in the same direction.'[5]

From the 1870s to the 1890s, the Pankhurst residences, first in
Russell Square and then in Manchester, served as a social centre for
radical agitators advocating an array of causes that embraced
republicanism, the reform of the House of Lords, women's rights,
agnosticism, socialism, and the new trades unionism. Guests
attracted to this circle ranged from the young Liberal parliamentar-
ian R. B. Haldane to Eleanor Marx, the young English socialists
Keir Hardie, Bruce Glasier, Enid Stacey, Ramsay MacDonald, and
the French Communards Rochefort and Louise Michel.[6] Unlike
the hosts and hostesses of liberal salon culture in the 1850s and
1860s, moreover, Pankhurst actively entered into the socialist
schemes of his eclectic company, standing as a parliamentary
candidate for the Independent Labour Party in 1895. Moderate
perhaps by the standards of continental socialism, his address to
electors spoke to the long tradition of social politics sustained by

[5]   R.M. Pankhurst to the Editor of the *Manchester Times and Examiner*, 9 June 1873,
      and 'The Manchester Republican Club', both in IISG, Pankhurst Family Collec-
      tion, Volumes of Newspaper Clippings, vol. 3 (98): 1863–79. Bright's speech at
      Glasgow is noted above, p. 251.
[6]   Sylvia Pankhurst, 'Synopsis of an Autobiography', IISG, Pankhurst Family
      Collection, folder 194, fol. 6, and Sylvia Pankhurst, 'Memories of Childhood',
      IISG, Pankhurst Family Collection, folder 199, fol. 9.

English working-class radicals in the face of classical liberalism after 1848. 'This party is absolutely right in its principles', he asserted. 'Its resolution to always unite the social and political problems is justified by historical experience.'[7]

RADICALS, NEW LIBERALS, AND THE LAND

Although reduced in scale, working-class radical activity continued to exhibit considerable intellectual vitality in the late sixties. Faced with the failure of even a single working-class candidate to secure a seat in the general election of 1868 and alarmed by the rising tide of unemployment in London, metropolitan artisans and agitators established new leagues and committees to address the particular interests of labour. Moderate engineers, tailors, ironfounders, masons, carpenters, joiners, and members of other trades earlier active in the Reform League sought in forming the Labour Representation League in 1869 to ensure the future election of working-class MPs.[8] Less conciliatory in tone and intent were the Land and Labour and Unemployed Poor Leagues. Founded in October 1869 by a cohort of working-class radical activists with strong ties to the First International, the Land and Labour League advanced a programme that included land nationalization, a direct and progressive property tax, state-sponsored education, payment of MPs, a statutory limitation of the hours of labour, and abolition of the standing army.[9] Similar goals found expression in the Unemployed Poor League, established in the autumn of 1868 to promote state-sponsored general education, the abolition of the Poor Laws, and the institution of an 'organisation of labour'.[10] This organization, reinforced by artisans active in both the Reform League and the International, expanded into an International Democratic Association in 1869. Vociferous in exposing the plight of the unemployed, the members of the International Democratic Association combined

[7] Printed leaflet, 'Independent Labour Party', IISG, Pankhurst Family Collection, Volumes of Newspaper Clippings, vol. 4 (93), p. 90.
[8] Their initial manifesto is reprinted in James B. Jeffreys, *Labour's Formative Years* (London, 1948), pp. 147–9.
[9] Royden Harrison, 'The Land and Labour League', *Bulletin of the International Institute of Social History*, vol. 8 (1953), pp. 169–95. As Harrison notes on p. 174, eleven of the League's thirty-seven Council members were also members of the First International.
[10] *Eastern Post*, 31 October 1868, p. 4.

a defence of Irish nationalism with attacks on the land monopoly of the upper classes.[11]

These radical developments caused considerable private anxiety among liberal politicians. 'I had a long talk the other evening with Howell, one of the leaders of the Trades Unions and working men', the Liverpool liberal William Rathbone confided to his mother. 'He says the Liberal Party are losing ground much, for many reasons', Rathbone reported in distress, 'some of their Economies are considered harsh and partial'.[12] Although largely ignored by the Liberal party leadership, this concern commanded new public interest and sympathy among the more advanced middle-class representatives of liberal opinion. The editorials of the *Eastern Post*, a paper Gladstonian in its political preferences but tied through its East End constituents to the more popular inclinations of London radical culture, are illustrative of this trend. When confronted in 1868 with the demands of the Unemployed Poor Union, the *Eastern Post* both underscored the significance of social issues for parliamentary politics in the aftermath of the Second Reform Act and located the new social politics securely within the established framework of debate between the competing claims of class and nation. Citing Bright's speech at Glasgow in 1866 on the need to pit the 'nation' against purely class interests, the newspaper argued that with reform 'the nation has come into its inheritance'. 'It is entering even now into the enjoyment of its rights', the *Eastern Post* continued in a Mazzinian vein. 'It remains to be seen how it will discharge its duties.' These national duties clearly resided in the integration of social reform and parliamentary politics. For although the paper disavowed the programme of the Unemployed Poor League, it was sharply critical of Members of Parliament who remained indifferent to deteriorating economic conditions, and raised the spectre of Chartism to underline the need to counter the 'social mischiefs' of unemployment with legislation. 'As Chartism was more dangerous to the framework of the society in which we live than any preceding popular movement', it noted, 'so that conflict of forces which must come up in our generation, if it be not anticipated by the wisdom of statesmen, will be most formidable of all, because

[11] Fergus A. D'Arcy, 'Charles Bradlaugh and the English Republican Movement, 1868–1878', *Historical Journal*, vol. 25 (June 1982), pp. 369–70.
[12] Typescript of William Rathbone to his mother, 13 March 1870, University of Liverpool Archives, Rathbone Family Papers, IX.5.2.

it will be altogether disconnected from the ordinary politics of parties.'[13]

Rehearsing the *démoc-soc* arguments of late Chartism, this strain of polemic attracted a wide variety of middle-class reformers to radical campaigns that sought to amend the laws governing land ownership in Britain. Their efforts, which gained considerable attention from parliamentary leaders in the eighties and nineties, continued to exercise the liberal conscience and intellect into the twentieth century. Initially predicated upon traditional radical fears of the corrupt political influence of the landed aristocracy, these middle-class efforts to reform land tenures evolved from a laissez-faire economic base to encompass more novel economic aspirations. Without abandoning their fundamental conviction in the sacred character of private property in other goods, the proponents of these schemes came to generate 'a deviant tradition in nineteenth-century liberalism', a 'belief that land must be treated as a special kind of property, to which the normal justifications of exclusive individual ownership do not apply'.[14] Although boasting an intellectual lineage distinct from working-class radical agrarianism – few liberals had much veneration for the schemes of the Diggers, the followers of Thomas Spence, or the National Charter Association[15] – middle-class schemes for land reform created a common ground among rival radical groups for political dialogue on the role of the English state in the social and political life of the nation.

Foremost among the middle-class organizations that emerged in these years was the Land Tenure Reform Association, established in 1869 to promote agitation for the restriction of land accumulation by magnates. Building upon the liberal legacies of the Manchester School, the Land Tenure Reform Association took Richard Cobden's cry 'I would have a League for free trade in land just as we had

[13] *Eastern Post*, 31 October 1868, p. 4.
[14] Ursula Vogel, 'The Land Question: A Liberal Theory of Communal Property', *History Workshop*, no. 27 (Spring 1989), pp. 106–35, p. 106. Harold Perkin provides an overview of the political impact of these movements in 'Land Reform and Class Conflict in Victorian Britain', in J. Butt and I.F. Clarke (eds.), *The Victorians and Social Protest: A Symposium* (London, 1973), pp. 177–217; Clive J. Dewey details their economic context in 'The Rehabilitation of the Peasant Proprietor in Nineteenth-Century Economic Thought', *History of Political Economy*, vol. 6, (1974), pp. 17–47.
[15] See above, pp. 114–15, 132–3, for these more popular forms of radical agrarian thought.

a League for free trade in corn' as its point of departure.[16] Couched in these terms, the Association's programme appealed to a broad spectrum of middle-class liberal opinion: John Bright's brother Jacob, the economists Henry Fawcett and J.E. Thorold Rogers, P.A. Taylor, Edmond Beales, Frederic Harrison, and the former Christian Socialist Thomas Hughes all became members.[17] So too did John Stuart Mill, the Land Tenure Reform Association's leading light and guiding force. A close personal friend of Louis Blanc, Mill had flirted with French socialist doctrines since 1848 but had little sympathy for French – or English – arguments for universal manhood suffrage.[18] His distinctive interpretation of the science of political economy, a sensation when published in 1848, had lost much of its radical appeal two decades later. 'I am coming to think Mill's is a bad book morally', Frederic Harrison wrote to E.S. Beesly in 1868, ' – that he is tacitly sanctioning the economic selfishness.'[19] His political fears allayed by the limited enfranchisement of workers in 1867, Mill found in the land reform campaign an arena in which his abstract, cerebral socialism could merge with the more robust demands of popular radical culture. Moderate in comparison with many working-class exponents of land reform, he proved willing to negotiate with more radical artisans within both his own association and the competing Land and Labour League.

In its initial formulation, the programme of Mill's Land Tenure Reform Association emphasized the abolition of primogeniture as a means for preventing the large-scale accumulation of landed wealth, and thus gratified anti-aristocratic sentiments long central to the liberal reform tradition. The meliorist leaders of the secularist movement, anxious to forge links between their constituents and middle-class liberals, seized upon these anti-aristocratic

[16] Cobden's interest in free trade in land, expressed publicly in 1864 in his last speech at Rochdale, is discussed in Perkin, 'Land Reform and Class Conflict', pp. 196–7, and Vogel, 'The Land Question', pp. 109–111.

[17] *Bee-Hive*, 11 September 1869, p. 1.

[18] For Mill's complex relations with French socialist thought in 1848–49, see above p. 93 and his *Autobiography*, in *Collected Works*, vol I, p. 241. Broader analyses of these issues are provided in Iris Wessel Mueller, *John Stuart Mill and French Thought* (Urbana, 1956), pp. 175–215. Mill's support for political activity by only 'the élite of the working classes' is a commonplace of his correspondence in this period. See for example Mill to W.R. Cremer, 10 November 1868 and Mill to George Howell, 27 December 1868, in *Collected Works*, vol. XVI, pp. 1485, 1534.

[19] Harrison to Beesly, 2 June [1868], BLPES, Harrison Collection, 1/15/25.

arguments and lent their support to Mill's efforts. G.J. Holyoake was an early proponent of the Association; his successor to the secularist leadership, Charles Bradlaugh, combined references to Mill's economic theories and to Louis Blanc's social criticism with anti-aristocratic polemic in his arguments for the movement.[20] But the radical artisans who had emerged at the forefront of working-class reform earlier in the decade proved less amenable to the movement's moderate aims, and ultimately forced the Association to accept positive state intervention in the land market. Egged on by Marx, Robert Applegarth and W.R. Cremer convinced Mill and the Land Tenure Reform Association in 1870 to endorse 'the interception, by Taxation, for the benefit of the State, of the future Unearned Increase of the Rent of Land (so far as the same can be ascertained) or a great part of such increase, which is continually taking place without any effort or outlay by the proprietors, merely through the growth of population and wealth'.[21] Far less sweeping than the programme of compulsory land nationalization adopted by the Land and Labour League, the association's platform continued to suffer attack from radical artisans of the left, but it stands as a monument to the new liberal tendencies of the times nonetheless. Linking members of the International to aspiring parliamentary candidates, it served to introduce key middle-class liberals to the popular politics of social reform.

The role played in the radicalization of middle-class politicians by organizations such as the Land Tenure Reform Association is clearly evident in the evolution of the new liberal politics of Sir Charles Wentworth Dilke. Educated at Cambridge in the 1860s, Dilke studied under Henry Fawcett as an undergraduate, but declined to adopt his tutor's classical system of political economy. When assigned an essay in 1864 on forms of government, he turned for inspiration not to Adam Smith, Nassau Senior, and Samuel Smiles but rather to the writings of Louis Blanc, Etienne Cabet, and

---

[20] Holyoake Diary, November 1869, BI, Holyoake Collection; Charles Bradlaugh, *The Land Question: Large Estates Inimical to the Welfare of the People* (London, 1870), in BI, Bradlaugh Collection, 221(A).

[21] Harrison, 'Land and Labour League', pp. 172–3, discusses this struggle over the taxation of landowners' 'unearned increment'. For Marx's influence, see Applegarth to Marx, 2 December 1869 and 14 July 1870, IISG, Marx–Engels Collection, D., Letters to Marx, items 61–2.

Pierre Joseph Proudhon.[22] Blanc, indeed, became a personal friend, introducing Dilke to the Russian agrarian socialist Alexander Herzen later in the sixties.[23] But the English radical's socialist affinities, like those of Mill, were largely confined to his private correspondence in the era of reform. It was only with his election to represent Chelsea in 1868 that Dilke became a public advocate of state intervention in social life. This transformation was effected under the aegis of the Land Tenure Reform Association.

Active in the organization from its inception in 1868, Dilke became a key speaker on its behalf when the Land Tenure Reform Association began to sponsor public events in 1871. His speech in May at the Association's first public meeting began with a series of oratorical caveats, as Dilke sought to steer a middle road between liberal associations for the preservation of common lands on the one hand and the Land and Labour League's schemes for mandatory land nationalization on the other. Here Dilke adopted a broadly European perspective, and linked social welfare directly to the action of the state. The British system of land tenure, he argued, 'is of all known systems the only one in which the small proprietor has no place, and the one, too, in which the State has the least place'. Developing this theme further to explain the Land Tenure Reform Association's programme, Dilke advanced a line of argument that went beyond the shibboleths of Manchester School economics:

> Now, many land reformers would merely bring an end to the law of primogeniture and those other restrictions which are known as entails – a course which would only make our land tenure more commercial still, in making land more easily marketable. Cobden, for instance, was one of these, and his notion of reform in the land laws was that land should be sold as easily as a watch. We, too, desire that land should be sold as easily as a watch, but we desire, at the same time, to have securities against its too great accumu-

---

[22] Stephen Gwynn and Gertrude Tuckwell, *The Life of the Rt. Honourable Sir Charles W. Dilke*, 2 vols. (New York, 1917), vol. II, p. 25, notes Fawcett as a radical influence, but Dilke's abiding interest in French socialism suggests that Fawcett's teachings were less decisive than other, continental theories of political economy. Dilke's book-slips from the British Museum for autumn 1864 indicate that he read, among other works, Blanc's *Discours aux travailleurs* (1848), Proudhon's *Le Droit au travail et le droit de propriété* (1850), and the prospectus for Cabet's Icaria community (1852). BL, Dilke Papers, Add. MS 43,909, fols. 29, 30, 56.

[23] Louis Blanc to Alexander Herzen, [1869], BL, Dilke Papers, Add. MS 43,909, fol. 127.

lation, and to see also that the State should once more claim that reasonable share in the control of land which it should never have given up.

Denouncing extant systems of land tenure as 'new and unhistorical', Dilke – like the late Chartists of the 1850s – invoked the pattern of the English past to underline the need to link landed property with the performance of 'public duties' for the state, notably the administration of justice and the maintenance of the sick and the poor.[24]

In concluding his speech, Dilke reiterated the Land Tenure Reform Association's goal of taxing the 'unearned increase' of the value of land, affirming the programme imposed upon its middle-class liberals by its radical artisans. His critique of contemporary systems of land tenure, which contrasted modern systems of 'absolute' property unfavourably with the sixteenth-century concept of limited property rights, spoke to a long tradition of radical dissent from the teachings of the classical economists. Recalling in its tone the *Eastern Post*'s plea in 1868 for a 'national' politics to replace class rule, his final remarks urged not charity, abstinence, or self-help but rather active political intervention in social life. 'The life of the English labourer is a steady march down a hill, with a poor-house at the bottom', he concluded. 'At the same time, the observer finds, when he asks for the remedy, that, in these matters, there is not a pin to choose between the two parties in the State. Let them beware lest we people of the towns do not form one for ourselves.'[25]

Adumbrated in Mill's Land Tenure Reform Association in 1868, the gradual acceptance by new liberals of arguments for state intervention in social life soon extended beyond the land question, blurring but not erasing the class lines evident in English radical argument from 1848. Compulsory education was particularly successful in attracting a diverse array of radicals that ranged from middle-class parliamentarians to the radical artisanate. The political platform of the British Federation of the International, formed at Nottingham in 1872, called for 'education to be gratuitous, compulsory, and secular',[26] but middle-class liberals such as Dilke and the Birmingham radical Joseph Chamberlain were also vociferous in

[24] Sir Charles Dilke, *Speeches: By Sir Charles Wentworth Dilke: March, 1871 to March, 1872* (London, 1872), pp. 32–3, 36–7.
[25] *Ibid.*, pp. 37–8.
[26] 'Rules & Resolutions of the 1st Congress British Federation: Political Platform', IISG, Jung Collection, C. 166/12.

demanding state-sponsored education. Careful to distinguish between the needs of the individual and the needs of the nation, Dilke in October 1871 chose to emphasize the latter in his defence of compulsory national education:

> Without education the child will not merely not die, but may live as contentedly, though not perhaps as usefully as with it ... Education is necessary for wholly different reasons and in a wholly different degree. When the State interferes to save a child from death by starvation, it interferes to protect the life of a citizen who is incapable of protecting his own. Its interference is justifiable from the point of view of the individual. On the other hand, compulsory education is justifiable from the point of view of the State. The State suffers by crime and outrage, the result of ignorance. It interferes, therefore, to protect itself.[27]

Far removed from the liberal vision of Samuel Smiles, a vision in which the nation had consisted merely of an aggregate of its individuals and social regeneration lay outside the province of the state, this new liberalism dismissed the efficacy of private charity rather than exalting it. It thus challenged fundamentally received middle-class definitions of the radical programme. In sharp contrast to their predecessors, the 'Radicals' of the seventies, as Chamberlain noted in 1874, increasingly maintained 'that the evils themselves are caused, or at least increased, by bad legislation, and that more can be done in the way of remedy by Act of Parliament ... than by all the private charity and individual beneficence of the upper and middle class.'[28]

Although their record of political achievement pales before the legislative successes enjoyed by the new liberals of the 1890s and early twentieth century, middle-class radicals such as Mill and Dilke are of central importance to the history of mid-Victorian social and political thought. Their attempts from the later 1860s to establish a new social politics within liberalism marked a departure – and a retreat – from the dominant liberal precepts of the two preceding decades. The social mission of this new liberalism was, from a working-class perspective, not new. Nor, from a Marxian perspective, was it revolutionary. Its proponents sought to replace classical political economy not with a fully democratic socialism but rather

---

[27] Dilke, *Speeches*, p. 43.
[28] Joseph Chamberlain, 'The Next Page of the Liberal Programme', *Fortnightly Review*, vol. 16 (October 1874), p. 416. For Smiles on the nation, see above, p. 226.

with a socially conscious democracy. In doing so they travelled paths traversed since 1848 by the late Chartist leadership. The depth and significance of this commitment should not be ignored. For unlike the social sympathies of middle-class liberals of the 1840s, the new liberalism survived the onslaught of French revolutionary politics. The February revolution and the June Days of 1848 precipitated a class reaction in England, severing bourgeois reformers from both working-class radicals and their constituents; the Franco-Prussian War and the Commune neither divided radical culture neatly along perceived class lines nor demolished the social vision of radical politics tentatively advanced by middle-class liberals from 1868. Alienating some radicals of both classes, these events and their English response catapulted others toward socialism.

WAR, REPUBLICANISM, AND SOCIAL POLITICS

The outbreak of the Franco-Prussian War in 1870 served to catalyse and expand the tentative alliance forged in the aftermath of 1867 between liberal and radical reformers of the English middle and working classes. Precipitated by diplomatic wrangling over the fate of the Spanish monarchy, the Franco-Prussian War was, more fundamentally, predicated upon French fears of growing German unity and Bismarck's determination to solidify the German states' economic union in a patriotic war with a shared historic enemy. Against a backdrop of conservative opinion that both denounced France's role in the outbreak of the war and decried the potentially destabilizing impact of its course upon the working class, liberals and radicals in England voiced assessments of the conflict that stressed first its nationalist implications, then its republican potential, and finally its social democratic meaning.[29]

The burden of middle-class liberal and radical opinion, sympathetic to German aspirations for unity and sharply hostile to Louis Napoleon for his role in opposing republicanism in France and Italy, was firmly opposed to France in the first months of the hostilities. 'God save Germany!', Goldwin Smith wrote to James Bryce upon the outbreak of war. 'She is the leading school now of European civilization', he concluded, while 'the French empire is

---

[29] P.K. Martinez provides an excellent overview of the response, and particularly its conservative manifestation, in 'Paris Communard Refugees in Britain, 1871–1880' (DPhil thesis, Sussex University, 1980), pp. 1–17.

reaction and barbarism'.[30] Anti-Catholic sentiments earlier evident in middle-class support for Mazzini and Garibaldi encouraged liberals to support Germany in its battle with France; a conviction that patriotic warfare would forge a German nation from Prussia and the lesser states complemented this longstanding Protestant radical prejudice. James Stansfeld's wife Caroline, schooled by Mazzini to counter French revolutionary politics with nationalist fervour, was quick to denigrate 'the iniquitous war'. 'Of course, I am *German* – (not Prussian) – to the last degree', she wrote to Karl Blind's wife in July, 'and hope the Brigand L.N. may have such a defeat at once as to bring matters to the concrete [end] with as little mischief as possible – but it is a sin and a shame that it is allowed at all.'[31]

Liberal politicians who habitually associated themselves with the aspirations of the French left voiced much the same opinion. John Stuart Mill, informed of the French declaration of war, reportedly struck his chair and exclaimed 'what a pity the bombs of Orsini missed their mark, and left the crime-stained usurper alive'.[32] The liberals Charles Dilke and Auberon Herbert, inspired by similar sentiments, travelled to Germany and served, for three weeks, with an ambulance team attending the army of the Crown Prince of Prussia.[33] Even English Positivists, normally Francophile in sympathy, were of this persuasion. 'Like nearly all English politicians, certainly all Liberals to a man, I had been a hearty opponent of the French pretext for commencing war', Frederic Harrison later recalled. 'And all through the summer and autumn, along with all my Liberal friends, I had warmly hoped for German victories, with the final extinction of the Imperial dynasty and the Napoleonic Legend.'[34]

The decisive defeat of Louis Napoleon's forces at Sedan on 1 September 1870 shattered this liberal interpretation of the war. For with the fall of the French empire and the declaration by Paris

[30] Smith to Bryce, 16 July 1870, BODL, James Bryce MS, Correspondence with Goldwin Smith, item 16.
[31] Stansfeld to Blind, 27 July 1870, BL, Blind Papers, Add. MS 40,125, fol. 86. Belfort Bax noted the influence of anti-Catholicism upon middle-class opinion in this regard in his *Reminiscences*, p. 15.
[32] John Morley, *Recollections*, 2 vols. (New York, 1917), vol. I, p. 55.
[33] Charles Dilke, 'Notes for an Autobiography', BL, Dilke Papers, Add. MS 43,929, fols. 71–4.
[34] Harrison, *Autobiographic Memoirs*, vol. II, pp. 2–3.

patriots of a new republic on 4 September, sympathy for France rose swiftly in liberal circles. Germany, hailed only weeks before as an emergent nation engaged in a just and defensive war, now figured in English polemic as an aggressive military machine determined to destroy at any cost the citizens of the young French republic. Charles Dilke, who reported that he and Auberon Herbert had begun 'to wish to desert [the Germans] when we saw how over-bearing success had made the officers', was one among the many English liberals who travelled to France to witness the long-awaited fall of the second empire. In Paris he marched with a republican crowd singing the Marseillaise, and dined with both Blanqui and Louis Blanc. Unlike middle-class liberals in 1848, Dilke was unper-turbed by the spectre of the democratic and social republic, subsum-ing the socialist sympathies of his friends on the French left with the larger spirit of nationalism. The revolutionary crowd, in his analysis, had only 'Two shades: the patriots pure & simple, – & the *republican patriots*.'[35]

Far from representing the sympathies of a handful of isolated individuals, these republican sentiments contributed to a critique of contemporary social relations that came to pervade the more advanced wings of liberal opinion. In London the liberal editor John Morley now used the pages of his *Fortnightly Review* to elaborate an English interpretation of the Franco-Prussian War that reflected arguments current in the new liberal response to unemployment and land tenure reform. Citing the influence of the International and the Land and Labour League as examples of English workers' growing disillusion with 'parliamentary instruments and representatives of patrician obstruction', Morley argued that the role of the French republic was to act as a salutary 'leavening element in England', a force stirring all classes of the nation to reform. Like the liberals of 1848, Morley was quick to equate perceived working-class sympathy for the republic in France with a desire for social reform at home, claiming that to 'the believer in democracy' the 'unmistakable and deep-lying sympathy with France' displayed by London workmen 'proves their confidence in French social ideas, as meeting most fully their own requirements'. Far from denouncing these tendencies at

---

[35] Charles Dilke, 'Notes for an Autobiography', BL, Dilke Papers, Add. MS 43,929, fols. 76–82. Henry Labouchere, in Paris with Dilke in September, entertained himself by lecturing to the revolutionary crowd under various guises – as an American visitor, as a citizen of Marseilles, and as an English sympathizer.

home and abroad, Morley set 'the highest value upon these French social ideas, which a republic would bring into more prominence than ever, and upon the influence which a French republic would have upon our own movement – an influence, I would repeat, so valuable, as to be worth any sacrifice on our part to strengthen it'. Predictably, the instrument of England's regeneration in his analysis was the force of patriotic sentiment. 'If an end is to be put, without open breach and revolution, to the want of energetic and self-respecting action in England, we shall have to begin at the beginning; and the beginning is an undivided nation', he concluded. 'England, like Germany, has need to pray for, and to effect, national unity.'[36]

Morley's encomium to the principles of national unity and social reform testified to the intellectual impact of the new French republic upon middle-class thinkers in 1870; the burst of public speeches, meetings, and processions that celebrated the fall of the empire demonstrated the broader popular appeal of French social politics in England at this time. Encompassing both London and the provinces, the wave of French republican enthusiasm that swept reform circles from September drew substantial force from nationalist and internationalist sympathies forged in the continental revolutions of 1848. The arguments of liberals and radicals whose activism dated from the Chartist era were prominent in this response, acting to incorporate the new revolutionary developments into an established oppositional tradition already freighted with precise patriotic meanings and tactical implications. Joseph Cowen, the Newcastle industrialist whose generous contributions had sustained continental refugees throughout the fifties, was swift to extend his congratulations to the new French republic, which he linked directly to the cause of national independence in Italy and Poland.[37] Birmingham patriots were equally eager to link national unity, the revolution of 1848, and the declaration of the third French republic. The *Birmingham Daily Post*, reporting a public meeting held in the town hall to express sympathy with the new republic, threw its support behind the French 'in their change from a system of repression to one of freedom – from the Government of the Country by one man for the

---

[36] John Morley, 'England and the War', *Fortnightly Review*, vol. 8 (October 1870), pp. 480, 482–8. The leavening imagery was common in the liberal response. Beesly wrote to Marx on 20 September 1870 that 'all this excitement is leavening the mass for us'. IISG, Marx–Engels Collection, D., Letters to Marx, item 249.

[37] Typescript of a speech by Cowen, 6 September 1870, T&WAD, Cowen Collection, 634/A910, fol. 1.

interests of a dynasty, to a Government . . . for the benefit of the nation'. In his speech to the assembled crowd, the Reverend Arthur O'Neill recalled attending a similar meeting in the town hall to celebrate the republic of 1848 and moved that the audience petition the English government to accord diplomatic recognition to the new republican government of France. Joseph Chamberlain, although too young himself to have participated in the response to the February revolution, supported O'Neill's resolution with a cry for 'Liberty, Fraternity, and Equality', words crafted to recall the aspirations of earlier generations of French and English radical reformers.[38]

Just as earlier manifestations of sympathy for democratic and nationalist causes on the continent had encouraged the elaboration of militant internationalist sentiments by English radicals, the declaration of the Third Republic fostered radical efforts to persuade the English government to intervene in the Franco-Prussian War on behalf of France. Developing alongside the social interpretation of the French republic, middle- and working-class calls for intervention alienated radicals affiliated with the pacifist movement, to which both the heirs to the Manchester School tradition and a growing sector of the liberal working class subscribed.[39] But as in earlier decades, a significant portion of radical opinion stood as intransigently opposed to laissez-faire tendencies in foreign affairs as it did in economic relations. English members of the First International played a key role in promoting this spirit of militant interventionism. When George Howell and the moderate liberal workers of the Labour Representation League called a meeting on 13 September to express sympathy for the French republic, Robert Applegarth moved that this republican sympathy be backed by the armed force of British troops. Telegraphing to the office of the General Council for support, Applegarth mustered the members of the International, who ran to the meeting, supported his motion, and triumphantly forced its passage over the objections of less strident reformers.[40]

---

[38] *Birmingham Daily Post*, 12 September 1870, p. 5; 13 September 1870, p. 5.
[39] For the growth of working-class interest in the pacifist movement, see Sager, 'Social Origins of Victorian Pacifism'. When, however, Edmond Beales convened a public meeting of workers in London to celebrate the declaration of the Third Republic and urge against British intervention, he found that the latter argument still alienated a significant cohort of the working-class leadership. See *Birmingham Daily Post*, 9 September 1870, p. 5.
[40] *General Council Minutes*, vol. IV, p. 498.

Public meetings to urge diplomatic recognition of the new republic served to link these demands with the traditions of earlier
movements that had tied English popular politics to national
independence and socialist reform on the continent. The procession
that preceded a republican demonstration in Hyde Park late in
September included marching bands, men bearing the banners of the
red republic, and a cohort of émigrés carrying the red, green, and
white tricolour of Italian independence. Participants voted to send
the French republic a message of congratulations, elected to send a
deputation to Gladstone urging English recognition and protection
of the republic, and joined in singing the Marseillaise.[41] The 10,000–
12,000 republican sympathizers who gathered at Trafalgar Square to
participate in another meeting, organized by a committee of London
working men, mixed republican and socialist themes at their celebration. Participants brandished the French tricolour, the flag of the
red republic, and the American stars and stripes, and greeted with an
outburst of enthusiasm Robert Applegarth's resolution that the
meeting invite the new French government to dispatch Louis Blanc to
explain the implications of the war to the English population.[42]

Commenting in the press on the import of the meeting at
Trafalgar Square, the liberal journalist Justin McCarthy discerned
both established working-class oppositional sentiments and a new
spirit of radical reform from within the ranks of the middle class.
McCarthy's description of the event began by emphasizing elements
of the gathering long typical of working-class associational life,
dwelling on the red caps of liberty raised aloft on poles by artisans
singing the Marseillaise. But in comparing the English response to
the events of 1870 with the response to 1848, McCarthy – who was
equally antagonistic to Chartism and the new republicanism of the
day – was careful to underline the different social compositions of
the two phases of English radical activity. For in sharp contrast to
earlier working-class radical causes, republicanism in the 1870s, he
asserted, commanded the allegiance of sections of the respectable
middle class. This 'fraternization' with workers McCarthy rightly
judged 'one of the most remarkable phenomena of English political
life'.[43] Other observers were forcibly convinced of the same novel

[41] *Nonconformist*, 28 September 1870, p. 932.
[42] *The Penny Bee-Hive: The People's Paper*, 24 September 1870, p. 502.
[43] Justin McCarthy, 'Republicanism in England', *The Galaxy*, vol. 12 (July 1871), pp.
    30–40.

development. One newspaper, preparing a facetious 'Provisional Government' for an imminent English republic, mixed former Chartists, members of the International, Manchester School economists, and new liberals indiscriminately in its hypothetical cabinet. Presided over by 'citizen' Charles Dilke, the mock republican government boasted the former Owenite and Christian Socialist Patrick Lloyd Jones as Foreign Secretary, the Chartist James Finlen as Minister of Education, the secularist G.J. Holyoake as Minister of Public Worship, and George Howell as Secretary-at-War. Middle-class citizens were equally prominent. Jacob Bright was designated Commander-in-Chief, P.A. Taylor as Colonial Secretary, and Goldwin Smith as Indian Secretary, while John Stuart Mill, Edward Beesly, and Auberon Herbert occupied the Post Office, the Commission of Works, and the Poor-Law Board.[44]

Like the rhetoric and symbolism that pervaded the radical response to the Franco-Prussian War, the composition of metropolitan republican gatherings reflected patterns of radical allegiance that had persisted from earlier decades of oppositional activity. Crafts and trades active in radical movements since at least the Chartist era provided the wellspring of support of the new wave of French republican enthusiasm: bookbinders, bootmakers, hatters, gilders, carpenters, cabinetmakers, masons, painters, plasterers, and ironfounders were prominent in the deputation that petitioned Gladstone for English diplomatic recognition of the French republic on 27 September. The Positivist intellectuals, now fully prepared to abandon the Manchester liberalism of their youth for a militant internationalism, joined with these radical unionists in the attempt to ally England's liberal ministry with the republican government of France.[45] Rebuffed by Gladstone, these middle- and working-class radicals united in October to establish the Anglo-French Intervention Committee, a body determined to impress the public mind with the common virtues of militant internationalism, French revolutionary politics, and English social reform.[46]

[44] Unidentified press clipping, [1870], BI, Bradlaugh Collection, item 223.
[45] *Penny Bee-Hive*, 1 October 1870, p. 513.
[46] *General Council Minutes*, vol. IV, pp. 499, 502. For the Positivist interpretation of this cause, see Edward Spencer Beesly, *A Word for France: Addressed to the Workmen of London* (London, 1870). Here Beesly compared the Prussian sovereigns to the Stuarts, defended the French revolutionary tradition, and endorsed 'the Reorganisation of Labour'.

The interventionist efforts of this coalition, anachronistically described by Frederic Harrison as 'entirely in accord with Liberal traditions',[47] served both to introduce new liberal converts to the public platforms of popular politics and to generate a new constellation of alliances among different generations, classes, and interest groups of the English radical leadership. In London, the signatories of a petition that urged Gladstone's cabinet to protect the French republic with British troops included F. A. Maxse – a retired naval officer whose radical passage had begun in the ranks of Mill's Land Tenure Reform Association – former Chartists such as J.B. Leno, and the Christian Socialist J.M.F. Ludlow.[48] In the provinces too interventionist sentiment revived radical convictions and alliances by invoking a national heritage of militant patriotism. Julian Harney, writing in Joseph Cowen's *Newcastle Chronicle* in January, urged that '*national* duty, fully performed, would three months ago have placed England's forces by the side of those who were on our side in the Crimea'. Burdened with 'costly' and 'absurd' aristocratic institutions and thwarted by a ministry pledged to the old liberal policy of 'peace at any price', the old Chartist concluded, the nation stood diverted from the path 'which assuredly she would have taken, had . . . a Cromwell wielded the scepter of her power'.[49] Earlier loath to air their antagonism to classical political economy before the popular audiences attracted to metropolitan public platforms, the Positivists now entered the campaign against the tenets of the Manchester School with open enthusiasm. E.S. Beesly, chairing a meeting of workers at St James's Hall in January, characterized Cobden as 'very narrow and ignorant on such questions' as war, while urging English labourers that they could not 'afford to see French liberty crushed, for every blow struck at it by German despots would tell against the social interests of working men all over the world'.[50]

Far from commanding the undivided allegiance of middle-class reformers, the new liberal efforts to integrate English politics with French republicanism revived old radical antagonisms entrenched in the aftermath of the February revolution. As in 1848, the editors of the *Nonconformist*, although staunchly determined to remove aris-

[47] Harrison, *Autobiographic Memoirs*, vol. II, pp. 10–11.
[48] *Times*, 30 December 1870, p. 7.
[49] *Newcastle Weekly Chronicle*, 7 January 1871, p. 4.
[50] *Times*, 11 January 1871, p.3.

tocratic privileges and abuses from the English constitution, remained firmly opposed to the marriage of social and political radicalism. Contemplating the declaration of the republic, this organ of radical Dissent urged its subscribers to view the political enthusiasm of 'the operative class' with considerable caution, for 'amongst this class, an inclination to Red Republicanism, or, in other words, to a Republic based upon social democracy, has for many years past had its chief strength'.[51] Manchester liberals were increasingly exercised by the implications of this development for Liberal party politics. Rallying behind Gladstone at a meeting at the Free Trade Hall in February, delegates representing over 200 branches of the Reform Union met to demonstrate their continued allegiance to the liberal legacies of Cobden and Bright. The chairman began by calling upon his listeners to uphold 'civil and religious freedom' and to support 'the policy of peace and non-intervention', a policy that Richard Marsden Pankhurst subsequently endorsed in his own speech. Equally hostile to aristocratic landholding and government expenditure, the speakers sought to locate their pacifism securely within the framework of an indigenous, liberal radical tradition. The chairman chided Beesly for his antagonism to Gladstone's policy of non-intervention, and noted that the French 'in going to war ... only acted in accordance with the traditions of France'. The organist, capturing the dominant mood of the occasion, refused to gratify scattered calls from the audience for the Marseillaise.[52]

As the tenor of the Reform Union meeting made clear, philosophical differences could divide English radicals as deeply in 1871 as they had in 1848. Indeed the Manchester liberals' principled opposition to intervention testified to the continued purchase of precisely those ideological distinctions that had emerged most sharply in the aftermath of the February revolution. But whereas the evolving trajectory of French politics in 1848 had increasingly forced English radicals to choose between intervention and laissez-faire, between a social democratic politics and an ideology of separate spheres, the course of popular politics after the French republic's submission to

---

[51] *Nonconformist*, 5 October 1870, p. 953.
[52] National Reform Union, *Report of the Great Meeting in Support of Mr Gladstone's Government and Non-Intervention in the Free Trade Hall* (Manchester, 1871), pp. 4, 8, 10–12, 15–16, 22.

Prussian forces in January 1871 saw English radicals choose among a shifting array of radical options in which elements of liberal and labour ideologies were often intertwined. Rooted in the myriad republican clubs that galvanized the political nation from January, this expanded radical platform strengthened the ties between working-class political agitators and the new liberal activists. Exploiting the enduring appeal of eighteenth-century radical traditions, it added to their classical lineaments varieties of radical argument and forms of symbolic representation earlier confined to working-class manifestations of popular politics and reform.

Anti-monarchical sentiment, fuelled by the widowed queen's self-imposed exile from the public sphere, animated the new republican clubs that sprang to life in 1871; anti-aristocratic convictions long integral to both middle- and working-class radical movements complemented and reinforced these republican tendencies. Royal dowries and annuities provided an immediate impetus for the formation of republican clubs in this context. Gladstone's proposed £30,000 dowry and £6,000 annuity for Princess Louise raised radical resentment in February, and his proposed annuity of £15,000 for Prince Arthur met with radical opposition in August.[53] The fifty-odd republican clubs established in these months united middle- and working-class reformers in regions as various as Birmingham, Leicester, Middlesbrough, Newcastle, Nottingham, Sheffield, Sunderland, and London.[54] The activities of their adherents ranged from public meetings to denounce the age-old abuses of the Civil List to attempts to foment novel social and economic legislation. Affording the radical wing of the Liberal party with an opportunity to voice in the House of Commons radical sentiments cherished by their more strident constituents, opposition to the royal dowry and annuities also connected republican MPs to vigorous expressions of republican sentiment out of doors. Henry Fawcett, P.A. Taylor, and Sir Charles Dilke received votes of thanks for their parliamen-

---

[53] For the broad context of the monarchy's waning popularity, see David Cannadine, 'The Context, Performance and Meaning of Ritual: The British Monarchy and the "Invention of Tradition", *c.* 1820–1977', in Eric Hobsbawm and Terence Ranger (eds.), *The Invention of Tradition* (Cambridge, 1983), pp. 101–64, esp. pp. 108–20. William Kuhn provides an excellent analysis of the anti-monarchical element of the republican movement in 'Ceremony and Politics: The British Monarchy, 1871–1872', *Journal of British Studies*, vol. 26 (April 1987), pp. 133–62.

[54] *Eastern Post*, 18 March 1871, p. 4, notes republican clubs in these locations.

tary opposition to Princess Louise's dowry from the Brighton Radical Association, a meeting of working men in Northampton, and the Birmingham Labour Representation League.[55] In Nottingham, 10,000 persons gathered before a platform decorated with tricolour flags at a republican demonstration to thank Dilke, Fawcett, and Taylor for their republican efforts.[56]

The republican clubs that organized and sustained these activities from February provided venues for both old and new radical critiques of government. For while some republicans confined themselves to traditional diatribes against the evils of 'Old Corruption', the republican movement grew to accommodate critiques of liberal economics as well. Birmingham's Republican Club, established by the secularist Charles Cattell late in January, chose to uphold republican virtues as instruments with which to combat aristocratic extravagance, rather than to endorse the principles of social democratic reform.[57] Under the guidance of Daniel Merrick, the Sock and Top Union's leader, the Republican Association of Leicester – P.A. Taylor's parliamentary constituency – similarly eschewed new liberal politics. Firmly committed to universal manhood suffrage, its members trusted to the devices of individual efforts 'to educate the people in the principles of political economy, moral virtue and social advancement'.[58]

But by March, working-class efforts to expand the meaning of republicanism by embracing social democratic goals were also evident in both London and the provinces. In Newcastle T.J. Bayfield, a working man candidate for the School Board, suggested the formation of a republican association in February 'to help curb extravagance and expenditure'. Successfully enrolling over a hundred members two weeks later in the Newcastle Republican Club, Bayfield invoked new liberal themes familiar from the land tenure reform campaigns of the late sixties. 'It was not only the

[55] *Reynolds's Newspaper*, 26 February 1871, p. 5.

[56] *Nottingham and Midland Counties Daily Express*, 28 February 1871.

[57] George J. Barnsby, *Birmingham Working People: A History of the Labour Movement in Birmingham 1650–1914* (Wolverhampton, 1989), pp. 154–62, details Cattell's efforts. D'Arcy, 'Bradlaugh and the Republican Movement', esp. pp. 372–3, analyses the wider growth of republican clubs at this time. As the quotation from Cattell's treatise on *The Land*, p. 62 above, indicates, this Birmingham radical had himself embraced social democratic principles by the end of the decade.

[58] Bill Lancaster, *Radicalism, Cooperation and Socialism: Leicester Working-Class Politics 1860–1906* (Leicester, 1987), p. 79.

question of the throne which they as Republicans would have to consider', he concluded, 'they wanted wiser agrarian laws than they now had.'[59] At the Wellington Music Hall in London, the same tendency was evident at a republican meeting chaired by a compositor. Speakers began by blaming royal pensions for the plight of the poor, and ended by twitting the queen as a devotee of the 'Political Economists'.[60] Tentative, episodic, and inchoate in their early expression, the economic themes adumbrated by radicals in early 1871 expanded dramatically in response to the declaration of the Paris Commune at the end of March. Reinvigorating working-class debate on the social meaning of radical democracy, they captivated the middle-class liberal imagination as well.

THE COMMUNE AND ITS AFTERMATH

Like the February revolution and June Days of 1848, the rise and fall of the Paris Commune forced English radicals to reassess their commitment to the varied political ideals expressed in their interpretations and celebrations of the French revolutionary tradition. A reaction against military defeat and the election by provincial voters of a predominantly conservative National Assembly, the autonomous Parisian government of the Commune unleashed a battery of attacks on the institutions of monarchy, centralized government, and private property in France. Lacking a consistent, overarching ideology, the Commune offered English observers a more malleable political template than had the French events of 1848, providing a loose framework around which radical reformers constructed a diverse, often contradictory array of symbolic meanings. The brutal suppression of this revolutionary government by Adolphe Thiers and the National Assembly – 20,000 persons died when the French army invaded Paris in May – brought a new wave of continental refugees to England's shores. Becoming intertwined with extant republican sentiments, the diffuse legacy of their Communard cause resonated with established labour traditions, lent an added impulse to the new liberal convictions cherished by a growing sector of the middle class, and ultimately came to inform the rituals and beliefs of the early socialist movement.

---

[59] *Newcastle Weekly Chronicle*, 18 February 1871, p. 4; 4 March 1871, p. 3.
[60] *Eastern Post*, 11 February 1871, p. 5.

Denounced, like the Provisional Government before it in 1848, as a seedbed of communism and atheism, the Commune offered English and continental radicals of the middle class an opportunity to reiterate their earlier opposition to the ideal of the social and democratic republic. The aging Giuseppe Mazzini, writing in June, indicted the Commune at one and the same time as an agent of class antagonism and a brake to nationalist development. A phenomenon informed by 'the old sectarian socialism', a materialist philosophy that could only pervert the true political life of the working class, the Commune in this analysis stood opposed to the sovereign nation, and 'the nation alone possesses the secret, the inspiration of her own life and mission'.[61] The tone struck by the *Nonconformist* was less philosophical, but conveyed essentially the same charge. Although willing, like much of the liberal press, to concede the virtues of the Commune's emphasis on municipal self-government, the Dissenting conscience declined to entertain any sympathy for its perceived socialist politics. Conflating the Commune with communism and communism with social democracy, the journal was confident already in March that 'The Communistic Revolution' would suffer 'the inevitable collapse which Social Democracy is destined to endure'.[62]

This reaction rehearsed themes that had dominated the bourgeois radical response to the February revolution, and now commanded the allegiance of many moderate working-class radicals as well. Charles Bradlaugh, who had gained a considerable working-class following as president of London's Republican Club, explicitly warned his adherents against the use of the red flag at republican gatherings, and sought by emphasizing the abolition of Old Corruption and the English monarchy to disassociate his own movement from events in France.[63] He was not alone in this endeavour. The proposal to organize a mass demonstration in honour of the

---

[61] Giuseppe Mazzini, *The War and the Commune* (London, 1871), pp. 34, 38–9, 47. Reprinted from the *Contemporary Review* (June 1871).

[62] *Nonconformist*, 29 March 1871, p. 304. For liberal endorsements of the Commune as a reaction against centralized government, a theme that struck a deep chord in many English radicals, see for example *ibid.*, 24 May 1871 pp. 516–17, and *Newcastle Weekly Chronicle*, 25 March 1871, p. 4.

[63] *Eastern Post*, 14 May 1871, p. 5; D'Arcy, 'Bradlaugh and the Republican Movement', esp. pp. 373–5. As D'Arcy notes, Bradlaugh's moderation did not prevent him from being tarred with the brush of 'Red Republicanism' by conservative opinion.

Communards created a heated debate among rival republican factions meeting at Clerkenwell Green in June, as Irish republican sympathizers sought to convince the audience 'that the working classes, through paying too much attention to foreign politics, had paid too little attention to what was going on in their own land'.[64] Although this attempt to turn radical attention from international to national affairs proved unavailing, other efforts to this end enjoyed considerable success. In August Bradlaugh exploited a purely national vein of republican enthusiasm in convening a crowd of 20,000 to protest the 'robbery' of the people occasioned by the £15,000 annuity granted to Prince Arthur.[65]

Vocal and articulate sectors of working-class radical opinion contested this insular vision, refusing to disown either the Commune or the succession of French revolutionary episodes that had preceded it. Here the continued force of the late Chartist traditions was conspicuously evident. In sharp contrast to the moderate upstart Bradlaugh, *Reynolds's* worked to interweave old and new, English and French, radical cries in its response to the Commune. 'The sympathies of the English working classes should be, and doubtless are already, strongly enlisted on the side of their brethren in France, now struggling to emancipate themselves from the odious and tyrannous fangs of royalty, aristocracy, and capital', *Reynolds's* proclaimed early in April. Denouncing 'the pestiferous influences of rank, property and profit [which] infect the body politic there, as here', the paper predicted that the suppression of the Commune would deliver the French people yet again into the hands of those 'who sought in blood to discount the Republic, as once before it was done in June, 1848'. This analysis struck squarely at the tenets of classical liberalism. 'Industry will be asked to pay the fine' imposed by corrupt government, *Reynolds's* concluded, 'and property will seek to excuse itself under the doctrines of political economy, from any contribution that is not paid out of the enhanced rents and profits earned by industry.'[66] More recently established journals also embraced this neo-Chartist worldview. First issued in September 1870, the *Republican* magazine reprinted odes and addresses by Bronterre O'Brien and endorsed the proposals of the Land and Labour League – heir, it claimed, to the doctrines of Robespierre,

---

[64] *The Potteries Examiner*, 17 June 1871, p. 2.   [65] *Ibid.*, 5 August 1871, p. 3.
[66] *Reynolds's Newspaper*, 2 April 1871, p. 1.

who had recognized 'that the only way to secure a lasting peace or Republic that shall be good for all, is to commence with social justice'. By June 1871, these strands of argument were intermingled with articles sympathetic to the Commune, and were accompanied by advertisements for both Marx's *Civil War in France* and a treatise on 'social innovators' such as Louis Blanc.[67]

Public demonstrations throughout London mobilized working-class radicals behind these social democratic interpretations of the Commune, lending the force of popular politics to the abstract analyses offered in the radical press. 'A republic, to be of any use to the masses of the people, must deal with the social questions affecting their interests', the carpenter John Weston proclaimed early in April, standing beneath a red flag surmounted by a cap of liberty at an East End republican meeting. The following speaker reiterated this theme with words familiar from the late Chartist era. Underscoring the need for 'social regeneration' in England and France, he proclaimed that 'the land question would never be thoroughly solved in the interest of the people until the social and democratic Republic existed'.[68] James Murray, a disciple of Bronterre O'Brien and member of the International, led a procession of several thousand, preceded by the requisite marching band and caps of liberty, to Hyde Park later in April to express fraternal sympathy alike for Communards and communists. Proclaiming that the Commune represented 'the liberation of labour from the trammels of capital', his address ended, predictably, with the cry 'Long live the universal Republic, democratic and social.'[69]

Continental members of the International laboured energetically to infuse social democratic interpretations of the Commune with a Marxian analysis of class relations, an effort that proved of only limited appeal to English workers. *The Civil War in France*, Marx's strident interpretation of the Commune as an attempt by labour to supplant capital, attracted new members to the International only to alienate some stalwarts of the radical agitation. In Nottingham, Feargus O'Connor's parliamentary constituency in the forties, working-class republicans collected funds for Communard refugees, established a local branch of the International, and engaged in a

[67] *Republican*, esp. 1 September 1870, pp. 5–6; 1 October 1870, p. 5; 15 June 1871, p. 1; 15 September 1871, pp. 7–8; 1 January 1872, pp. 2–3.
[68] *Reynolds's Newspaper*, 16 April 1871, p. 6.
[69] *Ibid.*, 23 April 1871; *Eastern Post*, 23 April 1871, p. 3.

lively correspondence with Marx himself in the months that followed Edward Truelove's publication of his tract in June.[70] The
response of working-class radicals in London was more problematic. Both George Odger and Benjamin Lucraft resigned from the
Council of the International when their names were appended to the
Civil War in France without their prior approval, a decision that
prompted acrimonious debate within both the International and the
wider radical community.[71] Like Charles Bradlaugh's success at
channelling portions of the republican movement into narrowly
English political directions, these disputes over the social and
economic implications of French events limited working-class radical leaders' ability to claim a distinctively working-class meaning for
the Commune in England. In the face of liberal encroachments and
radical defections, the labour leaders of 1871 were unable to rebuild
the semblance of unity successfully manufactured by diverse Chartist factions in 1848.

Working-class radicals thus presented a fractured visage in their
response to the Paris Commune. But so too did liberals and radicals
of the middle class. Far more striking, indeed, than the erosion of
the *démoc-soc* consensus within working-class radical circles was the
extension of social democratic lines of argument to middle-class
liberal and radical opinion. For although many middle-class
reformers joined the general English outcry against the Commune
and Marx's *Civil War in France*, vocal opponents of this reaction
declined to repeat the historical pattern traced by the middle-class
radicals of 1848. The *Eastern Post* warned its readers that the
Commune and its 'Communist atrocities' were intended 'to inaugur-
ate the rule of the working classes pure and simple'; the *Nonconformist* urged 'the teaching of sound political economy' to combat the
rising influence of the International.[72] But Cowen's *Newcastle
Chronicle* expressed the new tolerance for French social politics in
liberal circles. Printing extracts from the *Civil War in France*, the
paper found the International's pronouncements on the Commune
'ably and defiantly written', if not perhaps 'in all respects . . . very

[70] Peter Wyncoll, 'The First International and Working Class Activity in Nottingham 1871–73', *Marxism Today*, vol. 12 (December 1968), pp. 372–9, and *idem*,
'Thomas Smith: A Working Class Defender of the Commune', *Marxism Today*,
vol. 15 (March 1971), pp. 86–9.

[71] For these divisions, see esp. *General Council Minutes*, vol. IV, pp. 216–18;
Republican, 1 August 1871, p. 6.

[72] *Eastern Post*, 17 June 1871, p. 4; *Nonconformist*, 4 October 1871, p. 977.

prudent'.[73] Other middle-class proponents of radical reform built upon these new liberal tendencies. Refusing to disown the Commune, they sought to use French precedents as instruments with which to secure social reform within the pale of liberal politics.

The English Positivists naturally seized upon the Commune as a long-awaited vindication of their social doctrines. 'I was almost hopeless of it [the Republic] for a generation', Frederic Harrison wrote to John Morley in March. 'Now I am of good cheer.' Discerning in the Commune a working-class cry for a government that would serve as 'the protector of the weak & the helper of the suffering', Harrison embraced the Commune as labour's reaction against 'the hell on earth of political economy', 'an attempt to free Society from . . . the Gospel of Free Trade'.[74] Interwoven with the response of working-class partisans of the Commune, this sympathy publicly united the left wings of the labour and liberal radical movements. Beesly and his fellow Positivist J. H. Bridges published a series of articles in the *Bee-Hive* upholding the Commune as an embodiment of both 'social progress' and internationalist sentiment. The latter sentiment, 'the fraternal spirit growing up between the working classes', was a force nicely illustrated, Beesly noted, by Garibaldi's election to the National Assembly by Parisian workers.[75] Although rejecting working-class radicals' insistence on the necessarily democratic basis of the social republic – Comte's system of social organization relied upon scientific expertise and had little respect for popular democracy – the Positivists worked actively to blend their vision of reform with the response of labour leaders who remained committed to the union of social, democratic, and economic change. Sympathy for socialists, if not for socialism, flourished in this milieu, a seeming contradiction that Beesly justified to Marx in June:

> I know very well that you are radically opposed to us Positivists nor do I suppose it to be at all likely that you will ever alter your views. The one point we & you have in common is our indignation against the individualist theories of the propertied classes & their anti-social conduct . . .

[73] *Newcastle Weekly Chronicle*, 17 June 1871, pp. 4–5.
[74] Harrison to Morley, 22 March 1871 and [April 1871], BLPES, Harrison Collection, 1/53/19–26, and 1/53/32.
[75] *Bee-Hive*, 8 July and 22 April 1871. Both articles are reprinted in Royden Harrison (ed.), *The English Defence of the Commune: 1871* (London, 1971), pp. 123, 76–7.

No doubt, whenever it becomes a practical question whether private property is to be abdicated you will find us opposed to you firmly. But it is likely that long before then we & you shall have been crushed side by side by our common foe.[76]

Earlier distanced from other middle-class radicals by their Francophile social sympathies, the Positivists now found themselves surrounded by middle-class enthusiasts of the Commune. In Oxford the newly established Republican Club abandoned the established precepts of classical economics in 1871, adopting resolutions that departed from the traditions of late Chartism only in fixing a prohibitive membership fee of 10s per annum. Merging nationalist and socialist impulses, their resolutions drew upon the Mazzinian language of rights and duties, but were not constrained by it. 'By a republic', the Oxford republicans explained, 'shall be understood that form of Commonwealth which, by means of political and social equality, will combine the utmost liberty of the individual with the strongest bonds of national union, and commit to the people the duties and rights of self-government.' Meshing easily with the arguments of the new liberalism, the club's sixth resolution called for 'the establishment of a system of national education, a better distribution of land, a more satisfactory relation between labour and capital, and legislation in general for the benefit of the working classes'. Internationalist sympathies were a logical corollary of these aspirations. The club's honorary secretary, A.P. Richards of Wadham College, wrote to Hermann Jung to ascertain the principles of the International. 'If as I do not doubt, they are such as the Club also has in view', Richards promised Jung, 'it will endeavour to cooperate with you & other bodies in effecting them.'[77]

Public support for the Communard refugees complemented this middle-class republican enthusiasm, knitting together diverse cohorts of middle-class radicals and extending into the wider middle- and upper-class population. Beesly and Harrison joined forces with the members of the International, soliciting funds and employment from sources to which the trade union leadership had little access. Writing to thank John Morley for a contribution to the cause,

[76] Beesly to Marx, 13 June 1871, IISG, Marx–Engels Collection, D., Letters to Marx, item 258.
[77] 'Oxford Republican Club: Resolution', and A.P. Richards to Hermann Jung, 10 April 1871, IISG, Jung Collection, C. 942/1–2.

Harrison noted in February 1872 that he had now found employment for over a hundred Communards:

> I live a strange life. Every day brings me 40 letters in which the British public is displayed in all its colours ... Pinching housewives write ... for a 'distressed' maid of all work at £7 a year ... Oxford men want a Communist by the next train to live with them. Well to do people offer a home and their friendship. An M.P. sends £100 an 'old housekeeper' sends £5.[78]

Drawing upon networks and traditions of mutual aid established by Chartists and French socialists in 1848, these efforts succeeded in winning broad-based support for the Communards from the varied precincts of the middle-class radical community. Bourgeois radicals of the Chartist period had rushed to the aid of Italians, Poles, and Hungarians while ignoring French *démoc-soc* émigrés, but Dilke, Fawcett, Mill, Taylor, and others united to aid the Communards of 1871.[79]

Even some liberals who repudiated the putatively socialist politics of the Commune came in the months that followed its fall to sympathize with its social tendencies. The liberal economist J.E. Cairnes, writing in Morley's *Fortnightly Review* in July, rehearsed received liberal wisdom in tracing the fall of the Commune to 'the spectre of socialism – that rank growth of economic ignorance'. 'Other causes, no doubt, have contributed to the terrible catastrophe which we now witness and deplore', he wrote, echoing the analysis of an earlier generation of economists in 1848, 'but most assuredly economic ignorance is deeply responsible in the matter.' Yet Cairnes's analysis departed radically from the bourgeois critique of his predecessors, for his liberal outlook was rooted in a new system of political economy. Cairnes thus acknowledged the pervasive liberal equation of laissez-faire with political economy only to attack it. Far from constituting a scientific law, impartial and immutable in its

---

[78] Harrison to Morley, 13 February [1872], BLPES, Harrison Collection, 1/53/7. See also Harrison to F.A. Maxse, 24 February [1872] and 27 May 1872, WSRO, Frederick Augustus Maxse Papers, item 203.

[79] The persistence of patterns of mutual aid established in 1848 is evident for example in the efforts of old radicals such as Thomas Allsop and Louis Blanc to raise funds for the refugees. See Thomas Allsop to Marx, 1871–8, IISG, Marx–Engels Collection, D., Letters to Marx, items 7–39, and Louis Blanc to Charles Dilke, 25 November 1871, BL, Dilke Papers, Add MS 43,884, fol. 42. For the new middle-class response, see Harrison to Dilke, 6 July [1871], BL Add MS 43,898, fols. 151–2, and Maltman Barry to John Stuart Mill, 20 April 1872, BLPES, Mill–Taylor Collection, vol. 2, item 208.

operation, laissez-faire emerged from Cairnes's analysis as a useful precept whose day had long passed. 'The truly significant circumstance', he reasoned, 'is that the policy in question, the policy expressed by *laissez-faire*, has been steadily progressive for nearly half a century, and yet we have no sign of mitigation in the harshest features of our social state.' The role of the new political economy and the new liberalism, in this view, lay in 'ends to be compassed in social and industrial life which can only be reached through the action of society as an organised whole ... a work of positive and reconstructive reform still lies before us'.[80]

POPULAR LIBERALISM AND THE REPUBLICAN IMPULSE

Accelerated by the republican enthusiasm unleashed by the Franco-Prussian War and Paris Commune, middle-class academics' growing willingness to explore the social and economic implications of democratic politics impressed contemporary observers as both a deep challenge and a decisive intellectual turning point for English liberal culture. Sir Charles Dilke, writing of his membership in the Political Economy Club in the sixties and seventies, noted that 'the son of the Club's founder, John Stuart Mill, lived to lead the way out of the doctrine of his father, James Mill, Malthus, and Ricardo, against the opposition of his own disciple Fawcett, into the new land which he just lived to see'. 'In the debates which I regularly attended', Dilke recalled, 'Mill, who had become semi-socialist in his views, was usually at odds with his own disciple Fawcett, who had remained an individualist.'[81] As the political careers of liberal politicians such as Dilke demonstrated, moreover, this expression of liberal doctrine extended beyond the abstract musings and rarefied atmosphere of the middle-class debating society. Becoming implicated with the public spectacles and pronouncements of popular and electoral politics, the republican impulse served to create links between working-class radical associations and liberal politicians of the middle and upper class.

---

[80] J.E. Cairnes, 'Political Economy and Laissez-Faire', *Fortnightly Review*, vol. 10 (July 1871), pp. 80–97, esp. pp. 97, 89, 86.
[81] Political Economy Club, *Political Economy Club Centenary Volume* (London, 1921), pp. 309–10.

Dilke himself played a central role in mediating a popular republican marriage of the radical and liberal traditions in this period. Inspired by French and English developments, he undertook a tour of the provinces in the autumn of 1871 to deliver a series of radical speeches in the towns of the industrial north. Stridently anti-monarchical in tone, his rhetoric relied upon received radical antagonism to the evils of Old Corruption rather than suggesting novel democratic mechanisms for social and economic change. Speaking at a public meeting in Newcastle on 6 November, Dilke thus occupied himself with an extended calculation of the cost to the British taxpayer of the royal family, a cost that he estimated at £1,000,000 per annum. 'Well, if you can show me a fair chance that a republic will be free from the political corruption that hangs about the monarchy', he concluded after deprecating this charge upon the public purse, 'I say, for my part – and I believe that the middle classes will say – let it come.'[82] Couched in familiar radical tones, these assertions meshed easily with the established hagiographies of the radical patriotic tradition. One ode to 'Citizen Dilke' in the *Republican* compared the liberal MP to 'the old heroic leaders / In Hampden's holy war'.[83]

If the text of Dilke's speech against the monarchy played upon well-established radical themes, the circumstances of its delivery lent his rhetoric novel republican meanings. For although the substance of Dilke's speech was confined to arguments against excessive government expenditure, the radical symbolism that enveloped it evoked recent memories of working-class protests against insufficient government surveillance of the social and economic sphere. The preceding months had seen the inauguration of Bayfield's Newcastle Republican Club – an institution whose purpose George Odger described in his inaugural speech as 'a solemn protest against all class government'.[84] More substantially, this period had witnessed the escalation of trade union protest throughout the north. In August a mass demonstration of South Durham miners had applauded cries for government 'protection against the unfeeling avarice of employers and the negligence of parents, which caused so

---

[82] Sir Charles Dilke, *Sir Charles Dilke on the Cost of the Crown* (London, 1871), esp. pp. 11, 23.
[83] *Republican*, 1 January 1872, p. 4.
[84] *Newcastle Weekly Chronicle*, 17 June 1871, p. 3.

much suffering and hardship' among children in the mines.[85] The same month saw concerted efforts by Odger, Joseph Cowen – now a Liberal MP for Newcastle – and members of the International to win the nine-hours day for Newcastle's striking engineers.[86] London workers had used the symbols of French republicanism in celebrating the successful resolution of this conflict for their northern brothers in October. When an estimated 20,000 engineers, cordwainers, painters, plasterers, carpenters, and masons gathered for a victory demonstration in Trafalgar Square, Charles Murray and John Nieass delivered speeches for the International, Joseph Cowen's efforts on behalf of the engineers received due recognition, and 'the Republican flag and cap of liberty were also prominent'.[87]

Dilke's appearance at Newcastle in November formed the capstone of this series of radical events. At his speech on 'Representation and Royalty', the platform became a meeting place for representatives of both the liberal and labour radical traditions. Here Cowen, in the chair, sat alongside both Bayfield of the Newcastle Republican Club and John Burnett, president of the Nine Hours League. Lest liberals' new sympathy for organized labour appear in doubt, Dilke also spoke at the inaugural soirée of the Ouseburn Engine Works, a cooperative workshop established in Newcastle to employ workers turned out by their employers for supporting the nine-hours movement during the strike.[88] Conservative critics of the republican movement seized upon these social and economic associations in their efforts to discredit Dilke's antimonarchical campaign. Ballads lambasting his speech on royalty interpreted Dilke's message as a 'Communist' attack on property, rooted in the subversive doctrines of the Paris Commune.[89] Patriotic

[85] *Ibid.*, 5 August 1871, p. 5. The speaker clearly articulated a positive conception of liberty. 'If people persisted in sending their sons [to work] for fifteen or sixteen hours per day', he concluded, 'why should not the laws of the country emphatically prohibit such oppression and such tyranny.'

[86] *General Council Minutes*, vol. IV, pp. 252–5. Odger, although officially estranged from the Council over the *Civil War in France*, was active in recruiting the International Working Men's Association's assistance for the engineers.

[87] *Reynolds's Newspaper*, 15 October 1871, p. 3.

[88] *Newcastle Weekly Chronicle*, 11 November 1871, p. 5.

[89] Jackdaw, *The Dilkiad: Or The Dream of Dilke: An Anti-Republican Lay* (London, 1872). 'Twas in those days when all the land beneath a rash did lie, / A Gallic inflammation from a ruined realm hard by. / From Leicester Square the "Commune" had spit its noxious slime, / And English fools the slaver caught and quaffed it off like wine; / No land, no gold, no wives, no laws, *no nothing evermore*, /

defences of the monarchy emerged as a natural counterbalance to this pernicious internationalist threat. One conservative ballad, 'Dedicated to Patriotism and Loyalty', urged the superior, if ethereal, claims of the nation against the vulgar demands of economic materialism. 'Nations, like man, have a *soul*, / – Nations that are not dead', it asserted staunchly, 'Which never can live on the pitiful dole / Of mere abundance of bread!'[90]

Popular disturbances in both London and the provinces lent fire to these attacks, but problematized conservative efforts to lodge an exclusive claim to British patriotic traditions. In Chelsea, Dilke's constituency, conservative electors convened a predominantly working-class assembly of several hundred to express their disapproval of his attack upon the queen. But when organizers of this event sought to bring the meeting under the direction of one Mr Taylor, radical workers intervened, and succeeded in forcing John Nieass of the International into the chair. Conservative participants' efforts to sing 'God Save the Queen' met with 'Rule Britannia' – with emphasis falling on 'Britons never, never shall be slaves' – cheers for Dilke, and verses of the Marseillaise. After 'chairs were thrown about and broken', the *Newcastle Chronicle* noted in its account, 'free fighting became general'.[91]

Workers in Bolton brought this conflict to a violent peak when Dilke lectured there in November. Boasting a Republican Club convinced that 'as capitalists were everywhere banded together, it was of the first importance that the workmen of the world should combine to advance their interests', Bolton witnessed anti-republican disturbances when George Odger delivered a speech to 400 radicals on 25 November.[92] Dilke's arrival in Bolton five days later further fanned these flames. Invited to speak by a group of reformers

---

But Odger for a President, and lush and blood galore! / Such was the programme kindly brought from Paris' sanguine den . . . / When Communists in fustian were, and Communists in silk, / And rarest among Communists was shining Charley Dilke.'

[90] Anon., *'What Is the Use of Kings?' and How the Question Was Answered: A National Ballad for the Times: Together with 'Chelsea Buns', or, The Story of Young Carlo Dolci: A Political Satire: and 'Chant de la Commune'* (London, 1872), p. 7.

[91] *Newcastle Weekly Chronicle*, 2 December 1871, p. 8.

[92] *Reynolds's Newspaper*, 15 October 1871, p. 2; *Bolton Evening News*, 27 November 1871. At this inaugural tea party for the Bolton Republican Club, loyalists singing the national anthem were interrupted by republicans crying 'three cheers for Sir Charles Dilke'. The police were brought in to restore order, and allow Odger to deliver his speech.

that included both local liberals and the cotton spinner Joseph Mellor, Dilke became the object of patriotic attention as conservatives placarded the town demanding that all 'true born Englishmen' resist the republican siren. His local sponsors, fearing that riot would prevent the delivery of Dilke's speech, issued tickets to limit attendance to the Temperance Hall to their own followers, a decision that further enraged Dilke's antagonists. At the meeting itself, the building and its audience of several hundred suffered continuous attack from the excluded conservatives, who threw successive volleys of stones through the windows and attacked the doors with hammers, bludgeons, and other available weapons. Requests for police protection went unanswered for an hour by the borough magistrates, who watched the attack from a distance of only 300 yards. The eventual return of order could not erase the consequences of their delay. William Shofield, a planer who sustained serious head injuries as a member of Dilke's audience, died within the week.[93]

In London, loyalists and republicans continued the battle begun by Dilke's speech at Newcastle throughout the early months of 1872. Organizers of a meeting held in the Duke of Wellington Riding School, Knightsbridge, issued tickets to their followers in an effort to prevent 'Democrats' from attending the loyalist gathering. But the forty or fifty Dilkite partisans who succeeded in joining the audience of 1,000 thwarted this attempt to orchestrate a concerted patriotic defence of the monarchy. Advancing on the platform to demand the admittance of excluded radicals grouped outside, these republican patriots seized chairs, benches, and railings and forced their antagonists to retreat from the podium. Once in command of the platform, Dilke's supporters secured their position with barricades constructed from the chairs and benches and placed one Mr Bickley, a master plasterer, in the chair. Raising a red flag from the platform, the radicals gave three cheers for Dilke and three cheers for the Republic. Class sentiments complemented continental influences in the radical resolutions that followed. Votes of confidence passed on Dilke's behalf thanked the liberal republican 'for his efforts on behalf of justice to the hard-working oppressed working men of this country'. When the loyalists finally succeeded in

---

[93] For the decision to invite Dilke to speak, see *Bolton Evening News*, 25 November 1871 and 30 April 1872. For the event itself, see *ibid.*, 1 and 7 December 1871, and 'Petition to the Rt. Hon. Henry Austin Bruce, from Inhabitants of Bolton, in the County of Lancashire', December 1871, HO 45/9391/2.

clearing the hall – they were reduced to lowering the gas – Dilke's followers formed a procession of 150 which marched down Sloane Street to his residence, singing the Marseillaise.[94] The same French symbolism pervaded Dilkite agitation in February. Denied the use of the Freemasons' Hall by proprietors chary of republican excess, a large assembly of supporters brought flags inscribed with French republican emblems and the cap of liberty to a public meeting in Trafalgar Square on the night of 5 February and protested the Bolton outrage.[95] Dilke himself, speaking to his constituents later in the month, publicly defended the republican convictions of Louis Blanc.[96]

Popular sympathy for the monarchy, bolstered since December 1871 by the Prince of Wales's illness with typhoid, acted to erode metropolitan republicanism in the ensuing months, but the impress of French revolutionary traditions continued to mark the course of English politics as new Liberal candidates sought to win radical support in urban constituencies. The career of Frederick Augustus Maxse provides a case in point. Born to an affluent family, Maxse enjoyed a gentlemanly education enriched by study abroad at a Parisian boarding school in 1845–6. A successful naval career that included service in the Crimean War then occupied Maxse until his retirement to private life in the sixties.[97] Extensive reading in these years provided him with a liberal education centred on issues of social justice. The notes written in his commonplace books reveal radical literature emanating from the revolutions of 1789 and 1848 to have been a formative influence on his intellectual development. A devotee of Paine and detractor of Burke, Maxse was intrigued by the societies established by adherents of Thomas Spence – 'so similar to our Land & Labour League societies!'. Intrigued by Mill's defence of the February revolution in the *Westminster Review*, he consulted the works of Pierre Leroux on French socialism and considered the

---

[94] *Eastern Post*, 20 January 1872, p. 3; *Newcastle Weekly Chronicle*, 20 January 1872, p. 3.
[95] *Newcastle Weekly Chronicle*, 10 February 1872, p. 7. The *Chronicle* estimated the crowd at 10,000.
[96] *Ibid.*, 24 February 1872, p. 5. Tom Nairn misses the significance and persistence of French symbolism in his analysis of the Dilkite campaign, which he depicts as a critique of monarchy lacking in social or economic meaning. See Tom Nairn, *The Enchanted Glass: Britain and Its Monarchy* (London, 1988), pp. 328–30.
[97] J. Morrison Davidson, *Eminent Radicals In and Out of Parliament* (London, 1880), pp. 231–9, provides an introduction to Maxse and his politics. For his French schooling, see the letters in WSRO, Maxse Papers, item 142.

Positivist philosophy of Auguste Comte.[98] By 1868, Maxse was prepared to test his distillation of these novel doctrines in the arena of parliamentary politics. Although defeated as a Liberal candidate at Southampton, he declined to abandon or temper his growing conviction of the social mission of politics. His lectures on political duty in 1869 defended the political career of Ernest Jones, 'a man actuated by the highest motives and chivalry', and refused to accept the common liberal demarcation between the social and political spheres. 'Charity may here and there palliate our wide spread suffering, but it is unable to strike at its causes', Maxse concluded from an extended survey of the economic ills of the day. 'These can only be dealt with by the *politician*.'[99]

Denied a parliamentary forum by his defeat at Southampton, Maxse found a public platform for his social democratic views in the radical campaign for English intervention in the Franco-Prussian War. His speech at a gathering of workers in December, later published by Edward Truelove, derided middle-class fears of both abstract political theories and 'the terrible Reds' who expounded them, while finding in English sympathy for 'democratic France' grounds for 'the solution of those social and political problems which now entangle us in their meshes'. Maxse interwove nationalist and internationalist themes throughout this analysis. Comparing France under German rule to 'a new Poland', he upheld the foreign policy of the First International and borrowed Mazzini's language of rights and duties to explain England's interventionist imperative.[100] A vocal advocate of Paris's republican government during the Commune, Maxse was active in efforts to aid Communard refugees from 1871.[101]

An unsuccessful bid for Parliament in 1872, standing now for the Tower Hamlets, brought Maxse 3,000 votes.[102] Defeat in this election only served to drive him further to the political left. Lectures

---

[98] Commonplace and pocket books, n.d. but ca. 1864–73, WSRO, Maxse Papers, items 149, 151–54.

[99] F.A. Maxse, *Our Political Duty: A Lecture Delivered by Captain Maxse, R.N. at Fareham and Southampton* (London, 1869), in WSRO, Maxse Papers, item 304.

[100] Frederick Augustus Maxse, *A Plea for Intervention: An Address Delivered by Captain Maxse, R.N.* (London, 1871), pp. 2, 4–7.

[101] See esp. his correspondence with Frederic Harrison in WSRO, Maxse Papers, item 143, and the correspondence relating to his pamphlet, *The Suppression of the Commune*, in WSRO, Maxse Papers, item 189.

[102] *Nonconformist*, 18 February 1872, p. 165.

and writings designed to promulgate his political views embraced and intermingled a constellation of radical arguments familiar to working-class protest since 1848. Taking the Commune as his immediate inspiration, Maxse sought with *The Causes of Social Revolt* (1872) to explicate the nature of political relations in a society 'founded upon a recognition of Class divisions'. Here he launched a sustained attack upon 'the Individual Competitive Theory', citing a French republican of 1848 as his authority when he railed against 'the infallible nostrums' of 'political economy'. 'Ignorance in the upper and middle classes, I place as a prime cause of social revolt', Maxse commented in endorsing mandatory, state-sponsored education. 'I often think that a little compulsory education among the governing classes upon what is called the Social Question, would exercise a most beneficial effect.' Maxse defended Dilke from the aspersions cast by his Bolton detractors, and situated the English republican in an eclectic pantheon of radical leaders that included Ernest Jones, Edmond Beales, E.S. Beesly, Mazzini, and Garibaldi. He concluded by calling upon workers to support the cause of land tenure reform, trade unionism, and the eight-hour workday.[103]

The diminution of republican ardour in the metropolis failed to reduce Maxse's social democratic enthusiasm after 1872. Wooed by Joseph Chamberlain throughout 1872–3 as a likely candidate to run as a liberal representative of the principles of the National Education League, Maxse chose instead to pursue an independent radical line that would link him more directly to the cause of labour.[104] Determined to win acceptance by a popular constituency, he sought the support of the Tower Hamlets Radical Association and Radical Electoral Committee in 1873. Both institutions boasted venerable radical affiliations. The Radical Association, established in June 1871, had been active in the republican campaigns of Dilke and P. A. Taylor, and included a former Leicester Chartist among its members. The associated Radical Electoral

---

[103] Frederick Augustus Maxse, *The Causes of Social Revolt: A Lecture, Delivered in London, Portsmouth, and Greenwich* (London, 1872), pp. 3, 16, 21, 43–4, 49, 53, 72–3, 78.

[104] For Maxse's relations with Chamberlain, see their extensive correspondence in WSRO, Maxse Papers, item 205. In the impending campaign, Chamberlain argued, the National Education League's principles of secular, gratuitous education 'must [be] put ... in the foreground, although other questions may have their place'. Chamberlain to Maxse, 26 June 1873, WSRO, Maxse Papers, item 205, fol. 18.

Committee often met, appropriately, at the Sidney Arms, a venue shared with the local branch of the Land and Labour League, to which the committee lent its support.[105] In July John Hales of the International Working Men's Association raised the possibility of Maxse's candidature at a meeting of these Tower Hamlets radicals, and was asked to provide an indication of the liberal's political views. Hales seized this opportunity with alacrity, depicting Maxse as a social democrat of the deepest hue, a radical committed to a range of labour issues that included land reform, universal manhood suffrage, the protection of trade unions, and legislation to preserve the health of workers in factories and mines. 'I said you were a man of position who for some time past had devoted yourself to the work of ameliorating the condition of the People', he informed Maxse. 'That you were eminently a *Social Reformer* that you looked upon political power as the means to improve the Social condition of the mass.' The seventy assembled radicals responded by voting unanimously to invite the 'author of the "Causes of Social Revolt"' to contest the Tower Hamlets 'in the Radical and Labour interest'.[106]

Maxse embraced this challenge with enthusiasm in the following months. Supported by John Morley, E.S. Beesly, and Edmond Beales, 'whose successor he regarded himself', he offered Tower Hamlets' electors a social democratic definition of radical politics with patriotic overtones. 'Influential people regarded class legislation as good, and Radicals desired to upset it, and substitute national legislation', Maxse proclaimed in December. 'External circumstances', not individual moral character, figured centrally in his anatomy of the workman's dilemma. A critique that reached a crescendo in condemning 'the "laissez faire" or "leave everything alone" political economists – those scientific apologists for the strong, and laborious exponents of a fatalist creed – these gentlemen [who] taunt us with encouraging working men to rely too much on the State', Maxse's address broke decisively from the liberal traditions of previous decades. 'Superficial thinkers were wont to say that it was impossible to make men good by Act of Parliament', Maxse commented, 'but he contended that bad laws made bad men,

---

[105] *Eastern Post*, 27 July 1872, p. 5; 31 August 1872, p. 5; 11 January 1873, p. 5.
[106] John Hales to Maxse, 20 July 1873, WSRO, Maxse Papers, item 185. Hales was a weaver by trade.

and good laws went a great way towards making good men.'[107] His election posters reiterated these points, depicting pauperism and 'our class system' as direct consequences of defective parliamentary institutions (Ill. 5).[108]

This political platform, successful in addressing the issues put to Liberal candidates by restive trade unions, failed, however, to gain Maxse a parliamentary seat. 'The thoroughness of Captain Maxse alarmed the many electors', the *Eastern Post* noted wisely in February. 'He was essentially the working men's candidate.'[109] Continuing to participate in the activities of the Land Tenure Reform Association until it folded in 1876, Maxse remained committed to a social vision of politics into the following decade. Louis Blanc, an admirer of the English liberal's pamphlets on the Franco-Prussian War, wrote to accept Maxse's offer to translate his writings in 1881.[110]

If Maxse's persistent failure to gain a parliamentary seat in the seventies illustrates the limited influence exercised by social democrats within the liberal fold, the electoral tribulations of less advanced Liberal candidates nonetheless attest to the growing influence of these radical tendencies. J.E. Thorold Rogers, schooled in the Cobdenite tradition, encountered difficulties when he sought to stand for Oldham in 1872. Although in receipt of generous funds from Samuel Morley, who had since 1868 transferred his financial assistance from the Reform League to middle-class candidates pledged to Gladstonian liberalism, Rogers found himself hard pressed by the demands of Oldham's workers. Local liberals insisted that he support a legislative reduction of the hours of female and child labour in the mills to gain their support; when Rogers declined to address the labour issue in his address to the electors, they chose

[107] *Eastern Post*, 9 February 1873, p. 7; F.A. Maxse, *The Radical Candidature for the Tower Hamlets: First Speech by Capt. Maxse, R.N.* ([London], n.d.), in WSRO, Maxse Papers, item 184.

[108] 'Captain Maxse's Address', [1873–4], WSRO, Maxse Papers, item 184.

[109] *Eastern Post*, 8 February 1874, p. 4. The United Kingdom General Post Office and Telegraph Service Benefit Society wrote in January to ask whether Maxse would agree to support their union; he pledged in his campaign speeches to work for parliamentary protection of organized labour. See E. Hawkins to Maxse, 28 January 1874, WSRO, Maxse Papers, item 186, and *Eastern Post*, 31 January 1874, p. 5.

[110] Printed circular from Humphrey Sandwith, Howard Evans, and F.A. Maxse to the Land Tenure Reform Association, 30 October 1876, and Louis Blanc to Maxse, 13 May 1881, WSRO, Maxse Papers, items 307 and 203.

CAPTAIN MAXSE'S ADDRESS.

TO THE ELECTORS OF THE TOWER HAMLETS.

GENTLEMEN,

        I beg to offer myself as a Candidate for the Parliamentary Representation of the Tower Hamlets.

I desire to call your attention to the following facts, which concern you as Voters.

PAUPERISM.

In England and Wales during the course of a single year

Above 2,000,000 Persons receive Parochial Relief.

EDUCATION.

Out of 2,000,000 children on the School Register less than 9000 pass the sixth standard, or, in other words, receive the rudiments of education, and only

150,000 leave School able to read and write decently.

THE LAND SYSTEM.

With food increasing in price, towns shamefully crowded, and an exodus of agricultural labourers in the course of arrangement, there are, at a moderate estimate, in the United Kingdom,

10,000,000 Acres of Waste Fertile Land,

and immense, almost uninhabited tracts lie in a state of semi-cultivation for want of the capital and industry which our class system of land tenure effectually excludes. Under this system the industrious poor have been gradually superseded by the only class which can afford to waste good land and now monopolizes it everywhere.

GOVERNMENT BY A MINORITY OF ELECTORS.

Under the present electoral system

    30,000 Electors—in small boroughs—elect 44 Members of Parliament.

    546,000 Electors—in large boroughs—elect 35   ditto

therefore

30,000 Electors govern 546,000 Electors.

    16,000 Electors in the Tower Hamlets return 1 Member.

    16,000 Electors in various rural districts return 30 Members.

Such is the distribution of political power imposed upon the credulity of voters as the foundation of a National Assembly.

Furthermore, the cost of admission to Parliament ranges at from £1000 to £10,000; the system of registration seems expressly devised to disenfranchise working men; and the lodger franchise is so complicated with forms and disqualifications that it is virtually inoperative.

All these humiliating facts are intimately connected. Pauperism, high rates, dear food, and huddled populations, are the result of bad education, bad land laws and Government by the Minority. My politics are founded upon the conviction that it is within the province of Parliament to remedy the evils I have set forth. I shall, if returned as your Member, advocate a truly National system of Education; alteration of the Land system, including the Preservation and Nationalization of the Commons; and Electoral Reform based upon equal representation, assimilated town and county franchise, preferential voting, and triennial Parliaments.

The present system of direct taxation presses unfairly upon precarious incomes, while the indirect taxation (by diminishing the value of wages) falls heavily upon the working classes. I am in favour of the readjustment of the former, so as to relieve small temporary incomes, and to permit the gradual abolition of taxes upon articles of consumption commencing with the immediate repeal of the tea and sugar duties.

I do not come forward as a Party Candidate, except so far as party is founded upon principle. I am opposed to the Tories, because I perceive in them the active supporters of wrong and oppression, and it is their fixed policy to preserve the unjust principles which disturb society and alienate Ireland. I am with the Liberals so long as they promote a truly progressive policy; but when Liberalism degenerates, as official Liberalism has recently done, into Toryism, I claim the right to independent action.

67, CROMWELL ROAD,—S.W.   FREDK. A. MAXSE.

    26th January, 1874.

CENTRAL COMMITTEE ROOMS, "YORK MINSTER," PHILPOT STREET, COMMERCIAL ROAD.

5   Maxse election poster (1873)

in his place the Honourable E.L. Stanley, who 'pledged himself to all the working men's programme'.[111] 'Just now any man, instructed & honest in his political economy, will find his virtues an obstacle to his getting into Parlt.', John Bright wrote to Rogers in consolation. Railing bitterly against the pernicious effect upon the work force of trade unions and high wages, Bright perceived that 'the "war of classes" is apparently extending – not a political war so much as a social & industrial one'.[112] Other provincial Liberals discerned the same trend, and greeted even the defeat of their own party by the Conservatives with considerable relief. The origin of the Conservative reaction, Samuel Greg wrote to Liverpool's George Melly, lay in 'the thought & attitude of the working classes'. In this context, Greg confessed, he was more satisfied with the Conservative win than he could have been with a 'Revolutionary' Liberal victory.[113]

Historians of the labour movement typically emphasize the successful liberalization of working-class politics in the mid-Victorian period, underlining the respectable character and moderate aims of even radical artisans in these years. The evolving pattern of relations among working-class radicals, middle-class liberals, and continental revolutionaries suggests, however, a different perspective. As the riots that surrounded the Dilkite agitation of 1871–2 clearly demonstrate, moderation and respectability represent only one end of the spectrum of behaviour displayed by English labour radicals. And if twentieth-century scholars are preoccupied by the failure of a Marxist politics to evolve in the mid-Victorian years, the liberal academics who lived through the national and international contests of these times were forcibly convinced that English workers had fallen under the baneful influence of continental socialism. Lecturing to undergraduates at Cambridge as Professor of Political Economy, Henry Fawcett voiced a pervasive liberal concern in finding 'Modern Socialism' to characterize a growing segment of the radical artisanate. Interpreting socialism, as a generation of liberal reformers had done before him, as

[111] Samuel Morley to Rogers, 27 June 1868, and James Newton to Rogers, 20, 25, and 28 May 1872, BODL, Thorold Rogers Papers, Correspondence, Box 2, items 493, and 518–20.
[112] John Bright to Rogers, 18 July 1872 and 28 January 1873, BODL, Thorold Rogers Papers, Correspondence, Box 1, item 141.
[113] Greg to Melly, 7 February 1874, LCL, Melly Collection, 920 MEL, 25/vol. 19, fol. 4882.

government intervention in social life, Fawcett traced the working-class abandonment of the political economy of liberal individualism to 'Continental ideas'. As the February revolution clearly demonstrated, 'the Continental workman was constantly looking to the State as he would to a powerful friend, or benefactor, to aid and reward him'. Under the influence of this pernicious force, of which Marx's International represented only 'the extreme party', the English worker's natural preference for cheap and skeletal government had been vitiated. 'It can scarcely have escaped notice that during the last two or three years English workmen have with much greater frequency asked for Government assistance', Fawcett noted dourly, 'and demands for State intervention are consequently enlarging.'[114]

Stark and simplistic, Fawcett's analysis of the intellectual origins of English socialism is nonetheless significant, for it points to both a dominant line of argument dividing the working and the middle class in mid-Victorian England and a source of this conflict's resolution. Socialism – defined by Nassau Senior in 1849 as 'the belief that the inequality of conditions is remediable' through legislation and as 'reliance upon state intervention' by Fawcett in 1873 – divided the radical artisanate from the liberal bourgeoisie in England for two decades after 1848, creating two distinct political cultures delimited by perceptions of class difference. But although it assumed the form of a class movement, the so-called socialism of these years was not itself predicated upon a consistent class analysis of society. Grounded rather in the conviction that national prosperity and social welfare required the positive freedoms of constructive parliamentary legislation, the socialism of the *démoc-soc* ideal became 'the political economy of the poor', in Nassau Senior's phrase, by virtue of the middle-class reaction to 1848.[115] As middle-class radicals came to question the rigid allegiance to classical political economy forged in their response to the continental revolutions, the class configuration of English popular politics became less obvious. Mediated by the participation of both middle- and work-

---

[114] 'Modern Socialism', in Henry and Millicent Fawcett, *Essays and Lectures on Social and Political Subjects* (London, 1872), pp. 6–22.

[115] For Fawcett's definition, see *ibid.*, p. 12; for Senior on socialism and 1848, see Nassau W. Senior, *Journals Kept in France and Italy from 1848 to 1852: With a Sketch of the Revolution of 1848*, ed. M.C.M. Simpson, 2 vols. (London, 1871), vol. I, pp. 150–2.

ing-class radicals in a series of nationalist and internationalist political movements, this reconciliation of the two classes radicalized Liberal politics even as it liberalized sectors of the labouring population.

Conclusion

Thirty years ago, in the 'fifties, the old orthodox Economy was
dominant; it received the superstitious veneration of the whole
capitalist class; and it more or less overawed the leaders of the
labouring class. To-day the old orthodox Economy – the Gospel,
or Sophism, of Supply and Demand, absolute freedom for Individual Exertion, and so forth – all this is ancient history. 'We are all
Socialists now', cries an eminent Statesman in jest or in earnest.
And the jest has earnest in it, if we take Socialism to mean, not the
substitution of some communistic utopia for the old institutions
of Capital and Labour, but rather the infusion of all economic
and political institutions with social considerations towards social
ends. Thirty years ago Socialism was a mere outlandish day-
dream. It is now, in the new vague sense, as a modifying tendency,
a very real force.[1]

Twentieth-century historians conventionally date the modern
socialist movement in England from the 1880s and 1890s, locating the origins of the Labour party in organizations such as the
Fabian Society, the Social Democratic Federation, and the Independent Labour Party.[2] This chronology coincides nicely with the
emergence of Marxist thought in Britain – serialized translations
of the first chapters of *Capital* appeared in radical periodicals
from 1883, and an English edition of the first volume appeared in

[1] Frederic Harrison, 'Socialist Unionism', in his *National and Social Problems*
(London, 1908), pp. 421–39, p. 422. Reprinted from *The Nineteenth Century*, vol.
26 (1889).
[2] See for example Henry Pelling, *The Origins of the Labour Party, 1880–1900*, 2nd
edn (Oxford, 1965); Stanley Pierson, *British Socialists: The Journey from Fantasy to
Politics* (Cambridge, Mass., 1979); and Paul Thompson, *Socialists, Liberals and
Labour: The Struggle for London, 1885–1914* (London, 1967).

1887[3] – and thus affirms common assumptions about the logical relationship between Marxism and the evolution of socialist politics. But it departs significantly from the perceived experience of contemporaries. For as both the life and the writings of Frederic Harrison suggest, contemporary observers traced the roots of British socialism not to the popularization of Marxist theory, but to the breaking of classical political economy that accompanied the reintegration within liberal culture of the social, economic, and political spheres. Viewed from this perspective, the origins of English socialism may be seen to reside less in the formation of the first formally socialist organizations than in the earlier radical agitations of the 1860s and 1870s, deriving their initial impetus not from German historical materialism but from French social democratic thought and English working-class radical patriotism. Initially embraced by the radical spokesmen of the late Chartist movement, French social democratic tendencies were located within a richly textured fabric of radical nationalism and internationalism in which Marxist theory figured as only a single, often isolated strand.

An understanding of the course and character of mid-Victorian radical relations, indeed, suggests that the emergence of socialism in the 1880s was rooted in an intensification and acceptance of radical trends associated since 1848 with the cause of labour. Far from marking the end of a profound caesura in working-class consciousness begun with the decline of the mass platform in 1848, the evolving trajectory of social democratic and socialist thought grew from the very soil of late Chartism. The term 'liberalization' fails to convey the force and the complexity of political relations among radical representatives of the middle and working classes in this period. Successful in capturing the sharp diminution of mass protest that characterized working-class politics after 1848, it obscures both the persistence of working-class opposition to economic liberalism after Chartism and the varied radical hues that marked the liberal complexion itself in these years. Until the advent of the Reform League in 1865, the agitations mounted by radical workers offered little threat to the formal structures of the Victorian state. But together the arguments of the radical press, the cycle of ceremonial

---

[3] Kirk Willis details this development in 'The Introduction and Critical Reception of Marxist Thought in Britain, 1850–1900', *Historical Journal*, vol. 20 (June 1977), pp. 417–59.

observances that celebrated the confluence of the French and the English revolutionary traditions, and the episodic groundswells of radical support for continental nationalist causes helped to sustain an abiding antagonism to liberal economics among a vocal sector of the English working class.

Middle-class radical culture was governed by a rather different dynamic in these years. While effectively united in endorsing market mechanisms, middle-class radicals repeatedly confronted the limits of liberal consensus when they turned from domestic issues to the pressing concerns of continental politics. Captivated (like radicals of the working class) by movements for national independence, bourgeois reformers grappled with the antinomies of their liberal conscience when they sought to extend the principles of laissez-faire from English social and economic relations to the realm of international diplomacy. The willingness of some ardent liberal patriots to support English government intervention in the domestic affairs of continental nations generated conflict with those liberal reformers who upheld strict laissez-faire at home and abroad. For a significant sector of the radical middle class, the resolution of this conflict ultimately lay in the acceptance of a political philosophy in which parliamentary intervention figured as the linchpin of both national and international well-being. In embracing this social democratic interpretation of liberal politics, these new liberal reformers embraced the peculiar logic of the post-Chartist working-class radical tradition.

No single event or development initiated this fundamental transformation of English liberal culture, which derived from sources as diverse as academics' growing dissatisfaction with Ricardian theories of the wages fund, social reformers' rising consciousness of urban poverty, and Liberal party preoccupations with the implications of an increasingly democratic franchise.[4] To radical democrats, the passage of the Second Reform Act was particularly significant, and acquired added importance as the halcyon days of Gladstone's first ministry gave way to the less sanguine political prospects signalled

---

[4] For the changing intellectual fortunes of political economy and socialism within liberal culture, see Freeden, *New Liberalism*, pp. 25–75. Stedman Jones, *Outcast London*, and Gertrude Himmelfarb, *Poverty and Compassion: The Moral Imagination of the Late Victorians* (New York, 1991), address the growing perception of poverty. For the tenor of Liberal party politics in the aftermath of 1867, see Michael Bentley, *The Climax of Liberal Politics: British Liberalism in Theory and Practice 1868–1918* (London, 1987), esp. pp. 133–7.

by the Liberal electoral defeat of 1874. For although the escalation of the Irish problem and the defection of key businessmen to the Tory fold dampened many liberals' enthusiasm for domestic reform, it ignited the radical aspirations of others. Convinced of the growing imperative to expand the party's electoral base, this radical wing of liberalism continued to pursue the social democratic themes adumbrated by the new liberals of 1868–74.[5]

The fortunes of the National Reform Union in the late Victorian era suggest the lineaments of this radicalization of liberal culture. Heir to the traditions of the Anti-Corn Law campaign, the Reform Union had served in its early years as an instrument of the Manchester School. Led by men of substance pledged to property qualifications for the franchise, the early Reform Union upheld a programme of liberal economics at home and diplomatic non-intervention abroad.[6] The death in 1871 of George Wilson, who had served as president of both the Reform Union and the earlier Anti-Corn Law League, initiated a period of decline for the organization, but the Liberal defeat in 1874 brought the Union back to life with a new radical agenda. In July 1875 the Reform Union's executive produced a revised constitution that called for the extension of household suffrage from the boroughs to the counties, a more equitable distribution of parliamentary seats, a revision of the laws governing land ownership, security for agricultural occupiers, reform of the game laws, and promotion of religious equality for Dissenters.[7] Earlier hostile or indifferent to the claims of organized labour, Reform Union liberals now worked with trade union leaders to attract workers to their ranks. The summer of 1876 saw the Reform Union, assisted by the officers of the National Agricultural Labourers' Union, stage a series of large open-air meetings in Oxfordshire to explain their liberal programme to unenfranchised labourers. By December, sympathetic liberal reformers had contributed over £1,700 to this cause.[8]

---

[5] These trends are explored in relation to high politics in Thomas William Heyck, *The Dimensions of British Radicalism: The Case of Ireland 1874–95* (Urbana, 1974).

[6] See above, pp. 235–40.

[7] Printed notice, 'The National Reform Union Constitution. As revised by the Executive Committee, July, 1875', University of Newcastle upon Tyne, G.O. Trevelyan Papers, GOT 193.

[8] National Reform Union, 'Statement of Receipts and Expenditures May 1875-December 2, 1876', Sheffield City Libraries, H.J. Wilson Collection, M.D. 5890, Correspondence of the Sheffield Liberal Association and Reform Union.

The following years saw the Union's membership rise significantly: 173 branches sent delegates to the Reform Union conference in Manchester's Free Trade Hall in 1875, but by 1891 the organization boasted 423 active branches.[9] An expansion of the Union's ideology paralleled this increase in its membership. The constitution adopted in 1875 had offered a programme designed to wean agricultural workers from the corrupt influences of an aristocratic landed class; the popularization of socialist doctrines in the 1880s encouraged the Union to address the interests of urban workers as well. In decided contrast to the liberal reaction to the Chartist challenge in 1848, these years witnessed a sustained attempt on the part of liberal activists to meet the perceived threat of working-class socialism by incorporating socialist themes into the Liberal platform. The works chosen for inclusion in the Reform Union's recommended 'Social Science Series' in 1891 are instructive in this respect. Here radical classics with a liberal bent appeared alongside the early writings of the British socialist movement. J.E. Thorold Rogers's *Work and Wages* offered readers the arguments of a liberal thinker deeply marked by the teachings of Richard Cobden; G.J. Holyoake's *Self-Help a Hundred Years Ago* and W.J. Linton's *English Republic* represented the opinions of the sector of the late Chartist leadership most sympathetic to Liberal party politics. Works by avowed socialists expanded the scope of the series well beyond these tentative efforts at social democratic thinking. In Ernest Belfort Bax's *Religion of Socialism*, Sidney Webb's *Socialism in England*, Edward Aveling and Eleanor Marx's *Working-Class Movement in America*, and Paul Lafargue's *Evolution of Property*, Reform Union readers could engage with the premier writings of contemporary socialist thinkers at home and abroad.[10]

The strands of historical memory invoked and interwoven in this Liberal bid for working-class support demonstrate the enduring influence and appeal of the patterns of working-class radical belief established in the mid-Victorian years. Crafted to incorporate the Chartist legacy into the liberal tradition, the Reform Union's distinctive interpretation of the liberal past combined a rejection of the stark liberal doctrines of Cobden and Bright with repeated

[9] Printed programme for 'National Reform Union. Lecture Season, 1891–92', BODL, Johnson Collection, Creeds, Parties, Policies: Box 21.
[10] 'The Publication List of the National Reform Union, August 1891', BODL, Johnson Collection, Creeds, Parties, Policies: Box 21.

efforts to integrate Liberal party politics with the cause of radical patriotism in England and on the continent. While continuing to uphold free trade in goods, the Union now disowned earlier liberal antagonism to trade unions, insisting that the nineteenth century had seen 'Tory laws' against organized labour countered by 'the efforts of the Whigs and Radicals to emancipate the working classes from oppression'.[11] The Liberal party's relations with nineteenth-century workers figured in this mythic recreation of the liberal past as integral contributions to a seamless web of radical activity designed to uphold the integrity of the nation-state. The topics included in S. Lloyd's lectures for the Reform Union in 1891–2 ranged from 'John Hampden and England's Fight for Freedom', to 'John Bright and National Progress', 'Richard Cobden and the Struggles for Cheap Bread', 'The Rise and Progress of English Liberalism', and 'The Political and Moral Aspects of Modern Labour Movements'.[12] Lectures on European patriots were a mainstay of the Reform Union programme, serving to link the Union both to the radical traditions cherished by earlier generations of English workers and to the line of radical succession constructed by the new generation of socialist speakers active in working men's clubs. The life of Mazzini, like that of Cromwell a common topic of veneration at Reform Union meetings, provided a popular ideological common ground with working-class radical traditions. In 1884 *The Liberal*, the journal of the London and Counties Liberal Union, advertised lectures on 'Richard Cobden' and 'The Cost of Government' alongside W. Bruce's 'Mazzini' and the socialist H.M. Hyndman's 'What is Law, or How the Workers are Legally Robbed'.[13]

Juxtaposed against this litany of English and continental patriots were the figures and the emblems of the late Chartist movement. By the 1890s, indeed, the radical tradition traced in Reform Union lectures departed from the norms of late Chartist hagiography primarily in its insistence that Chartist and social democratic

---

[11] I.S. Leadman, *Trade Unions and Parliament: A Short History of Working Men's Combinations*, National Reform Union Pamphlets no. 30 (n.p., *ca.* 1893), in BODL, Johnson Collection, Creeds, Parties, Policies: Box 21.

[12] Printed programme, 'National Reform Union: Lecture Season 1891–92', BODL, Johnson Collection, Creeds, Parties, Policies: Box 21.

[13] For the Reform Union on Cromwell and Mazzini, see the lecture titles offered by S. Firth, D.S. Prosser, and W. Whitham in *ibid.* For the Liberal Union, see *The Liberal*, vol. 1 (January 1884), in BODL, Johnson Collection, Creeds, Parties, Policies: Box 17.

developments formed an integral component of the liberal heritage rather than a reaction against it. W.T. Postlewaite cultivated these associations in 'The New Charter, or Liberalism of To-day'; W.H. Chadwick offered lectures on both 'My Trial and Imprisonment for Chartism in 1848' and 'Mr Gladstone: His Services to his Country'. The trajectory implied in J. Middleton's lecture topics was clear. Beginning with 'Habeas Corpus: How We Got It, and What It Is Worth', it extended to 'Chartism: Its Influence on Modern Politics', and concluded with 'Socialism: Practical and Unpractical'.[14] Attempts to incorporate Ernest Jones, by far the most radical of the late Chartist leaders, into the pantheon of liberal patriots complemented the efforts of these lecture campaigns. Annual celebrations of the deceased Chartist's birthday emerged as a common component of northern reform culture in the 1870s, and continued into the twentieth century (Ill. 6). Adducing 'patriotism' as Jones's most salient political characteristic, reform-minded liberal speakers repeatedly conflated Chartism and liberalism, constructing an interpretation of the liberal past that bore little relation to the radical history of the previous years – not least in ignoring Jones's two-year imprisonment under a Liberal government for his Chartist activities in 1848. Richard Pankhurst, who would later leave the Liberal fold for the Independent Labour Party, chaired a meeting of Manchester reformers which commemorated Jones in 1879. Having toasted 'The Commonwealth', he led the audience in a rendition of Jones's 'Song of Cromwell's Time'. 'To privilege he opposed the people, and to class he opposed the country', Pankhurst eulogized. 'The Anniversary of the Birthday of Ernest Jones', the meeting concluded, 'should be a red-letter day in the History of English Liberalism.'[15]

Social democratic interpretations of Jones's patriotism enriched these lines of liberal argument in the following decades, but also rendered them increasingly contentious. R. Bax of the Rawtenstall

[14] Printed programme, 'National Reform Union: Lecture Season 1891–92', BODL, Johnson Collection, Creeds, Parties, Policies: Box 21.
[15] Ernest Jones Commemoration Committee, Burnley, *In Memoriam: Ernest Jones* (Manchester, 1874), in BODL, Johnson Collection, Leaders of Reform: Box 7. For the 'Song of Cromwell's Time', see above, p. 128. The argument that Jones was a quintessential liberal clearly demanded a selective reading of the radical and liberal traditions. The 'advanced Liberals' who in 1877 honoured Jones for taking 'such a prominent part in the Chartist agitation, and indeed in all Liberal movements' identified Major Cartwright, not Adam Smith, as 'the father of English liberalism'. See *The Bacup Times*, vol. 10 (February 1877), in Scrapbook of Newspaper Cuttings on Ernest Jones, MCRL, MSF 923/2/J/8.

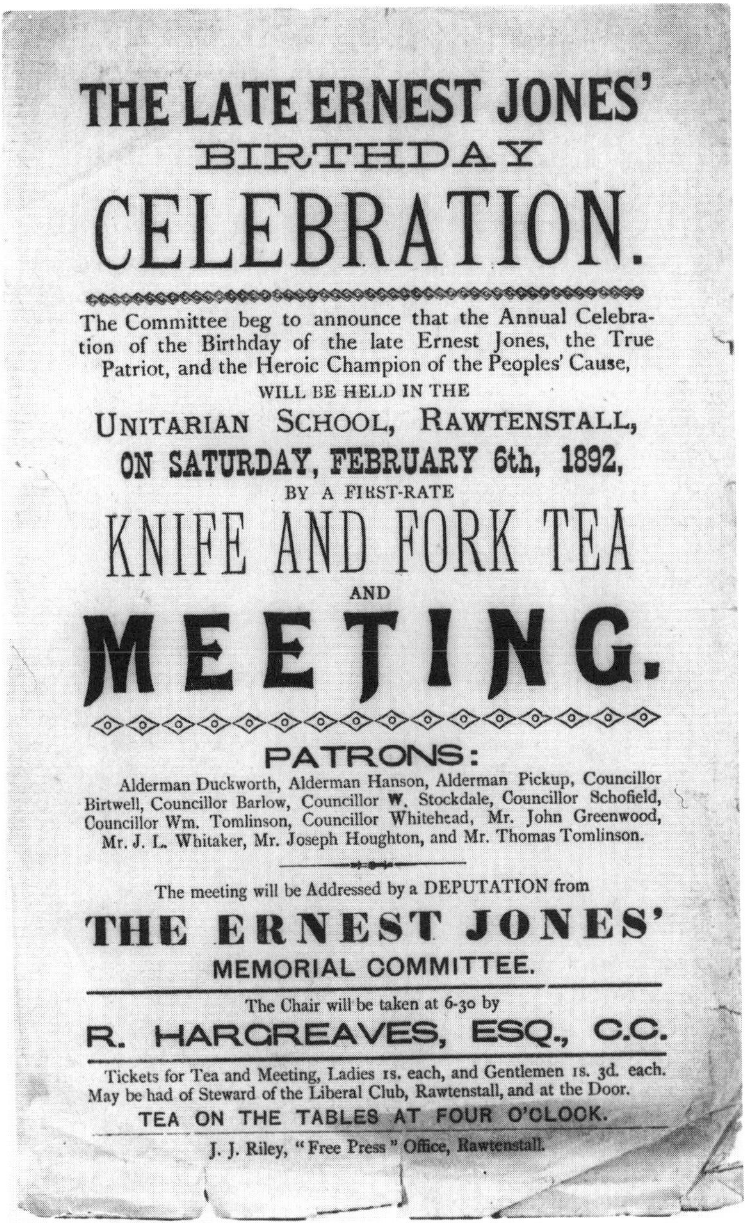

THE LATE ERNEST JONES'
BIRTHDAY
CELEBRATION.

The Committee beg to announce that the Annual Celebration of the Birthday of the late Ernest Jones, the True Patriot, and the Heroic Champion of the Peoples' Cause,
WILL BE HELD IN THE
UNITARIAN SCHOOL, RAWTENSTALL,
ON SATURDAY, FEBRUARY 6th, 1892,
BY A FIRST-RATE
KNIFE AND FORK TEA
AND
MEETING.

PATRONS:
Alderman Duckworth, Alderman Hanson, Alderman Pickup, Councillor Birtwell, Councillor Barlow, Councillor W. Stockdale, Councillor Schofield, Councillor Wm. Tomlinson, Councillor Whitehead, Mr. John Greenwood, Mr. J. L. Whitaker, Mr. Joseph Houghton, and Mr. Thomas Tomlinson.

The meeting will be Addressed by a DEPUTATION from
THE ERNEST JONES'
MEMORIAL COMMITTEE.

The Chair will be taken at 6-30 by
R. HARGREAVES, ESQ., C.C.

Tickets for Tea and Meeting, Ladies 1s. each, and Gentlemen 1s. 3d. each.
May be had of Steward of the Liberal Club, Rawtenstall, and at the Door.
TEA ON THE TABLES AT FOUR O'CLOCK.

J. J. Riley, "Free Press" Office, Rawtenstall.

6 Ernest Jones: birthday celebration (1892)

Liberal Club praised Jones in 1891 for 'his sacrifices, his sufferings
and noble patriotic deeds for the emancipation of his fellow-
countrymen from political and social thralldom',[16] arguments that
underlined advanced liberals' new willingness to unite social and
political reform. Socialist orators proved, however, as eager as
liberals to appropriate the Chartist leader for their own evolving
radical traditions. Their determination to seize upon Jones's social
democratic tendencies to argue that he was a founding father of their
own movement made the late Chartist legacy a contested ideological
terrain, as amenable to invocation by the Independent Labour Party
as to liberal panegyric.[17]

If contests with socialists for the right to inherit the Chartist
mantle troubled the course of the new liberalism, so too did the
refusal of all liberals to subscribe to social democratic interpretations of politics. For although the 'socialist' agendas of the new
liberalism – calls for an eight-hour workday, land tenure reform,
compulsory education, and other measures of legislative interference
in social and economic life – paled before the demands of Marxian
revolution, they offered a clear and palpable insult to the liberal
sensibilities of thinkers and politicians who continued to uphold the
negative conceptions of freedom that had dominated the radical
liberalism of the previous decades. Auberon Herbert, who with
Charles Dilke had transferred his allegiance from the Prussian
patriots to the French republicans in the autumn of 1870, found
himself increasingly hostile to the radical trajectory of advanced
liberal opinion in England as the decade progressed. By 1877
Herbert had become a vocal antagonist of creeping socialism within
the liberal ranks. As Honorary Secretary of 'The Personal Rights &
Self-Help Association', he sought to convince reform-minded liberals of the compelling need to 'protect and enlarge personal liberty
and personal rights' while opposing 'the multiplication of laws and
the tendency to control and direct through Parliament the affairs of
the people'.[18]

Pledged to 'the general principle of liberty as against restraint or

[16] Cited in Ernest Jones Jr to A.B. Wakefield, 4 February 1891, MCRL, MSQ
923/2/Jo4.
[17] B. Wilson, 'The Independent Labour Party and Mr Ernest Jones', cutting from the
Halifax Courier [1891], in 'Scrapbook of Newspaper Cuttings Etc. on Ernest
Jones', MCRL, MSF 9223/2/J/8.
[18] Auberon Herbert to J.E. Thorold Rogers, 14 December [1877], BODL, Thorold
Rogers Papers, 364/1–2.

protection', the Personal Rights & Self-Help Association joined a growing circle of liberal organizations that urged 'the working people of this and of every other country' to embrace 'self-abnegation as regards the resources of the state, and to pursue their own special aims by means other than those of legislation'.[19] Herbert Spencer, hailed by these younger reformers as the true keeper of the liberal faith, was especially vociferous in defending conventional, negative conceptions of liberty against the socialist encroachments of positive freedom. Describing socialism as 'the coming slavery' in 1884, Spencer was determined to expose the particular dangers that social democracy posed to received liberal traditions of individualism. 'The belief, not only of socialists, but also of those so-called Liberals who are diligently preparing the way for them, is that by due skill an ill-working humanity may be framed into well-working institutions', he explained. Legislation 'proper to liberalism', in contrast, consisted in constraints preventing the citizen 'from directly or indirectly aggressing on his fellows – needful, that is, for maintaining the liberties of his fellows against his invasions of them: restraints which are, therefore . . . negatively coercive, not positively coercive'.[20]

As Spencer's diatribe against social democracy suggests, the implications of the middle-class defection from orthodox political economy had by the 1880s extended from the Liberal party to the new politics of socialism. Here, as throughout the mid-Victorian period, radical interpretations of nationalism and internationalism were of central importance. For the patterns of allegiance forged by working-class radicals after 1848, patterns in which *démoc-soc* ideals elided with nationalist and class ideologies, persisted in the socialist parties of the 1880s and 1890s, expanding their appeal alike to working- and middle-class radical activists. Permitting artisans to affirm their allegiance to the English radical tradition of the elect nation while upholding the particular rights and duties of labour within the international order, the patriotic politics of the 1850s, 1860s, and 1870s had both allowed working-class leaders to cooper-

---

[19] Printed circular, 'The Personal Rights & Self-Help Association', 14 December 1877, and printed leaflet, *Self-Help and Personal Rights Association, Paper No. II* [1877], in BODL, Thorold Rogers Papers, 364/3–4. For the broader context of liberal opposition to socialist tendencies in this period, see Mason, 'Political Economy and the Response to Socialism in Britain'.

[20] Herbert Spencer, 'The Coming Slavery' and 'The New Toryism', reprinted in his *The Man versus the State* (London, 1894), pp. 43, 15–16.

ate with middle-class liberals and insulated them from the full force of liberalization. As trends within liberalism and the perceived implications of the increasingly democratic franchise forced the radical wing of the Liberal party toward social democracy in the succeeding decades, radical patriotism continued to function as both a repository of working-class values and a bridge to reformers of the middle class.

Historians of English socialism have underlined the paucity of Marxist thinking within the early socialist parties, but have failed adequately to explore the corresponding strength of these organizations' patriotic traditions.[21] Throughout the mid-Victorian years, the heroes of continental nationalist movements had figured in the working-class radical imagination as proponents of political intervention in social and economic life. As such, they were readily accommodated by later socialist movements. The *Labour Prophet* selected Mazzini's injunction 'Let Labour Be the Basis of Civil Society' to adorn its masthead in 1893; in 1913 the Independent Labour Party's publications ranged from Eden Paul's *Karl Marx and Modern Socialism* to Louis Blanc's *Evils of Competition* and Mazzini's *Duties of Man*.[22] When requested in 1906 to name authors whose works had influenced their political development, Labour Members of Parliament ignored Marx but cited Mazzini – and Milton – often.[23] The socialist engraver Walter Crane, attempting to trace his own political evolution, neatly captured the spirit and the contradictions of this radical passage to socialism. He traced his rejection of liberal politics from a boyhood apprenticeship to William James Linton – 'Chartist, and poet, and friend of Mazzini and Kossuth ... *really* a Socialist' – through Mill's discussion of French socialism in his *Political Economy* and the events of the franchise reform movement in the sixties, to membership in the Social Democratic Federation, the Socialist League, the Fabians, and the Hammersmith Socialist Society.[24]

Significantly, a similar vein of international patriotism marked the

[21] 'Common sense', Ross McKibbin argues in a characteristic vein, suggests that nationalism acted to moderate the political outlook of the working class, 'but the evidence *that* it did is thin, or thinnish'. McKibbin, 'Why Was There No Marxism?', p. 23.

[22] *Labour Prophet*, August 1893; 'I.L.P. Diary for 1913', IISG, Max Nettlau Collection, I.L.P. and Fabian File, folder 1614.

[23] 'The Labour Party and the Books that Helped Make It', *Review of Reviews* (June 1906), pp. 568–82.

[24] *How I Became a Socialist: A Series of Biographical Sketches* (London, n.d.), pp. 23–5.

political evolution of the middle-class socialists with whom Crane associated in the 1880s and 1890s. Edward Carpenter, like Crane a key figure in socialist artistic circles in this period, was born to a liberal family committed to the Philosophical Radicalism of Mill and Fawcett, but began to embrace a new radical vision at Cambridge, where he read Mazzini's *Duties of Man*.[25] H.M. Hyndman, founder of the Marxist Social Democratic Federation, traced his socialist awakening to Mazzinian influences as well. A 'philosophic Radical, with a great admiration for John Stuart Mill', Hyndman evinced little interest in social issues as a young man. 'Although I had read a good deal of political economy at Trinity, I should say that my first serious interest in social questions was due to my visits to the East End of London ... at the time when the shipping trade was leaving the Thames for the Tyne', he later recalled. 'What I saw then ... coming at the same time as my acquaintance with Mazzini, which became very intimate, might perhaps be reckoned as the first inkling I obtained of unscientific Socialism.' Hyndman devoted two chapters of his autobiography to Mazzini, Garibaldi, and Italian unification.[26]

The early history of Hyndman's Social Democratic Federation – the organization's name is significant – drew upon and perpetuated these patriotic traditions. Begun in 1881 as an effort to revive the Chartist movement, the Democratic Federation boasted Hyndman, Joseph Cowen, and the O'Brienite radicals James and Charles Murray among its initial members: as Hyndman noted with satisfaction in October, 'all the old '48 men are heartily with us'. Although the Federation had embraced a fully socialist programme by 1884, Hyndman's efforts to court middle-class radical support for his movement continued to underline his nationalist credentials. 'We have got a most remarkable body of people together most remarkable', he wrote to Helen Taylor in July, 'and I am not talking of what I don't know, for I numbered Marx & Mazzini among my intimate acquaintance, & I knew Garibaldi & his surrounders well; so I can make a fair comparison.'[27]

If nationalist traditions, as the memoirs of Hyndman, Carpenter,

[25] Edward Carpenter, *My Days and Dreams* (London, 1916), pp. 38, 60, 61.
[26] *How I Became a Socialist*, pp. 3–4, and H.M. Hyndman, *Record of an Adventurous Life* (London, 1911).
[27] H.M. Hyndman to Helen Taylor, 2 October 1881 and 25 July 1884, BLPES, Mill–Taylor Collection, vol. 18, items 28 and 32. For the early history of the Social Democratic Federation, see M.S. Wilkins, 'The Non-Socialist Origins of England's First Important Socialist Organization', *International Review of Social History*, vol. 4 (1959), pp. 199–207.

and Crane suggest, helped to precipitate the evolution of English socialism in the 1880s and 1890s, internationalist traditions helped to sustain social democratic convictions in this period as they had in previous decades. The Paris Commune figured as the central symbol of socialist internationalism in these years; exiled Communards both embodied this internationalist spirit and served to acquaint a new generation of radical reformers with its significance. Ernest Belfort Bax traced his socialist conversion to sympathy for the Commune and friendships with émigré Communards, while George Bernard Shaw, serving his socialist apprenticeship in London's debating clubs, received his introduction to both the French language and the anarchist theories of Proudhon from a Communard exile.[28] The Commune, in the interpretations of this new generation of English radicals, served as an international symbol of the necessary union of the social, economic, and political spheres. Precipitating 'the final rupture between working-class democracy and the ruling middle class ... the workmen ... were bringing to birth a new world – the world of the independent and free organisation of industrial and commercial labour', Belfort Bax, Victor Dave, and William Morris proclaimed in 1886. Viewed 'in its true light', the Commune thus served 'as a torch lighting us on our way towards the complete emancipation of labour, and the breaking down of the wall of national rivalries which foretells that consummation'.[29]

Just as ritualized anniversary celebrations of the French revolution of 1848 had allowed English working-class radicals to express their *démoc-soc* convictions in an international context, ritualized celebrations of the Commune encouraged socialists of later decades to affirm their commitment to 'the struggle of workers under capitalism'.[30] Extending from London to the provinces, these annual celebrations united representatives of otherwise divergent

---

[28] For Bax, see *How I Became a Socialist*, pp. 10–11 and his *Reminiscences*, p. 30; for Shaw and the Commune, see Willard Wolfe, *From Radicalism to Socialism: Men and Ideas in the Formation of Fabian Socialist Doctrines, 1881–1889* (New Haven, 1975), p. 117.

[29] Ernest Belfort Bax, Victor Dave, and William Morris, *A Short Account of the Commune of Paris* (London, 1886), pp. 59, 79.

[30] For the initial celebration, see *General Council Minutes*, vol. V, p. 414. For celebrations in the following decades, see the printed announcements in IISG, Nettlau Collection, Social Democratic Federation files, folders 1615, 1616, and 1618. The citation is from an announcement in folder 1616.

socialist groups in shared international ceremonies. Prince Kropot-
kin joined Hyndman and Annie Besant for the Social Democratic
Federation's celebration of the nineteenth anniversary of the Commune; the twenty-second anniversary saw Frederick Engels together
with Keir Hardie, diverse Fabians, and members of the Independent
Labour Party.[31] No less significantly, these anniversary celebrations
– in sharp contrast to Chartist commemorations of the French
revolution of 1848 – succeeded both in eliciting the participation of
advanced liberals and in securing the use of liberal venues for
socialist celebrations. When the Social Democratic Federation sponsored a course of lectures on the French revolutionary tradition in
1890, Hyndman lectured on the Paris Commune, and the new liberal
Graham Wallas expatiated upon the significance of the February
revolution of 1848.[32] South Place Chapel, the preserve of Unitarian
nationalists in the mid-Victorian era, now emerged as a popular
location for Commune celebrations, 'to commemorate the glorious
struggle then made to emancipate the workers from the tyranny
and oppression of the landlord and capitalist class'.[33] Without
erasing the lines that divided socialists from radical liberals, these
rituals clearly acted to blur the perception of such differences. 'We
had a splendid meeting to celebrate the Commune', John Bruce
Glasier wrote to a friend in 1892. 'The large Hall of the Liberal
Association was filled about 300 being present: the SDF holding
another commemoration at the same time ... After the meeting,
we had a dance – confined to avowed socialists which went off
brilliantly.'[34]

The Labour party that emerged from these radical traditions
rightly traces its lineage to democratic conceptions of government
and society that owe as much to the nation-state as they do to class.

---

[31] Printed notices of Commune celebrations in IISG, Nettlau Collection, Social
Democratic Federation files, folders 1615 and 1618.

[32] Printed announcement of 'A Course of Three Lectures on Three Revolutionary
Epochs of French History' [1890], IISG, Nettlau Collection, Social Democratic
Federation files, folder 1615.

[33] Printed announcement of Commune celebration, 1887, IISG, Nettlau Collection,
Socialist League file, folder 1607. South Place Chapel's visitors' book for this
period testifies to the institution's new spirit of liberal accommodation: it contains
the signatures of Henry Fawcett, Auberon Herbert, John Morley, Frederic
Harrison, E.S. Beesly, F.A. Maxse, Joseph Cowen, Henry George, and William
Morris. See Book of Autographs, South Place Ethical Society, London.

[34] J. Bruce Glasier to James Brown, 21 March 1892, University of Liverpool Library,
John Bruce and Katherine Glasier Papers, I.1.1892/6.

Its centenary edition of the *Communist Manifesto* locates the origins of Labour politics in the patriotic efforts of the Levellers, the Chartists, and the Christian Socialists,[35] a line of descent repeatedly invoked in twentieth-century socialist polemic. 'What is important about the English Revolution', Eric Heffer argued as recently as 1980 in introducing a new edition of Eduard Bernstein's *Cromwell and Communism*, 'is that before Marx ... an English text on socialist thought was clearly to be seen.' 'Socialism in Britain is not a foreign import', he proclaimed. 'It is inherently British, in reality as British as the Union Jack or the hymn "Abide with Me".'[36] The historical relationship between the development of socialism and these early radical phenomena was of course contingent rather than inherent or self-evident. As the dominant trends within mid-Victorian bourgeois radicalism made abundantly evident, seventeenth-century patriotic traditions were as easily used in the nineteenth century as instruments of classical liberal economics as they were as agents of social democratic reform. The truth encapsulated within socialists' fictional radical genealogies derives from the success with which Chartists and their followers impressed their own distinctive marks upon the template of the English revolutionary tradition. Accepting the fundamental legitimacy of parliamentary structures as a given, these radical reformers sought to transform the character of social and economic life through the rule of law. Viewed from the perspective of classical Marxism, their efforts were tokens of liberalization; viewed from the perspective of classical liberalism, their achievements were rank communism.

The constraints imposed upon the English radical tradition by its patriotic heritage were not insignificant. As historians of English working-class culture have repeatedly argued, a commitment to the received institutions and practices of the state limited workers' ability to conceptualize both political and economic alternatives to the status quo.[37] Their preoccupation with 'Old Corruption' further limited the scope of their radical vision. A fundamental conviction, shared by middle- and working-class radicals alike, that the evils of

---

[35] Harold J. Laski (ed.), *Communist Manifesto: Socialist Landmark* (London, 1948), p. 6.

[36] Eric Heffer (ed.), *Cromwell and Communism: Socialism and Democracy in the Great English Revolution* (London, 1980), foreword.

[37] See above, pp. 5, 50, and McKibbin, 'Why Was There No Marxism?', esp. pp. 16–26.

the age were best attributed to the perversion of established government structures clearly impeded radicals' willingness to elaborate or entertain sustained critiques of industrial capitalism. Although the late Chartists generated a rich and diverse body of polemic in opposition to the liberal economic tenets that dominated the political discourse of their age, they lacked an overarching economic ideology of their own that lay outside their understanding of the nation-state. They thus lacked, like later liberals disillusioned by classical economics, a coherent programme beyond the extension of the suffrage. If Victorian radicals' successive efforts to achieve democratic reform obscured the perception of this liability in their own time, the history of English socialism in the twentieth century has made it conspicuously evident.

But although working-class radicals failed to elaborate a consistent theory of economic exploitation, the history of mid-Victorian radicalism was centrally informed by the perception of class relations. Class was clearly not the sole category by which members of the upper orders interpreted the experience of Victorian workers. Nor was class the only perspective from which workers sought to understand themselves. Rather, English workers interpreted their lives within a variety of parameters – as representatives of an international brotherhood of labour, as constituents of 'the people', as men and women, and as members of a nation with a distinctive radical history of birthrights and freedoms.[38] A conviction that the labouring population shared a fundamental class outlook was nonetheless a commonplace of Victorian public opinion. This pervasive belief was not least among the achievements of working-class radical agitation after 1848. For while the late Chartists and their successors failed to articulate an incisive critique of capitalism, they succeeded in convincing many observers that even their most patriotic agitations embodied a powerful working-class antipathy to liberal economics. Labour historians who question the extent of the working-class contribution to the formation of the welfare state have underlined the impediments that limited workers' acceptance of social welfare schemes, notably their antagonism to bureaucratic officialdom and increased taxation. But the same historians note that by the later nineteenth century, middle- and upper-class politicians believed the welfare state to be, in Sidney Webb's phrase, the

---

[38] Joyce, *Visions of the People*, details these myriad identities with particular force.

'economic obverse of democracy'.[39] The working-class radical leaders who sustained popular protest after Chartism laboured to construct precisely this interpretation of the fundamental unity of the social, economic, and political spheres.

The full force of this challenge to the Victorian liberal order is apparent only if one attends at once to the nationalist and the internationalist themes of working-class radical argument. The genesis of radicals' patriotic identities lay in the seventeenth-century revolutions. They thus anticipated the development of continental nationalism, and preceded the development of class consciousness. The nineteenth century saw these received conceptions of nationhood evolve within a broader European context, as English radicals came to identify their revolutionary traditions with struggles for independence waged in Hungary, Italy, Poland, and France. In extending their own national consciousness to encompass the aspirations of these continental peoples, English radicals articulated internationalist conceptions that contained both nationalist and class sentiments. The interplay of these themes, derided by contemporary polemicists and ignored by subsequent historians, structured popular politics in the aftermath of the Chartist movement, altered the course of Victorian liberalism, and informed the evolution of organized socialism in England.

Marx recognized the primacy of horizontal divisions within industrial society, divisions that united the workers and the bourgeoisie of England more closely with corresponding classes on the continent than with each other. Contemporary liberal theorists reversed this schema, advancing the vertical integration of the nation-state as an alternative to international working-class solidarity. Neither model adequately describes the peculiar blend of agitation and acquiescence that characterized radical culture in mid-Victorian England, for class and national affinities operate concurrently in historical experience. In nineteenth-century England, the antagonism of their relationship was not axiomatic. In the popular movements of the day, labour leaders wilfully deployed the guise of liberal nationalism to promote systems of political economy closely associated in the public mind with a conscious working class. They

---

[39] Webb is cited by José Harris, 'Did Workers Want the Welfare State?: G.D.H. Cole's Survey of 1942', in Jay Winter (ed.), *The Working Class in Modern British History* (Cambridge, 1983), pp. 200–14, citation from p. 200, which also provides a survey of the debate on workers and the welfare state.

thereby laid the foundations of social democracy in contemporary Britain. To describe this complex series of negotiations as an anomaly, to dismiss it as false consciousness, is to deny the reality and logic of a variety of historical experience that reaches, through radical nationalism and internationalism in England, from the Reformation to the present.

Bibliography

I MANUSCRIPT SOURCES

Great Britain

Bedlay Castle, Chryston, by Glasgow
  John McAdam Papers
Birmingham Reference Library
  George Dawson Collection
  William Lovett Collection
  Joshua Toulmin Smith Collection
Bishopsgate Institute, London
  Charles Bradlaugh Collection
  Thomas Cooper Collection
  George Jacob Holyoake Collection
  George Howell Collection
Bodleian Library, Oxford
  James Bryce MS and Uncatalogued Papers
  John Johnson Collection
  J.E. Thorold Rogers Papers
Bradford Central Library
  Bradford Freehold Land Society Plan (1852)
British Library, London
  Karl Blind Papers
  John Bright Papers
  Richard Cobden Papers
  Sir Charles Dilke Papers
  Leigh Hunt Papers
  Harriet Martineau Papers
  Francis Place Collection
  Joseph Sturge Papers
British Library of Political and Economic Science, London School of
    Economics
  Thomas Allsop Collection
  Frederic Harrison Collection
  John Stuart Mill–Harriet Taylor Collection
  Henry Solly Collection
  Webb Trade Union Collection

Cambridge University Library
  John Malcolm Forbes Ludlow Correspondence and Papers
Churchill College Archives, Cambridge
  Dilke Family Papers
Girton College Archives, Cambridge
  Bessie Rayner Parkes Papers
Lancashire Record Office, Preston
  Burnley Lodge Operative Joiners and Carpenters Minute Book, 1850–73
Liverpool City Library, Archives Division
  George Melly Papers
Manchester Central Reference Library, Archives Division
  Richard Cobden Papers
  Ernest Jones: Letters to A.B. Wakefield relating to Ernest Jones, 1886–91
  Ernest Jones: Scrapbook of Newspaper Cuttings on Ernest Jones
  Manchester and Salford Equitable Co-operative Society Minute and
    Attendance Book, 1859–62
  J.B. Smith Papers
  George Wilson Papers
Manchester Co-operative Union Library
  George Jacob Holyoake Collection
  Robert Owen Collection
Modern Records Centre, University of Warwick
  Amalgamated Society of Carpenters and Joiners, Financial Reports and
    Minutes
  Friendly Society of Ironfounders, Minute Books and Monthly Reports
  London Society of Compositors, Quarterly Reports
National Labour History Museum and Labour Party Archives, Manchester
  James Bronterre O'Brien Papers
  Wolverhampton Tin Plate Workers' Society, Minute Book, 1867–84
Public Record Office, Kew
  Foreign Office Papers FO 27/1094
                         FO 519/172
                         FO 519/177
  Home Office Papers HO 45/2410 A–B
                      HO 45/4085H
                      HO 45/4547A
                      HO 45/5128
                      HO 45/6188
                      HO 45/6794
                      HO 45/7691
                      HO 45/7854
  Metropolitan Police Papers MEPO 2/43
                              MEPO 2/62
                              MEPO 2/68
Sheffield City Archives
  Robert Leader Collection
  Saw Makers' Protection Society Minute Book, 1860–96
  H.J. Wilson Collection

South Place Ethical Society, London
  Book of Autographs
  Minute Book of South Place Chapel, 1852–62
  Music Committee Book, 1878–89
Tyne and Wear Archives Department, Newcastle
  Joseph Cowen Jr Collection
University College, London
  E.S. Beesly Papers
  John Bright Papers, Ogden MS 65
  Brougham Collection
  Edwin Chadwick Collection
  Francis Newman Papers
University of Liverpool Archives
  John Bruce and Katherine Glasier Papers
  Rathbone Family Papers
University of London Library
  Herbert Spencer Collection
University of Newcastle upon Tyne Special Collections
  Manuscript Album
  G.O. Trevelyan Papers
University of Sheffield Library
  A.J. Mundella Papers
West Sussex Record Office, Chichester
  Richard Cobden Papers
  Frederick Augustus Maxse Papers
West Yorkshire Archive Service, Bradford
  Bradford Freehold Land Society, Handbill
  W.E. Forster Correspondence

France

Bibliothèque Historique de la Ville de Paris
  Papiers Ledru-Rollin

Italy

Istituto Giangiacomo Feltrinelli, Milan
  William James Linton Papers
Istituto per la Storica del Risorgimento, Rome
  Archivio Jessie White Mario

The Netherlands

Internationaal Instituut voor Sociale Geschiedenis, Amsterdam
  Eng. 2 File (Correspondence of Ernest Jones)
  Hermann Jung Collection
  Marx–Engels Collection

Max Nettlau Collection
Pankhurst Family Collection

II NEWSPAPERS AND PERIODICALS

Beacon: A Journal of Politics and Literature
Bee-Hive: And Trades', Friendly Society, and Co-operative Journal
Birmingham Daily Post
The Birmingham Journal and Commercial Advertiser
Birmingham Mercury
Bolton Evening News
Bookbinders Trade Circular
British Miner and General Newsman: A Publication Devoted to the Interests of the Working Miners of the United Kingdom
Cabinet Newspaper: The Union of Classes and the Liberty of Man
Cause of the People: A Political History of Nine Weeks
Christian Socialist
Commonwealth: The Organ of the Reform Movement
Cooper's Journal: Or, Unfettered Thinker and Plain Speaker for Truth, Freedom, and Progress
Daily News
Democrat and Labour Advocate: The Rights of Labour
Democratic Review of British and Foreign Politics, History, and Literature
Demokrata Polski
Douglas Jerrold's Weekly Newspaper
Eastern Post
Edinburgh Review
Eliza Cook's Journal
English Republic: God and the People
Examiner
Fortnightly Review
Freethinker's Magazine: And Review of Theology, Politics and Literature
Friend of the People: Equality, Liberty, Fraternity
Glasgow Sentinel
L'Homme: Journal de la Démocratie Universelle
Howitt's Journal: Of Literature and Popular Progress
Illustrated London News
Investigator: A Journal of Secularism
Irish Felon
Irish Tribune
Jerrold's Weekly News: And Financial Economist
Labour League: Or, Journal of the National Association of United Trades
Leader
Liverpool Mercury
London News
Louis Blanc's Monthly Review: The New World of Politics, Arts, Literature, and Sciences

Manchester Examiner and Times (subsequently *Manchester Weekly Examiner and Times*, *Manchester Weekly Times and Examiner*)
The Miner and Workman's Advocate
Monthly Record of the Society of the Friends of Italy
Morning Chronicle
National Instructor
The National Reformer
Newcastle Chronicle
Newcastle Weekly Chronicle
Nonconformist
Northern Star
Northern Tribune: A Periodical for the People
Notes to the People
Nottingham and Midland Counties Daily Express
Le Nouveau Monde: Journal Historique et Politique
The Operative Bricklayers' Society Trade Circular and General Reporter
The Penny Bee-Hive: The People's Paper
People's Paper: The Champion of Political Justice and Universal Right
Politics for the People
The Potteries Examiner
Power of the Pence
Preston Chronicle
Le Proscrit: Journal de la République Universelle
The Puppet Show
The Reasoner
Red Republican: Equality, Liberty, Fraternity
The Republican: A Magazine Advocating the Sovereignty of the People
La République Exilée: Revue Démocratique
Reynolds's Political Instructor
Reynolds's Weekly Newspaper (subsequently *Reynolds's Newspaper*)
Saturday Review
Secular World: And Social Economist
Sheffield and Rotherham Independent
Sheffield Free Press
Social Reformer
Spirit of the Age: Journal of Political Education and Industrial Progress
Spirit of the Times: Or Social Reformer
Star of Freedom: Journal of Political Progress, Trades' Record and Co-operative Chronicle
Stockport Advertiser
Times
Vanguard: A Weekly Journal of Politics, Biography, and General Literature
The Voice of the People: A Supplement to All Newspapers
La Voix du Proscrit: Organe de la République Universelle
Westminster Review
The Working Man: A Political and Social Advocate of the Rights of Labour, and a Monthly Record of Co-operative Progress

The Working Man's Friend and Family Instructor
Workman's Advocate

III PUBLISHED DIARIES, LETTERS, AND MEMOIRS

Adams, W.E. *Memoirs of a Social Atom*. 2 vols. London, 1903.
Arch, Joseph. *From Ploughtail to Parliament: An Autobiography*. London, 1898; London, 1986.
Bamford, Samuel. *Early Days*. London, 1849.
　Passages in the Life of a Radical. 2 vols. London, 1844.
Bax, Ernest Belfort. *Reminiscences and Reflections of a Mid and Late Victorian*. London, 1918.
Black, Frank G., and Black, R.M., eds. *The Harney Papers*. Assen, 1969.
Bright, John. *The Diaries of John Bright*. Edited by R.A.J. Walling. New York, 1931.
Buckle, George E., ed. *The Letters of Queen Victoria*. 2nd ser., 3 vols. New York, 1926.
Burn, James Dawson. *Autobiography of a Beggar Boy*. London, 1855.
Burnett, John, ed. *Annals of Labour: Autobiographies of British Working-Class People 1820–1920*. Bloomington, 1974.
Butler, Josephine. *Josephine E. Butler: An Autobiographical Memoir*. Edited by G.W. Johnson and L.A. Johnson. London, 1928.
Carpenter, Edward. *My Days and Dreams*. London, 1916.
Chancellor, Valerie E., ed. *Master and Artisan in Victorian England: The Diary of William Andrews and the Autobiography of Joseph Gutteridge*. New York, 1969.
Conway, Moncure Daniel. *Autobiography: Memoirs and Experiences*. 2 vols. Boston, 1904.
Evans, Howard. *Radical Fights of Forty Years*. London, 1913.
Faure, Philippe. *Journal d'un combattant de février*. Jersey, 1859.
Fawcett, Millicent Garrett. *What I Remember*. London, 1924.
Frost, Thomas. *Forty Years' Recollections: Literary and Political*. London, 1880.
Gladstone, William. *The Gladstone Diaries: 1861–1868*. Edited by H.C.G. Matthew. Oxford, 1978.
Harrison, Frederic. *Autobiographic Memoirs*. 2 vols. London, 1911.
Holyoake, George Jacob. *Sixty Years of an Agitator's Life*. 2 vols. London, 1893.
How I Became a Socialist: A Series of Biographical Sketches. London, n.d.
Howitt, Mary. *Mary Howitt: An Autobiography*. Edited by Margaret Howitt. 2 vols. London, 1889.
Hyndman, H.M. *Records of an Adventurous Life*. London, 1911.
Jevons, W. Stanley. *Letters and Journal of W. Stanley Jevons*. Edited by Harriet A. Jevons. London, 1886.
King, Mrs Hamilton. *Letters and Recollections of Mazzini*. London, 1912.
Leno, John Bedford. *The Aftermath: With Autobiography of the Author*. London, 1892.

Lessner, Frederick. *Sixty Years in the Social-Democratic Movement: Before 1848 and After, Recollections of an Old Communist.* London, 1907.

Linton, William James. *European Republicans: Recollections of Mazzini and His Friends.* London, 1893.

  Threescore and Ten Years: 1820 to 1890 Recollections. New York, 1894.

McAdam, John. *The Autobiography of John McAdam (1806–1883): With Selected Letters.* Edited by Janet Fyfe. Edinburgh, 1980.

McCarthy, Justin. *Reminiscences.* 2 vols. London, 1899.

Mazzini, Giuseppe. *Mazzini's Letters to an English Family: 1844–1872.* Edited by E.F. Richards. 3 vols. London, 1920–2.

Meysenbug, Malwida von. *Memoiren einer Idealisten.* 2 vols. Stuttgart, 1922.

Morley, John. *Recollections.* 2 vols. London, 1917.

Place, Francis. *The Autobiography of Francis Place.* Edited by Mary Thrale. Cambridge, 1972.

Schwabe, Julia Salis, ed. *Reminiscences of Richard Cobden.* London, 1895.

Senior, Nassau W. *Journals Kept in France and Italy from 1848 to 1852: With a Sketch of the Revolution of 1848.* Edited by M.C.M. Simpson. 2 vols. London, 1871.

Smith, Charles Manby. *The Working Man's Way in the World.* London, 1857.

Smith, Goldwin. *Reminiscences.* Edited by Arnold Haultain. New York, 1910.

Solly, Henry. *These Eighty Years: Or, The Story of an Unfinished Life.* 2 vols. London, 1893.

Soutter, Francis. *Recollections of a Labour Pioneer.* London, 1922.

Tuchkova-Ogareva, N.A. *Vospominaniia [Reminiscences].* Edited by V.A. Putintseva. Leningrad, 1929.

Vincent, David, ed. *Testaments of Radicalism: Memoirs of Working-Class Politicians 1790–1885.* London, 1977.

IV PAMPHLETS, SPEECHES, AND WORKS

Anon. *'What Is the Use of Kings?' and How the Question Was Answered: A National Ballad for the Times: Together with 'Chelsea Buns', or, The Story of Young Carlo Dolci: A Political Satire: and 'Chant de la Commune'.* London, 1872.

Bax, Ernest Belfort, Dave, Victor, and Morris, William. *A Short Account of the Commune of Paris.* London, 1886.

Beesly, Edward Spencer. 'The History of Republicanism in France'. *Fortnightly Review*, vol. 16 (October 1874), pp. 471–94.

  The Social Future of the Working Class: A Lecture Delivered to a Meeting of Trades' Unionists, May 7, 1868. London, 1869.

  A Word for France: Addressed to the Workmen of London. London, 1870.

Bentham, Jeremy. 'Principles of International Law'. In *The Works of Jeremy Bentham*, vol. II, pp. 535–60. Edited by John Bowring. Edinburgh, 1843.

Blanc, Louis. *Letters on England.* 2 vols. London, 1866.

Observations on the Recent Manifesto of Kossuth, Ledru-Rollin, and Mazzini. London, 1855.

Blatchford, Robert. *Merrie England.* London, 1893.

Bradlaugh, Charles. *The Land Question: Large Estates Inimical to the Welfare of the People.* London, 1870.

Bright, John. *Speeches on Parliamentary Reform, &c., by John Bright, Esq., M.P.* Manchester, [1866].

Speeches on Questions of Public Policy by the Right Honourable John Bright, M.P. Edited by James E. Thorold Rogers. London, 1880.

Buxton, John. *English Aid to Garibaldi, On His Invasion of the Sicilies: Is It Lawful and Just? Correspondence between the Manchester Foreign Affairs Association and Mark Philips, Esq. and also between the Former and R.P. Greg.* Manchester, [1860].

Cairnes, J.E. 'Political Economy and Laissez-Faire'. *Fortnightly Review,* vol. 10 (July 1871), pp. 80–97.

Some Leading Principles of Political Economy Newly Expounded. New York, 1875.

Cattell, Charles C. *The Land: How to Make It Feed the People and Pay the Taxes. Second Edition with Reply to the Rt. Hon. John Bright, M.P.* Birmingham, [1879].

Chamberlain, Joseph, 'The Next Page of the Liberal Programme'. *Fortnightly Review,* vol. 16 (October 1874), pp. 405–29.

Cliffe Leslie, J.E. 'The Political Economy of Adam Smith'. *Fortnightly Review,* vol. 8 (October 1870), pp. 549–63.

Cobden, Richard. *Speeches on Questions of Public Policy by Richard Cobden, M.P.* Edited by John Bright and James E. Thorold Rogers. London, 1903.

Speeches of Richard Cobden, Esq., M.P., on Peace, Financial Reform, and Other Subjects: Delivered during 1849. London, 1849.

Cooper, Jerym. *Three Letters to the Conservatives of England, and through Them to the People of England, on the Subject of Garibaldi and Revolution.* London, 1864.

Cooper, Thomas. *Eight Letters to the Young Men of the Working Classes.* London, 1850.

Cromwell, Oliver. *The Letters and Speeches of Oliver Cromwell, with Elucidations by Thomas Carlyle.* Edited by Sophia C. Lomas. 3 vols. London, 1904.

Dalberg-Acton, John Emerich Edward. 'Nationality'. In his *Essays on Freedom,* pp. 166–95. Edited by Gertrude Himmelfarb. Boston, 1948.

The Democratic and Social Almanac for 1850. London, 1849.

Dilke, Sir Charles. *Sir Charles Dilke on the Cost of the Crown.* London, 1871.

Speeches: By Sir Charles Wentworth Dilke: March, 1871 to March, 1872. London, 1872.

Fawcett, Henry. *The Economic Position of the British Labourer.* London, 1865.

Manual of Political Economy. 2nd edn. London, 1865.

Fawcett, Henry, and Millicent. *Essays and Lectures on Social and Political Subjects*. London, 1872.

Fox, W.J. *Lectures: Addressed Chiefly to the Working Classes*. 4 vols. London, 1846–9.

The General Council of the First International: 1864–1872. 5 vols. Moscow, 1964.

Haller, William, ed. *Tracts on Liberty in the Puritan Revolution 1638–1647*. 3 vols. New York, 1934.

Hansard's Parliamentary Debates, 3rd ser.

Harrison, Frederic. 'The Fall of the Commune'. *Fortnightly Review*, vol. 10 (August 1871), pp. 129–55.

'The Iron Masters' Trade Union'. *Fortnightly Review*, vol. 1 (1865), pp. 96–116.

'The Limits of Political Economy'. *Fortnightly Review*, vol. 1 (1865), pp. 356–76.

National and Social Problems. London, 1908.

The Political Function of the Working Classes: A Lecture Delivered at the Cleveland Street Institution, on March 25, 1868. London, 1868.

Harrison, Royden, ed. *The English Defence of the Commune: 1871*. London, 1971.

Henderson, W., ed. *Victorian Street Ballads: A Selection of Popular Ballads Sold in the Street in the Nineteenth Century*. London, 1937.

Herzen, Alexander. *Desiatiletie Volnoi Russkoi Tipografii v Londone: 1853–1863 [Ten Years of the Free Russian Press in London: 1853–1863]*. London, 1863.

L'Etoile Polaire sur la mort de Stanislaus Worcell. London, 1857.

Holyoake, George Jacob. *A History of the Fleet Street House*. London, 1856.

The Liberal Situation: Necessity for a Qualified Franchise, A Letter to Joseph Cowen, Jun. London, 1865.

The Life and Character of Henry Hetherington. London, 1849.

Life of Dr. Bernard: With Portrait and Judgment of the Press on His Trial. London, 1858.

What May England Do for Italy? London, 1861.

Working-Class Representation: Its Conditions and Consequences. London, 1868.

The Workman and the Suffrage: Letters to the Right Honourable Lord John Russell, M.P. and to the 'Daily News'. London, 1859.

Howell, George. 'The History of the International Association'. *The Nineteenth Century*, vol. 4 (July 1878), pp. 19–39.

Hume, David. *The History of England*. 6 vols. London, 1778.

Jackdaw. *The Dilkiad: Or the Dream of Dilke: An Anti-Republican Lay*. London, 1872.

Jevons, William Stanley. *The Theory of Political Economy*. London, 1871.

Jones, Ernest. *The Battle-Day: And Other Poems*. London, 1855.

Evenings with the People. London, 1856–7.

Kerns, Thomas. *Chartist Sunday Meetings: Correspondence between the*

Rev. Thomas Kerns, M.D., Incumbent of Brightside, and the Chartists of Sheffield. Sheffield, [1848].

Kingsley, Charles. *Alton Locke, Tailor and Poet: An Autobiography.* London, 1850.

Kossuth, Louis. *Kossuth: His Speeches in England.* London, 1852.

Kossuth, Louis, Ledru-Rollin, Alexandre, and Mazzini, Giuseppe. *Manifesto of the Republican Party.* London, 1855.

Labour Party. 'The Labour Party and the Books that Helped Make It', *Review of Reviews* (June 1906), pp. 568–82.

Laski, Harold J., ed. *Communist Manifesto: Socialist Landmark.* London, 1948.

Linton, William James. *James Watson: A Memoir.* New Haven, 1879.

'Prose and Verse: Written and Published in the Course of Fifty Years'. 20 vols. A collection of Linton's published writings in the British Library, press mark 12269. g. 11.

Literary Association of the Friends of Poland. *Report of the Twenty-Third Annual Meeting of the Literary Association of the Friends of Poland.* London, 1855.

Lovett, William. *Justice Safer than Expediency: An Appeal to the Middle Classes on the Question of the Suffrage.* London, 1848.

Ludlow, John Malcolm Forbes. *Labour and the Poor.* 2nd edn. London, 1852.

Ludlow, John Malcolm Forbes, and Jones, Patrick Lloyd. *Progress of the Working Class, 1832–1867.* London, 1867.

Lyly, John. *The Complete Works of John Lyly.* Edited by R. Warrick Bond. 3 vols. Oxford, 1902.

McCarthy, Justin. 'Republicanism in England'. *The Galaxy*, vol. 12 (July 1871), pp. 30–40.

Macaulay, Thomas Babington. *The Works of Lord Macaulay.* 12 vols. London, 1898.

Manning, Henry Edward. *The Visit of Garibaldi to England: A Letter to the Right Honourable Edward Cardwell, M.P.* London, 1864.

Marx, Karl, and Engels, Frederick. *Karl Marx, Frederick Engels: Collected Works.* New York, 1975–.

Maxse, Frederick Augustus. *The Causes of Social Revolt: A Lecture, Delivered in London, Portsmouth, and Greenwich.* London, 1872.

A Plea for Intervention: An Address Delivered by Captain Maxse, R.N. London, 1871.

Mayhew, Henry. *London Labour and the London Poor.* 4 vols. London, 1861–4.

The Unknown Mayhew: Selections from the Morning Chronicle 1849–1850. Edited by E.P. Thompson and Eileen Yeo. Harmondsworth, 1984.

Mazzini, Giuseppe. 'The Commune in Paris'. *Contemporary Review*, vol. 17 (June 1871), pp. 307–18.

M. Mazzini's Lecture, Delivered at the First Conversazione of the Friends of Italy. London, 1852.

The War and the Commune. London, 1871.

334   *Bibliography*

Melly, George. *Self-Help: The Future of the Working Classes*. Liverpool, 1864.

Mill, John Stuart. *The Collected Works of John Stuart Mill*. General editor F.E.L. Priestley. 25 vols. Toronto, 1963–86.

Morley, John. 'England and the War'. *Fortnightly Review*, vol. 8 (October 1870), pp. 479–88.

National Reform Union. *Report of the Great Meeting in Support of Mr. Gladstone's Government and Non-Intervention in the Free Trade Hall*. Manchester, 1871.

Neale, Edward Vansittart. *May I Not Do What I Will with My Own?: Considerations on the Present Contest between the Operative Engineers and Their Employers*. London, 1852.

Newman, Francis W. *An Appeal to the Middle Classes: On the Urgent Necessity of Numerous Radical Reforms, Financial and Organic*. London, 1848.

Political Economy Club. *Political Economy Club Centenary Volume*. London, 1921.

Price, Richard. *A Discourse on the Love of Our Country, Delivered on Nov. 4 1789, At the Meeting House in the Old Jewry, to the Society for Commemorating the Revolution in Great Britain*. London, 1790.

Pyat, Félix, Besson, A., and Talandier, Alexandre. *Letter to the Parliament and the Press*. London, 1858.

Rochefort, Henri. 'The Revolution of September, 1870'. *Fortnightly Review*, vol. 16 (August 1874), pp. 216–25.

Rogers, James E. Thorold. *Cobden and Modern Political Opinion*. London, 1873.

Sandwith, Humphrey. 'Earl Russell, the Commune, and Christianity'. *Fortnightly Review*, vol. 10 (July 1871), pp. 35–44.

A Short History of the South Place Ethical Society and an Urgent Appeal. London, 1927.

Smiles, Samuel. *Self-Help: With Illustrations of Character and Conduct*. 2nd edn. Boston, 1866.

Smith, Joshua Toulmin. *Parallels between the Constitution and Constitutional History of England and Hungary*. London, 1849.

Spencer, Herbert. *The Man versus the State*. London, 1894.
   The Works of Herbert Spencer. 20 vols. Osnabrück, 1966.

Stansfeld, James. *The Italian Movement and Italian Parties*. London, 1862.

Taylor, Peter Alfred. *Burning a Theological Book: Libraries of Mechanics' Institutes: Should They Be Free, or Subject to Theological Censorship?* London, 1858.

Thornton, William Thomas. *On Labour: Its Wrongful Claims and Rightful Dues, Its Actual Present and Possible Future*. 2nd edn. London, 1870.

Venturi, Emilie A. *Joseph Mazzini: A Memoir*. London, 1875.
   'Religious Republicanism: Joseph Mazzini as a Religious Teacher'. *Contemporary Review*, vol. 18 (September 1871), pp. 189–211.

Wright, Thomas. *Our New Masters*. London, 1873.
   Some Habits and Customs of the Working Classes: By a Journeyman Engineer. London, 1867.

V PUBLISHED SECONDARY WORKS

Adamson, J.S.A. 'Oliver Cromwell and the Long Parliament'. In *Oliver Cromwell and the English Revolution*, pp. 88–98. Edited by John Morrill. New York, 1990.

Altick, Richard. *The English Common Reader: A Social History of the Mass Reading Public, 1800–1900*. Chicago, 1957.

Anderson, Benedict. *Imagined Communities: Reflections on the Origins and Spread of Nationalism*. London, 1983.

Anderson, Olive. 'The Janus Face of Mid-Nineteenth-Century English Radicalism: The Administrative Reform Association of 1855'. *Victorian Studies*, vol. 8 (March 1965), pp. 231–70.

A Liberal State at War: English Politics and Economics during the Crimean War. London, 1967.

Anderson, Perry. *Arguments within English Marxism*. London, 1980.

'Components of the National Culture'. *New Left Review*, no. 50 (July–August 1968), pp. 3–57.

'Origins of the Present Crisis'. *New Left Review*, no. 23 (January–February 1964), pp. 26–51.

Ashcraft, Richard. *Revolution Politics and Locke's Two Treatises of Government*. Princeton, 1986.

Ashton, Robert. 'Tradition and Innovation in the Great Rebellion'. In *Three British Revolutions: 1641, 1688, 1776*, pp. 208–23. Edited by J.G.A. Pocock. Princeton, 1980.

Ashton, Rosemary. *Little Germany: Exile and Asylum in Victorian England*. Oxford, 1986.

Aspinall, Arthur. *Politics and the Press, c. 1780–1850*. London, 1949.

Backstrom, Philip N. 'The Practical Side of Christian Socialism in Victorian England'. *Victorian Studies*, vol. 6 (June 1963), pp. 304–24.

Bailey, Peter. ' "Will the Real Bill Banks Please Stand Up?": Towards a Role Analysis of Mid-Victorian Working-Class Respectability'. *Journal of Social History*, vol. 12 (Spring 1970), pp. 336–53.

Banks, Olive. *The Biographical Dictionary of Modern British Feminists: Volume One, 1800–1930*. Brighton, 1985.

Barnard, F.M. 'National Culture and Political Legitimacy: Herder and Rousseau'. *Journal of the History of Ideas*, vol. 44 (April–June 1983), pp. 231–53.

Barnsby, George J. *Birmingham Working People: A History of the Labour Movement in Birmingham 1650–1914*. Wolverhampton, 1989.

Bauckham, Richard. *Tudor Apocalypse*. Appleford, 1978.

Baylen, Joseph O., and Gossman, Norbert J., eds. *Biographical Dictionary of Modern British Radicals*. 2 vols. Brighton, 1984.

Beales, Derek. 'Garibaldi in England: The Politics of Enthusiasm'. In *Society and Politics in the Age of the Risorgimento*, pp. 184–216. Edited by John A. Davis and Paul Ginsborg. Cambridge, 1991.

Beer, Max. *A History of British Socialism*. 2 vols. London, 1921.

Behagg, Clive. 'Myths of Cohesion: Capital and Compromise in the

Historiography of Nineteenth-Century Birmingham'. *Social History*, vol. 11 (October 1986), pp. 375–84.

Politics and Production in the Early Nineteenth Century. London, 1990.

Belchem, John. 'Chartism and the Trades, 1848–1850'. *English Historical Review*, vol. 98 (July 1983), pp. 558–87.

'1848: Feargus O'Connor and the Collapse of the Mass Platform'. In *The Chartist Experience: Studies in Working-Class Radicalism and Culture, 1830–1860*, pp. 269–310. Edited by James A. Epstein and Dorothy Thompson. London, 1982.

'Henry Hunt and the Evolution of the Mass Platform'. *English Historical Review*, vol. 93 (October 1978), pp. 739–73.

Industrialization and the Working Class: The English Experience, 1750–1900. Aldershot, 1990.

'Orator' Hunt: Henry Hunt and English Working-Class Radicalism. Oxford, 1985.

Bell, Aldon D. 'Administration and Finance of the Reform League, 1865–67'. *International Review of Social History*, vol. 10, pt 3 (1965), pp. 385–409.

Bellamy, Joyce M., and Saville, John, eds. *The Dictionary of Labour Biography*. London, 1972–.

Bellamy, Richard, ed. *Victorian Liberalism: Nineteenth-Century Political Thought and Practice*. London, 1990.

Bentley, Michael. *The Climax of Liberal Politics: British Liberalism in Theory and Practice 1868–1918*. London, 1987.

Berenson, Edward. *Populist Religion and Left-Wing Politics in France, 1830–1852*. Princeton, 1984.

Berg, Maxine. *The Machinery Question and the Making of Political Economy 1815–1848*. Cambridge, 1980.

Berlin, Isaiah. 'Two Concepts of Liberty'. In his *Four Essays on Liberty*, pp. 118–72. Oxford, 1969.

Best, Geoffrey. *Honour among Men and Nations: Transformations of an Idea*. Toronto, 1982.

Bestor, Arthur E., Jr. 'The Evolution of the Socialist Vocabulary'. *Journal of the History of Ideas*, vol. 9 (June 1948), pp. 259–302.

Biagini, Eugenio. 'British Trade Unions and Popular Political Economy, 1860–1880'. *Historical Journal*, vol. 30 (December 1987), pp. 811–40.

Bloom, Solomon F. *The World of Nations: A Study of the National Implications in the Work of Karl Marx*. New York, 1941.

Borochov, Ber. *Nationalism and the Class Struggle: A Marxian Approach to the Jewish Problem*. Edited by Abraham G. Duker. Westport, Conn., 1972.

Boyle, Thomas. *Black Swine in the Sewers of Hampstead: Beneath the Surface of Victorian Sensationalism*. New York, 1989.

Braddick, Michael. 'State Formation and Social Change in Early Modern England: A Problem Stated and Approaches Suggested'. *Social History*, vol. 16 (January 1991), pp. 1–17.

Bradley, James E. 'Whigs and Nonconformists: "Slumbering Radicalism" in English Politics, 1739–89'. *Eighteenth Century Studies*, vol. 9 (1975), pp. 1–27.

Brandenburg, Alexander. 'Der Kommunistische Arbeiterbildungsverein in London'. *International Review of Social History*, vol. 24 (1979), pp. 341–70.

Braunthal, Julius. *History of the International*. Translated by Henry Collins and Kenneth Mitchell. 3 vols. London, 1966.

Breuilly, John. 'Artisan Economy, Artisan Politics, Artisan Ideology: The Artisan Contribution to the 19th Century Labour Movement'. In *Artisans, Peasants and Proletarians 1760–1860*, pp. 187–225. Edited by Clive Emsley and James Walvin. London, 1985.

Nationalism and the State. Manchester, 1982.

Brewer, John. *Party Ideology and Popular Politics at the Accession of George III*. Cambridge, 1976.

The Sinews of Power: War, Money and the English State, 1688–1783. New York, 1989.

'The Wilkites and the Law, 1763–74: A Study of Radical Notions of Governance'. In *An Ungovernable People: The English and Their Law in the Seventeenth and Eighteenth Centuries*, pp. 128–171. Edited by John Brewer and John Styles. London, 1980.

Briggs, Asa. 'The Language of "Class" in Early Nineteenth-Century England'. In *Essays in Labour History*, pp. 154–72. Edited by Asa Briggs and John Saville. London, 1960.

'Middle-Class Consciousness in English Politics, 1780–1846'. *Past and Present*, no. 9 (April 1956), pp. 65–74.

Bristow, Edward. 'The Liberty and Property Defence League and Individualism'. *Historical Journal*, vol. 18 (December 1975), pp. 761–89.

Brock, Peter. 'The Polish Revolutionary Commune in London'. *Slavonic and East European Review*, vol. 35 (December 1956), pp. 116–28.

'Zeno Świętosławski, A Polish Forerunner of the *Narodniki*'. *American Slavic and East European Review*, vol. 13 (December 1954), pp. 566–87.

Brown, Lucy. 'Chartists and the Anti-Corn Law League'. In *Chartist Studies*, pp. 342–71. Edited by Asa Briggs. London, 1959.

Victorian News and Newspapers. Oxford, 1985.

Burrow, John. *A Liberal Descent: Victorian Historians and the English Past*. Cambridge, 1981.

Calhoun, Craig. *The Question of Class Struggle: Social Foundations of Popular Radicalism during the Industrial Revolution*. Chicago, 1982.

Calman, Alvin. *Ledru-Rollin après 1848 et les proscrits français en Angleterre*. Paris, 1921.

Cameron, Rondo. *A Concise Economic History of the World: From Paleolithic Times to the Present*. New York, 1989.

Campanella, Anthony P. *La Legione Britanica nell' Italia Meridionale con Garibaldi nel 1860*. Palermo, [1964].

Cannadine, David. 'The Context, Performance and Meaning of Ritual: The British Monarchy and the "Invention of Tradition" *c.* 1820–1977'. In

The Invention of Tradition, pp. 101–64. Edited by Eric Hobsbawm and Terence Ranger. Cambridge, 1983.

Chartist Biographies and Autobiographies, London, 1986.

Chase, Malcolm. *'The People's Farm': English Radical Agrarianism 1775–1840*. Oxford, 1988.

Claeys, Gregory. *Citizens and Saints: Politics and Anti-Politics in Early British Socialism*. Cambridge, 1989.

Machinery, Money and the Millennium: From Moral Economy to Socialism 1815–1860. Princeton, 1987.

'Mazzini, Kossuth, and British Radicalism, 1848–1854'. *Journal of British Studies*, vol. 28 (July 1989), pp. 225–61.

'Reciprocal Dependence, Virtue and Progress: Some Sources of Early Socialist Cosmopolitanism and Internationalism in Britain, 1750–1850'. In *Internationalism in the Labour Movement, 1830–1940*, vol. I, pp. 235–58. Edited by Frits van Holthoon and Marcel van der Linden. 2 vols. Leiden, 1988.

Clark, J.C.D. *English Society 1688–1832: Ideology, Social Structure and Political Practice during the Ancien Regime*. Cambridge, 1985.

Clarke, Peter. *Lancashire and the New Liberalism*. Cambridge, 1971.

Liberals and Social Democrats. Cambridge, 1978.

Clements, R.V. 'British Trade Unions and Popular Political Economy, 1850–1875'. *Economic History Review*, 2nd ser., vol. 14 (August 1961), pp. 93–104.

Clifton, Robin. 'The Popular Fear of Catholics during the English Revolution'. *Past and Present*, no. 52 (August 1971), pp. 23–55.

Cohler, Ann. *Rousseau and Nationalism*. New York, 1970.

Coleman, D.C. *Courtaulds: An Economic and Social History*. 3 vols. Oxford, 1969–80.

Colley, Linda. 'The Apotheosis of George III: Loyalty, Royalty and the British Nation 1760–1820'. *Past and Present*, no. 102 (February 1984), pp. 94–129.

In Defiance of Oligarchy: The Tory Party 1716–60. Cambridge, 1982.

'Eighteenth Century English Radicalism before Wilkes'. *Transactions of the Royal Historical Society*, 5th ser., vol. 31 (1981), pp. 1–19.

'Whose Nation?: Class and National Consciousness in Britain 1750–1830'. *Past and Present*, no. 113 (November 1986), pp. 97–117.

Collins, Henry. 'The English Branches of the First International'. In *Essays in Social History*, pp. 242–75. Edited by Asa Briggs and John Saville. London, 1967.

Collins, Henry, and Abramsky, Chimen. *Karl Marx and the British Labour Movement: Years of the First International*. London, 1965.

Collinson, Patrick. *The Birthpangs of Protestant England: Religious and Cultural Change in the Sixteenth and Seventeenth Centuries*. New York, 1988.

'England and International Calvinism 1558–1640'. In *International Calvinism 1541–1715*, pp. 197–223. Edited by Menna Prestwich. Oxford, 1985.

Coltham, Stephen. 'George Potter, the Junta, and the *Bee-Hive*'. *Internation-*

al Review of Social History, vols. 9 and 10 (1964–5), pp. 391–432, 23–65.

Corrigan, Philip, and Sayer, Derek. *The Great Arch: English State Formation as Cultural Revolution*. Oxford, 1985.

Cowling, Maurice. *1867, Disraeli, Gladstone and Revolution: The Passing of the Second Reform Bill*. Cambridge, 1967.

Crafts, N.F.R. *British Economic Growth during the Industrial Revolution*. Oxford, 1985.

Cressy, David. *Bonfires and Bells: National Memory and the Protestant Calendar in Elizabethan and Early Stuart England*. London, 1989.

Crossick, Geoffrey. *An Artisan Elite in Victorian Society: Kentish London 1840–1880*. London, 1978.

Crossick, Geoffrey, and Haupt, Heinz-Gerhard, eds. *Shopkeepers and Master Artisans in Nineteenth-Century Europe*. London, 1984.

Cummings, Ian. *Marx, Engels and the National Movement*. London, 1980.

Cunningham, Hugh. 'The Language of Patriotism, 1750–1914'. *History Workshop Journal*, no. 12 (Autumn 1981), pp. 8–33.

   The Volunteer Force: A Social and Political History, 1859–1908. Hamden, Conn., 1975.

Daniels, Elizabeth Adams. *Jessie White Mario: Risorgimento Revolutionary*. Athens, Ohio, 1972.

Dann, Otto, and Dinwiddy, John, eds. *Nationalism in the Age of the French Revolution*. London, 1988.

D'Arcy, Fergus A. 'Charles Bradlaugh and the English Republican Movement, 1868–1878'. *Historical Journal*, vol. 25 (June 1982), pp. 367–83.

Davidson, J. Morrison. *Eminent Radicals In and Out of Parliament*. London, 1880.

Davis, Horace B. *Nationalism and Socialism: Marxist and Labor Theories of Nationalism to 1917*. New York, 1967.

Davis, Horace B., ed. *The National Question: Selected Writings by Rosa Luxemburg*. New York, 1976.

Davis, John. *Reforming London: The London Government Problem 1855–1900*. Oxford, 1988.

de Bertier de Sauvigny, G. 'Liberalism, Nationalism and Socialism: The Birth of Three Words'. *Review of Politics*, vol. 32 (April 1970), pp. 147–66.

De Kray, Gary Stuart. *A Fractured Society: The Politics of London in the First Age of Party, 1688–1715*. Oxford, 1985.

   'Political Radicalism in London after the Glorious Revolution'. *Journal of Modern History*, vol. 55 (December 1983), pp. 585–617.

Deák, Istvan. *The Lawful Revolution: Louis Kossuth and the Hungarians, 1848–1849*. New York, 1979.

Deane, Seamus. *The French Revolution and Enlightenment in England: 1789–1832*. Cambridge, Mass., 1988.

Dentith, Simon. 'Political Economy, Fiction and the Language of Practical Ideology in Nineteenth-Century England'. *Social History*, vol. 8 (May 1983), pp. 183–99.

Derry, John. 'The Opposition Whigs and the French Revolution'. In *Britain and the French Revolution 1789–1815*, pp. 35–59. Edited by H.T. Dickinson. Basingstoke, 1989.

Deutsch, Karl W. *Nationalism and Social Communication: An Inquiry into the Foundations of Nationality*. London, 1953.

Dewey, Clive S. 'The Rehabilitation of the Peasant Proprietor in Nineteenth-Century Economic Thought'. *History of Political Economy*, vol. 6 (1974), pp. 17–47.

Dickinson, H.T. *Liberty and Property: Political Ideology in Eighteenth-Century Britain*. London, 1977.

Dickinson, H.T., ed. *Britain and the French Revolution 1789–1815*. Basingstoke, 1989.

Dobb, Maurice. *Theories of Value and Distribution since Adam Smith: Ideology and Economic Theory*. Cambridge, 1973.

Dozier, Robert R. *For King, Constitution, and Country: The English Loyalists and the French Revolution*. London, 1983.

Driver, Cecil. *Tory Radical: The Life of Richard Oastler*. New York, 1946.

Edsall, Nicholas C. 'A Failed National Movement: The Parliamentary and Financial Reform Association, 1848–54'. *Bulletin of the Institute of Historical Research*, vol. 49 (May 1976), pp. 108–31.

Richard Cobden: Independent Radical. Cambridge, Mass., 1986.

Eley, Geoff. 'Nationalism and Social History'. *Social History*, vol. 6 (January 1981), pp. 83–107.

Ellegård, Alvar. *The Readership of the Periodical Press in Mid-Victorian Britain*. (Göteborg, 1957).

Elton, G.R. 'English National Selfconsciousness and the Parliament in the Sixteenth Century'. In *Nationalismus in vorindustrieller Zeit*, pp. 73–82. Edited by Otto Dann. Munich, 1986.

The Tudor Revolution in Government: Administrative Changes in the Reign of Henry VIII. Cambridge, 1953.

Emsley, Clive. *British Society and the French Wars, 1793–1815*. London, 1979.

'Nationalist Rhetoric and Nationalist Sentiment in Revolutionary France'. In *Nationalism in the Age of the French Revolution*, pp. 39–52. Edited by Otto Dann and John Dinwiddy. London, 1988.

Epstein, James A. 'The Constitutional Idiom: Radical Reasoning, Rhetoric, and Action in Early Nineteenth-Century England'. *Journal of Social History*, vol. 23 (Spring 1990), pp. 553–74.

'Feargus O'Connor and the *Northern Star*'. *International Review of Social History*, vol. 21 (1976), pp. 51–97.

The Lion of Freedom: Feargus O'Connor and the Chartist Movement, 1832–1842. London, 1982.

'Understanding the Cap of Liberty: Symbolic Practice and Social Conflict in Early Nineteenth-Century England'. *Past and Present*, no. 122 (February 1989), pp. 75–118.

Epstein, James A., and Thompson, Dorothy, eds. *The Chartist Experience: Studies in Working-Class Radicalism and Culture, 1830–60*. London, 1982.

Finer, S.E. 'The Transmission of Benthamite Ideas 1820–50'. In *Studies in the Growth of Nineteenth-Century Government*, pp. 11–32. Edited by Gillian Sutherland. London, 1972.

Finn, Margot C. ' "A Vent Which Has Conveyed Our Principles": English Radical Patriotism in the Aftermath of 1848'. *Journal of Modern History*, vol. 64 (December 1992).

Fisher, Chris. *Custom, Work and Market Capitalism: The Forest of Dean Colliers, 1788–1888*. London, 1981.

Fletcher, Anthony. 'Oliver Cromwell and the Godly Nation'. In *Oliver Cromwell and the English Revolution*, pp. 209–33. Edited by John Morrill. New York, 1990.

Foner, Eric. *Tom Paine and Revolutionary America*. New York, 1976.

Fontana, Biancamaria. *Rethinking the Politics of Commercial Society: The Edinburgh Review 1802–1832*. Cambridge, 1985.

Foster, John. *Class Struggle and the Industrial Revolution: Early Industrial Capitalism in Three English Towns*. 2nd edn. London, 1977.

Fox, Alan. *History and Heritage: The Social Origins of the British Industrial Relations System*. London, 1985.

Frame, Robin. *The Political Development of the British Isles 1100–1400*. Oxford, 1990.

Fraser, Derek. *The Evolution of the British Welfare State: A History of Social Policy since the Industrial Revolution*. 2nd edn. London, 1984.

Fraser, W. Hamish. *Trade Unions and Society: The Struggle for Acceptance 1850–1880*. London, 1974.

Freeden, Michael. *The New Liberalism: An Ideology of Social Reform*. Oxford, 1978.

Furniss, Edgar. *The Position of the Laborer in a System of Nationalism: A Study in Labor Theories of the Later English Mercantilists*. Boston, 1920.

Gammage, R.G. *History of the Chartist Movement: 1837–1854*. London, 1854.

Gash, Norman. *Politics in the Age of Peel: A Study in the Technique of Parliamentary Representation 1830–1850*. London, 1953.

Gauthier, Florence. 'Universal Rights and National Interest in the French Revolution'. In *Nationalism in the Age of the French Revolution*, pp. 27–38. Edited by Otto Dann and John Dinwiddy. London, 1988.

Gellner, Ernest. 'Nationalism and the Two Forms of Cohesion in Complex Societies'. In his *Culture, Identity, and Politics*, pp. 6–28. Cambridge, 1987.

   Nations and Nationalism. Ithaca, New York, 1983.

George, Timothy. 'War and Peace in the Puritan Tradition'. *Church History*, vol. 53 (December 1984), pp. 492–503.

Gillespie, Frances. *Labor and Politics in England, 1850–1867*. Durham, N.C., 1927.

Gilley, Sheridan. 'The Garibaldi Riots of 1862'. *Historical Journal*, vol. 16 (December 1973), pp. 697–732.

Godechot, Jacques. 'Nation, patrie, nationalisme et patriotisme en France au xviiie siècle'. *Annales historique de la Révolution française*, vol. 43 (October–December 1971), pp. 481–501.

Goldie, Mark. 'The Roots of True Whiggism 1688–94'. *History of Political Thought,* vol. 1 (1980), pp. 195–234.

Goldman, Lawrence. 'A Peculiarity of the English?: The Social Science Association and the Absence of Sociology in Nineteenth-Century Britain'. *Past and Present,* no. 114 (February 1987), pp. 133–71.

'The Social Science Association 1857–1886: A Context for Mid-Victorian Liberalism'. *English Historical Review,* vol. 101 (January 1986), pp. 95–134.

Goldman, Lawrence, ed. *The Blind Victorian: Henry Fawcett and British Liberalism.* Cambridge, 1989.

Goodway, David. *London Chartism 1838–1848.* Cambridge, 1982.

Goodwin, Albert. *The Friends of Liberty: The English Democratic Movement in the Age of the French Revolution.* London, 1979.

Gosden, P.H.J.H. *The Friendly Societies in England 1815–1875.* Manchester, 1961.

Gossman, Norbert J. 'British Aid to Polish, Italian, and Hungarian Exiles 1830–1870'. *South Atlantic Quarterly,* vol. 68 (Spring 1969), pp. 231–45.

Gray, Robert Q. *The Labour Aristocracy in Victorian Edinburgh.* Oxford, 1976.

Greenleaf, W.H. 'Toulmin Smith and the British Political Tradition'. *Public Administration,* vol. 53 (Spring 1975), pp. 25–44.

Griffiths, Ralph A. 'The Later Middle Ages'. In *The Oxford Illustrated History of Britain,* pp. 166–222. Edited by Kenneth O. Morgan. Oxford, 1984.

Gunn, J.A.W. *Beyond Liberty and Property: The Process of Self-Recognition in Eighteenth-Century Political Thought.* Kingston and Montreal, 1983.

Gwynn, Stephen, and Tuckwell, Gertrude. *The Life of the Rt. Honourable Sir Charles W. Dilke.* 2 vols. New York, 1917.

Habermas, Jürgen. *The Structural Transformation of the Public Sphere: An Inquiry into a Category of Bourgeois Society.* Translated by Thomas Burger with the assistance of Frederick Lawrence. Cambridge, Mass., 1989.

Hadfield, Alice Mary. *The Chartist Land Company.* Newton Abbot, 1970.

Haight, Gordon S. *George Eliot: A Biography.* Oxford, 1968.

Hall, Catherine, and Davidoff, Leonore. *Family Fortunes: Men and Women of the English Middle Class 1780–1850.* London, 1987.

Haller, William. *Foxe's Book of Martyrs and the Elect Nation.* London, 1963.

Hamburger, Joseph. *Intellectuals in Politics: John Stuart Mill and the Philosophic Radicals.* New Haven, 1965.

Hammond, J.L. and Barbara. *James Stansfeld: A Victorian Champion of Sex Equality.* London, 1932.

Hampsher-Monk, Iain. 'John Thelwall and the Eighteenth-Century Radical Response to Political Economy'. *Historical Journal,* vol. 34 (March 1991), pp. 1–20.

Harris, José. 'Did British Workers Want the Welfare State?: G.D.H. Cole's

Survey of 1942'. In *The Working Class in Modern British History*, pp. 200–14. Edited by Jay Winter. Cambridge, 1983.

Harris, Tim. *London Crowds in the Reign of Charles II: Propaganda and Politics from the Restoration until the Exclusion Crisis*. Cambridge, 1987.

Harrison, Brian. ' "A World of Which We Have No Conception": Liberalism and the English Temperance Press 1830–1872'. *Victorian Studies*, vol. 13 (December 1969), pp. 159–80.

Harrison, Brian, and Hollis, Patricia. 'Chartism, Liberalism and the Life of Robert Lowery'. *English Historical Review*, vol. 82 (July 1967), pp. 503–35.

Harrison, J.F.C. *Robert Owen and the Owenites in Britain and America: The Quest for the New Moral World*. London, 1969.

Harrison, Royden. *Before the Socialists: Studies in Labour and Politics, 1861–1881*. London, 1965.

'British Labour and the Confederacy'. *International Review of Social History*, vol. 2 (1957), pp. 78–105.

'The British Working Class and the General Election of 1868'. *International Review of Social History*, vol. 5 (1960), pp. 424–55, and vol. 6 (1961), pp. 74–109.

'The Land and Labour League'. *Bulletin of the International Institute of Social History*, vol. 8 (1953), pp. 169–95.

Harrison, Royden, Woolven, Gillian, and Duncan, Robert, eds. *The Warwick Guide to British Labour Periodicals 1790–1970: A Checklist*. Brighton, 1977.

Harrison, Royden, and Zeitlin, Jonathan, eds. *Divisions of Labour: Skilled Workers and Technological Change in Nineteenth Century Britain*. Brighton, 1985.

Harvie, Christopher. *The Lights of Liberalism: University Liberals and the Challenge of Democracy 1860–86*. London, 1976.

Hay, Douglas. 'Property, Authority and the Criminal Law'. In *Albion's Fatal Tree: Crime and Society in Eighteenth-Century England*, pp. 17–63. Edited by Douglas Hay, Peter Linebaugh, John Rule, E.P. Thompson, and Cal Winslow. London, 1975.

Hayes, Carlton J.H. *The Historical Evolution of Modern Nationalism*. New York, 1931.

Hechter, Michael. *Internal Colonialism: The Celtic Fringe in British National Development, 1536–1966*. Berkeley, 1975.

Heffer, Eric, ed. *Cromwell and Communism: Socialism and Democracy in the Great English Revolution*. London, 1980.

Hewitt, Martin. 'Radicalism and the Victorian Working Class: The Case of Samuel Bamford'. *Historical Journal*, vol. 34 (December 1991), pp. 873–92.

Heyck, Thomas William. *The Dimensions of British Radicalism: The Case of Ireland 1874–95*. Urbana, 1974.

Hill, Christopher. *The Collected Essays of Christopher Hill*, vol. II: *Religion and Politics in 17th Century England*. Brighton, 1986.

'The Norman Yoke'. In *Democracy and the Labour Movement: Essays in Honour of Dona Torr*, pp. 11–66. Edited by John Saville. London, 1954.

Reformation to Industrial Revolution: A Social and Economic History of Britain 1530–1780. London, 1967.

The World Turned Upside Down: Radical Ideas during the English Revolution. Harmondsworth, 1972.

Hilton, Boyd. *The Age of Atonement: The Influence of Evangelicalism on Social and Economic Thought 1795–1865*. Oxford, 1988.

'The Role of Providence in Evangelical Social Thought'. In *History, Society and the Churches: Essays in Honour of Owen Chadwick*, pp. 215–33. Edited by Derek Beales and Geoffrey Best. Cambridge, 1985.

Himmelfarb, Gertrude. *The Idea of Poverty: England in the Early Industrial Age*. New York, 1983.

The New History and the Old. Cambridge, Mass., 1987.

Poverty and Compassion: The Moral Imagination of the Late Victorians. New York, 1991.

Hinde, Wendy. *Richard Cobden: A Victorian Outsider*. New Haven, 1987.

Hinton, James. *Labour and Socialism: A History of the British Labour Movement 1867–1974*. Brighton, 1983.

Hobsbawm, Eric. *Labouring Men: Studies in the History of Labour*. London, 1964.

Nations and Nationalism since 1789: Programme, Myth, Reality. Cambridge, 1990.

Worlds of Labour: Further Studies in the History of Labour. London, 1984.

Hobson, J.A. *Richard Cobden: The International Man*. London, 1919.

Hodder, Edwin. *The Life and Work of the Seventh Earl of Shaftesbury, K.G.* 3 vols. London, 1886.

The Life of Samuel Morley. 2nd edn. London, 1887.

Hont, Istvan, and Ignatieff, Michael. 'Needs and Justice in the Wealth of Nations: An Introductory Essay'. In *Wealth and Virtue: The Shaping of Political Economy in the Scottish Enlightenment*, pp. 1–44. Edited by Istvan Hont and Michael Ignatieff. Cambridge, 1983.

Howe, Anthony. *The Cotton Masters: 1830–1860*. Oxford, 1984.

Hroch, Miroslav. *Social Preconditions of National Revival in Europe: A Comparative Analysis of the Social Composition of Patriotic Groups among the Smaller European Nations*. Translated by Ben Fowkes. Cambridge, 1985.

Humphries, Anne. 'G.W.M. Reynolds: Popular Literature and Popular Politics'. *Victorian Periodicals Review*, vol. 16 (Fall and Winter 1983), pp. 78–89.

Hunt, Lynn. *Politics, Culture, and Class in the French Revolution*. Berkeley, 1984.

Jacob, Margaret and James, eds. *The Origins of Anglo-American Radicalsim*. London, 1984.

James, Louis, and Saville, John. 'George William MacArthur Reynolds (1818–1879)'. In *The Dictionary of Labour Biography*, vol. III, pp. 146–7. Edited by Joyce M. Bellamy and John Saville. London, 1976.

Jeffreys, James B. *Labour's Formative Years*. London, 1948.

Jenkins, Roy. *Victorian Scandal: A Biography of the Right Honourable Gentleman Sir Charles Dilke*. New York, 1965.

Jones, Charles A. *International Business in the Nineteenth Century: The Rise and Fall of a Cosmopolitan Bourgeoisie*. New York, 1987.

Jones, David J.V. *The Last Rising: The Newport Insurrection of 1839*. Oxford, 1985.

Jones, Evan Rowland. *The Life and Speeches of Joseph Cowen, M.P.* (London, 1885).

Joyce, Patrick. *Visions of the People: Industrial England and the Question of Class, 1840–1914*. Cambridge, 1991.

'Work'. In *The Cambridge Social History of Britain 1750–1950*, vol. II, pp. 158–68. Edited by F.M.L. Thompson. 3 vols. Cambridge, 1990.

Work, Society and Politics: The Culture of the Factory in Later Victorian England. Brighton, 1980.

Kadish, Alon. *Historians, Economists, and Economic History*. London, 1989.

Kamenka, Eugene, ed. *Nationalism: The Nature and Evolution of an Idea*. New York, 1976.

Karsten, Peter. *Patriot-Heroes in England and America: Political Symbolism and Changing Values over Three Centuries*. Madison, 1978.

Kearney, Hugh. *The British Isles: A History of Four Nations*. Cambridge, 1989.

Kedourie, Elie. *Nationalism*. London, 1960.

Kent, Christopher. *Brains and Numbers: Elitism, Comtism, and Democracy in Mid-Victorian England*. Toronto, 1978.

'Presence and Absence: History, Theory, and the Working Class'. *Victorian Studies*, vol. 29 (Spring 1986), pp. 437–62.

'The Whittington Club: A Bohemian Experiment in Middle-Class Social Reform'. *Victorian Studies*, vol. 18 (September 1974), pp. 31–55.

Kenyon, J.P. *Revolution Principles: The Politics of Party 1689–1720*. Cambridge, 1977.

Kirk, Neville. 'In Defence of Class: A Critique of Recent Revisionist Writing upon the Nineteenth-Century English Working Class'. *International Review of Social History*, vol. 32 (1987), pp. 2–47.

The Growth of Working Class Reformism in Mid-Victorian England. London, 1985.

Klevensky, M. 'Gertsen Izdatel' i ego sotrudniki' ['Herzen the Publisher and His Colleagues']. *Literaturnoe Nasledstvo* [*Literary Heritage*], nos. 41–2 (1941), pp. 572–620.

Koditschek, Theodore. *Class Formation and Urban Industrial Society: Bradford, 1750–1850*. Cambridge, 1990.

Kohn, Hans. 'The Genesis and Character of English Nationalism'. *Journal of the History of Ideas*, vol. 1 (January 1940), pp. 69–94.

The Idea of Nationalism: A Study in Its Origins and Background. New York, 1944.

Koss, Stephen. *The Rise and Fall of the Political Press in Britain: The Nineteenth Century*. Chapel Hill, 1981.

Kramer, Lloyd S. 'The Rights of Man: Lafayette and the Polish National Revolution, 1830–1834'. *French Historical Studies*, vol. 14 (Fall 1986), pp. 521–46.

Kramnick, Isaac. *Bolingbroke and His Circle: The Politics of Nostalgia in the Age of Walpole*. Cambridge, Mass., 1968.

    Republicanism and Bourgeois Radicalism: Political Ideology in Late Eighteenth-Century England and America. Ithaca, New York, 1990.

Kuhn, William. 'Ceremony and Politics: The British Monarchy, 1871–1872'. *Journal of British Studies*, vol. 26 (April 1987), pp. 133–62.

Kutolowski, John F. 'Victorian Provincial Businessmen and Foreign Affairs: The Case of the Polish Insurrection, 1863–1864'. *Northern History*, vol. 21 (1985), pp. 236–58.

Lake, Peter. 'Anti-Popery: The Structure of a Prejudice'. In *Conflict in Early Stuart England: Studies in Religion and Politics 1603–1642*, pp. 72–106. Edited by Richard Cust and Anne Hughes. London, 1989.

Lancaster, Bill. *Radicalism, Cooperation and Socialism: Leicester Working-Class Politics 1860–1906*. Leicester, 1987.

Large, David. 'London in the Year of Revolutions, 1848'. In *London in the Age of Reform*, pp. 177–211. Edited by John Stevenson. Oxford, 1977.

Lehning, Arthur Müller. *The International Association 1855–1859: A Contribution to the Preliminary History of the First International*. Leiden, 1938.

Levack, Brian P. *The Formation of the British State: England, Scotland and the Union 1603–1707*. Oxford, 1987.

Leventhal, F.M. *Respectable Radical: George Howell and Victorian Working Class Politics*. Cambridge, Mass., 1971.

Lewis, Jane. 'The Working-Class Wife and Mother and State Intervention, 1870–1918'. In *Labour and Love: Women's Experiences of Home and Family, 1850–1940*, pp. 99–120. Edited by Jane Lewis. Oxford, 1986.

Lloyd-Jones, Hugh, Pearl, Valerie, and Worden, Blair, eds., *History and Imagination: Essays in Honour of H.R. Trevor-Roper*. London, 1980.

Lovett, Clara M. *The Democratic Movement in Italy 1830–1876*. Cambridge, Mass., 1982.

Lowe, W.J. 'The Chartists and the Irish Confederates: Lancashire, 1848'. *Irish Historical Studies*, vol. 24 (November 1984), pp. 172–96.

Lubenow, William C. *The Politics of Government Growth: Early Victorian Attitudes toward State Intervention, 1833–1848*. London, 1971.

Lyons, F.S.L. *Internationalism in Europe 1815–1914*. Leyden, 1963.

McCabe, Joseph. *Life and Letters of George Jacob Holyoake*. 2 vols. London, 1908.

McCalman, Iain. *Radical Underworld: Prophets, Revolutionaries and Pornographers in London, 1795–1840*. Cambridge, 1988.

    'Ultra-Radicalism and Convivial Debating Clubs in London, 1795–1838'. *English Historical Review*, vol. 102 (April 1987), pp. 309–33.

    'Unrespectable Radicalism: Infidels and Pornography in Early Nineteenth-Century London'. *Past and Present*, no. 104 (August 1984), pp. 74–110.

Maccoby, Simon. *English Radicalism 1762–1785: The Origins*. London, 1955.

    English Radicalism 1853–1886. London, 1938.

McCord, Norman. *The Anti-Corn Law League, 1838–1846*. London, 1958.

MacDonagh, Oliver. *Early Victorian Government, 1830–1870*. London, 1977.

McGiffert, Michael. 'God's Controversy with Jacobean England'. *American Historical Review*, vol. 88 (December 1983), pp. 1151–74.

MacKay, Donald F. 'Joseph Cowen e il Risorgiménto'. *Rassegna Storica del Risorgimento*, vol. 51 (January–March 1964), pp. 5–26.

McKenzie, Robert, and Silver, Allan. *Angels in Marble: Working Class Conservatism in Urban England*. Chicago, 1968.

McKibbin, Ross. 'Why Was There No Marxism in Great Britain?'. In his *Ideologies of Class: Social Relations in Britain 1880–1950*, pp. 1–41. Oxford, 1990.

MacLeod, Roy, ed. *Government and Expertise: Specialists, Administrators and Professionals, 1860–1919*. Cambridge, 1988.

Mason, John W. 'Political Economy and the Response to Socialism in Britain, 1870–1914'. *Historical Journal*, vol. 23 (September 1980), pp. 565–87.

Matskumura, Takao. *The Labour Aristocracy Revisited: The Victorian Flint Glass Makers, 1850–80*. Manchester, 1984.

Maurice, Frederick, ed. *The Life of Frederick Denison Maurice: Chiefly Told in His Own Letters*. 2 vols. London, 1884.

Meinecke, Friedrich. *Cosmopolitanism and the Nation State*. Translated by Robert B. Kimber. Princeton, 1970.

Merriman, John M. *The Agony of the Republic: The Repression of the Left in Revolutionary France, 1848–1851*. New Haven, 1978.

Miller, Naomi. 'John Cartwright and Radical Parliamentary Reform 1808–1819'. *English Historical Review*, vol. 83 (October 1968), pp. 705–28.

Mitchell, Charles. *The Newspaper Press Directory*. London, 1858.

Moorhouse, H.F. 'The Marxist Theory of the Labour Aristocracy'. *Social History*, vol. 3 (January 1978), pp. 61–82.

Morelli, Emilia. *L'Inghilterra di Mazzini*. Rome, 1965.

Morgan, Edmund S. *Inventing the People: The Rise of Popular Sovereignty in England and America*. New York, 1988.

Morgan, Kenneth O. *Keir Hardie: Radical and Socialist*. London, 1975.

Morley, John. *Death, Heaven and the Victorians*. London, 1971.

Morley, John. *The Life of Richard Cobden*. 2 vols. London, 1905.

Morrill, John, ed. *Oliver Cromwell and the English Revolution*. New York, 1990.

Morris, R.J. *Class, Sect and Party: The Making of the British Middle Class, Leeds 1820–1850*. Manchester, 1990.

    'Samuel Smiles and the Genesis of Self-Help: The Retreat to a Petit Bourgeois Utopia'. *Historical Journal*, vol. 24 (March 1981), pp. 89–109.

Moss, Bernard. *The Origins of the French Labour Movement, 1830–1914: The Socialism of Skilled Workers*. Berkeley, 1976.

Mueller, Iris Wessel. *John Stuart Mill and French Thought*. Urbana, 1956.

Mulligan, Lotte, and Richards, Judith. 'A "Radical" Problem: The Poor and the English Reformers in the Mid-Seventeenth Century'. *Journal of British Studies*, vol. 29 (April 1990), pp. 118–46.

Nairn, Tom. *The Break-Up of Britain: Crisis and Neo-Nationalism*. London, 1977.

   The Enchanted Glass: Britain and Its Monarchy. London, 1988.

   'The English Working Class'. *New Left Review*, no. 24 (March–April 1964), pp. 43–57.

Neal, Larry. *The Rise of Financial Capitalism: International Capital Markets in the Age of Reason*. Cambridge, 1991.

Newman, Gerald. *The Rise of English Nationalism: A Cultural History 1740–1830*. New York, 1987.

Nicolaevsky, B. 'Toward a History of "The Communist League" 1847–1852'. *International Review of Social History*, vol. 1 (1956), pp. 234–52.

Norman, Edward. *The Victorian Christian Socialists*. Cambridge, 1987.

O'Brien, Conor Cruise. *God Land: Reflections on Religion and Nationalism*. Cambridge, Mass., 1988.

O'Gorman, Frank. *The Whig Party and the French Revolution*. London, 1967.

Ozouf, Mona. *La Fête révolutionnaire 1789–1799*. Paris, 1976.

Partridge, Monica. 'Alexandr Gertsen i ego angliiskie sviazi' ['Alexander Herzen and His English Ties']. In *Problemi izucheniia Gertsena* [*Problems in the Study of Herzen*], pp. 348–69. Edited by V.P. Volzin. Moscow, 1963.

Patterson, A. Temple. *Radical Leicester: A History of Leicester 1780–1850*. Leicester, 1954.

Paul, Ellen Frankel. *Moral Revolution and Economic Science: The Demise of Laissez-Faire in Nineteenth-Century British Political Economy*. Westport, Conn., 1979.

Pelczynski, Z.A. 'Nation, Civil Society, State: Hegelian Sources of the Marxian Non-Theory of Nationality'. In *The State and Civil Society: Studies in Hegel's Political Philosophy*, pp. 262–78. Edited by Z.A. Pelczynski. Cambridge, 1984.

Pelling, Henry. *A History of British Trade Unionism*. 3rd edn. Harmondsworth, 1976.

   The Origins of the Labour Party, 1880–1900. 2nd edn. Oxford, 1965.

   'The Working Class and the Origins of the Welfare State'. In his *Popular Politics and Society in Late Victorian Britain*, pp. 1–18. London, 1968.

Pemble, John. *The Mediterranean Passion*. Oxford, 1987.

Perkin, Harold. 'Land Reform and Class Conflict in Victorian Britain'. In *The Victorians and Social Protest: A Symposium*, pp. 177–217. Edited by J. Butt and I.F. Clarke. London, 1973.

   The Origins of Modern English Society. London, 1969.

   'The Origins of the Popular Press'. In his *Structured Crowd: Essays in English Social History*, pp. 47–56. Brighton, 1981.

Peters, Marie. *Pitt and Popularity: The Patriot Minister and London Opinion during the Seven Years' War*. Oxford, 1980.

Petler, D.N. 'Ireland and France in 1848'. *Irish Historical Studies*, vol. 24 (November 1985), pp. 493–505.

Pierson, Stanley. *British Socialists: The Journey from Fantasy to Politics*. Cambridge, Mass., 1979.

    Marxism and the Origins of British Socialism: The Struggle for a New Consciousness. Ithaca, 1973.

Plummer, Alfred. *Bronterre: A Political Biography of Bronterre O'Brien 1804–1864*. London, 1971.

Pocock, J.G.A. *The Ancient Constitution and the Feudal Law: A Study of English Historical Thought in the Seventeenth Century*. Cambridge, 1957.

    'England'. In *National Consciousness, History, and Political Culture in Early Modern Europe*, pp. 98–117. Edited by Orest Ranum. Baltimore, 1975.

    The Machiavellian Moment: Florentine Political Thought and the Atlantic Republican Tradition. Princeton, 1975.

    Virtue, Commerce, and History. Cambridge, 1985.

Pocock, J.G.A., ed. *Three British Revolutions: 1641, 1688, 1776*. Princeton, 1980.

Pollard, Sidney. 'Nineteenth-Century Co-operation: From Community Building to Shop Keeping'. In *Essays in Labour History*, pp. 74–112. Edited by Asa Briggs and John Saville. London, 1960.

Porter, Bernard. *The Refugee Question in Mid-Victorian Politics*. Cambridge, 1979.

Porter, Roy. *English Society in the Eighteenth Century*. Harmondsworth, 1982.

Prest, John. *Liberty and Locality: Parliament, Permissive Legislation, and Ratepayers' Democracies in the Nineteenth Century*. Oxford, 1990.

Prestwich, Menna, ed. *International Calvinism 1541–1715*. Oxford, 1985.

Prothero, I.J. *Artisans and Politics in Early Nineteenth-Century England: John Gast and His Times*. Folkestone, 1979.

Pugh, Martin. *The Tories and the People: 1880–1935*. Oxford, 1985.

Quinault, Roland. '1848 and Parliamentary Reform'. *Historical Journal*, vol. 31 (December 1988), pp. 831–51.

Raven, Charles E. *Christian Socialism 1848–1854*. London, 1920.

Read, Donald. *Press and People, 1790–1850: Opinion in Three English Cities*. London, 1961.

Renan, Ernest. *Qu'est-ce qu'une nation?*. Paris, 1882.

Richardson, R.C., and Ridden, G.M., eds. *Freedom and the English Revolution: Essays in History and Literature*. Manchester, 1986.

Richey, Russel E. 'The Origins of British Radicalism: The Changing Rationale for Dissent'. *Eighteenth Century Studies*, vol. 7 (1973–4), pp. 179–92.

Robbins, Caroline. *The Eighteenth-Century Commonwealthsman: Studies in the Transmission, Development, and Circumstance of English Liberal Thought from the Restoration of Charles II to the War with the Thirteen Colonies*. Cambridge, Mass., 1959.

Robbins, Keith. *John Bright*. London, 1979.

Nineteenth-Century Britain: England, Scotland, and Wales, the Making of a Nation. Oxford, 1989.

Rogers, Nicholas. 'Popular Protest in Early Hanoverian London'. *Past and Present*, no. 79 (May 1978), pp. 70–100.

Whigs and Cities: Popular Politics in the Age of Walpole and Pitt. Oxford, 1989.

Rose, Mary B. *The Gregs of Quarry Bank Mill: The Rise and Decline of a Family Firm, 1750–1914.* Cambridge, 1986.

Rothstein, Theodore. *From Chartism to Labourism: Historical Sketches of the English Working Class Movement.* London, 1929.

Royle, Edward. *Radicals, Secularists and Republicans: Popular Freethought in Britain, 1866–1915.* Manchester, 1980.

Victorian Infidels: The Origins of the British Secularist Movement 1791–1866. Manchester, 1974.

Rubinstein, W.D. 'The End of "Old Corruption" in Britain 1780–1860'. *Past and Present*, no. 101 (November 1983), pp. 55–86.

Rudman, Harry W. *Italian Nationalism and English Letters: Figures of the Risorgimento and Victorian Men of Letters.* New York, 1940.

Russell, Conrad. *Parliament and English Politics, 1621–1629.* Oxford, 1979.

Ryan Alan. *Property and Political Theory.* London, 1984.

Rzadkowska, Helena. *Działalność Centralizacji Londyńskiej Towarzystwa Demokratycznego Polskiego 1850–1862* [*The Activities of the London Centralization of the Polish Democratic Society 1850–1862*]. Warsaw, 1971.

Saab, Ann Pottinger. *Reluctant Icon: Gladstone, Bulgaria, and the Working Classes, 1856–1878.* Cambridge, Mass., 1991.

Sager, Eric W. 'The Social Origins of Victorian Pacificism'. *Victorian Studies*, vol. 23 (Winter 1980), pp. 211–36.

Samuel, Raphael. 'The Workshop of the World: Steam Power and Hand Technology in Mid-Victorian Britain'. *History Workshop Journal*, no. 3 (Spring 1977), pp. 6–72.

Samuel, Raphael, ed. *Patriotism: The Making and Unmaking of British National Identity.* 3 vols. London, 1989.

Sarvasy, Wendy. 'A Reconsideration of John Stuart Mill's Socialism'. *Western Political Quarterly*, vol. 38 (June 1985), pp. 312–33.

Saville, John. *1848: The British State and the Chartist Movement.* Cambridge, 1987.

Ernest Jones: Chartist. London, 1952.

Saville, John, ed. *Democracy and the Labour Movement: Essays in Honour of Dona Torr.* London, 1954.

Schlereth, Thomas J. *The Cosmopolitan Ideal in Enlightenment Thought: Its Form and Function in the Ideas of Franklin, Hume, and Voltaire, 1694–1970.* Notre Dame, 1977.

Schoyen, A.R. *The Chartist Challenge: A Portrait of George Julian Harney.* 2 vols. London, 1908.

Schwartz, Pedro. *The New Political Economy of J.S. Mill.* London, 1968.

Schwarzkopf, Jutta. *Women in the Chartist Movement.* New York, 1991.

Scott, Jonathan. *Algernon Sidney and the English Republic, 1623–1677.* Cambridge, 1988.

Seccombe, Wally. 'Patriarchy Stabilized: The Construction of the Male Breadwinner Wage Norm in Nineteenth-Century Britain'. *Social History*, vol. 11 (January 1986), pp. 53–76.

Seed, John. 'Gentlemen Dissenters: The Social and Political Meaning of Rational Dissent in the 1770s and 1780s'. *Historical Journal*, vol. 28 (June 1985), pp. 299–326.

    'Unitarianism, Political Economy and the Antinomies of Liberal Culture in Manchester, 1830–50'. *Social History*, vol. 7 (January 1982), pp. 1–25.

Seton-Watson, Hugh. *Nations and States: An Enquiry into the Origins of Nations and the Politics of Nationalism.* London, 1977.

Sewell, William H. *Work and Revolution in France: The Language of Labor from the Old Regime to 1848.* Cambridge, 1980.

Shaen, M.J. *William Shaen: A Brief Sketch.* London, 1912.

Shannon, Richard. *Gladstone: 1809–1865.* London, 1982.

Shapiro, Ian. *The Evolution of Rights in Liberal Theory.* Cambridge, 1986.

Shipley, Stan. *Club Life and Socialism in Mid-Victorian London.* Oxford, 1971.

Smail, John. 'New Languages for Labour and Capital: The Transformation of Discourse in the Early Years of the Industrial Revolution'. *Social History*, vol. 12 (January 1987), pp. 49–71.

Smith, Anthony D. *Theories of Nationalism.* London, 1971.

Smith, Francis B. *The Making of the Second Reform Bill.* Cambridge, 1966. *Radical Artisan: William James Linton 1812–98.* Manchester, 1973.

Smith, R.J. *The Gothic Bequest: Medieval Institutions in British Thought, 1688–1863.* Cambridge, 1987.

Sommerville, Johann. 'Oliver Cromwell and English Political Thought'. In *Oliver Cromwell and the English Revolution*, pp. 234–58. Edited by John Morrill. New York, 1990.

Spall, Richard Francis, Jr. 'Free Trade, Foreign Relations, and the Anti-Corn Law League'. *International History Review*, vol. 10 (August 1988), pp. 405–32.

Spiers, Edward M. *Radical General: Sir George de Lacy Evans.* Manchester, 1983.

Stedman Jones, Gareth. *Languages of Class: Studies in English Working Class History 1832–1982.* Cambridge, 1983.

    Outcast London: A Study in the Relationship between Classes in Victorian Society. Oxford, 1971.

    'Society and Politics at the Beginning of the World Economy'. *Cambridge Journal of Economics*, vol. 1 (March 1977), pp. 77–92.

Steele, E.D. *Palmerston and Liberalism, 1855–1865.* Cambridge, 1991.

Sykes, Robert. 'Early Chartism and Trade Unionism in South-East Lancashire'. In *The Chartist Experience: Studies in Working-Class Radicalism and Culture, 1830–60*, pp. 152–93. Edited by James A. Epstein and Dorothy Thompson. London, 1982.

352   *Bibliography*

Szporluk, Roman. *Communism and Nationalism: Karl Marx versus Friedrich List*. New York, 1988.

Taylor, Miles. 'John Bull and the Iconography of Public Opinion in England *c.* 1712–1929'. *Past and Present*, no. 134 (February 1992), pp. 93–128.

'The Old Radicalism and the New: David Urquhart and the Politics of Opposition, 1832–1867'. In *Currents of Radicalism: Popular Radicalism, Organised Labour and Party Politics in Britain, 1850–1914*, pp. 23–43. Edited by Eugenio F. Biagini and Alastair J. Reed. Cambridge, 1991.

Tchernoff, I. *Le Parti républicain au coup d'état et sous le second empire*. Paris, 1906.

Tholfson, Trygve. *Working Class Radicalism in Mid-Victorian England*. New York, 1977.

Thompson, Dorothy. *The Chartists: Popular Politics in the Industrial Revolution*. New York, 1984.

'Women and Nineteenth Century Radical Politics'. In *The Rights and Wrongs of Women*, pp. 112–38. Edited by Juliet Mitchell and Ann Oakley. London, 1976.

Thompson, E.P. 'Eighteenth-Century English Society: Class Struggle without Class?'. *Social History*, vol. 3 (May 1978), pp. 133–65.

The Making of the English Working Class. Harmondsworth, 1963.

'The Peculiarities of the English'. In *The Socialist Register: 1965*, pp. 311–62. Edited by Ralph Miliband and John Saville. London, 1965.

William Morris: Romantic to Revolutionary. 2nd edn. New York, 1976.

Thompson, Noel W. *The People's Science: The Popular Political Economy of Exploitation and Crisis, 1816–34*. Cambridge, 1985.

Thompson, Paul. 'Liberals, Radicals and Labour in London 1880–1900'. *Past and Present*, no. 27 (April 1964), pp. 73–101.

Socialists, Liberals and Labour: The Struggle for London, 1885–1914. London, 1967.

Tiller, Kate. 'Late Chartism: Halifax 1847–58'. In *The Chartist Experience: Studies in Working-Class Radicalism and Culture, 1830–60*, pp. 311–44. Edited by James A. Epstein and Dorothy Thompson. London, 1982.

Trevelyan, G.M. 'Englishmen and Italians: Some Aspects of Their Relations Past and Present'. In his *Clio, a Muse: And Other Essays*, pp. 104–23. Freeport, N.Y., 1968.

Garibaldi and the Making of Italy. London, 1911.

Garibaldi and the Thousand. London, 1909.

Underdown, David. *Revel, Riot, and Rebellion: Popular Politics and Culture in England 1603–1660*. Oxford, 1985.

Van der Linden, W.H. *The International Peace Movement, 1815–1874*. Amsterdam, 1987.

Van Holtoon, Frits, and Van der Linden, Marcel, eds., *Internationalism in the Labour Movement, 1830–1940*. 2 vols. Leiden, 1988.

Vicinus, Martha. 'Chartist Fiction and the Development of a Class-Based Tradition in Literature'. In *The Socialist Novel in Britain: Towards the*

Recovery of a Tradition, pp. 7–25. Edited by H. Gustav Klaus. Brighton, 1982.

Independent Women: Work and Community for Single Women, 1850–1920. Chicago, 1985.

The Industrial Muse: A Study of Nineteenth Century British Working Class Literature. London, 1974.

Vincent, Andrew, and Plant, Raymond. *Philosophy, Politics and Citizenship: The Life and Thought of the British Idealists*. Oxford, 1984.

Vincent, John. *The Formation of the British Liberal Party, 1857–1868*. London, 1966.

Vogel, Ursula. 'The Land Question: A Liberal Theory of Communal Property'. *History Workshop*, no. 27 (Spring 1989), pp. 106–35.

Vogeler, Martha S. *Frederic Harrison: The Vocations of a Positivist*. Oxford, 1984.

Weaver, Stewart Angas. *John Fielden and the Politics of Popular Radicalism 1832–1847*. Oxford, 1987.

Webb, R.K. *The British Working-Class Reader 1790–1848*. London, 1955.

Weiler, Peter. *The New Liberalism: Liberal Social Theory in Great Britain 1889–1914*. New York, 1982.

Weill, Georges. *Histoire du parti républicain en France: 1814–1870*. Paris, 1928.

Weisser, Henry G. *April 10: Challenge and Response in England in 1848*. Lanham, 1983.

British Working-Class Movements and Europe: 1815–1848. Manchester, 1975.

'Chartist Internationalism, 1845–48'. *Historical Journal*, vol. 14 (March 1971), pp. 49–66.

Wicks, Margaret. *The Italian Exiles in London, 1815–48*. Manchester, 1937.

Wiener, Carol Z. 'The Beleaguered Isle: A Study of Elizabethan and Early Jacobean Anti-Catholicism'. *Past and Present*, no. 51 (May 1971), pp. 27–62.

Wiener, Joel. *William Lovett*. Manchester, 1989.

Wilkins, M.S. 'The Non-Socialist Origins of England's First Important Socialist Organization'. *International Review of Social History*, vol. 4 (1959), pp. 199–207.

Willis, Kirk. 'The Introduction and Critical Reception of Marxist Thought in Britain, 1850–1900'. *Historical Journal*, vol. 20 (June 1977), pp. 417–59.

Wilson, Kathleen. 'Empire, Trade, and Popular Politics in Mid-Hanoverian Britain: The Case of Admiral Vernon'. *Past and Present*, no. 121 (November 1988), pp. 74–109.

'Inventing Revolution: 1688 and Eighteenth-Century Popular Politics'. *Journal of British Studies*, vol. 28 (October 1989), pp. 349–86.

Wolfe, Willard. *From Radicalism to Socialism: Men and Ideas in the Formation of Fabian Socialist Doctrines, 1881–1889*. New Haven, 1975.

Worden, Blair. 'The Commonwealth Kidney of Sir Algernon Sidney'. *Journal of British Studies*, vol. 24 (January 1985), pp. 1–40.

Wright, T.R. *The Religion of Humanity: The Impact of Comtean Positivism on Victorian Britain*. Cambridge, 1986.

Wyncoll, Peter. 'The First International and Working Class Activity in Nottingham 1871–73'. *Marxism Today*, vol. 12 (December 1968), pp. 372–9.

'Thomas Smith: A Working Class Defender of the Commune'. *Marxism Today*, vol. 15 (March 1971), pp. 86–9.

Yeo, Eileen. 'Robert Owen and Radical Culture'. In *Robert Owen: Prophet of the Poor: Essays in Honour of the Two Hundredth Anniversary of His Birth*, pp. 84–114. Edited by Sidney Pollard and John Salt. London, 1971.

Yeo, Stephen. 'A New Life: The Religion of Socialism in Britain, 1883–1896'. *History Workshop Journal*, no. 4 (Autumn 1977), pp. 5–56.

Zagorin, Perez. *The Court and the Country: The Beginning of the English Revolution*. London, 1969.

VI UNPUBLISHED THESES

Berridge, Virginia. 'Popular Journalism and Working Class Attitudes, 1854–86: A Study of *Reynolds's Newspaper, Lloyd's Weekly Newspaper*, and the *Weekly Times*'. PhD thesis, University of London, 1976.

Claeys, Gregory. 'Chartism, Democratic Theory and Political Radicalism: An Investigation of Aspects of the Relationships between Socialism and Politics in Britain, 1820–1852'. PhD thesis, Cambridge University, 1983.

Finn, Margot C. 'After Chartism: Nationalist Sentiment in English Popular Radicalism, 1848–1871'. PhD thesis, Columbia University, 1987.

Martinez, P.K. 'Paris Communard Refugees in Britain, 1871–1880'. DPhil thesis, Sussex University, 1981.

Pincus, S.C.A. 'Protestantism and Patriotism: Ideology and the Making of English Foreign Policy 1650–1665'. PhD thesis, Harvard University, 1990.

Ramos, Benedict. 'Recruitment to Italy in 1860'. MA thesis, Birkbeck College, University of London, 1984.

Smith, Philip T. 'The London Metropolitan Police and Public Law and Security, 1850–1868'. PhD thesis, Columbia University, 1975.

Index

Allsop, T., 68, 291 n. 79
American Civil War, 198, 204, 213, 234
ancient constitution, 17, 44
anniversary celebrations, 122, 135, 147;
 of Commune, 318–19; of E. Jones,
 312–13; of February revolution, 125–
 6, 134, 136, 137, 230; of June Days,
 137, 192; of Polish revolutions, 124–
 5, 137, 192, 230, 231; of Robespierre,
 122–4, 191
Anti-Corn Law League, 58–9, 94, 147,
 149, 235, 250
Applegarth, R., 196, 237, 247, 269, 277,
 278
Arch, J., 36
aristocracy, opposition to, 172, 213,
 215, 216, 310; and E. Jones, 139, 191;
 and land reform, 268, 281; and
 Reynolds, 138, 205, 219; *see also* Old
 Corruption
Ashurst, W., 160, 190, 208, 219

Bamford, S., 56–7
Barbès, A., 85, 91, 136
Bax, E., 310, 318
Bayfield, T. J., 283–4, 293, 294
Beales, E., 255, 268, 300; and
 Garibaldi, 219, 220, 241; and
 parliamentary reform, 224, 237, 243,
 244; and Poland, 215, 216
Bee-Hive, 195, 216, 220, 232, 246;
 establishment of, 192, 193–4;
 Positivists and, 202, 214, 289
Beesly, E. S., 199, 202, 223, 279, 300;
 and Marx, 289–90; radicalization of,
 244–5, 257–9, 280
Bentham, J., 27–8, 50, 79
Bernard, S., 182–4, 190, 191
Birmingham, 148, 166, 169; and 1848,

78–9; and Kossuth, 99, 126–7; and
 parliamentary reform, 243, 245; and
 republicanism, 276–7, 282–3
Blanc, L., 68, 104, 191, 203–4, 229, 278,
 287; and Chartists, 84, 85, 90, 114,
 116, 118, 120, 121, 176; and
 Christian Socialists, 153, 155–6; and
 Mazzini, 162, 170–1; middle-class
 opposition to, 75, 76, 77, 79, 91, 249;
 middle-class support of, 258, 269–70,
 275, 297, 301
Bolton, 295–6
Borochov, B., 31–2, 228
Bradford, 64, 165, 235
Bradlaugh, C., 36, 134, 186, 211, 269,
 285, 286
Brewer, J., 16, 49, 50
Bridges, J. H., 199, 289
Bright, Jacob, 268, 279
Bright, John, 58, 162, 213, 303, 311;
 and Chartists, 94, 97, 103, 181; and
 Crimean War, 173, 174; and
 Pankhurst, 263–4; and parliamentary
 reform, 96, 197, 224, 240, 244, 249–
 51, 266; *see also* Manchester School
Bristol, 120, 186, 208, 254
British Legion, Garibaldian, 206–8
Bryce, J., 200, 273
building trades, 192, 195, 202, 211, 258;
 see also trade unions

Cabet, E., 68, 86, 91, 114, 120, 269
Cairnes, J. E., 237, 260, 291–2
Carpenter, E., 317
Cartwright, J., 35, 49, 54
Catholicism, 70, 274; and Italy, 167,
 204, 205–6, 208, 210, 211; and
 national consciousness, 17, 19–20, 38,
 44–5, 153

responses to, 63, 64, 67; middle-class responses to, 73, 74–7, 79, 146; *see also* anniversary celebrations and June Days

Finlen, J., 137–8, 139, 140, 242, 279

Forster, W. E., 147, 166

Fortnightly Review, 275, 291–2

Foster, J., 3, 6

Fourier, C., 75, 79, 114

Fox, W. J., 71, 102, 163, 164, 181, 186

Foxe, J., 19–20, 60

Franco-Prussian War, 196, 273–82, 298

Fraternal Democrats, 58, 63, 119, 122, 135–6, 232

French revolution (1789), 23, 24–7, 33, 52–5

French revolution (1848), *see* February revolution and June Days

Friend of the People, 109, 113, 115, 116, 119

Friends of Italy, 166–71, 176, 191, 208

Frost, J., 85, 127–8

Garibaldi, G., 118, 161, 166, 203, 289, 317; British Legion and, 206–8; in England, 217–25; English interpretations of, 204–5, 209–13; and parliamentary reform, 236, 241–2

Gellner, E., 11, 23, 25

Germany, 73–4, 79, 86, 92, 149; *see also* Franco-Prussian War

Gladstone, W. E., 7, 223, 278, 279, 281, 282, 308

Glasgow, 251, 264, 266

Glasier, J. B., 264, 319

Glorious Revolution, 45, 99, 206

Green, T. H., 260

Greg family, 94–5, 197, 207, 210, 303

Halifax, 120–1, 151–2, 165, 166

Hampton, J., 36–7, 47, 54, 177; and Chartists, 60, 67, 85, 101, 179; and liberals, 146, 180, 293, 311

Hardie, J. K., 264, 319

Harney, G. J., 83, 86, 120, 130, 133, 156, 237; and Cowen, 175, 176, 280; and *démoc-soc* ideal, 88, 112–13, 170; and Fraternal Democrats, 58, 63, 119, 122, 135; and Hungary, 101–2; and Jersey coup, 178, 179; and radical press, 108–12, 115, 116, 121, 157

Harrison, F., 199–202, 214, 257, 268, 306–7; and Commune, 290–1; and Franco-Prussian War, 274, 280; and Garibaldi, 223–4

Harrison, R., 2, 238

Herbert, A., 274, 275, 279, 314–15

Herzen, A., 117, 125, 130, 138, 162, 270

Hetherington, H., 101, 130

Hobsbawm, E., 1, 2, 11 n. 24, 31

Holyoake, G. J., 103, 129, 130, 184, 237, 269; and Chartism, 83, 128, 132, 133; and *démoc-soc* ideal, 69, 90–1, 139, 170–1; and Italy, 165, 166, 207, 219, 258; and liberals, 151–2, 163, 176, 190, 202, 210, 310; and radical press, 109, 116, 117

Howell, G., 119–20; and Chartism, 134, 193; and International, 231, 277; and political economy, 193, 196, 266; and Reform League, 237, 245

Hughes, T., 153, 158, 237, 268

Hugo, V., 130, 178

Hume, D., 13, 47

Hume, J., 95–6, 97, 101, 164

Hungary, 91, 164, 165, 174–5; and middle class, 73, 79, 92, 147, 149; sympathy meetings for, 98–102, 126–7

Hunt, H., 36–7, 49, 97

Hunt, T., 71, 151

Hyde, Park, 212, 244, 278, 287

Hyndman, H. M., 311, 317, 319

Independent Labour Party, 264–5, 306, 312, 314, 316

International Association and Committee, 136–40, 177, 189

International Working Men's Association, 227–34, 237, 277; Commune and, 287–8, 290; Marx and, 298, 300; origins of, 136–7, 217; republicanism and, 294, 295

internationalism, 10–12, 26–33, 51–2, 57–8; *see also* Fraternal Democrats, International Association and Committee, and International Working Men's Association

Ireland, 8, 16, 22, 211–12, 286; Chartists and, 63, 64, 79, 122, 124

Ironside, I., 69, 76, 93

Israel, as symbol, 18, 36, 42

Italy, 66, 73–4, 188–9; *see also* Garibaldi and Mazzini

Past and Present Publications

General Editor: PAUL SLACK, *Exeter College, Oxford*

* Published also as a paperback
† Co-published with the Maison des Sciences de L'Homme, Paris